BUSINESS

A Novel Approach

BUSINESS

A Novel Approach

by Richard N. Farmer
INDIANA UNIVERSITY

Ten Speed Press
BERKELEY, CALIFORNIA

*To all the W100 A.I.'s,
from 1970 to the present,
who have made teaching this course
so much fun.*

1☯

TEN SPEED PRESS
P O Box 7123
Berkeley, California 94707

Library of Congress Catalog Number: 84-50041
ISBN: 0-89815-128-7

Book Design by Hal Hershey
Cover Design by Brenton Beck

Printed in the United States of America

10 9 8 7 6 5 4 3 2 1

CONTENTS

PREFACE

A young friend of mine, Al Faber, recently completed an assignment to study a big company, RVA Incorporated. Al is a journalist, and his boss sent him to RVA for four months. His job was to turn the company inside out, and to discover just what made a big company function. After he had spent all that time figuring out the company, he had to write a series of articles explaining what it was all about for his magazine, NEWSWORLD.

I got to know Al pretty well during his assignment, since he spent a lot of time in Bloomington, visiting with the Masters' family (for reasons which you will discover in Chapter 4 and beyond). He is a capable young fellow, but he really didn't know much about business. I gather that his boss picked him for this assignment for exactly this reason. He wanted an inquisitive, intelligent young reporter, not an expert. Al went to work, and in the end, he turned out his articles. You may have seen some of them if you are a NEWSWORLD reader.

But Al also kept very good notes, and he wrote out some of his adventures in RVAland for his own amusement. I think that he is an aspiring novelist, among other things. A short while back he sent me his manuscript, telling me to do whatever I wanted with it. While Al often got confused by business terminology, it seemed well worth presenting to you, since, somewhat to my surise, he ended up writing a rather good business textbook. You might enjoy seeing how a serious, intelligent young person can learn a lot in a short time. I have taken the liberty of reorganizing some of his materials and adding some questions at the end of the chapters. Al tends to get carried away with personal elements, so this material is necessary to keep you on track.

Even though some one else wrote most of this book, it was still a lot of work to put together, and I had lots of help. Thanks go to Dan Farmer, who revised and worked out the statistical materials for the RVA Annual Report; to Leslie Shaw, Chris Mossing, Susan Peters, Carolyn Vick, Larry Yinger, Carlos Enriquez, Alan Fishman, Laura Anderson, and John Steele, all of whom helped prepare the glossary and bibliography; and to Andrea LePere, who helped in numerous ways with these materials. Thanks also goes to Chuck Forney, who taught me a lot about recycling and small business.

Al can't defend himself, since he didn't put the story together in precisely this way, so all errors, omissions, and other problems are my responsibility entirely.

Richard N. Farmer

Bloomington, Indiana
September, 1984

1

INTRODUCTION

Mr. McKeever is expecting you, Mr. Faber," the secretary said. "Go right in."

Al Faber tried to stay calm as he walked toward the huge door to Jason McKeever's office. He had never been up here on the 44th floor, to the big boss's office. The publisher of *Newsworld* simply didn't deal with junior staff reporters, no matter how ambitious they were.

He pushed the door open, to see a large, well dressed, fit-looking gray-haired man coming out from behind a gigantic desk, a desk that could have been the size of Al's whole cubicle downstairs.

"Come in, Al, come in." The publisher extended a well-manicured and tanned hand. "Let's sit over here where we can be comfortable. Coffee?"

"No thank you, sir."

"I'm glad you could come up on such short notice."

It had been three quarters of an hour since Al's editor had grabbed his arm at the coffee machine. "Get up to the 44th floor right now. I don't know what you blew this time, but Jason McKeever wants you front and center, pronto!" Al had spent most of the last half hour cooling his heels and watching McKeever's secretary handle phone calls.

"It's no problem, really, Mr. McKeever, no problem at all," Al said as they settled into arm chairs set around a coffee table. So this is executive country, he thought. A guy at the top gets an office so big he can have a whole conference area away from his desk.

"You did a fine job on that tax assessment scandal study," Mr. McKeever said. "A fine job. *Newsworld* was proud and happy to run your series."

"Thank you, sir. I had a lot of help." Maybe this was a break?

"I'll get right to the point. I need you for a new assignment. Are you free right now?"

Al supposed that you never told the big boss you had nothing to do. He would certainly never let his editor think he was loafing. "I've just got a few odds and ends going."

"Fine. Something happened over at my club that bothered me. I ran into Bill Wilson, who's head of the RVA Corporation. Have you ever heard of it?"

"It's a big conglomerate, isn't it?"

"Right," Mr. McKeever said. "Mines, oilfields, supermarkets, toolmaking ... you name it and RVA has a group doing it. In the first hundred of the *Fortune* 500, in term of sales. Higher than that in terms of profits."

"The *Fortune* 500?"

"Every year, *Fortune* magazine prints a list of the 500 largest corporations in the U.S.," Mr. McKeever explained. "RVA is one of the biggest private corporations in the world. Bill Wilson is the CEO ... chief executive officer. Nice fellow ... I've known him since college days. He's one of the two or three men who are responsible for building RVA. Started back in 1946 with a little tool and die company in Detroit and took off from there. By 1970, sales were over $3 billion per year, and it's been straight up from there. Brilliant fellow. But he gave me a problem." Mr. McKeever stared out the window. The view of Manhattan was phenomenal.

"Yes, sir." Al thought that it might be better to listen than to talk.

"It's this. Bill was chiding me for running a bunch of anti-business articles in *Newsworld*. Almost every week we've had something ... bribery, exploitation of workers in Mexico, shoddy production for consumers." McKeever grinned at Al. Al had written a sidebar on citizens' groups protesting a major auto manufacturer's quality control problems, six months ago. Had McKeever been reading Al's file? He felt that we were giving business a bad name. So I told him that we just reported what was happening. Business is giving itself a bad name. But he didn't buy that. He said that there was plenty of good news, if we only took the trouble to find out."

"But sir, we try to find stories, not public relations releases."

"I know, and I told him that. But he kept on arguing, and, well, he's a very persuasive guy. He made a few points I hadn't thought about." Mr. McKeever got up and began to walk back and forth in his huge office. "Do you know what's been happening to business school enrollments?"

"No sir, I don't."

"They more than doubled during the 1970's," Mr. McKeever said. "Doubled! You know, we're supposed to be taking the pulse of the American public, and *Newsworld* has always prided itself on picking up the first signs of change among American young people. Have we ever run a story on that simple fact?"

Al waited.

"No, we haven't. Those young people may know something we don't. And here's another fact for you. The number of women in business schools has gone up from perhaps five percent in the 1960's to over thirty percent now. We're supposed to be covering the women's rights movement, and somehow we never went back to see what women are doing to get those rights economically. We should.

"And another thing." Mr. McKeever stopped pacing. "Some of the best students, the very smartest, are now in business schools. Back in the 1960's, smart people stayed away from such dreary places ... now, lots of business schools have the very best students and the highest standards. What do you think of that?"

"Well, I ..." Al wasn't sure what to think, since when he was in college, not too many years ago, the B-school at his university didn't have all that good a reputation.

"We're missing something here. Oh, lots of people still don't think much of private business and free enterprise. Look what happened when the oil companies made those huge profits. There was lots of criticism. But if so many young people are going into business, why? What's going on out there? Where are we headed? Newsworld is supposed to know, and we don't."

"Yes, sir." If the boss said it was true, it might be wise not to disagree until some evidence was in.

"Bill Wilson and I talked for quite a while about this. Something's happening in the U.S. Oh, like most things, it's ambivalent ... some good, some bad. But I want to find out exactly what's going on."

Mr. McKeever seemed to want a response now, so Al said, "How about the move back to conservative political principles ... things like the tax revolt in California, and the moves toward decontrol of business. Could this be part of it?"

McKeever smiled. "Exactly. Remember, you can't stay under thirty forever. In ten or fifteen years, these young people of today will be running lots of things, and a very high percentage of them will be trained in business. What are the implications?" He paused and looked out his huge picture window. "Well, Bill and I kept talking, and finally he offered me something that was too good to pass up."

Was this Al's break?

"He told me that we should send an investigative reporter to RVA to really find out what was going on. Look at everything, the good and the bad. He'd open all doors, make sure that our reporter could talk to anyone about anything. That's why I called you in."

"Me? Why? You have dozens of good business reporters."

"That's exactly what I don't want for this assignment. I want someone who is more like the general public. You're twenty-seven, right? You majored in journalism in college, right?"

"Yes, sir." Old McKeever must really have studied that file.

"Have you ever studied business?"

"I never even took the Introduction to Business Course at college. I don't know a thing about business. Look, Mr. McKeever, it really seems that you should get an expert ..."

"Nonsense! I want a smart young person to do this job. And I want it done thoroughly. Take three or four months to do it. I want you to start from scratch, to look at every corner of RVA. Wilson will make sure that you can talk to anyone. Get your background materials as complete as you can. Find out where the skeletons are buried, and find out what's good about a major, modern corporation too. Bill's like myself . . . he's too old to pick up just what's happening to young people, even though he claims he hires only the best. Besides, he's won big, and he forgets that most people don't. Find out what it is in business that attracts young people. Find out what makes people criticize big companies, too. And when you're done, you should have a series of articles that no one ever really did before. RVA, from the ground up! Let's see what kind of animal a huge conglomerate is. Are you interested?"

"Yes, I am," Al said, "but I still wonder if I'm qualified."

"Al, business is easy. You buy low and sell high. Those accountants, marketing experts, engineers, and all the rest are just confusing the issues. But something is going on here, and *Newsworld* should be in on it. Why do young people major in business? Why do they figure that a career in business is better than traditional things? I want to know."

"So I write about the rights and wrongs?"

"Don't hide anything. I want an unbiased story. Get to it as soon as you can. I'll make sure that your present assignments are covered."

"Well, all right."

"You're not married, and you should be able to travel around a bit. You'll have to, with RVA. The company is all over the world. Make sure you have a valid passport . . . they're on four continents and in thirty countries."

"Yes, sir!" Al wondered if they had a Paris branch.

"Don't take too long abroad, since RVA is an American company. And don't spend two months in the Paris branch!"

"No, sir!"

McKeever stood in front of Al. The interview was over. Al stood up, they shook hands, and McKeever steered Al to the door. As Al was passing the secretary's station (a U.S. Senator's press aide was just standing to go in), McKeever called after him, "Oh, Al, Bill and I have a bet on this, but don't let that concern you."

Back at his desk, Al thought, wow, where do you start on an assignment like this? He had visited the morgue, pulled *Newsworld*'s few clips on RVA, and read them. Not much there. How was he going to even begin to figure out how a company operates that has over 65,000 employees?

Why not start at the top? he reasoned, and put in a call to Bill Wilson's office. But it turned out Wilson had other ideas. His secretary, who was waiting to hear from *Newsworld*, said that Mr. Wilson thought RVA's long history would provide an excellent perspective, and the secretary gave Al the phone number of RVA's resident archivist and historian, one Dr. Ronald Robertson. It might be useful to start with him; he was at RVA's head office, just across town.

After lunch? Nope—dillydallying would never get Al back to executive country, and certainly not on a permanent basis. He picked up the phone and dialed again.

2

THE FORMATION
AND GROWTH
OF A NEW BUSINESS

I'm sorry I'm late," Al said. "I had trouble finding your office."

"Everybody does, Mr. Faber." Dr. Robertson was a gray haired, round little man who looked like a professor Al had once had. "It's not exactly a choice location, back here behind building maintenance. Corporate offices always seem to reflect what's important, from the bottom up. The president and chief executive officer is on the fortieth floor; the vice presidents are on the 39th floor; and here we are on the sixth floor. That's about right. Just behind a small department, in the worst corner of the building."

"I would think that a company would be a bit more interested in its own history."

"Nonsense. Companies live for tomorrow, not yesterday. You can't change the past, but you can influence the future. Everyone in this corporation, except me, is worrying about what is going to happen, and trying to do something about it. If you worry about tomorrow, you get a big office and a competent staff. You don't end up in a small place like this, with stacks of documents of no particular importance piled up all over." Dr. Robertson waved his pipe around his small, untidy office. "I'm supposed to keep track of what happened, but few care. You're the first visitor I've had for weeks. Now, what exactly do you want, young man?"

Al explained why he had come.

"Finding out all about RVA, eh? Not looking for the latest scandal, or hint of disaster? Unusual, to say the least. Young people, indeed everyone these days, seem to revel in what is, not what was. Strange. What do you know?"

"Almost nothing. But I figured that RVA must have come from someplace, and maybe where it came from might explain a bit about what it is."

"A most commendable attitude, Mr. Faber. Very shrewd. People these days seem to assume that the RVAs of this world emerge fully blown from the womb, or maybe by act of Congress, or something. They don't. It takes decades to develop an organization as big and complex as this."

"So where did it start?"

"Many places, I suppose, but the key original company was the Ross Machine Tool Company, which started back in 1924."

"What was that? I never heard of it."

"Few have. But William Ross was a genius. He was an engineer, and he invented things. He was a rather impractical man, but he kept coming up with improved machine tools. You never worry about the shock absorbers on your car, do you?"

"Rarely," Al said.

"Back in 1924, most cars didn't even have shock absorbers. They ran quite badly, I can assure you. I'm old enough to remember my own father taking us out for rides in our Packard Six, and we bounced all over the place. A few auto companies, including Hudson, had developed a good shock absorber, but the internal mechanisms require some very tricky machining. No one could do it right. William Ross figured out how to do it fast and cheaply and invented a machine to do it. He built one in his garage and sold it to a supplier for Hudson, who made those shocks. It all began there."

Al thought that over. "Look, how do you start a company? Just begin, like that, in your garage? I mean, I would think that it would be pretty complicated."

"Then and now, it is easy, Mr. Faber. You just, ah, start, as you say. Mr. Ross had a bit of money . . . I believe that his grandmother left him four or five thousand dollars, which was a good sum in those days, and he quit his job, bought some materials, and began his company."

"Five thousand bucks! I bet that was like a million now, what with inflation and everything."

Dr. Robertson smiled. "I see that you are not an economist. No, it was, ah, equivalent to about $30,000 now. Believe it or not, most price inflation since 1776 has been within the past thirty years. Prices are now about six times what they were in the 1920's, so five then is about thirty now."

"What about licenses and permits? Didn't this Ross have to . . ."

"No permits, no licenses, not anything. Mr. Ross started a proprietorship. You can do it too, if you have anything to sell, even today. Of course there are some things that do require licenses to operate, such as a trucking company, a bank, a bus line, or a law firm. But to start a manufacturing or retailing company, you just begin. Mr. Ross had a proprietorship the day he began."

"What's a proprietorship?" Al asked.

Dr. Roberston sighed and looked out the window for a while. Al felt stupid. But Dr. Robertson explained, and Al carefully wrote it down.

"So then what?" Al asked.

"Mr. Ross sold a lot of machines, prospered, and got into trouble."

"How do you get into trouble when you're doing well?"

"Very easily. It took about two thousand dollars of materials and labor

A PAGE FROM AL'S NOTEBOOK

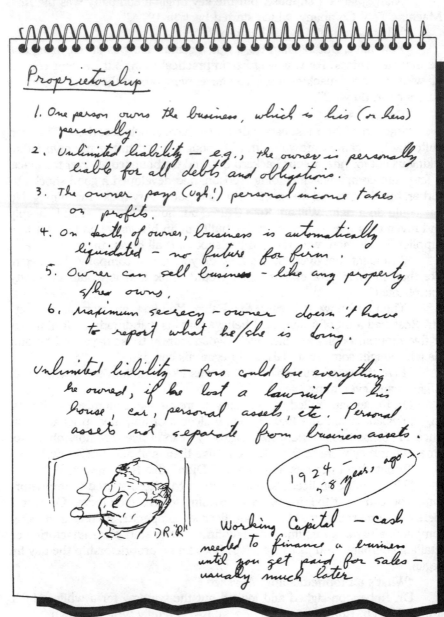

Proprietorship

1. One person owns the business, which is his (or hers) personally.

2. Unlimited liability — e.g., the owner is personally liable for all debts and obligations.

3. The owner pays (ugh!) personal income taxes on profits.

4. On death of owner, business is automatically liquidated — no future for firm.

5. Owner can sell business — like any property s/he owns.

6. Maximum secrecy — owner doesn't have to report what he/she is doing.

Unlimited liability — Ross could lose everything he owned, if he lost a lawsuit — his house, car, personal assets, etc. Personal assets not separate from business assets.

DR. "R"

1924 — 58 years ago

Working Capital — cash needed to finance a business until you get paid for sales — usually much later to build one of his special tools. Remember, these were very large and complicated, with electric motors, special grinding attachments, and much more. The Ross and Vogel Machine Tool Division of RVA, up in Bridgeport, has one on display at its headquarters, if you want to look at it. Very ingenious, really. Our grandfathers were not dumb."

"So Ross is making money and selling tools, and he's in trouble?"

"He almost went bankrupt. He had orders for fifty machines. That meant that he needed over $100,000 to finance the orders to make them. People, including big companies, don't normally pay for things until they are delivered. So Mr. Ross needed working capital, and as a small proprietorship, no one would lend him money. Supposing he died, or became incapacitated? Supposing that he was a crook, so when you lent him money he just took it and ran? Even a firm order from General Motors, which Mr. Ross had, was not enough to convince a suspicious banker."

"Gee, I would think that a brilliant, serious engineer could talk a bank into a loan with an order like that," Al said. "And couldn't he sell stock, or something?"

"There are two problems with that, Mr. Faber. A proprietorship cannot sell stock, remember. Besides, how would an engineer be expected to know anything about the stock market? Mr. Ross was a brilliant man, but like so many brilliant men, he knew very little about finance. All he knew was that he needed lots of money in early 1926, and his bank would not lend it to him.

"Then, too, you are assuming that Mr. Ross was serious. He most decidedly was not. Indeed, he was quite a ladies' man. There was quite a scandal around 1927 ... but never mind. In short, he was not a person that a sober banker would lend much money to. So, enter Mr. Peter Vogel."

"Who was he?"

"Mr. Vogel was what you might call an entrepreneur, financier, or perhaps even a sharpshooter. He looked for potentially profitable deals and financed them. In 1926, he had just sold his electric railway properties near Boston, and he was looking for an opportunity. He was what you would call now a venture capitalist. He owned a big Chalmers ..."

"A what?"

"It was a nice upper-middle-class car. Please don't interrupt, young man."

"Sorry."

"... that had poor shock absorbers. He obtained a set that Hudson was making, and he was impressed. In the end, he traced the manufacturer back to the machine maker, and found Mr. Ross in Bridgeport. When he discovered that Mr. Ross had a financial problem, he got interested. Finally, in early 1927, they formed the partnership of Ross & Vogel."

"Now what is the difference between a proprietorship and a partnership, if any?" Al asked.

Dr. Robertson sighed and told him, and Al wrote it down.

"OK, now we have a partnership. What next?"

"Mr. Vogel was very shrewd. He recognized that Mr. Ross was, well, a bit erratic, so he got him back into his garage ... actually a development center ... where he could piddle around and develop things. This really was what Mr. Ross wanted to do anyhow. Mr. Vogel did the managing and financing. He was smart enough to hire some very capable subordinates, too, which Mr. Ross would never do. Too individualistic, Mr. Ross was. Mr. Vogel was smart enough to realize that he didn't know everything. It was a good combination. Mr. Ross developed a whole new line of sophisticated machine tools for the auto industry before 1934, when he died. Every time he came up with something good, Mr. Vogel and his associates did the necessary work to put the machine into production and get some sales."

"So the partnership prospered, and they lived happily ever after," Al said.

"No, actually the partnership was quite short-lived."

"Why?"

Dr. Robertson waved his pencil at Al. "Don't you see? Partnerships are fragile things, and that unlimited liability was beginning to bother Mr. Vogel. Sales were over a million dollars in 1927, and profits were over $100,000. A law suit, a death, anything, could cause trouble. Then there was Mr. Ross's ex-wife, who was beginning to cause trouble, but that's another story. No, it was time to form a corporation. Besides, Ross & Vogel needed some extra cash."

"Hey, 1929 was the great boom, wasn't it?" Al asked. "That was when clerks made millions in the market."

"Not quite, Mr. Faber, but it was a time when the stock market was quite buoyant, and the economy was booming. Investment bankers were looking for a chance to invest in interesting new ventures. Mr. Vogel talked to several, and in 1928, Ross & Vogel became a corporation."

Dr. Robertson stopped and looked at Al. "Well?"

"OK," Al said sheepishly, "What's a corporation? I think that I know, but you tell me correctly."

After explaining, Dr. Robertson went on. "They sold four million dollars' worth of stock to the public and held on to a bit over fifty percent of the shares for their own use. Hence they could control the corporation. The other fifty percent was in widely scattered holdings. Suddenly Ross & Vogel was a very nice company, with a lot of capital. It was able to expand rapidly, just in time to get overextended in the great crash."

"1929 and it all went down the drain, huh?"

"Not quite, but it was difficult. Auto sales dropped almost eighty percent between 1929 and 1932, and Ross & Vogel were selling their machine tools to the auto industry. But Mr. Ross came through. He developed a new line of tools to meet the needs of the new all steel bodies that were just being introduced."

What's a partnership?
1. Two or more people contract to do business.
2. Unlimited liability - like a proprietorship
3. Owners pay personal income taxes on shares of profit.
4. On death of one owner, partnership is dissolved legally.
5. Partners typically can't sell their share without permission of other partners.
6. Mutual agency - i.e., either partner can commit the company.

(a) Investment banker — one whose main business is lending money to companies for investment purposes

(b) Commercial bank - handles all normal banking activities for companies and individuals, such as handling checking and savings accounts. Also makes short term loans.

(Watch this - since 1934, (a) separate from (b) by law, but a new banking ehe, revolution is a' coming - Now accounts, how?? branch banking, money market funds, etc., etc. — check out later)

"What did they make auto bodies out of before?"

Dr. Robertson fumbled with his pipe. "Wood, mainly, with steel panel overlays. But in the late twenties and early thirties, steel was coming in, and that meant lots of welding. Ross & Vogel developed a line of special welding tools that could do fifty or more welds simultaneously. Even in the Great Depression, those tools sold."

A corporation —
1. Legal person — can conduct business as a person. Can sue and be sued, own property, etc. Can be immortal- organizations don't die like people!
2. Chartered by a state, under state law (50 ways!). No Federal charters. Big companies tend to get charters in tolerant states (eg., Delaware).
3. Issues stock. Anyone with money can buy shares. Stockholders are owners.
4. One share = one vote. Biggest sharehol'ers can control.
5. Limited liability — stockholders can only lose value of shares if company goes broke. Makes stockholding much more willing to invest.
6. Share value depends on what company does. Big profits (or good expectations) can cause share prices to go way up.
7. Can issue other securities like bonds (which are debt). Pays fixed annual interest to bondholders, who are not owners, but creditors

What a mess! No wonder they have B-schools!

"So the company beat the crash?"

"The stockholders didn't get a dividend from 1931 to 1935, but they survived. Mr. Ross had also developed some very excellent die injection casting equipment, and zinc alloy die casting was coming in at that time as well. He was well along on that work when he died in 1934. Quite young, too. Perhaps if he had lived a more quiet life ..."

8. If company goes under, creditors get paid first, before stockholders. These include workers, suppliers, and bondholders

9. Stockholders elect a board of directors, who hire managers, who are responsible for running the company.

10. Most laws applying to real persons apply to corporations.

11. Corporations pay corporate income tax, which is different from personal income tax. If it pays dividends to stockholders, then stockholders must pay personal income tax on these (double taxation).

12. Corporations are required to make financial reports to the state in which they are chartered. PUBLIC corporations (those with many owners) have complex and detailed reporting requirements.

13. Since owners can easily sell stock, transfer of ownership is easy.

WHEW!

"Say, this Ross was really important to the company, wasn't he?" Al asked. "I mean, if it wasn't for him, nothing much would have happened."

"You're right, but remember that Mr. Vogel was important too. If it wasn't for him, Mr. Ross would never have gotten off the ground. Literally tens of thousands of companies tried to get started in the 1920's. It was the right time, since the economy was booming, and industries like autos were growing even faster. A man with a good idea could get ahead. But most failed. They lacked some critical element for success. Ross & Vogel needed both technical and managerial skills, to say nothing of marketing and finance, and Mr. Vogel supplied the missing link. Even the stock market helped. Remember, when the company was losing money, the stockholders got nothing. If the company had nothing but bank loans, with interest to pay, it would have gone under."

"But Ross & Vogel must have been a small company at that time?"

Dr. Robertson dug a paper out of a pile on his desk. "It was, let's see ... by 1940, they only had four million dollars in sales. About the same as 1929. A typical story, stagnation through the Great Depression."

"But how did they get big? Who took over from Ross?"

"Nobody did. The company ran on his technical genius for ten years. But World War II started in Europe in 1939, and Ross & Vogel made machinery that made weapons. Orders soared. When the U.S. entered the War in 1941, sales soared again. By 1944, sales were over $80 million per year."

"And then the company took off," Al said.

"It did not. Mr. Vogel retired in 1945, just as the war ended. The company had some good men, but no one with any imagination. Besides, you have to realize what kind of world it was, back then. Everyone expected another depression. The unemployment rate had ranged from ten to forty percent from 1930 to 1941, and most respected observers felt that as soon as the war was over, another crash would occur."

"Forty percent! Now with nine percent unemployment we feel threatened."

Dr. Robertson nodded. "You young people don't know the meaning of unemployment. Now, what would you do as a manager, if you felt that your sales were about to nosedive, and your workers would be laid off?"

"Be pretty conservative, I guess," Al replied.

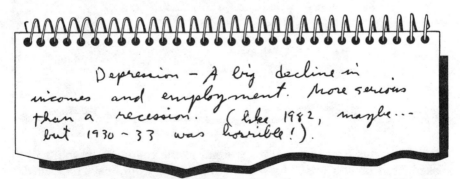

Depression — A big decline in incomes and employment. More serious than a recession. (like 1982, maybe... but 1930-33 was horrible!).

"Ross & Vogel had been very conservative in the 1930's, and they planned to be that way again in the 1940's. They had made profits when many others were going under. They did this by not expanding very fast. Remember the trouble they had in the early 1930's, when their sales collapsed. They hung onto cash and made as few investments as they could. Most of the wartime expansion was financed by the Federal Government, through various war emergency measures. Ross & Vogel operated new plants, but the government actually owned them."

"So they decided to sit tight after the War?"

"Exactly. Most of the government plants were given up, even though the company had a chance to buy them at a big discount. The new management decided to stick with their auto tooling business, and car sales would determine just about what the company could do."

"Hey, Dr. Robertson, this doesn't sound like the story of a huge, successful company. All you've told me is about a little tool company that just sits around. Are you sure that you have the right company?"

"Oh, yes, and it is important to understand just how things got started. You see, Ross & Vogel actually was a pretty good sized company right after the War, by standards of the time. They were stagnating technically, although no one really knew it. They were deep into specialized welding, die casting, and other machine tools used in mass production industries, and surprisingly enough, that 1934 technology, modestly developed, was very useful in 1948. Of course they had excellent engineers and production people, and their technical salesmen knew as much about their customers' business as they did. Mr. Vogel was always strong on finance, and the company was extremely well run. Profits were high, even though wartime taxes were fierce. It was a nice medium sized company, like hundreds of others."

"Something must have happened."

"John Tavis happened," Dr. Robertson said. "Have you ever heard of him?"

"No."

Dr. Robertson sighed. "So much for fame. One of the world's most distinguished business managers, and you never heard of him. John Tavis was an unusual man. He had been a paratrooper during the War, and he once said that nothing in business was nearly as dangerous as jumping out of a plane over Europe during the War with various people shooting at you. He took risks that few took in business during the 1950's."

"Where did he come from?" Al asked.

"A very distinguished eastern family. He went to Harvard Business School just before the War. His uncle owned a few hundred shares of Ross & Vogel stock, and Mr. Tavis noticed some Ross & Vogel equipment during the war. He thought highly of it, so he used his uncle's influence to get a job interview in 1946. He joined the company in finance, and by 1950 he was president. Then things began to change."

"I suppose that the company was in bad shape by 1950, with that sit-tight attitude." Al said.

"No, it was not. Instead of depression, there was a postwar boom. Auto sales reached an all-time high, as did household appliance sales. Ross & Vogel just got bigger, doing what came naturally to them. They even built two new plants to handle the business, and by 1950 they were doing $120 million in sales. Their customers had pulled them along."

"That's sort of funny. You do nothing, but you win anyhow."

"You would be surprised, Mr. Faber, at how many companies make big profits by just performing well in the small field in which they have competence. Ross & Vogel had a worldwide reputation for being the best in their field. If you were building an auto plant anywhere, or a component plant, you naturally bought machinery from Ross & Vogel. They had over 60 percent of the business in their lines, and exports were very high. Remember that Europe was rebuilding at this time, and many auto plants were being built or reconstructed. Ross & Vogel equipment was in most of them. And really, that was one of the company's problems."

"It doesn't sound like a problem to me, Dr. Robertson. It must be fun to dominate a market and squeeze the competition."

"It may be nice, but we do have antitrust laws. Ross & Vogel really could not expand much in their own fields. If they did, the Company could expect an antitrust suit."

"So how do you expand under those conditions?" Al asked. "I had expected that Ross & Vogel would just go on growing within the auto industry."

"Oh, no. Mr. Tavis saw right away that this was impossible. But he did have a very profitable company, and he did have a cash hoard of almost $60 million of retained earnings. So he began to expand in other fields."

"By starting new companies?"

"No, that would have been too difficult. Remember how long it took Ross & Vogel to get to any size. No, he began to buy companies. A lot of conservative firms were around at that time, and Mr. Tavis could buy them fairly cheaply. Remember, most people still expected stagnation, even though the economy was moving ahead rather nicely."

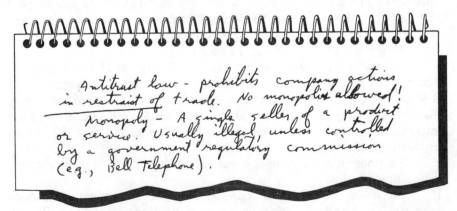

Antitrust law - prohibits company actions in restraint of trade. No monopolies allowed! Monopoly - A single seller of a product or service. Usually illegal, unless controlled by a government regulatory commission (eg., Bell Telephone).

"Say, what did the New Deal have to do with all of this?" Al asked. "I seem to remember that the New Deal was very anti-business."

"You are thinking of the period from 1933 to 1940, Mr. Faber. Perhaps the New Deal was anti-business, but much of what it did had the effect of stimulating demand and making companies better off. But one key problem was uncertainty. The new legislation sometimes tried to fix prices, and it often helped labor. The labor laws were changed to make union organizing very easy, as compared to previous times. Minimum wage legislation came in, as did Social Security. New economic regulation for such industries as motor trucking and airlines also came along, and agriculture got price supports and other special legislation. Conservative businessmen saw in each new law something that would destroy them, so they were nervous even as their profits and sales rose. Of course taxes, particularly income taxes in the higher brackets, were raised, and that didn't make anyone feel any better.

"But remember that in 1950, the fifty-year-old businessman had been thirty when the Great Depression started. That, and the New Deal, were not history to him, but something he had lived through. The war was only five years back, and many such men had been in the Army or Navy. These people were sure that something horrible was going to happen, and soon. This is why they were so convinced that the American economy was in for deep trouble."

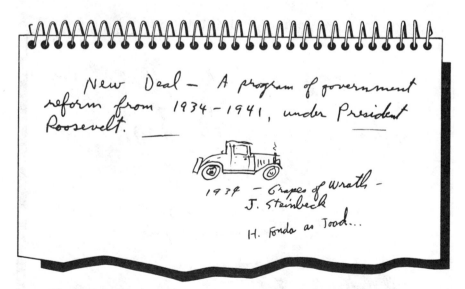

New Deal — A program of government
reform from 1934 – 1941, under President
Roosevelt.

1934 — Grapes of Wrath —
J. Steinbeck
H. Fonda as Jood...

"So Mr. Tavis took his risks, only they weren't as dangerous as most people thought?"

"Exactly. He began by buying a small customer, Ace Engine Company. It made small aircraft engines. Then he acquired Neutro Fibers, a major synthetic company, Peters Coal Company, Kine Lumber, and many others. By 1960, what is now RVA owned a dozen other companies, all in different fields."

"I suppose that Tavis's $60 million didn't last long," Al said, "if those companies were any size."

"Oh, he usually didn't need cash. He paid for companies with Ross & Vogel stock, and he sold bonds."

"He did? Why would anyone want to get stock, when he could have cash?"

"Because Ross & Vogel has long been listed on the New York Stock Exchange."

Al was puzzled, so Dr. Robertson explained what that meant: "You see, a group of owners could sell out, get stock, and either hold on and hope that the stock price went up, or that dividends would rise, or both. After all, the expanded Ross & Vogel would be making more money with their new companies. If the price went up, then the stockholder could sell and take his capital gains."

"His what?"

Dr. Robertson explained. "That tax advantage, particularly to a wealthy person, could be very attractive. If the acquired company was privately held, that is, its stock was not listed, such a strategy for selling could be worth literally millions of dollars."

NYSE - New York Stock Exchange, the largest and most prestigious stock exchange. The "BIG BOARD"

Prices listed daily in THE WALL STREET JOURNAL and most metropolitan newspapers.

Capital Gains - buy an asset at $100, then sell later for $300 -
The $200 is a capital gain, not income (taxed lower, so attractive to those in high tax brackets).

"This Tavis was a smart guy then."

"He was brilliant. But he did more. He recognized that Ross & Vogel knew all about their own industry, but they knew very little about other fields. So he tried to keep the existing management of the firms he acquired. A good man in a stodgy company could be a great manager if he were encouraged to expand. Often it was the owners, not the managers, that were the conservative ones."

"So what did Tavis do?"

"By 1960, what is now RVA was doing $600 million a year in sales. By 1970, it was doing $1.4 billion. Mr. Tavis just kept on adding companies and expanding his old ones. He went for growth and profits, and he got both."

"What about antitrust? Was all of this legal?"

"Oh, yes," Dr. Robertson said. "You see, buying a company in a completely different field than the one you are in is usually all right."

"I can see the strategy now," Al said. "You just keep buying up companies, and make sure that you don't monopolize anything. But there are lots of industries, so you can keep right on going."

"Don't forget that by doing this, you get the other companies' markets, technology, and most importantly, managers." It's called a conglomerate, and Mr. Tavis was a genius to put it all together. Lots of people have tried, and only a few succeeded. Most businessmen were content to stay small. In the end, they either remained unimportant, or they got taken over." Dr. Robertson stuffed his pipe again. "But the game is running out now."

"Why? It sounds like a game that could go on forever."

"When you're a hundred million dollar company, it is easy enough to find a few twenty million dollar companies to buy. Your sales then go up perhaps forty percent per year. But RVA is now a $4.7 billion company. To get forty percent increase per year, you have to find a few billion dollar companies. There just aren't very many of those around. Moreover, if they do exist, they probably have some business in some of your fields, so you get back to antitrust problems. The government may not let you acquire them. No, this particular road is about ended for RVA, Mr. Faber. The 1950's and 1960's were real growth years for the American economy, so Mr. Tavis had his golden opportunity. He took it. But now, RVA will have to figure out other strategies."

"How about international business? RVA is big overseas, but so far all you've told me about is the American side."

"Ross & Vogel built a small plant in Canada in 1940. The Canadians put in a high tariff on certain machinery in 1938, so the company invested there to hold on to their market. It was not exactly a huge move, since the Detroit plant put a building in Windsor, Ontario, which is all of two miles across the river. Besides, Canada is not totally alien to Americans. But this plant prospered, and in 1948, the company built another, bigger plant in

Toronto. Then when Mr. Tavis bought the Ace Engine Company, he discovered that this firm had a small engine plant in what is now West Germany. It had been built by the Ace founder, who had a cousin over there in the 1920's. Strangely enough, the plant had been taken over and rapidly expanded by the Nazis during the war. The U.S. Government wanted the plant continued, so Mr. Tavis agreed. A bit of horse trading occurred, I believe. There was a small antitrust question about acquiring Ace. By agreeing to help out with German reconstruction after World War II, Mr. Tavis avoided a potentially awkward legal question."

"I thought that the law is the law," Al observed dryly.

"It is, but the prosecutor has to decide what to do. In this case, the Attorney General's Office had several options."

"I see. So what happened in Germany?"

"The Ace Plant was a huge success. It expanded rapidly as the West German Auto industry expanded. Actually, it does not make engines, but rather braking systems and certain transmissions and components. But when European auto sales go from perhaps 5,000 per year in 1946 to over ten million now, it is nice to be a supplier for the industry."

"How much of RVA's business is foreign, Dr. Robertson?"

"About 35 percent. That is typical of the larger companies these days. Some go over 50 percent. In the 1960's RVA expanded a lot overseas, both by acquiring companies with foreign operations, and by expanding existing companies."

"I suppose that you get lots of cheap labor over there?"

Dr. Robertson laughed. "We used to, but in the countries we are in, we typically pay more. West Germany, Switzerland, and Norway, for example. Wage rates in all these countries are higher than here."

"How about India and Taiwan?"

"We have a Taiwanese electronics assembly plant, but we aren't in India. What for? The market for our products there is very small. Yes, labor is cheaper in Taiwan, which is one reason we are there. But I believe that this plant accounts for less than one percent of total sales. The big ones are in rich, sophisticated countries where big markets exist, like West Germany."

Al made a note to check this out later. He had heard so much about American companies running away to cheap labor countries that he felt this story was not complete, but it could wait.

"How about the 1970's, Dr. Robertson? You've told me how RVA got that far."

"The 1950's and 1960's were probably unique. Everywhere, economies were expanding. It was easy to acquire conservative, good companies and make them grow. Energy was cheap, and lots of what we do involves substituting energy for people. It pays off in high productivity and higher wages. In spite of many local wars, there was no World War III, which probably would have destroyed us all. Mr. Tavis saw the opportunities, and he took them. But you can't just go on expanding a finite world forever without running into trouble. In 1973, the first energy crisis hit. Prices for energy quadrupled in a month, and then in 1979–80, they doubled again. We had a big recession in 1974–75, and suddenly expansion was hard. We had another one in 1982 that really was rough. In the late 1970's, we began to get double digit inflation, and while we get big sales increases, we don't gain much. After all, if sales go up in dollars by ten percent, but prices go up by ten percent too, you're standing still. RVA is treading water right now, although we're still moving ahead a bit in most years.

"Besides, we have new problems. Have you heard of corporate social responsibility?"

"Yes, but what does it mean to you?"

"It means plenty, and I don't just mean what we do to be nice people. Since the mid-1960's, our country has evolved a new idea about what big companies should be doing. We have new and tough laws on pollution, product safety, worker welfare and safety, equal employment rights, and even pension rights. We have to observe these laws, like it or not. Such things cost money, and of course they take lots of highly skilled staff to work out."

"Are they bad?"

"Few things in this world are purely good or bad, Mr. Faber. If we save some lives in one of our plants because of new safety devices, but as a result we have to raise prices, is this good or bad? If a woman is hired because of equal opportunity legislation, but a man is not, who wins? Any company always has to live in the world it is in, and big companies are always required to follow the rules fairly closely. If they don't, disaster is certain. Remember what happened to those firms that made illegal overseas payments. Worse, remember what happened to their managers. They got fired."

"Some of them did."

"You must have lots of opportunity to check out such things over at *Newsworld*, Mr. Faber."

"I will, too."

"Fine. But I think that the world of RVA that you find now will be a bit different from the world we have been talking about. Things have changed, and RVA is trying to change with them."

Al turned over a page in his notebook, wrote for a moment, then tapped his pen on his teeth.

"What are the big changes, then?" he asked.

"Well," Dr. Robertson said, "I think that there are a few really important things to remember. One is the much extended government role in business, particularly in big business. It has come in fast in the 1970's, although of course government has always regulated companies in various ways. But the new ways are important, expensive, and perhaps somewhat disturbing to older people.

"Then there is the fact that educational levels are so much higher than

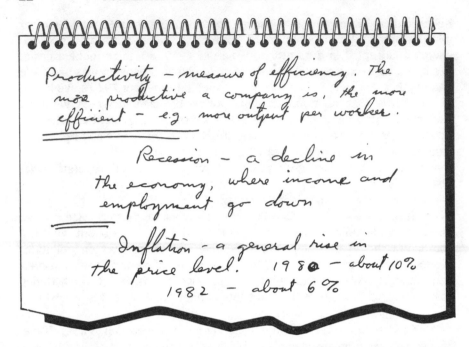

Productivity – measure of efficiency. The more productive a company is, the more efficient – e.g. more output per worker.

Recession – a decline in the economy, where income and employment go down

Inflation – a general rise in the price level. 1980 – about 10%
1982 – about 6%

they used to be. People are so much better informed ... and I might add, more productive. When Ross & Vogel started back in 1928, less than five percent of young Americans started college. Now more than 40 percent do, and high school education is all but universal. This makes a big difference in labor markets and in many other ways.

"Slow growth in the economy since the early 1970's is a real problem, too. Our recessions seem to get worse, and the unemployment rate often goes above ten percent these days. This is not only an American problem, since all industrialized countries share low growth and rising unemployment, but it does make it very difficult for job seekers, particularly younger people and reentering women." Dr. Robertson stared at Al. "Not every young person can expect to get as good a job as you have, Mr. Faber, not by a long shot."

Al nodded. He knew he was lucky—but he'd worked for it, too.

Dr. Robertson toyed with his pencil. "I suppose that the growing share of government in the economy would be another factor. In 1930, all government took about five percent of national income. Now it takes over thirty percent. Such change does make a difference.

"Finally, I think that the new change in expectations is important. In the old days, like 1925, people did not really expect to win. Now we expect equality, opportunity, economic gains, and perhaps even perfection in our somewhat messy social situation. RVA, as a major supplier of jobs, goods, and services, is expected, even required to give more people more of everything."

Al was scribbling furiously. He wasn't quite sure how all of this fit in, but he would find out later. "Dr. Robertson, it seems to me that the 1980's might be a bit different. I mean, people aren't so naive about expectations now, and recent government moves seem to be to scale back regulations, not expand them."

Dr. Robertson nodded. "Yes, perhaps we have discovered that we cannot gain utopias easily. Young people in particular seem to be disillusioned. We have seen a little scaling back of government expenditures, and even a few modest tax cuts. Even inflation has slowed a bit in recent years. But we are not dismantling all those government controls, not by a long shot. We have spent almost fifty years changing the way big business operates, and we are not likely to go back to the beginning soon. Indeed, much of what happens in the 1980's and 1990's will depend on what we do now, and remember that those 1950 managers saw the 1930's personally. The 1960 managers are still here, and they saw all these new changes personally. Those experiences will not go away."

"Dr. Robertson, if you were trying to figure out RVA, how would you do it?"

"You mean, if I had your job? Try this." Dr. Robertson doodled on a legal pad for a moment, then tossed it over. "You have to go beyond RVA, young man. Talk to those people I've shown there. Oh, and go talk to RVA people too, but you won't understand it all until you see who else is involved."

Al glanced at the diagram and put it in his pocket. "Thank you." He thought for a moment. "Dr. Robertson, in effect you've told me that RVA was the creation of three men. Can that really be true? I mean, here is a multi-billion dollar company, with over 65,000 employees, and yet you've only talked about three of them. Were Ross, Vogel, and Tavis such supermen really?"

DR. ROBERTSON'S DIAGRAM

Dr. Robertson threw up his hands. "How should I know? You asked about RVA. I told you what the history is. History is always selective. I could have told you about highly skilled Bridgeport machinists in 1928, who made the tools that Ross invented. If they hadn't done their jobs, the company would have folded early. I could have told you about those accountants who developed better audit systems in 1935. If they hadn't, someone might have stolen the company long ago. I could have told you about the engineers in 1946 who refined some of Mr. Ross's ideas and made them better. I could have talked about the technical salesmen, who talked reluctant customers into sales for their own good in 1955. I could have even talked about assembly line workers in Detroit, who were absolutely necessary to get the products manufactured. Of course everyone was necessary and critical, and Ross & Vogel, and RVA, has been blessed with first rate talent all up and down the line. If the company didn't need every one of its 65,000 employees, it wouldn't have them. But when you ask about history, you normally ask about strategy, not tactics."

"It's like a chain, isn't it? I mean, if one link breaks, then the chain fails totally."

"Of course, but there is always someone who figures out what the chain is for. That's the strategy, and that's why Vogel, Ross and Tavis are so important."

"Suppose none of them had lived, or suppose they had never met. Then what?"

"You're talking about *if* history, Mr. Faber. If we had never invented railroads, what would the country look like? Someone actually wrote such a book. But history has one key characteristic. You can think what you want about anything that happened, but you can never change it. Mr. Tavis, Mr. Vogel, and Mr. Ross did what they did. As a result, RVA exists and is here, right now. You can't change that fact, although you can change the future." Dr. Robertson's round face was troubled. "That is why we pay historians so little. They only report what has been, and few care very much. But managers can and do change the future. If they are good, they get ten times what a historian gets paid. Perhaps it is just, but still . . . well, you will not find much discussion of those three people around the company now. They are dead and buried, and they are only a part of history. But they do matter."

Dr. Robertson tossed a copy of RVA's latest annual report across the desk.* "Read this carefully. It will tell you what is, or at least what was a few months ago. Perhaps it will give you an idea of where to go next."

*See Appendix 2.

DISCUSSION QUESTIONS

1. What is a corporation? What are its key characteristics?

2. What is a proprietorship? What are its key characteristics?

3. What is a partnership? What are its key characteristics?

4. RVA's predecessor company went from proprietorship to a partnership to a corporation as it grew. Why? What was wrong with staying a proprietorship?

5. Dr. Robertson stated that anyone could start a business just by going out and doing it. It this really true now? Look around your own area and find a fairly new small business. What is it doing? Do you think that it just started?

6. What is working capital?

7. Mr. Ross almost went broke by being a big success. Do you think that the same sort of thing might happen today? Why or why not?

8. Things looked pretty rough in 1945, when World War II ended, but they turned out pretty well. Things look terrible now. Do you think that they will turn out pretty well, as they did after 1945, or will they just keep getting worse? Why?

9. What is a capital gain?

10. Is it fair that millionaires owning small but highly profitable companies could sell out to RVA for stock and avoid taxes on most of their gains? Why or why not?

11. What is a conglomerate?

12. What is the NYSE? Where can you find out more about it?

13. Dr. Robertson mentioned four things he felt were important in the past few decades. What were these? Are there any other major changes going on that you think might affect us all in the near future? What?

3

WHAT DO MANAGERS DO?

Al had no trouble finding Donald Beeman's office. He was of course on the 39th floor with the other five executive vice presidents. Al had to negotiate two competent secretaries, who carefully checked his appointment before he got in. Getting to see a VP was almost as hard as getting to see the president of the United States. Al wondered why.

Mr. Beeman himself did not turn out to be particularly intimidating. He was in his fifties, gray-haired, very carefully dressed and groomed in what Al had come to recognize as the executive style. His hair was neither too long nor too short, and his clothes were hand tailored and conservative. His huge office had a great view and contained a desk, but nothing much was on it. Mr. Beeman gave Al a firm, two-handed handshake, and led him to a comfortable sofa in the corner.

Mr. Beeman gazed at Al intently for a moment (Al became very aware of the ink stain on his best coat) before saying, "Well, we've been wondering what a journalist like you had on Bill Wilson that would make him give you the open door treatment. But Bill is impetuous. I suppose he thought that it would do some good. Now, what can I do for you? Bill told me to give it to you straight, whatever it was you wanted. What kind of scandal are you after? Dirty food? Defective washing machines?"

"I know that you're in charge of the consumer durables and the retailing group," Al said, "but I'm not really after scandal. That's not my job."

"It seems to be for most journalists."

"Yes, I know, but, well ..." Al was not sure how to proceed. "Look, Mr. Beeman, I looked up your salary in *Business Week*. You made $286,000 in salary, plus bonus ... $327,500 last year. I suppose we could start with what you do to earn that kind of money."

Mr. Beeman smiled. "It is a lot of money, isn't it? I'm not sure anyone earns that kind of money, really, although a few of us get paid that much. I'm a manager. I manage."

"And what exactly does that mean?"

"One scholar recently said that management is getting things done through people. I guess that is a part of it, but there's lots more. I make sure that my divisions of RVA do well, and hopefully do better every year. If they don't, I'm in deep trouble."

"What do you mean, better?"

"Bottom line performance. That means profitability. I try to make more money for the company every year. Oh, my boss looks at a few other things, like growth rates of sales, return on assets, and these days even some public responsibility issues get looked at. I wouldn't last long if Ralph Nader attacked our divisions, or we had black boycotts, or women agitated against our employment policies."

"But basically it's just money?"

"Sure, does that bother you?"

"Well, yes." Mr. Beeman was certainly frank, Al thought. He cast around for his next question, but Mr. Beeman went ahead for him.

"You wanted to know how I earned my money. Maybe if I tell you about a few projects we have been working on, you might see what managers do, and what management is."

"Go ahead."

"Let's see . . . about twenty-five years ago, the Wide West Grocery chain was an independent company. It had grown slowly but steadily by renting stores on main streets all over the Western U.S., in the 10,000 to 20,000 square foot range. Because it was a big chain, it could bulk buy items and keep prices lower than independent stores. Ever since the 1930's, the chain had been operating this way. But in the late 1950's, sales gains slowed rapidly. Then RVA bought the chain. At that time, I was a regional manager for twenty stores in California. I figured that I would probably get fired when the chain was taken over, but Mr. Tavis called me to RVA's New York headquarters. I had no idea what he wanted."

"I gather this Tavis was the fellow who made RVA great. Did you work with him very often?"

"I only saw him twice in my life. That first time in 1958, and once more in 1970, just before he died. But he was a genius. He asked just one question and gave one order that first time. 'Wide West is in deep trouble,' he said. 'You look like a bright young man. Find out why and tell me. I want a long-term plan to get the chain back on the growth track. Give me that, too.'"

"Why you? I mean, he must have had lots of people around."

"He did. He never told me why I was chosen. He was a prodigious worker, and he had the ability to see through to the essence of things, to size up people properly. He had read the personnel files on all of the Wide West people. I was just a middle manager, fighting with store managers. I tried to avoid out-of-stock situations by getting trucks to deliver on time, and I tried to manage pricing. Somehow, Mr. Tavis felt that I could think strategically. Of course, I learned how to do it better than I had as a middle manager, so here I am."

"What did you do?" Al tried to imagine what he would have done, but no inspiration came.

"I moved to the Wide West headquarters in Denver and tried to figure out what the problem was. I must say that I really didn't have much good background in anything that mattered . . . I majored in English Lit in college. I took a job clerking in Wide West because it was the only job I could find, not because I loved the business. And in those days, we didn't have much data, since the computer was very new, and we didn't know how to use it properly."

"So you sat and thought?"

"Sure. What else was there to do? Oh, I talked to just about anyone who would talk to me, but no one really could put a finger on why our sales actually went down a bit in '58, and profits fell further. It was a recession year, but still, we were losing our market share. One thing I learned to do at that time was to talk to the people in the trenches . . . that is, the store managers, and even the store clerks. They had to handle the operational problems every day. I wasn't their boss at that time, but I sensed that if I ever did manage them, their motivation and performance were going to be critical to my success. Besides, I found that they had excellent ideas about why things were going wrong. But one night I had a drink with a fellow from a drug store chain, and he gave me the right idea."

"Which was?"

"Back then, the move to the suburbs was just beginning. Shopping centers were very new, for the most part, and we hadn't paid much attention. Most of our customers had always shopped on Main Street, but they were beginning to move out. And when they moved, they changed their shopping patterns. That's where our market share was going. This drug company had built a few new drug stores in new shopping centers, and sales were so high that management didn't believe it. It was like owning the mint."

"So you moved to the shopping centers and got rich?"

Mr. Beeman smiled. "We had over 600 stores then. No, you just don't move the 8,000 or so employees and the stores out by next week. We owned many properties, and we had long-term leases on most of the others. If we moved in a hurry, we would lose our shirts on leases alone. Besides, one key factor as it turned out was store size. A 30,000 to 50,000 square foot unit seemed right for the new ones. Now, take a store manager who was used to a small operation with maybe five to ten employees, and what might happen? He could have lots of trouble handling such a big operation.

"Besides, there weren't many good shopping centers around in those days. Even if we wanted to move, we couldn't find places to go. No, if we did make a move, it would take many years."

"So that's what you told Tavis?"

"Not right away. I got all the data I could, and I had some young bright business school people to help me. We tried to figure out if this was really the problem."

"What do you mean? It seems pretty obvious to me."

"It may now, Mr. Faber, but it wasn't too obvious in 1958. There could have been a lot of things wrong. Suppose that our prices were wrong for our market ... say, a bit too high. Say that our stores just needed restructuring, in terms of where to put the meat or milk. Suppose that sales were slipping because we had neglected personnel training, and our clerks were surly and impolite? Suppose that the people moving to the suburbs were going to get tired of that life and move back to the city? Lots of people thought that this might happen back then. If I was wrong on my original idea, Wide West could lose tens of millions of dollars. It could even go broke, and I could lose my job. It has happened, and often, when a supposedly sharp manager makes a major blunder."

"Let's see ... in effect, you tried to figure out what the problem was, right?"

"Right, Mr. Faber. That really is step one of management. You have to know what the question is before you can begin to answer it. But then the next step is critical too. You have to plan your answer."

"So you set up a plan?"

"Right. Actually it was a simple one. It only took up a few pages. But we tried it, and it worked. It took over fifteen years, though, before we were sure that we were on the right track."

"What was the plan?"

"We decided to go slowly into bigger stores in major shopping centers. Every year, we would try a few new stores, but we were to go slowly. This was in part because we had to, given the shortage then of good new shopping centers, and partly because we wanted to. If we were off on the wrong foot, we could find out fairly fast, without losing our shirts."

"Are you saying that that idea is worth $286,000 per year?" Al asked.

"We're not done yet, Mr. Faber. I sent the plan to Mr. Tavis, and he approved it. I was appointed planning officer for Wide West in Denver. I was supposed to help the line managers do their jobs right."

"Line managers?"

Mr. Beeman explained the difference between line and staff, and Al carefully wrote it down. "I didn't have much authority, but I did have information, and my reports were being forwarded to New York. We began to carry out the plan."

Al thought for a while. "Hey, that must have been a job. You have to change 600 stores, move people, change managers. How did you do it?"

"That wasn't the half of it. When a plan gets going, everything has to be dovetailed so it fits. We had to worry a lot about real estate leases, which I mentioned before. The stores we moved at first were the ones whose leases were running out. Have you any idea of how long it takes just to read 500 leases to see what is going on? Then we had to approach shopping center builders and negotiate new leases. Lots of lawyers and real estate specialists worked for years on this one aspect alone.

Bottom line - the last line on the income statement, which is net profit.

Out of stock - Not having an item in the store that the customer wants.

Market share - ~~$~~ (1) - (get it right, guy!) percent of the total sales in a given market that a company has.

Lease - a contract to rent a property, subject to conditions in writing

PLAN - A proposed course of action for the future. Without plans, no one can manage! (Football - game plans)

$327,000/year - wow! For this?

"We had to revise completely our trucking system as the shift got under way as well. We eventually had to change all of our warehousing practices, because they were set up on the basis of shipping goods to small stores. The big new ones took truckloads. In the end, we built new, larger warehouses, and we even changed the types of trucks and trucking contractors we used.

"We had to set up a completely new store managers' training program. The first store we had almost collapsed, because the manager, who was a whiz with twelve people, fell apart with ninety.

"We had to change our basic organization. With bigger stores, my old job disappeared. One new store did the business that six to ten old ones did, so the store manager was really doing much of what I used to do."

"Who did all of these things?" Al asked. You couldn't cover all the bases."

"No, I didn't. Remember, I didn't even know how to do some of the things that had to be done. I'm not a lawyer ... I couldn't tell you if a given lease was valid or not. I'm not a transportation or physical distribution specialist ... I couldn't say what kinds of warehouses or trucks to build or buy. But that gets at another dimension of being a manager. A good manager knows how to hire and keep good people, and he knows how to figure out if they are fooling him or not."

"How do you know?"

Mr. Beeman sighed. "I don't think that I really do. A junior manager gives you a report, saying that he needs $3.7 million in capital to build a new warehouse which is absolutely necessary. You look at the summary ... you can't even read the whole report, through sheer lack of time ... and you ask him and some others questions. After a while, if you've had some experience, you begin to smell out the phonies. You learn to sense when something is not quite right.

"I remember that warehouse report. The fellow wanted a huge, plush office for himself, and he buried it in the specifications, which ran 320 pages. I asked a couple of our in-house architects about it, and they smelled it out. Saved $167,000 on that one item alone." Mr. Beeman laughed. "Oh, then it turned out that there was an error in the handling requirements. The warehouse was built for tonnage for stores that weren't going to be built for ten years. Lots of things. That expert is no longer with us, I'm afraid. He was rather careless with our money."

"In effect, your two-page plan led to lots of other plans."

"Right. Have you ever seen the specs on one new store? They can run to hundreds of pages. The electrical materials alone are enormous. You see, this is a big part of what I do. I have a big, simple plan, and then I get hundreds, even thousands of people to carry it out. If they do their job right, the big job gets done correctly, and we make money. The only way we can make money is to have a customer voluntarily walk into one of our stores and buy something. Suppose that we did everything right, except that the junior manager responsible for stocking the new store goofed up? We would have a great new building, a hundred employees getting paid, and no business. Suppose that the utility expert didn't check with the electric power company, to find out if they could handle our electrical needs? We can't run a store without power."

"I see a pyramid of plans, up and down the line," Al said. "You say, let's build some new stores in good locations! The troops salute, and they go do their things all over the place. And their subordinates do their things. And on and on."

"Right again. And if anyone down the line goofs up, I'm responsible. You can't delegate responsibility, only authority."

Authority — given the right to make
decisions and manage.
Line manager — one who is in charge.
Responsible for results.
Staff — advisors to managers. Examples:
Lawyers, real estate experts, design engineers,
etc.
AUTHORITY WITHOUT RESPONSIBILITY
IS DISASTROUS!

"What do you mean, Mr. Beeman?"

"I can give a person I choose the authority to plan for our electric power requirements. But if he fails, I am always responsible. Sure, I can fire him, but I could get fired too."

"I see what you mean," Al said thoughtfully. "I write a story, but if *Newsworld* gets sued for libel, the magazine, and my boss, take the heat, along with me."

"Exactly. They are responsible, even though you wrote it. If it ever is different, you have chaos, not management."

"But that means that you're responsible for men and women you probably never even met," Al said. "I mean, how do you handle that?"

"I make sure that those people's bosses are good. One odd definition of a manager is one who can choose his own people, period. If he can't choose his people, he is an administrator, not a manager."

"But what about all the rest? The planning, the activities, and the organizing?"

"All critical, but in the end it's people who do things, not organizations. And if I can trust my people, and they trust me, our company works fine."

"OK," Al said, "I begin to see what you do. But really, there's nothing much to it, is there? I mean, your company is running fine, and your junior managers are good. Once you get it all organized you just sit here and talk to outsiders like me."

Mr. Beeman smiled. "Sometimes. But I am giving you just one small example of what I do. Do you think that I had only one good idea? We have dozens of problems, including the one that some of those first shopping

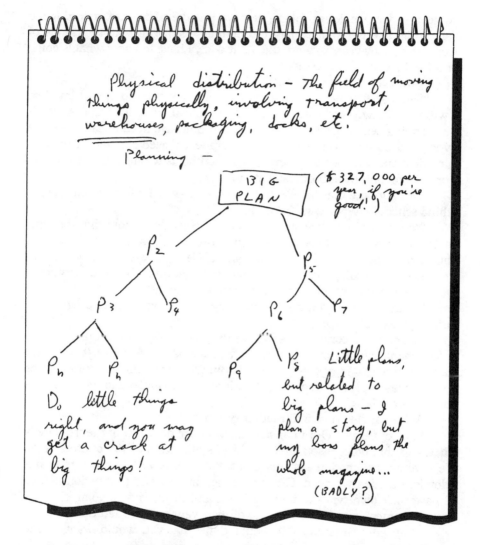

Physical distribution — The field of moving things physically, involving transport, warehouses, packaging, docks, etc.

Planning —

BIG PLAN   ($327,000 per year, if you're good!)

P_2 P_5

P_3 P_4 P_6 P_7

P_h P_h P_9 P_8 Little plans, but related to big plans — I plan a story, but my boss plans the whole magazine... (BADLY?)

Do little things right, and you may get a crack at big things!

center stores we opened back in the early 1960's are now too small and obsolete, and we have to go back and do it again. But our durable goods division is facing new competition from Japan and Taiwan, and we have a dozen new products to decide about putting into production. One might cost $30 million to develop, and what if it doesn't sell? And on and on. But there really is more."

"Dr. Robertson said that management is future, while history has already happened. I don't think that he makes $200,000 per year."

"No he doesn't, not by a long shot. But Dr. Robertson can take a close look at what we managers have done, and try to decide whether we did it right or not. He doesn't make the key decisions. I've pointed out to you that we get an idea, we set up plans, and we put the plans into action. If the plan is big, like our shift to larger supermarkets, it can take thousands of people and many years to work out. As it does, I have to know what is going on. I need feedback on results."

"How would that work out?" Al asked.

"Suppose that we are planning just one new store to open May first. It will take a few years' early work before we can even open that store ... the shopping center has to be designed and built, we need a lease with the owner, and so on. As all those events happen, I need reports on what is going right and what is going wrong. If something is wrong, I have to correct it or have one of my subordinates do it."

"OK, suppose that the electrical contractor was fouling up, and he got behind schedule. What would you do?"

"You missed one key step, Mr. Faber. How do I know that the contractor is fouled up? I have to have an information system to tell me that. This store might be in Illinois, and I am in New York. I may never see it. One very critical thing that I do is make sure that my information system is good, or I and the company could get into trouble fast."

"So in this case you have someone report to you about progress on various phases of the project?"

"Exactly. In a company as large as this, we have a very complex system to feed managers information. Quite often, we barely glance at it, since we are pretty sure that things are going well. But when something horrible comes up, hopefully we know about it before it gets impossible, and we do something about it."

"Who handles your information system?"

"Lots of people. Our financial materials are done out of the treasurer's office, and that office also handles a lot of statistical material of other sorts. We have an information systems group that works with computers to develop information we need. Our marketing, finance, and production people all have their own types of information to tell them what is going on. And often I see mere summaries of some of their very complicated data."

"Why only summaries? I would think that you would want to see everything."

"I would, but there are only twenty-four hours in a day. We have sales reports on every item sold in every store we have. Take 600 stores times 25,000 items, and I would have to read 15 million items a day. Even I can't read that fast ... and that report comes out daily. No, store managers, or even store division heads have to take care of that item. If sales of some key item start declining, they have to know what to do. That's why they get paid quite well. They do manage."

"So you only look at important things, right?"

"Right, Mr. Faber. And one of the key tricks of management is knowing what is important. If I keep looking at the wrong feedback, I will get into deep trouble very quickly."

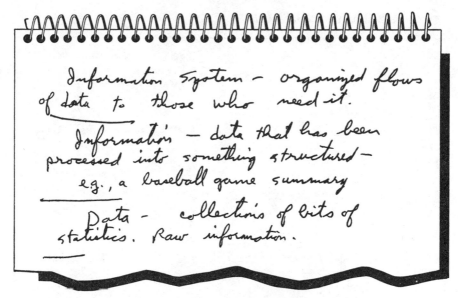

Information system - organized flows of data to those who need it.

Information - data that has been processed into something structured - e.g., a baseball game summary

Data - collections of bits of statistics. Raw information.

"How do you know what's important, Mr. Beeman?"

"Oh, I can see quite a few things that really matter, like costs for major items and overall sales. But I doubt that any management book will tell you five simple rules for deciding what is important. As you move along, you work it out. This is one reason why most top managers are fairly old. It takes quite a while to figure out such things."

Al glanced over at Mr. Beeman's empty desk. "You seem to have very little to worry about today."

"No, I have plenty on my mind, but all the routine stuff is being handled by others. Red tape is often nothing more than bad management, in the sense that the top people have to do too much. Some states, for example, require by law that the head of their Motor Vehicle Division personally sign all new licenses. This means that the top person, among other things, should sign perhaps 25,000 licenses every working day. If he or she really did it, nothing else would happen. It is quite common to find long delays in both government and business because no one ever figured out what should be delegated down to subordinates and what should be pushed to the top. Excess centralization means plenty of trouble, and usually it means that things get done very badly, with long delays."

Mr. Beeman grabbed Al's notebook and began drawing a little diagram. "This is the way it looks. See, it's a PARF loop. Planning, Activities, Results, and Feedback. If the feedback tells me that things are going wrong, I, or my subordinates, have to replan to take account of the difficulties."

Al studied the diagram. "It looks easy, but from what you've said, I suppose that it's not."

"Well, let's consider what can go wrong ... and believe me, lots can go wrong. First, you could have a bad plan. Supposing I told one of my

MR. BEEMAN'S DIAGRAM

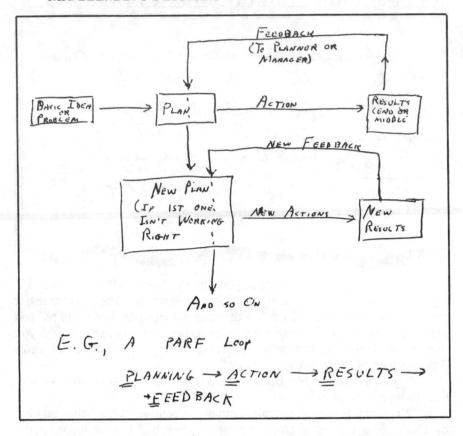

regional managers to build or open six new stores in excellent new shopping center locations in his territory within the next year. But in his whole territory, there are only three really good locations. We cannot achieve the plan, because it is unrealistic."

"So even if you fired him for non-performance, it wouldn't make any difference. You still wouldn't have six new stores."

"Right. Note that if the plan is either too easy or too difficult, we could be in trouble. Supposing he could open three stores, given our resources and what is possible, but we planned to open only one. Again, it is a poor plan."

"I see what you mean. If I'm a quarterback, and I plan to run off tackle, but the tackle against us there is 300 pounds and tough, we may not make a gain."

"Precisely. Even if you execute your plan or play perfectly, that big tackle makes the plan unrealistic. It won't work."

"OK, what else could go wrong?"

"Your plans have to have some numbers in them, or you never know what is going on. For example, we could plan to have those three new stores. That's a number ... we know when the plan is executed whether or not we have three. But it's not enough. We need to know what the stores will cost, how many employees each will have, and what kinds of people, and many other quantifiable things. We need to know times, such as just when a new store lease will be signed, when the store will be constructed, and when it will be opened. If we didn't have these time points built into the plan, we would never know where we stood."

"So if I said the store will be built, but I didn't say when, nothing much could happen, right?"

"That's it. Plans also have to be integrated with some action system. Plans without actions are daydreams. You might plan extensively to take a nice young lady out, but if you never get around to asking for a date, nothing will happen."

"In your case, this means that the people who actually do the work have to be pretty closely connected with the people who do the planning, right?"

"Often, Mr. Faber, they are the same people, but you are correct. If we don't coordinate all the activities we are doing, we get into trouble."

Mr. Beeman stood up and stretched. "How about some coffee? I could use a cup myself." Al said, "Sure," so Mr. Beeman went to his desk and used his inter-office phone to order some.

Al stood, stretching, too, and looked at Mr. Beeman's view while they made small talk about fishing, this morning's headlines, how the Yankees were doing, whatever, while they waited. Within a few minutes, the coffee was there. One advantage of being at the top, Al reflected, was that you got pretty good service. Managers did control their people, which meant that the people tried to please. Well, he tried to please his boss too. That was the way he got ahead. It figured.

"One more thing about planning," Mr. Beeman said, sipping his coffee. "It should be integrated with your information feedback system. By that I mean that you should have right in your plan some idea of the way that you are going to get feedback about results. If you know the key check points, and you tell the operators exactly how things will get checked, then you can get very good results. This is particularly true if the plan is realistic. Good people usually like to know that their work is being recognized."

"I can see that," Al said. "One thing that drives me nuts is to do something and discover that no one is paying attention, particularly if I did something right."

"I don't like being ignored either," Mr. Beeman said. "Oh, a good plan should have tolerance limits, too. You rarely want something done perfectly. Just good enough is fine. Perfection costs too much money."

"What do you mean? I would think that you do it right or else you fail."

"We make a toaster in our Consumer Durable Products Division. It has some parts that are accurate to plus or minus a hundredth of an inch. A few years back, we made them accurate to a thousandth of an inch. It turned out that a hundredth was quite accurate enough, in that if they were made this way, they always, well, almost always, worked fine. Changing that specification saved us almost a dollar a toaster. Careful machining and precision always cost big money. So do any other perfect specifications. If I insist that the trucking company deliver on May 4, without fail, they will, but I pay a premium. If I say, deliver in the week of May 4, I can get a cheap rate. A bit of slop always lets someone do the job cheaper."

"And if the slop doesn't really matter, why pay for something you don't need?"

"Right. I notice, Mr. Faber, that you have a rather cheap wristwatch. Why?"

"Well, I guess it's because I don't really need to have accurate time, say, within a second a day." Actually, it was a gift from his sister, but he didn't want to tell Mr. Beeman that.

"But if you worked for an airline or a railroad, you would need a $500 plus, very accurate watch. Such people need accuracy, and you don't. So they pay for it, and you don't have to."

"But lots of people buy expensive accurate watches they don't need."

"And lots of companies specify accuracies that they don't need as well. One program (which is a plan) that we are now carrying out in our manufacturing activities is to analyze carefully exactly what tolerances we really need. In some cases, we ask for a thousandth of an inch when a hundredth will do. Other times, we find the reverse. A part made too sloppily fails too often, and consumers are dissatisfied. Too often in the past, our tolerances were just stuck in by some engineer who did not really think through the implications of what he did.

"This program has already saved us over $500,000 per year for the past two years, and we hope to save still more in the future."

"So your profits go up, right?"

Mr. Beeman smiled ruefully. "For the most part our prices have gone down instead. Remember, the competition in consumer goods today is fierce. Those Japanese and Taiwanese imports ... tough. So we pass on most of the savings to the customer. I just wish we could have saved more for ourselves. But you see, it does no one any good to have overengineered parts inside his toaster that won't make any difference in the way the appliance works."

Al pondered his notes for a moment. "This planning business seems a lot more involved than I first thought."

"Some of our plans involve hundreds of millions of dollars, tens of thousands of people, and years of time. If they don't work, well, vice presidents can always resign. You can see it every week in the *Wall Street Journal*.

Planning Problems — or, what can go wrong!
1. Lousy plans - realism here.
2. Poor or no quantification —need numbers to tell you what's off
3. Plans need an action system — otherwise just daydreams.
4. Realism - no pipe dreams!
5. Plans must be integrated with feedback system - if not, you never know if you're carrying out plan.
6. Tolerance Limits - allow some reasonable fudge factor, but not too much.

Perquisites — non - money payments, e.g., good office, car, key to executive washroom, etc.

Or worse, the president resigns, because in the end, he can't delegate ultimate or complete responsibility either. If I fail, he has failed, and the top man is always vulnerable."

"So he pays you big money to make sure that you don't goof up."

"Money motivates, Mr. Faber. "So do perquisites ... you noted, I see, just how fast our coffee came, and you have been admiring my office and wondering why it's so nice. You haven't seen my company car and chauffeur, or my stock option plan, or lots of other things that come with this job. But such pay and perquisites only flow if I do what I am supposed to do, and do it right most of the time."

"OK, so planning is tough. What else is there?"

"Take another look at that sketch I gave you. See that action line? Once the plan is ready, you have to do things. Actions can be fouled up any number of ways, for any number of reasons. One example ... the cold winter of

1981–82 delayed construction on a number of shopping centers. As a result, although we planned to have stores open in May of 1982, they did not open until July or August. We lost three or four months' sales because of weather. Or we planned to stock a store completely by July, only one of our people failed ... a not uncommon event ... and the meats we intended to have available were not. This person forgot, or didn't care, so the long-term supply contract with the meat packer was not completed. The plan was great, but the action was terrible."

"Just like that football play. The guard is supposed to take out the linebacker, but he doesn't. So you gain a yard instead of thirty."

"Exactly. Most of our problems come from what might be called people problems. Finding really good people is always a strain. The textbooks say that a manager has to staff his operation and motivate his people, and the books are right. But as you noted, I have to motivate people I haven't even met."

"What else goes wrong?" Al asked, writing rapidly.

"Oh, many things. Organizational problems always are difficult. Who is in charge of what? Sometimes things fall between the cracks. A good plan should avoid this, but it happens. In one supermarket we built, no one noticed that installation of all the freezer equipment was simply not specified. The electrical contractor thought that the store manager was to be responsible, while the store manager thought that the contractor was responsible. As a result, we lost a month when we had a complete store, but no freezer equipment installed. Such things happen all the time, in spite of all we do to avoid them."

"I see what you are doing, Mr. Beeman." Al looked at the sketch. "You're just walking around this diagram. It looks simple, but I guess that lots of things are not as easy as they seem. Next comes feedback, I suppose."

"Yes, you can get into all kinds of feedback problems. We had one when you first walked in here. I did not have enough information (feedback) about why you were here. So I wasn't sure what to do with you. For all I know, we are talking about the wrong things. No one told me what was supposed to happen."

"Nobody told me, either," Al said. "But so far, I guess we're doing fine."

"Lack of feedback can be deadly, Al. Suppose that no one told me critical data about our new stores. I couldn't manage, because I wouldn't know what was going on. One major aerospace company some years ago simply did not have adequate feedback about the costs of a new aircraft they were building. Their cost accounting was so poor that the top managers did not know that costs were actually higher than the selling price. After a few years of good sales, this company was over a billion dollars in the hole. Lots of managers lost their jobs on that one, including a good friend of mine. But he did not know enough to insist on getting proper feedback."

"But most of the time you get some information, don't you?"

"Certainly. But it may be badly designed. The cost data can be so disorganized that I can't really figure it out, or the key figures may be buried somewhere down in the whole mess of unimportant materials. Sometimes you get noise in the feedback too, which makes it tough to figure out what is really happening."

"Noise? You mean folks shouting at you while you read reports?"

Mr. Beeman laughed. "Sort of. Did you ever try to listen to a distant radio station when there was static?"

"Sure. Sometimes you can barely understand what's going on. I was listening to a basketball game the other night, and it was just that way. I think that we won, but I'm really not sure."

"Well, my feedback often has noise in it too. I can hire, promote, or fire people, and one result is that they are very nice to me, even when they think that I'm nuts. I ask a subordinate for an opinion, and he hems and haws, tells me what a great person I am, and maybe, if I listen carefully, he buries in all the compliments what I want to find out, namely what is wrong." Mr. Beeman paused. "I'm not sure that women are better or worse on this point, really. We have quite a few female managers now, and they also give me lots of noise. But I can't read them quite as well as men ... lack of practice, I guess. Anyhow, the noise is in the system, and you have to be able to get through it and find out what is really going on. It takes practice."

"Let's see if I've got this right. The other day I got a speeding ticket. The cop said I was doing 35 in a 25 zone, but my speedometer was reading about 28. Would that be feedback system noise?"

"Your speedometer is a feedback device. Note that it takes some input (energy from the engine moving the car) and gives it back to the planner (the driver). But in this case, you were suffering from feedback distortion, not noise. Your feedback was just incorrect."

"I suppose that it happens all the time," Al said.

Mr. Beeman sighed. "More than anyone realizes. We just scrapped $40,000 worth of special die castings for our washing machine line because the measuring instrument that checked tolerances turned out to be off by a few thousandths of an inch. The technicians swore that it had never happened before, but every casting in that batch just wouldn't fit. We tossed them out. Our plan was great, our actions were excellent, but our feedback was distorted, so instead of washing machines, we get scrap metal."

"And I suppose that you have to pay for it."

"Of course. We can't raise prices in a competitive market like washing machines just because we don't know what we are doing."

"It sounds like the company that makes the fewest mistakes makes the most money."

"That's usually true. We all make mistakes, but we try to keep them down to some low level. But that $40,000 came right out of profits, I'm afraid ... and my bonus, too. We all pay for errors."

Feedback Problems —
1. No feedback (why didn't anyone
   tell me ! --- ?)
2. Noise — everything garbled
3. Disorganized — can't find the
   right stuff in the mess.
4. Distortion
5. Misdirection — goes to
   wrong person
6. Not quantified right — if you
   don't know what the
   numbers mean, you can't
   do much managing !

"So what else can go wrong? After all of this, I'm beginning to wonder how anything comes out right."

"Oh, you can get good feedback going to the wrong people for one thing. We had a beautiful report on freezer malfunctions being sent to the sales manager for the Wide West Division. Unfortunately, he was not responsible for fixing them. We have a store maintenance division reporting to another manager that does that. For a while, we couldn't figure out why so many stores were having freezer troubles that they couldn't get fixed. We were misdirecting feedback. When we finally got the reports to the right manager, we solved the problem."

"I still get a financial cost report for my section of *Newsworld*," Al said. "Although I have nothing to do with finances. I hope the person who does gets it."

"Note that such misdirections can waste a lot of time, too, Al. Do you read that financial report?"

"Sure, it's kind of interesting."

"On company time?"

"Yes. Oh, I see what you mean. Since it's none of my business, in effect my boss is paying me to do nothing that really matters."

"Exactly. Your boss is wasting time, which is money. One of the really tricky things I have to worry about is that all my managers know what they are supposed to know, but don't have to worry much about things they really can do nothing about."

"That could be tough, if the system is complicated, which yours is."

"Right. One more thing to worry about is that you can get correct feedback, but then you do the wrong thing. Remember the example of shifting our stores to the shopping centers? The feedback, which was correct, was that sales were declining. But we were not too sure what the correct replanning and actions should be. Even if you know the problem, being able to do something right about it can be a real difficulty."

Mr. Beeman looked away for a moment, then went on in a new tone of voice. "So much depends on how you set up your planning/control system, which really is this PARF loop system we've talked about. If we're working on something tangible, like a washing machine, it's complex, but not really too difficult. We can set quite tight quantifiable standards for parts, and give reasonable tolerances, and if we do our job right, the machines go together and work right. Remember, we have to set up all those feedback loops through the system to make sure that everything gets checked when it should. Our technical people are very good ... when something goes wrong, and they know about it, they can correct the problem fast.

"But how can I quantify what our lawyers do? Most of the time, they literally do nothing. That is, they keep us out of court. But I'm no lawyer, and I really can't tell when one of our lawyers has done a good job or not. I want to reward good men and women for good work, but it gets very tough to figure out what's good when you can't stick hard numbers on things."

"My boss has the same trouble," Al said. "I write a story, and I think it's good. Maybe he does too. But how do you know? I can see that if I had to produce a thousand toasters a day, you could figure out pretty fast how well I did my job. But if I work ten weeks on a story, how do you know that I couldn't have done it in five weeks?"

"Very astute, Al. In this country, we're very good at making toasters, and terrible at evaluating things that can't be measured. Inability to figure out what should be happening is the reason."

"So you set up this big system, and if you're good enough, and have enough good people, it runs like a fine watch, right? RVA must be at least 99 percent efficient."

Mr. Beeman laughed. "If we operate at seven percent efficiency, I'd be surprised. Most younger people don't really realize how badly systems function. If I could get RVA, or at least my part of it, up to eight percent efficiency,

More Things to go wrong —

I - Poor Actions —

   1. Foul ups by people

   2. Lousy organization — No one tells us to do a job, or how to do it

   3. Acts of God — fire, weather, wars, just plain bad luck

   4. Outsiders fail — truckers don't deliver, suppliers give you bad parts, etc.

from the present seven, I'd be one of the great managers of this century. Most systems barely function, and ours is no particular exception. Oh, we get along. Our products get produced, and our stores have products to sell. But every time you look closely at something you find all sorts of inefficiencies to be improved. Some activities are being done badly; some feedback is terrible; and often our planning is rather poor. Lots of our personnel are really not very good, as well."

"Why don't you fire the bad people and get some good ones?"

"Because we can't be sure that the next one will be any better than the one we have. Take a junior manager who really isn't all that good, who makes a lot of mistakes. But he is honest and trying, and he's been with us for a few years. When we hired him, we had high hopes, and I suppose that he did too. But we just aren't good enough to find another replacement that would be guaranteed to be better. Besides, there is the moral issue. If we made a mistake, should the individual suffer?"

"I suppose not. But it must be frustrating."

"There is another problem I have which is very frustrating to younger managers in our organization. I am supposed to see the whole organization. I know what kinds of talents we have, and my staff has a lot of projects that we could start. They all take money and talent and time. We run out of good people long before we run out of money, believe it or not, so my real problem is to decide how to use my talent.

"Now, the way we decide what to do is by rate of return. If a project looks like it will pay off at thirty percent per year, it is much more attractive than one that pays off at twenty percent per year. In effect, I have an order of priority for what plans will be executed in the near future.

"Many younger managers, however, don't see the big picture. They have a small section of the company, and they see that something can be done that would improve things. They are right, too. A $100,000 investment in say, some forklift trucks for a warehouse could yield twenty percent on investment. So they make the proposal to their boss, it eventually gets to me, and I turn it down."

"So they think you're nuts, huh?"

"Their precise terminology is, ah, sometimes more vivid than that." Mr. Beeman laughed. "I am regarded as an old fogy who doesn't understand his own company. What they don't know is that the engineering talent, the time, and the money is going into something else that will yield thirty-five percent on capital. Since they know nothing of this other area, they do not know this. All they can see is that RVA is not too smart."

"This order of priority thing turns out to be pretty important then, right?"

"It's critical, and it's one of the hardest things to learn. I suppose that you learn it only as you advance in management, and as you begin to see more and more of the company. Lots of people never do learn it. But if I spent all my time and effort doing things that weren't too important, the company would stagnate. Quite a few big companies do, you know. Their managers just can't figure out what really matters. And there's no book around to tell you what does."

"But they pay you big money to know."

"Right, or at least that is one thing they pay me for. A related problem is that it may take five, ten or even twenty years to figure out if you are right or not. Some big plans can take that long to work out. Right now, we are looking at possible production of some revolutionary new electronic consumer products. If I decide to start tomorrow, it will be ten or twelve years before we actually offer the product for sale. We have to build plants, buy custom-made machines, develop new marketing channels, and so on. I'm fifty-seven . . . I'll be dead before anyone really knows whether or not I made a good decision. If I'm right, the company will make hundreds of millions of dollars. If I'm wrong, we could lose that much. They pay me to be right more often than I'm wrong."

Mr. Beeman glanced at his very expensive watch. "We've run quite a bit overtime, Al. I hope that you got what you came for."

What do managers do, for
gosh sakes?

1. Plan

2. Staff

3. Direct — that is, give orders

4. Control — all that feedback
and such

5. Organize   — — —

<u>AND</u>

6. Figure out how to
spend $327,000 per year,
less taxes!

Al stood to go. "Thanks, Mr. Beeman. Unfortunately, my plan wasn't too good, and the feedback was defective. I'm not too sure what I expected, but I think that you've been a big help."

"Now, will I read an expose of RVA's managers? Or will you write a textbook on management?"

"I'm not sure what will come out of this," Al said. "This is just the beginning of what I'm supposed to do."

"Oh, did you decide that I'm worth what I get paid?" Mr. Beeman asked, smiling.

"Not really," Al said, grinning at him.

"If you decide, let me know. Good luck." Mr. Beeman walked with Al out of his office.

"Just one more thing, Mr. Beeman. Do you enjoy your work?"

"I've spent thirty-five years with RVA or one of its predecessors, Al. It's been my life. I work sixty to eighty hours a week, worry about the future of millions of dollars and tens of thousands of people. If I blow it, God knows how many lives could be ruined.

"I get attacked by everyone as being some sort of moral monster. Even my own children, who are now grown, are pretty dubious about the old man. But I can structure my own work, and I can try to figure out new problems in any way that makes sense. My own boss doesn't bother me much, as long as I produce. I suppose that I live a lifestyle that kings of old could not afford, and that is fun. Unlike folklore, I still have the charming wife I started with, and I don't have a blonde in every city. Frankly, I don't have the time. I feel the pressure, but again, counter to folklore, I don't have ulcers, a heart condition, or any other loathsome disease. I'm never bored, even talking to you."

"So?"

"I suppose that I like it just fine, Al, just fine. Indeed, I can't think of anything else that would be more fun. Nothing that pays over $200,000 per year, for sure." They shook hands, and Al left, clutching a bundle of notes. He chatted for a while with the quite attractive number two secretary and left, wondering just what he had learned, if anything.

DISCUSSION QUESTIONS

1. A football coach learned that his next opponent, State, was in trouble. Its All-American middle linebacker had been injured and probably could not play. So the coach made up a game plan based on the fact that the substitute was only a student and should be pretty easy to blast out of position.

Unfortunately the All-American turned up healthy for the game, and the coach lost, 21–7. Curiously, the coach's only touchdown came on the first play of the game, which was right up the middle. It was the first, and last, time that his center blocked out the guy. His team netted 84 yards rushing, as the All-American nailed play after play.

This coach's team went eight wins and three losses for the year, which earned him second place in the conference. If he had won that key game, he would have won the title and played in a major bowl game. He did get his team invited to a minor bowl, which he won easily. His school received $35,000 for playing,

while the major bowl game would have been worth over
$200,000.

Should the athletic director of this coach's school fire the
bum and get someone who could adapt more easily? Why or why
not?

What was wrong with the coach's game plan?

What feedback would the coach receive about critical points
as the game proceeded?

What was the critical assumption of the coach's plan?

2. What does a manager do? Be specific and complete.

3. What is a PARF loop? What does it mean?

4. What are staff personnel? What are line managers?

5. A manager of a student housing dorm once got fired
because one of his subordinates stole lots of money over a period
of four years. The culprit was caught, tried, and convicted, but the
manager also got fired. He was quite indignant about this.

"I delegated the authority to count the money to Sam," he
said. "After that, it was his responsibility. They asked me if I ever
checked it, but why should I? After all, it was his responsibility
and authority to keep track of the money. It wasn't fair to fire me
for what he did!"

Was this manager correct? Could he really delegate
responsibility? Could he delegate authority?

6. The dean of your business school has lots of duties,
including managing a staff of perhaps dozens or hundreds,
keeping track of curricula, making budgets, planning and
controlling the operation, and much more. However, one thing he
or she cannot do is fire tenured professors. Under typical college
rules, once a professor is tenured, he or she cannot be fired except
in cases of moral turpitude or extreme financial exigency. Mere
incompetence, failing to follow instructions or orders, or general
nastiness are not reasons for discharge.

Is your dean really a manager? Why or why not?

7. Is Mr. Beeman worth what he is paid? Is anyone worth
this much? Why or why not?

8. What is an information system?

9. The business class you are now taking has an
information system, complete with data, feedback, and all the rest.
What is it? Describe it in detail, and draw a diagram of it.

10. An instructor once stated that scores of over 90 on his
exams got A's. But it was a tough course, and he was a tough
grader, so for years no one got an A. As time went on, it became

more and more important for pre-med students to get A's, so they avoided his course in droves. The more tolerant instructor teaching the same course had 85 students, while this fellow had five or six.

The department chairman, to equalize teaching loads, demanded that students take the tough instructor's section. They were put in the section and told to stay there, or else. But what they did was go on strike, march on the president's house, and demand action. One over-anxious student actually filed a lawsuit against the school, demanding his rights. He pointed out that to get into medical school, you had to have a 4.0 average in this state, and one B meant being turned down.

The harassed president found himself with a lawnful of irate students, chaos all through the college, a lawsuit on his hands which looked like it might win, and a tenured, and hence unfireable professor who simply set high standards and was not about to change them.

Analyze this incident as a management problem. What kind of feedback was in this situation to tell the administrators that a problem was brewing? Whose plans were being fouled up by this situation? What activities were not being carried out well?

11. Al had a smudge on his coat when he saw Mr. Beeman. What kind of feedback was this to Mr. Beeman? Do you think that it meant anything? What?

12. Al was wearing a cheap watch, while Mr. Beeman had a very expensive one. Who cares? Does this sort of feedback tell you anything about these people? What?

13. To see Mr. Beeman, you had to get through two secretaries. What does this tell you about the vice president, if anything?

14. What types of poor actions are there? Give an example of one you have seen yourself.

15. Mr. Beeman mentioned that RVA runs at about seven percent efficiency, yet it is a good, profitable company. About how efficient is your school or college? Give two things it could do to be a bit more efficient.

16. You have a lot to do next week, so much that you probably won't get it all done.

What is your order of priorities? Why? What really has to be done to avoid disaster? Why? How do you really know?

4

CONTROL: ACCOUNTING

I'm really not sure that I should be bothering you, Mr. Harrington," Al said, "but I find this annual report pretty confusing."

"It's no bother, Mr. Faber. I received a note from Mr. Wilson telling me to extend to you every courtesy. You have a boss too, don't you?"

"Yes, and when he says jump, I guess I jump."

Wallace Harrington smiled. "Now what's your problem?"

Al flipped through RVA's *Annual Report* to the financial statements. "I never took a course in accounting, Mr. Harrington. That is, I started one, but I dropped it. It seemed pretty confusing and irrelevant."

"I know what you mean. I got a C minus in my first accounting course ... almost dropped the idea of becoming an accountant. But I stuck with it, and now I'm treasurer of one of America's biggest corporations. In the end, I enjoyed accounting. But I've always felt that it was taught backward. You start with the details of bookkeeping, and only after a few years of study do you get to the interesting part. Believe it or not, accounting can be fun."

"I'm not sure I believe *that*, but tell me, just what is accounting?"

"It could be defined in many ways, but I think of it as the art and science of keeping records of financial activities in generally accepted ways. It's a critical part of a company's total information system, which is its key feedback as to how it's doing. Without feedback on results, you'll never know how you're doing."

"The feedback part of the PARF loop, right?"

"I see that you've heard Don Beeman's lecture."

"Yes, I have," Al said. They both laughed. "He said that RVA was complicated, and I'm beginning to believe him. What a mess!"

"You've barely begun. Oh, come in Vicki." Mr. Harrington waved at the young woman at his door. "Vicki, meet Al Faber. This is Vicki Masters."

She certainly was attractive enough, Al thought, as he shook hands, even though her severely cut suit was not his idea of feminine attire. He glanced at Mr. Harrington. "Does Ms. Masters work for you?"

"She's my assistant. Most executives have at least one highly competent assistant these days ... we just can't cover all the bases. I thought that perhaps she could help you out on some aspects of this problem."

Al wondered if Mr. Harrington was about to dump him on some subordinate, but the older man made no effort to leave. Al asked him what kind of assistant Ms. Masters was.

"An 'assistant to' is not exactly what you may have in mind," Mr. Harrington said by way of an answer. "Vicki has an M.B.A. from Indiana University and she was in the top ten percent of her class. She's a thoroughly trained young executive. Majored in Accounting and Finance. I think that she can type, but I'm not sure, since we pay her far too much to worry about that. A lot of the analysis and legwork that went into those financial reports you're worried about was done by Vicki."

"What's worrying you?" Vicki asked Al.

"Well, I'm having trouble with the reports."

Vicki nodded. "Before we get into that, let's talk a bit about what accounting is supposed to do. A long time ago, accounting in its modern form was developed mainly to keep track of assets. Firms were small, and wealth was scarce. Owners wanted to know who, if anyone, was stealing what. In this kind of accounting, you check up and measure assets like inventories and cash. Then you prepare a statement of assets and liabilities, which are values owed. This is still important, and if you look at the balance sheet, you can see how it's done."

Al flipped to the balance sheet in the *Annual Report* (see Appendix II). "I see ... you start with assets and go on to liabilities." He studied the page for a moment. "How does this information get put together? It looks like a lot of work."

"It sure is," Vicki said. "Look at one item, Buildings, Machinery, and Equipment. We have eight divisions with factories, sales offices, and machinery all over the world. That one number represents a lot of arithmetic. Moreover, it has to be accurate, so we have both internal and external auditors checking each figure. Remember that we're a public corporation, owned by thousands of stockholders, and our legal obligation is to present as accurate a picture as we can."

"Excuse me, but what exactly is an auditor?"

Vicki looked startled, but told him, and Al wrote it down.

"There's another kind of accounting that is more modern," Vicki added. "Managers need lots of information about costs and revenues, and the balance doesn't show enough. You can't manage efficiently without excellent accounting information. Managerial accounting shows managers and even outsiders what is going on. Of course the managers generally get much more detailed information than what is shown here on the income statement."

Al studied the income statement for a while. "This material is very different from the balance sheet, isn't it? Let's see, you start with sales and deduct costs."

"Right," Vicki said. "Basically it's nothing more than subtracting total

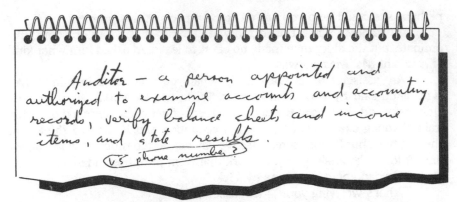

Auditor — a person appointed and authorized to examine accounts and accounting records, verify balance sheets and income items, and state results.

(vs phone number?)

costs from total sales. Then you get the famous bottom line ... namely profit."

"That's the one thing I keep reading about in the *Wall Street Journal*. Net profit seems to be the name of the game."

"So you read the *Wall Street Journal?*" Mr. Harrington asked.

"Well, since I started this assignment I do. It's kind of fun, even though I don't quite understand most of the numbers yet. And the quality of journalism is superb! But I do keep reading about profits."

"If we didn't make a profit, and a good one, we wouldn't be around very long," Vicki said.

Al took another look at the income statement. "This public statement lumps every division together just as the balance sheet did. I suppose that if the manager of one division wanted to know where he stood, he would want to have his own figures separated out, right?"

"Correct," Vicki said. "In fact, he would want to know a lot more. He needs each product costed, so he can tell what prices should be. He wants sales figures of every item in his line separately. We have over twenty profit centers in RVA, and each one of them has its own internal balance sheet and most importantly, its own income statement."

"What's a profit center?"

She told him, and he wrote it down. "I see what you mean. In effect you can tell how well each manager is doing by examining his own accounting statements. I suppose that not every manager is as good as the best."

"That's right," Mr. Harrington said. "One of our most important jobs in this office is to make sure that the accounting reports from every profit center and division are correct. We also have to make sure that they are produced rapidly. It won't help a manager to find out a year from now that he is doing badly today. If he knows something is going wrong, he can move quickly to correct problems."

"Fast and accurate feedback in the PARF loop, right?" Al asked.

"Right," Mr. Harrington said. "At present, we can get weekly summary statements out to division and profit center managers within three days." He leaned back in his big chair and pondered. "When I was young, it used to

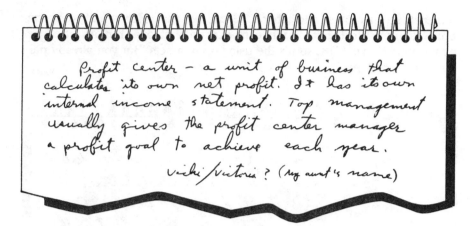

Profit center – a unit of business that calculates its own net profit. It has its own internal income statement. Top management usually gives the profit center manager a profit goal to achieve each year.

vicki/Victoria? (my aunt's name)

take months, and the data was really not very detailed. Thanks to computers and leased telephone lines, we can really work pretty fast nowadays."

Al glanced from Mr. Harrington back to Vicki. "You know, neither one of you looks like my idea of an accountant. I sort of thought they were as dry as dust, ancient, with green eyeshades and quill pens, nitpicking about one minor expense item."

Vicki laughed. "I suppose that such people exist someplace, but actually, modern accounting is really a form of information system construction and analysis. Our job is to provide proper and structured information to various people who need it to function well."

"When I started that accounting course, I remember that all we talked about were debits and credits and T accounts. It was really dull. But here you're talking about information systems, cost analysis, and all that. Are these things really both accounting?"

"Of course," Vicki said, "And don't sell all those debits and credits short. What you were beginning to learn was the structure of accounting, how things fit together in ways that anyone could understand. I guess in a way it's a lot like learning a language. We deal with various kinds of financial information in very precise ways, so that any accountant can take a look at any set of books and know what's going on. You can't run until you learn to walk, at least if you want to be a professional accountant."

"Al nodded. "I don't want to do that, but I do want to understand what's going on." He took another look at the income statement. "Let's see ... this says that the statement is for the year 1983."

Vicki nodded. "An income statement measures flows of cash and costs, like a river. It is for a period of time, not an instant. In this case, it reports for the whole year. Note that the balance sheet is for a moment, in this case, December 31, 1983. It's like a snapshot ... it tells you what the situation was at one moment in time."

"So you have total sales, and then you subtract costs. Inventories, materials and supplies, and labor ... I can see that. Hey, what's depreciation?" It took Vicki quite a while to explain that one, but Al jotted her explanation down. "OK, so it's the using up of assets. But you already paid for them, didn't you?"

Depreciation — Decrease in value due to wear, tear, decay, or obsolescence. If you buy an asset for $10,000, and it is expected to last 10 years, it will lose one tenth of its value per year. To report profits properly, you must write off (depreciate) this asset each year. Otherwise, you are using up your assets, and after ten years, you have nothing.

In theory, depreciation should cover the historic cost of the asset. This is a non-cash cost. That is, you deduct the cost, but you've already paid for the asset. You can have a positive cash flow, even though you're not making money.

But remember, if you expect to stay in business, this depreciation cash is going to be needed to buy replacement assets!

(story on V – ERA, MBA, or what?)

"Typically, yes, so this one is a cost that is not money, and it's called a non-cash cost. It's very real, though, as lots of poor businessmen have found out the hard way. Every year, you use up some of your assets, and if you don't remember this, when the asset is junk, you don't have money or credit to buy replacements."

"I think that happened to me," Al said. "I bought a car and ran the wheels off it for three years. I forgot that when it wore out, I had to come up with the cash to buy another one. That created some real cash problems for me. I borrowed the money, actually."

"If you wanted to, you could construct an income statement for yourself, just like this one," Vicki said. "Most people don't bother, but you have income and costs, just like a company does."

"And a net loss at the end of the year, unlike RVA," Al said. "This tax item I think I understand. RVA pays income taxes, too."

"And lots of others. They aren't shown here, but we pay payroll taxes, real estate taxes, excise taxes, and lots more." Vicki waved toward the offices on her left. "We have dozens of tax experts who do nothing but worry about what we pay and why. And of course our accounting system shows tax collectors just what we owe. One of our closest auditors is the IRS, and their people make very sure that we keep an honest set of books, I can assure you. Then the state tax people get in the act, as do foreign governments. Remember that we have lots of foreign business. Among other things, RVA is a very efficient tax collector for various governments."

"And then comes the bottom line, net profit," Al said. "Now, what's this *Opinion of Independent Auditors*?"

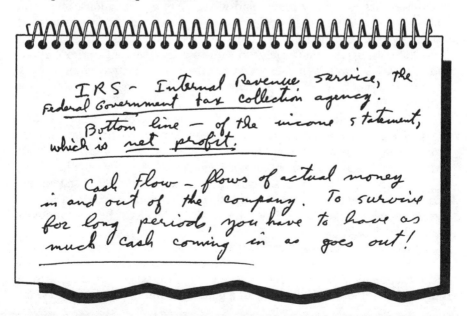

IRS - Internal Revenue service, the Federal Government tax collection agency.

Bottom line — of the income statement, which is <u>net profit</u>.

Cash Flow — flows of actual money in and out of the company. To survive for long periods, you have to have as much cash coming in as goes out!

"We're a public corporation," Vicki said. "Under American law, all such companies must have an outside audit every year. Actually, Radebaugh, Arpan, Schweikart, and Chung have their accountants working with us constantly. We pay them, but we really don't have much control over them. If they find something fishy, they have the duty to report it."

"Fishy like what?"

"Oh, suppose that we decide to depreciate an asset in ten years, and they feel that the proper length of time would be five years. They will raise this question with us, and if they really think that it is right to go five, they will insist. If we disagree, we get a qualified statement."

"I suppose that means that they would mention it in their opinion."

Vicki nodded. "And a qualified statement is poison. Security analysts and other possible stock buyers read our report very, very carefully. If there's any hint that we are finagling the books, then we could be in real trouble. So we might argue a lot, but we probably would come around."

"But who would care if you depreciated something over ten years instead of five? It doesn't sound like much of a problem to me."

Vicki scribbled a few figures on a piece of paper and handed it to Al. "See what happens to profits, if we take a big item and write it off over ten years? Profits go up. If we were having a bad year, we could play around and make it out to be a good year."

Al studied her page. "I suppose that there are lots of costs and revenues that can be finagled?"

"Right," Vicki said. "Sometimes it's called creative accounting. A company tries to take maximum advantage of the rules to gain bigger profits. But those rules are pretty tough, and while there are variations, investors, banks and other interested people don't like a company to keep changing around, even within the rules. Auditors *really* don't like it."

"Supposing you really disagreed with your independent auditor? Could you change?" It was a weird sensation talking to an attractive woman about accounting. Usually when he met someone like this, Al had other things on his mind.

Vicki waved her pencil. "Sure, there are many major public accounting firms who do these audits. But if we change firms, we better have a very good reason. Changing auditors is often interpreted as a slippery move to avoid something. And the next auditor might be tougher than the last."

"Remember, Al," Mr. Harrington put in, "that those independent auditors are very reputable and very prestigious. They can't afford to let any company make big mistakes. They are legally liable, and their accountants are the best."

"Where do you get accountants?" Al asked.

"From colleges that have accounting programs, mainly," Vicki said. "I had a chance to work for a public accounting firm when I graduated from Indiana, but I chose RVA instead. In a good accounting program, you learn

VICKI'S NOTE

Asset Cost: $100,000

A	B
10 year depreciation	5 year depreciation
(Dep. = $10,000/yr.)	(Dep. = 20,000/yr.)

	A	B
Revenue	$1,000,000	$1,000,000
All costs (except Dep.)	800,000.	800,000
	200,000	200,000
Depreciation	10,000	20,000
Net Profit	$190,000	$180,000

Tax Rate: 40%

In A: pays 40% of $190,000, or $76,000

In B: Pays 40% of $180,000, or $72,000

Make one little change in depreciation, and the IRS is out $4,000!

But remember this — in year 6, A still has depreciation left, and B doesn't — so A wins in the long run! Do you want your money now, or later?

the same tools and techniques." Vicki doodled a few notes. "I could have worked in government, too. The IRS and other agencies use lots of accountants. When we argue a tax question with the IRS, it's likely that the government person, our independent auditor's person, and I all went to similar schools."

"When I was young, accounting used to be pretty much a man's game, Al," Mr. Harrington said. "But as you can see, it's an open field now. And we always seem to need more accountants. Records and taxes get more complex every year."

Al turned to the balance sheet. "This one actually does balance," he said, after inspecting it.

"It does for a fact," Vicki said. "Assets equal liabilities plus the owner's equity."

"I can understand most of the items," Al said. "But how about receivables? Are these amounts due from customers and others?"

"Right," Vicki said.

"How do you know that they're any good? I mean, I have a few IOUs from some ex-friends that I doubt I'll ever collect."

"We check our credit customers pretty carefully," she said, "but we do have some bad debts. What you see there is the net amount, less provision for bad debts. Don't worry . . . our division managers are checked very carefully about letting poor customers have too much credit. This is another example of how we use our accounting data for managerial purposes."

Al thought for a moment. "Suppose you gave lots of credit to lousy customers. Then wouldn't that show up as sales on the income statement?"

Vicki smiled approvingly. She had a very nice smile. "You're a fast learner. That's another potential creative accounting act. Say a company wants to make sales grow for a year. Its managers can extend more credit to poorer risks, and sales go way up. So do accounts receivable over on the balance sheet. If you don't check carefully, all you see is a big sales and profit increase. But if those poor risks don't pay off, both your assets and your sales are smaller than they appear. Our independent auditor is always very interested in our bad debt record."

"It sounds like there are lots of ways to mess up the books," Al commented.

"That's why we need good accountants, and honorable ones. Remember, literally hundreds of thousands of people depend on getting accurate and timely information. If we foul things up, this company could collapse in a few years. Workers, stockholders, bankers, pension funds, and lots more people could be wiped out." Vicki leaned back in her chair and ran her fingers through her short brown hair. "That's why accounting is so interesting. It's even fun. If we don't do our job right, everyone's in trouble."

Mr. Harrington got up and excused himself, saying that he had another appointment. "Stay here with Vicki until you're satisfied, Al," he said as he left. "One more auditor, even a journalist, won't matter that much."

Al was looking at the *Annual Report* again. "There's one more statement that we haven't talked about. What's this *Sources and Uses of Funds* thing?"

"Remember those non-cash items in the income statement? If you work it through carefully, you could have a big profit, but no cash. And cash really is the lifeblood of the company. You have to meet payrolls, pay taxes, and pay suppliers with cash, not IOUs. Supposing you have big credit sales, legitimate ones from good accounts, but they aren't supposed to pay off for a few months. You have to meet your payroll now. Where does the money come from? If you haven't worked it all out, you're in trouble."

Al remembered that Mr. Ross had almost gone broke in 1927 over a cash shortage. "Where does the money come from?"

"Lots of places, but you have to know where it is or how to get it. We could borrow from our banks, for example. That cash inflow doesn't show up on the income statement. We might float a bond issue, and that would show up as a long-term account payable, but not on the income statement. Or we might draw down our cash reserves. Whatever we do, it's often difficult to trace what happens through these two basic statements."

"OK, so the *Sources and Uses of Funds* statement tells you where the cash is, and where it went, right?"

"Correct. Most companies have only published this statement in recent years, but it's extremely useful if you're interested in where the money is."

"Why only recently?"

"In the old days, there were many fewer non-cash items on the income statement. It wasn't too tough to make a few adjustments and see what was happening to cash. But as accounting got more sophisticated, lots of non-cash items began to show up. Credit got a lot more complicated, too, and remember that investment items don't show up on the income statement either. If you build a lot of plants, as RVA has done, you need lots of capital. A few companies that looked great on their income statements got into deep cash crises. It made sense to analyze cash flows separately."

Al studied the statements for a while, which wasn't really easy with Vicki beside him. "All of this stuff is history, really, isn't it? I mean, what we're looking at is what happened, not what's going to happen. A company could have a great year but fall apart the next year."

"It sure could, and many have. But this is just one part of the information system. I hope that you get into finance and budgets before you're done. There we get into financial planning for the future. Of course, what we plan for depends a lot on what's happened."

"I suppose that I will get there, before this crazy assignment is over," Al said. "I seem to be getting into all sorts of things that I never really thought much about."

"Actually, there is lots more we haven't even gotten into, because this business of keeping accurate records is pretty complicated. Everyone wants to have precise data, but it's tough to get it."

"Give me one more example."

"Accounting is culture bound."

"It's what?"

"Culture bound. That is, it's a part of a given country. The accounting rules, tax laws, and all the rest are basically local. But RVA operates in over 40 countries. One thing we have to do is to figure out how a set of Swedish books integrates into a set of American books."

"What's so exciting about that?"

Vicki was making another note. "It can make a huge difference in

VICKI'S INTERNATIONAL ACCOUNTING GAME

You build a plant for #1,000,000,

U.S.		Sweden	
Net profit, except depreciation	$2,000,000		#2,000,000
Depreciation (5 years)	200,000	Depreciation (1 year)	1,000,000
Net Profit	#1,800,000		#1,000,000

U.S. Tax @ 40% = $720,000 ; Profit = $1,080,000

Swedish Tax @ 40% = #400,000 ; Profit = $1,600,000

Visit sunny Sweden on your next business trip!

But remember — in year 2, Profits in Sweden will be _higher_ than in the U.S., since there is no more depreciation to take! So, invest more, or sigh and pay your taxes! This technique does not avoid taxes, but _postpones_ them.

profits. Take a look at this example. In Sweden, we can often depreciate an asset in one year. The same asset in the U.S., by law, can only be written off over five years. See what happens to profits in each case. Remember that we have lots of Swedish and American assets."

Al studied Vicki's example. "How do you reconcile this? I mean, you made either $1,080,600 or $1,600,000. Which one is correct?"

"It depends," Vicki said. "I'm right in the middle of a whole bunch of such adjustments right now. This gets into international accounting, which is a real growth field. Not too many local accountants know too much about how to do these things, let alone what the rules and laws are for fifty or more countries. I'm hoping to make a career in that field."

"It doesn't look like you'd run out of material," Al said. "You mean that you have to go through this whole business of preparing statements for each subsidiary in every country, each with different rules?"

"Right. And then after that, we have to consolidate those accounts, convert them to dollars, and get them into the main statement you see here."

Al thought for a moment. "Oh, I see. Each country has its own currency, so you have to translate into dollars. Ouch! Most currencies fluctuate in value every day."

"They do, and it's a pain to find an exchange rate that means anything. But we have to try. There's a lot more, but maybe you get the idea."

"So you have literally thousands of accountants, bookkeepers, and clerks all over the country—all over the world—trying to get your books in shape for literally thousands of users. And you do all this in a week, as Mr. Harrington said?"

"You'll have to visit our computer center. If you want, I can take you out there next Wednesday."

"I'll come. I always wondered what they do with those computers."

"They do lots of operations, including our materials. But there's more."

Al sighed. "I thought before that running a company was easy, but now I'm not so sure. It all seemed so simple. Oh well, live and learn." He glanced at his watch. "Hey, it's after five. I'm keeping you overtime."

"It's all right. The boss said to treat you right."

There was an awkward pause. Could he ask to see her outside of work? Were her eyes really hazel? He figured that someone so attractive would be booked up.

"Well," Al said.

"Look," she said, "let's go get a drink or something. There's a nice place nearby, maybe I can help you line up your questions for the computer division, or give you the low-down on other people you're seeing here. I can probably figure out a way to put it on my expense account."

"Well, sure," he said. "Actually, I was kind of thinking about dinner."

"We'll see about that." They picked up their coats. "You could have asked, you know."

"I was going to."

"But you didn't."

"Well, fine, but I'll get the tab. Magazines kind of run on expense accounts—entertainment for deep sources and that sort of thing."

Al had never dated an accountant, but then he had never known such an attractive one. They spent a lot of time talking about accounting problems at first, but after a while, after-work drinks turned into dinner, and they were talking about lots of other things.

As Al dropped her off, way too late, he said, "Well, your Mr. Beeman was wrong on one count, anyhow."

"What's that?"

"He said that plans without actions are daydreams. But I planned something without acting, and it came about anyhow."

"That's because when you plan, you have to take into account what you're planning for. Sometimes, the plannee can change a plan, too."

As Al drove home, he reflected that something useful could come out of accounting these days.

DISCUSSION QUESTIONS

1. Vicki said that you can make up an income statement for yourself. Do this for two one-month periods. Take your total income and subtract your total costs. How are you doing? Are you making a profit (saving) or a loss (borrowing)?

2. Consider the capital equipment you own, such as bicycles, stereos, cars, musical instruments, etc. How long will these items last, in your judgement? How much will they cost to replace? What depreciation should you charge on them each year?

3. Should you put in a depreciation item in your income statement for a given month? How much should this be, given that your assets will wear out or fall apart?

4. What is the bottom line?

5. The sales manager of a store selling consumer appliances such as TV sets, vacuum cleaners, stereos, refrigerators, etc., was put under terrific pressure by his boss to increase sales. This manager was promised a bonus if he could raise sales by 25 percent in the next month.

The manager increased his sales 38 percent by relaxing his credit standards. He allowed some pretty dubious customers to charge their purchases. He got his bonus, but the store went broke in three months because those dubious credit risks never paid their accounts on the merchandise the store had sent them.

On the income statement, what would sales look like in the month when this manager got his credit sales up?

What would accounts receivable look like on the balance sheet at the end of this month?

Would this big sales increase show up at all on the sources and uses of funds statement? Why or why not?

This store marked up its products 40 percent. A $100 item would be sold for $140. Of course, the store had to pay for its inventory, usually within 60 days.

Suppose sales went from $1,000,000 to $1,380,000 in this month that the manager had his big increase. How much cash would the company have to pay out in the next 60 days for merchandise sold?

6. What is the IRS?

7. What is a profit center in a big company?

8. What does an external auditor do?

9. What is a non-cash cost?

10. American business often tries to get depreciation times changed, usually to make them shorter. They note that countries like Sweden have much shorter depreciation times (asset lives) for major investments such as factories than the U.S. Why would these companies be interested in such problems? What effect on taxes and profit does depreciation time have?

11. Talk to someone around your school who is taking an introductory accounting class, and look at the textbook used in this class. What's going on here? Is it true that basic accounting is really a sort of language to be learned?

12. Go over to the placement center and find out how accounting majors are doing in the job market. Compare the accounting job offers with those for people in other fields.

13. What is a qualified statement of the independent auditors?

14. What is managerial accounting? Which financial statements show managers what is happening?

15. What is audit accounting? Which financial statement shows owners what is happening?

16. What is creative accounting?

17. Why is international accounting different from domestic accounting?

5

CONTROL: STATISTICS AND DATA PROCESSING

W hy on earth would RVA stick its main computer facility in Willow View, New Jersey?" Al asked, as he and Vicki cruised down the turnpike. "I would think that something important like that would be right in head-quarters in New York."

"What do you need to have a computer center?" Vicki replied.

"A computer, I guess. Electric power. Some very smart and well paid people. What else?"

"A set of cables to link your computers up with terminals all over the world, or perhaps a space satellite hookup for the overseas terminals." Vicki watched the forested land roll by. "Those very smart people like to live in a nice place, full of trees and parks. Since they do, why stay in the city? We can put the computer facility anyplace, since the other components can be hooked up anywhere. I use the main computer all the time in our accounting work in New York, but all I need is a terminal to tap the whole system. I really don't much care where it is, as long as it works."

"You know, lots of these modern industries seem to be located way out someplace, in a nice small city, or even in the mountains. I guess that if you only need people and some cables, then it really doesn't matter. Too bad for the cities, though. No wonder so many of them are in tough shape."

"Oh, it's not as bad as all that," Vicki said. "After all, most companies do have their headquarters in big cities. And remember, even though we do put some of our installations in places like Willow View, phone lines and other communications cost money."

"You put your factories out in the sticks."

"Sure, because modern factories need lots of space, including parking. In the old days, they built factories vertically, mainly because they were powered by big steam engines in the basement. Then came electricity and motor trucks, and factories were built horizontally. When you need lots of cheap land, you move way out."

Al glanced over at Vicki. He was impressed by the range of her knowledge. "It still seems like cities are losing ground," he said.

"They are. Factories are leaving, or they've already left, and lots of terminal activities, like railroads and ports, are also leaving. But cities still have the offices. Where you need face-to-face contact, you stay downtown. Like when you want to see us. You walk over from the *Newsworld* office to the RVA headquarters building. You don't spend time traveling, as we're doing now. But still, sometimes it makes good economic and social sense to put facilities way out someplace. So here we are, going way out. Does that bother you?"

"Well, if I have to travel, going with you is a nice way to do it."

"Flattery may get you someplace."

Al thought for a bit, then asked, "What are statistics, anyhow? I've used them all my life in one way or another, but they always come at me from someone who has something to sell."

"Basically, they're nothing more than properly ordered data. We have more data than we can possibly use, although we often don't have the right data. The problem is to get it put together so that someone can use it correctly."

"Give me an example."

"OK, suppose that we're selling baby cribs, which we do. One problem we immediately have is to figure out how big the market is. It wouldn't make much sense to make, say, 200,000 cribs per year when there are only 100,000 babies."

"So what do you do? Count babies?"

Vicki shook her head. "No, that would take too long. What should we do, just send someone out to collect all the names of babies that have been born in the past year? It would cost too much and take forever. Moreover, lots of people wouldn't buy a new crib. They may have one already, or they don't have the money, or perhaps their relatives lent them one. We would like to get some data on the people who will buy our cribs."

"So you start getting organized, right?"

"Right. In this case, there happen to be government agencies that do the organizing for us. Data exist, already sorted out, on babies born, where they are, and even what their parents' income is. You can also get information on how many babies are the first ones in the family, and how many are the fourth child."

"Why?" Al pondered. "Oh, I see. If the child is the first one, the odds are that the family will more likely buy a new crib. If the child is the second or third, then the parents probably already have a crib."

"You may get to be a manager yet."

"I'm not sure I'd like to be, but thanks anyhow. I see what you're driving at. You don't need raw data, like the numbers of babies born, but rather something organized to show you what you want to know."

"And what we want to know are the factors that would lead to the purchase of one of the cribs. If you order the data right, you can see more clearly how to plan your production and sales." She looked over at him. "Do you play poker?"

"Not much, but I'm pretty good at bridge."

"What are the odds that your next card will be an ace, if you have four cards already, and none is an ace?"

"Let's see, that leaves 48 cards, and four are aces, so it should be about twelve to one against."

"I thought you didn't know anything about statistics."

"I don't. That's just bridge, not statistics. If you didn't know things like that, you'd be a lousy card player."

"See, you already know some probability, which is statistics. Once again, the data are ordered, in this case along probabilistic lines. Now, are you a baseball fan?"

"Sort of."

"What was the batting average of your favorite player last year?"

"Jake Zeno? About .250. He had a bad year."

"And what does .250 mean?"

"That he got a hit, let's see, every fourth time at bat." Al thought that over. "I see where you're going with this. Don't tell me ... that average is another statistic. .250 is just another way of saying 25 percent."

"Here's another classic problem. We make light bulbs, and we guarantee them for 1,000 hours. Yet we obviously can't test them to destruction. How can we be sure that they will burn the right length of time?"

"No doubt with some statistical sleight of hand, although I can't imagine what that might be."

"We do random sampling. We select at random, say one out of every thousand bulbs we make, and burn it out. If we sample correctly, then we can state with quite good mathematical precision the probability that all the bulbs will burn 1,000 hours or more."

"I'll take your word for it. Where do you learn such things?"

"If you hadn't taken so much time studying journalism, you could have taken some statistics in college. We have hundreds of statisticians, and thousands of accountants. Both groups really are data organizers and sorters. Remember that you can't control anything unless you know what's going on."

"Lots of people try to lie with statistics, too," Al mused. "In my business, I see plenty of data put together by someone who wants to make a point."

"It can be done," Vicki agreed, sketching a couple of graphs. "Next time you pull off, you can take a look at these."

"Which is right now," Al said, moving off to a rest area.

Al studied Vicki's graphs. "Boy, I'm glad you're not selling me some-

VICKI'S GRAPHS (Or how to lie with statistics)

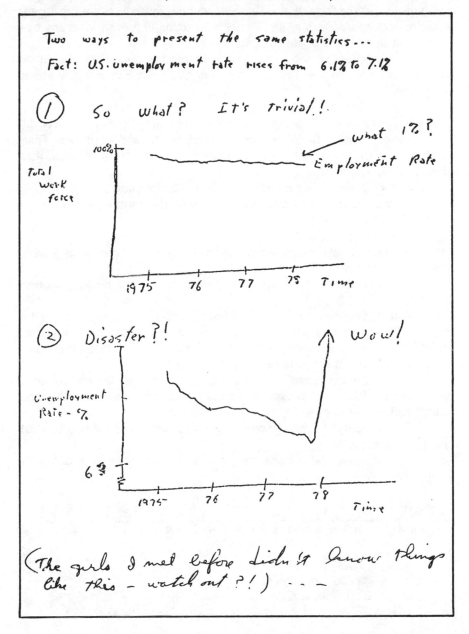

Two ways to present the same statistics...
Fact: U.S. unemployment rate rises from 6.1% to 7.1%

① So what? It's trivial!!.

what 1%?
← Employment Rate

100% —

Total work force

1975   76   77   78   Time

② Disaster?!   Wow!

Unemployment Rate - %

6% —

1975   76   77   78   Time

(The girls I met before didn't know things like this - watch out?!) --- -

thing. I've seen lots of stuff like this since I've worked for *Newsworld*."

"It's tempting to present your facts the right way," Vicki agreed. "I'm afraid that we do this too at times. It's the old story ... the optimist says the glass is half full, while the pessimist says that it's half empty. It depends on how you look at the facts. It also depends on how those facts are organized, so we're back to statistics again. The only meaningful feedback on any operation has to be some organized data."

Al started the car and moved back on the turnpike. "We should be there in about fifteen minutes. Tell me everything there is to know about computers."

"What do you know?"

"Nothing much. But computers sure seem to be taking over the world."

"Not quite. Essentially, they do basic arithmetic and store data. Then they can sort the data, print out information, and present it to users in a nice, neat manner."

"That's all, huh? That doesn't sound very threatening."

"It's the speed that's important. That, plus the enormous storage capacity of a modern computer."

"What do you mean?"

"You can retrieve information very fast. Have you ever seen a clerk look up information?"

"As a reporter? All the time. They spend lots of time messing around in the files."

"Well, if you ever watch a computer retrieve information, it's quite different. The clerk punches some coded instructions into a computer terminal, and within a few seconds the data is retrieved and either printed out or shown on the computer screen. It's really fast."

"I've seen that happen," Al said. "But I never really thought about it much. You're right ... it is fast, compared to fumbling around with some manila folders in a cabinet."

"The computer is merely replacing those folders and doing it a lot cheaper and faster."

"So in the end, the computer is just doing what we've been doing for a long time," Al said.

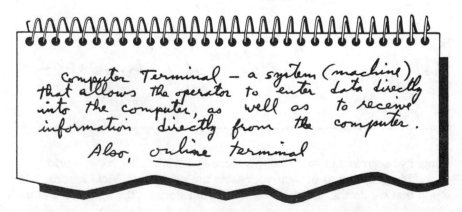

Computer Terminal — a system (machine) that allows the operator to enter data directly into the computer, as well as to receive information directly from the computer.

Also, online terminal

"Right," Vicki replied. "But computers do it fast. We've probably done more arithmetic and retrieved more information in the past month than mankind did in the first ten thousand years of figuring."

"What's so great about that?"

"If you can compute fast, you can find out what's going on fast. Did you ever watch a rocket launch?"

"Sure, I covered one for *Newsworld* last year."

"Did you notice how quickly the launch command was able to say that the mission was OK?"

"Within a few minutes, as I recall."

"There were billions of calculations in those few minutes. If some poor fellow had to sit down and do those trajectory calculations by hand, it would take ten years. Computers made rocket flights possible. Have you noticed those strange new cash registers in the supermarkets?"

"Sure, the ones with the light up dials to tell you the prices, and dozens of buttons for the checker to hit. I buy my groceries at a supermarket that has them."

"They aren't cash registers, they're computer terminals," Vicki said.

"What do they do?"

"The clerk punches in the inventory number for the product you're buying. The data goes to the computer, which notes that at store 126, someone just bought a ten-ounce jar of dill pickles. As sales are made, the computer can reorder inventory for the store without any humans bothering to check things. The order is automatically sent back to the warehouse, where it is filled, probably semi-automatically. Meanwhile, back in the store, you're getting a sales slip. It used to take days to do all of this, and now it's done almost instantaneously."

"Could that be the reason why your supermarket now has what I want?" Al asked. "I have some strange tastes, and it used to be that half the time the store was out of stock. I can't remember that happening for quite a while."

"Sure. In the old days, for some odd items, some clerk would have to go to the shelves and count things to see what to order. All the computer does is speed things up and make it nicer for the customer."

Al sighed. "Now, all you have to do is eliminate the clerks, and you can really save money."

"We're working on it. Have you noticed those black and white lines on most products?"

"Yes. It's some sort of product code, isn't it?"

Vicki nodded. "Those codes are machine readable. We already have the readers, and in a few years, you'll just slide your purchases under a scanner at the checkout counter. The clerk won't have to punch anything—it will be all automatic. And then, if you have the right kind of credit card, you will be able to slip it in a slot, and your purchase will automatically be deducted from your account and added to ours, unless of course you're overdrawn."

Al laughed. "And I suppose then a robot policeman will come up and grab me. Hey, without cash, the game will change. No money, no problems of theft. It's hard to hold up a credit card slot!"

Vicki laughed. "It sounds weird, but it's coming. Once we begin to think seriously about how many repetitive things we do, it's not hard to replace them with some computer or another."

"What happens to those poor clerks that get displaced?"

"Maybe they're working down here with the computer, or perhaps they're maintaining those terminals. One thing that has happened with computers is that a lot of dull jobs got eliminated, and a lot of interesting ones get created." Vicki watched the signs. "It's the next exit, slow down," she said. "Actually, on computers, I'm not sure which workers won and which ones lost in this transition. You see, computers are getting faster and cheaper every year, and they get simpler to use, too. Early computers were so complicated that you had to have advanced degrees in math just to figure out how to use them. Now you can learn to operate a terminal in a few minutes. Even you could figure one out." She nudged him in the ribs.

"I already have. I have one of those TV game things at home, and it's nothing more than a computer, right?"

"Correct. And I suppose that you have a pocket calculator, too?"

"Sure. That's not exactly hard to operate."

"But it's just another type of computer. These days, you can buy for a few thousand dollars the computational capacity that used to cost millions just ten years ago. Computing is so cheap that it doesn't pay not to compute."

"So RVA computes all the time?"

"Remember that we get daily accounting reports now, while in the old days, like five or ten years ago, we had to wait a month or more to find out where we were. It just makes our jobs easier." Vicki watched the road. "Turn left here, Al. This is the place."

Set back in a nice forested area, with lots of pleasant grass around, was an ultramodern building that looked more like a college campus than a company building.

They parked in the ample lot and went in. Jack Tribble, a senior computer specialist, was waiting for them. Vicki introduced Al to him, and Al said, "Vicki's been telling me all about computers, Mr. Tribble."

"She should know. Her department is one of our biggest users."

"Just how many terminals are connected to this facility?"

"Oh, about 425. RVA has offices and branches all over the world, and most of them use this central facility. Of course, lots of offices have their own micro-computers for special work, since they're so cheap nowadays, but we still route most of our work through this facility. That could change, though."

"What else happens here?"

"We do a lot of program design work. That is, we work up new ways of using computers." Mr. Tribble scratched his closely trimmed Afro. "Computers are funny things. They're totally logical. You have to tell them exactly what you want, and I mean exactly. Someone in RVA will ask us to figure out how to program their problem, and we try to help them out."

Al was staring at Tribble. "You'll excuse me for being blunt, but on the phone, when we set up this appointment, you didn't sound black, Mr. Tribble. Are you here through an affirmative action program, or, well, I'm not quite sure what else to ask, but is there a story in this?"

Tribble smiled. "Should I sound black? I wonder ... but the answer to your question is, no, I'm a computer technician, and I'm pretty good."

"He's right, Al," Vicki said. "We're not snowing you. Trib is the best person to take you around this facility. He's very good at his work, one of the best, in fact."

"I'm not the house black or the guy who sits in the window," Tribble added. "I majored in applied math at Rutgers, took my master's degree, and RVA hired me. If I can't produce, I'll be out of here, fast. See, computers are a field where competence will win for you—it's like sports, in a way. Computers don't have any racial bias. They are totally logical and very complex. If you can make them work, you have a job. Good programmers get paid very well, and they're scarce."

"I see," Al said. "You understand that I have to ask, for my story."

"Sure."

"OK, so the computer is logical. So what? I mean, what's the difference?"

"Right now, we're working on refining a program to allocate funds between all our branches, here and abroad. The idea is to figure out where we have surplus funds and where we need funds. Then we can cable transfer the surpluses to the deficit branches immediately. In the old days, each

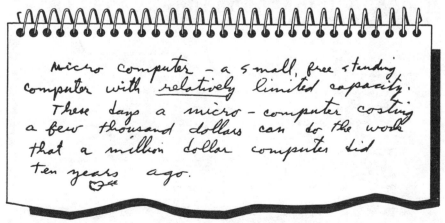

micro computer - a small, free standing computer with *relatively* limited capacity.

These days a micro - computer costing a few thousand dollars can do the work that a million dollar computer did ten years ago.

branch ran its own show. Say the French branch needed cash for working capital, while the English branch had surplus funds. That English cash would sit idle, while the French manager would have to go out and try to borrow money at high interest rates."

"It sounds logical to balance cash out," Al said. "What was the problem?"

"The first problem was that our branch managers were not very logical," Trib replied. "It took us two years to get them to agree to cooperate. The idea of taking the English manager's money didn't make him too happy, and the French manager didn't like the idea of the English manager knowing that he needed cash."

"Couldn't the boss just tell the troops to jump?"

"He could," Vicki said, "but that's not a good idea. Remember these local managers were running multimillion-dollar operations, and they are pretty creative people. We didn't want to shove them around and make them mad. So we tried to get them to agree voluntarily."

"And after two years, we finally did," Trib said. "By that time, I had worked up the computer program."

"These programs just tell the computer what to do?"

"Right," Trib said. "There are special computer languages, like COBOL and FORTRAN, that are used to give instructions. And if your logic is defective, the program won't even run. You have to go back and do it all over. Well, I had a great program, and it ran beautifully. It got input from every branch we had every day, giving their cash positions and needs for the next week, month, and year, as forecast."

"So you tried it, and you saved RVA millions of dollars?"

"We tried it and nearly got the company into very hot water," Trib said ruefully. "I got called on the carpet on that one."

"What happened?"

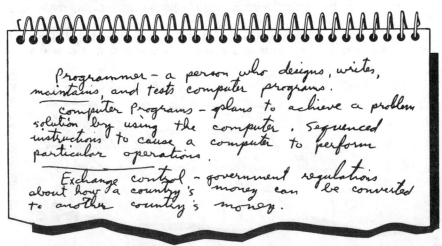

Programmer – a person who designs, writes, maintains, and tests computer programs.

computer Programs – plans to achieve a problem solution by using the computer. Sequenced instructions to cause a computer to perform particular operations.

Exchange control – government regulations about how a country's money can be converted to another country's money.

"I wasn't logical. I figured that you could change any foreign currency into any other one at any time, which is true in most countries most of the time. But just as I started my system, France imposed some exchange controls. It turned out that you couldn't take French francs out of the country without a special permit. So sure enough, in the first week, our program instructed the French manager to ship about 50 million francs to Sweden. He couldn't. The Swedish branch manager almost missed a payroll because of that, and I was in trouble."

"Your computer wasn't told about those French regulations, so it ignored them. I see. What did you do?"

"I got logical, and I built into the program all the exchange constraints that actually existed. Then it worked very well, and we did save the company several million dollars a year of excess financial costs and interest charges."

"Let's backtrack for a moment," Al said. "You mentioned COBOL and FORTRAN. What on earth are they?"

"You see, Al, computers don't speak English or any other human language. Specialists have developed these computer languages and many other special logical languages which the computer can read."

Trib explained about languages and Al carefully wrote it all down.

"How do you talk to a computer? I mean, how do you get your input into the thing?"

"Oh, there are several ways," Trib said. "Probably the most common is by using your computer terminal typewriter. But often we keypunch cards and prepare decks of instructions."

New words were flying thick and fast, Al thought, but he asked about

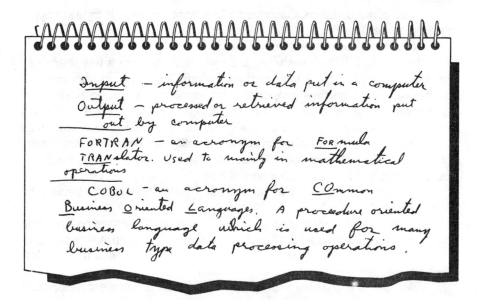

Input — information or data put in a computer
Output — processed or retrieved information put out by computer
FORTRAN — an acronym for FORmula TRANslator. Used to mainly in mathematical operations
COBOL — an acronym for COmmon Business Oriented Languages. A procedure oriented business language which is used for many business type data processing operations.

them and as Trib described them, he wrote them down. In the end, it seemed logical enough. What you did was tell your computer what to do, using a special language which it could read, and then you got back some output, which either was printed out for you or put on a TV-type screen. And the whole process was very fast. In this computer world, you were logical and rational, or things didn't work out too well.

"You see the kind of problem you run into," Vicki added. "Trib is a computer specialist, and he never took a course in international finance. The people in that area didn't know too much about computers, and they assumed that everyone knew about exchange controls. So they forgot to tell Trib the facts of international financial life. We've had the same problem in accounting, when we know a fact, and we assume that Trib and his people know it too. If they don't, we get into trouble."

"There's an old computer saying," Trib said. "GIGO. Garbage in, garbage out. Unless you make sense in your program you'll never make sense of your output."

"It sounds like you have to be a generalist," Al said.

"Maybe, but one thing I have to be careful about is that whoever I work with is thinking very logically. Actually one of the major gains that computers have given companies is just that. Before computers, it was easy to get into sloppy thinking habits. People just assumed that something was so, without ever checking it out. But when you start working out computer programs, you have to think through everything, and this is a real plus for managers."

"What else are you working on, Trib, besides money and finance?" Al asked.

"One of our divisions, Churchman Lumber Company, is trying to figure out how to cut logs."

"Cut logs? That sounds pretty easy."

Trib smiled. "That was what everyone thought until a few years ago. But then we took a close look at the problem. Prices for various types of lumber vary a lot, and not proportionally. Suppose a 2 × 6 in twelve-foot lengths sells for three times what a 2 × 4 is worth. But some 1 × 5's sell for proportionally more, while 1 × 4's are a drug on the market and going cheap. Now, here comes a log into the sawmill, and remember that every log is a bit different. How does the operator line up his cuts to maximize the revenue from the log? Does that sound easy?"

Al thought about it. "Not to me, but wouldn't a skilled operator be able to work that out?"

"That's the way they used to do it," Vicki said. "Then we realized that the operator had to do a lot of calculations in his head in a few seconds. The guys were surprisingly good, but not that good. We ended up with lots of cheap lumber."

"We are just finishing a program and related hardware development

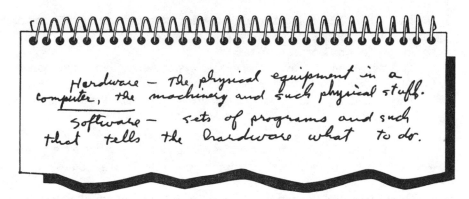

Hardware — The physical equipment in a computer, the machinery and such physical stuff.

Software — sets of programs and such that tells the hardware what to do.

to have the computer tell the operator where to make his cuts," Trib said.

"What's hardware?" Al asked. Trib's explanation went into Al's notes.

"You see," Trib was saying, "in this case we have to size the logs and get the grain straight before we could even begin to figure out what to do. We had to build a sophisticated measuring device, along with a grain reading gadget. Once the log was measured, grained, and set up, the computer could figure out what cuts to make, given the values of all the possible boards we could get from the log."

Al pondered. "Back to logic again. You can't cut a twelve-foot board from a ten-foot log."

"Right," Trib said. "You always have to build in the logical constraints, or you end up with GIGO."

"The pilot model is being tested now," Vicki said. "It should save us about twenty percent on our lumber, or give us twenty percent more revenue per log. Hey, Trib, when is the software going to be finalized for this project?"

"Next week, I hope. You accountants always want it yesterday. Don't worry, I'll let you know."

"OK, Trib, what else are you up to?" Al asked.

"Oh, a bunch of routine stuff. We make out all the payrolls for over 65,000 employees here, although the checks are printed up in each division. Remember, we're linked with all of them through remote terminals and printers. We keep track of inventories for most of our divisions. Such things have been routine for years. Where you need to count fast, we do it, and we save lots of time for all concerned." He paused. "There's one project I'm interested in which might even get into your business, Al. Have you heard much about office computerization?"

"A bit," Al replied. "You mean word processing, automatic filing, and all that? Our office manager has been talking about it, but so far, there's not been much action. Maybe *Newsworld* is a bit conservative."

"Come on," Trib said. "Let's take a look at the office of the future. It's here now, but so far few companies have taken advantage of it. My problem is to figure out what RVA really needs." They walked down the hall and into a, well, an office. Trib pointed to a micro-computer and screen. "Sit down. Let's see what a journalist can do with word processing."

Al sat. "Words I process for sure."

Trib turned on the power and got the system alive. "Now, type something."

The computer console was essentially a typewriter keyboard, so Al typed:

```
I am now viiting the RVA Computer Center to
see what the nwe wond3rs of computers may be . . .
```

He stopped and grinned up at Trib. "I can type, but not all that well." Three errors already, this was embarrassing.

"Well, let's process some words, then." He showed Al how to move the cursor around on the screen. When the cursor was over the 'viiting'—at the second i—Trib said, "Hit the s key."

Al did, and the word became 'visiting'. Then Trib showed him how to maneuver the cursor over 'nwe', and Al retyped 'new'. The computer obligingly corrected the word for him. Al stared at the screen. "Hey, with this gadget, I could be a great typist! You can correct anything you want!"

Trib smiled. "Computers even affect you, my friend. You could insert words, paragraphs, delete sentences, anything you want. But now let's print what you wrote." He punched a few keys, and a printer on a nearby table typed out his sentence.

"If you want, we can line justify too, just like a book. With this thing, you can write a story, make all the corrections you want, then print it out. You could make as many copies as you want. You could file a copy on a floppy disk for retrieval later. Printers could make plates from your copy, and it could go right to the magazine."

Al pondered this gadget. "A secretary could really be efficient with this thing, couldn't she?"

"Or he, Al," Vicki said. "Yes, no more carbon paper, files, correcting fluid, or anything. All your correspondence could be handled with this, and with a bit of extra storage, all the files can be made, too. *Newsworld* isn't the only group that prints things, Al. We have instruction manuals, policy statements, and dozens of other things to print. Now we can do it all in-house. And instead of having very highly skilled people do it, a trained typist can do it all."

"I know that the newspaper unions are always very nervous about innovations," Al said, "and now I see why. Wow, you can eliminate printers, editors, a whole group of people!" He thought of his own editor.

Trib said, "Word processing could lead to a totally different kind of office."

"It could eliminate the whole post office, couldn't it?" Al asked. "I mean,

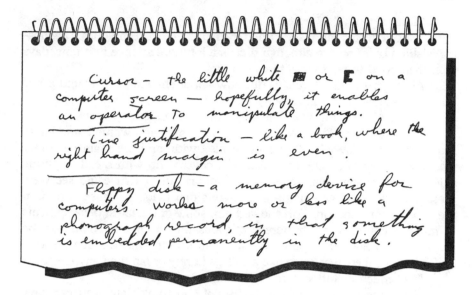

Cursor — the little white ▓ or ▐ on a computer screen — hopefully, it enables an operator to manipulate things.

———— Line justification — like a book, where the right hand margin is even.

Floppy disk — a memory device for computers. works more or less like a phonograph record, in that something is embedded permanently in the disk.

you could type a letter in New York, and through your leased lines, have it printed in San Francisco."

"It won't be soon, Al," Vicki said. "Everyone getting mail would have to have a terminal, and that won't come very soon. But yes, for companies, it's already happening. The post office itself has an experimental system in use for firms, and lots of private companies are trying to figure out the right hardware and software. So far, it's a bit expensive, but we're already doing a little."

"What are the limits?"

"There are a dozen possible systems, and not all of them are compatible," Trib said. "When we move, our San Francisco office has to be able to tie into New York. Right now, we're looking at several systems. Secretaries are expensive, and office productivity hasn't gone up nearly as much as factory productivity. We're going to change that."

"I believe you." Al looked again at the micro-computer keyboard, wondering if his own work wasn't in for some major changes. "What else do you have, Trib?"

"Oh, we did a diagnostic program for Lewis Hospital Supply Company. Someone would come in and say he was sick. They usually found out that it wasn't one thing that made him sick, but four or five factors. We constructed a program that enabled the computer to figure out just how those variables interacted. Doctors are very smart, but they can't handle five or six symptoms at once, when one depends on the other, and they all are interrelated. The patient gets measured in a dozen or more ways, and the computer program interrelates all the measurements and comes up with a good diagnosis."

"Does it work?" Al asked.

"Not perfectly, but it's a lot better than the older techniques. Diagnosing is still a bit of an art, although there's a lot more science in it nowadays than there used to be, thanks to computers."

Al glanced at his watch. "Trib, how about showing me around a bit? I'd like to see what you have here."

"Sure, Al, but you won't see very much. Come on."

Trib was right. There were lots of young men and women working in little cubicles, many with terminals to play with, and the main computer was just a hunk of machinery, most of it covered up with metal or plastic shields. A technician was repairing something, and all Al could see were masses of wires and various printed circuits that made no sense to him. In the experimental section, Trib showed him some of the latest developments in micro-circuitry, where hundreds of thousands of circuits could now be put on a chip the size of pinhead, but again it didn't make much sense to Al. The atmosphere was more like a college library or lab than anything else.

"Not much pollution here," Al commented.

"No, here we just think a lot. But if you think right, you can save yourself a lot of time and trouble. That's what we get paid to do."

Al was quiet and thoughtful on the way home. Vicki finally asked him what was bothering him.

"My dad was very sick last year, and his doctor really couldn't figure out what was bothering him. So they sent him to one of those computerized diagnostic centers, and it figured out what was wrong. They were able to do a relatively simple operation, and he recovered fast."

"So why does that bother you?"

"Your Lewis Hospital Supply Company is making money out of that kind of problem."

"Sure, and because we are, guys like Tribble are figuring out how to do the job better every year. You should see the latest model we have. It's so much better . . ."

"But it doesn't seem right to make money out of such things."

"If we didn't, who would bother? The better the job we do, the more patients we save, and the more money we make." Vicki thought for a while. "That bugs you, right? I mean, somehow we're doing the right things for the wrong reason."

"I guess that's it."

"Look, you write about the news, right?"

"Yes."

"Because people need to know what's going on, right?"

"Sure."

"And you get paid for it, and people pay for *Newsworld* magazine, right?"

He nodded.

"It's the same with business," Vicki said, "whether it's hospital supplies or truck tires or telephones. I don't think the 'wrong reason' really exists."

Al said, "It's tough. As I get into RVA, I'm beginning to see all sorts of complexities that I never thought existed. Boy, some of the stuff that Trib talked about. It looks so easy! But there's so much behind-the-scenes work that I don't even understand, and yet all that happens is that things seem to work pretty well."

"We get fouled up all the time," Vicki said, "but maybe we get a little better every year. We hope so, anyhow."

"How do I explain all this in two thousand words in a news story?" Al asked. "It's so easy to be glib about computers, and talk about how they're taking over the world, and all of that, but in the end, I probably just won't know what I'm talking about."

"Oh, I think that you'll come up with something, Al. But you still have a long way to go."

"Yeah, a long way to go."

Vicki patted his arm and smiled. "This really bothers you, doesn't it."

Al glanced over at her. "It sure does. How did I get into this mess, anyhow?"

"Don't worry. I'll be around to help out, if you'd like."

"Well, thanks, I probably will, Vicki. It's nice, hanging out with you."

He thought she was blushing.

DISCUSSION QUESTIONS

1. Take a look at your daily newspaper and find some statistics that are being used for something. How are these data organized? Is the user trying to prove something to you? Did he or she prove it?

2. Now go to the sports section of your newspaper and find some more statistics, such as the box score of a game. How are these data organized? What do they tell you about the team and individual performances?

3. If possible, pay a visit to your own school's computer center. What's going on here? What kinds of problems are being worked on? Why?

4. Find a small business person in your area and talk to him or her. Does s/he use a computer at all? Why or why not? Did s/he use one five years ago? What, if anything, does she or he do with the computer?

5. A few modern cars have computerized diagnostic systems built into them. When the car runs poorly, the technician plugs

the computer into special sockets built into the car, and within seconds the car's problems are diagnosed.

In this chapter, the problem of diagnosing illness was discussed. Go back and reread that section. Do you think that the program for these problems might work for car problems? Why or why not?

6. What is software?

7. What is hardware?

8. Your own college or university has many students to keep track of. Think a bit and write down the basic kinds of information your school has to have about you in order to keep the records straight.

How much of this data could logically be kept on a computer? Visit your registrar and ask, if you need to. Is any of the information actually computerized? Since when?

9. A trade union was trying to get a raise one year when inflation was 9 percent. The year before, inflation had been 5 percent, and the year before that, 6 percent. The union negotiating team wanted to present a graph which showed how dramatic this inflation had been. Help them out by drawing this graph.

Management wanted to show the same information, but of course it wanted to show that this 9 percent inflation really wasn't too important. Help them out by drawing a graph which shows how trivial this 9 percent really is.

Which group is really right? Why?

10. What is GIGO? What does it really mean?

11. Is it fair for RVA to make lots of money on their human diagnostic machine, when human lives are at stake? Why or why not?

RVA's diagnostic machine is estimated to save about 500 lives a year. The company makes a net profit of $1.8 million per year selling this machine. Is this fair? Why or why not?

12. Your company makes percussion caps for dynamite used in building roads and removing rocks. These percussion caps have to explode in exactly 3.1 seconds after being activated, or someone may get badly hurt. You obviously can't test every cap to destruction, since the caps have to be sold to customers. What can you do, besides hope that your manufacturing process is well done?

13. The next time you are in a big store buying something, take a good look at the checkout procedure. What kind of cash

register is being used? Is it really a computer terminal? Does the clerk just punch in prices, or does he or she also punch in inventory information?

If possible, talk to a store manager about his or her customer checkout information system. What is going on here besides the obvious taking of your money?

6

ORGANIZATION

Joe Chapman said, "Just a minute, Al," and got up to close the door. As he came back to his desk, Al watched him carefully. Joe was in his early thirties, very well groomed and dressed in a style that Al now recognized as corporate headquarters modern, and somewhat nervous.

"Thanks for taking the time to see me," Al said.

"You're supposed to have all doors open here. It's my pleasure. But I am surprised that you came this far down the corporate pyramid to talk to me. You've been nosing around the top dogs most of the time."

"I asked around, and they told me that you're the man to see about RVA organization."

"I'm just a staff man, and not even a top one. Just assistant to the chief long range planner." He lit a cigarette.

"Still, you're supposed to know all the answers." Al watched him. What was it about him? He realized that he had met other people like Joe before, when he was digging out that municipal bribery scandal. Joe might be perfectly in tune with this corporate environment, but something suggested that he was just a bit different.

"Well, Al, what do you want to know?"

"Just how is RVA organized? I mean, do you have an organization chart?"

"Sure." Joe reached in a drawer and fished out a bulky sheet. "Take a look. It really isn't worth much, but this is what we look like on paper. Remember, this is simplified. It's hard to get all the boxes on one sheet of paper. This is a big company."

Al studied the chart. "Where are you in this thing?"

"Over there, under staff reporting to Beeman."

"If you're long range planning for the whole company, why do you report to Beeman, and not the Chief Executive Vice President?"

Joe looked hard at Al. "You seem to know something about organization charts. It's history. Beeman was always interested in long range planning, and he did very well with it. I suppose that he told you a little about his career with Wide West Groceries. He pushed to get this group set up about eight years ago, so they left him in charge of it."

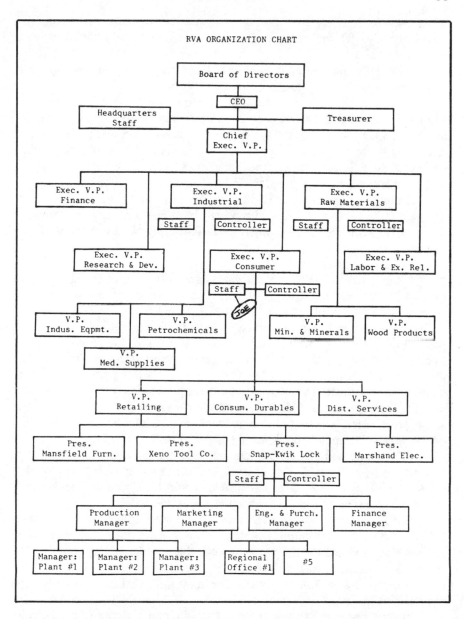

RVA ORGANIZATION CHART

"I see what you mean when you say it's simplified. Only the Consumer Durables Division shows what's below the group level."

"Right. If we stuck in every lower level organization for every group, we'd need a chart as big as the wall. Actually, the chart is a pyramid of power and authority. Note that as you work down from the CEO, every level has more people than the level above. Most companies and actually most organizations are like that. There's not much room at the top." Joe smiled grimly. "Darn little room. Every time you go up, you find fewer opportunities."

"OK, let's move down the chart. I see that the Treasurer and the headquarters staff report to the CEO."

"Actually, they have quite large pyramids of their own that aren't shown. Headquarters staff has about 125 people, and the Treasurer's office has about 55. Most of HQ staff are specialists of some sort, such as marketing research people, real estate experts, lawyers, pollution control guys, and so on. The financial people are in the Treasurer's office."

"And these are staff people? No line authority?"

Again Joe stared at Al. "Right. They're supposed to give advice only. They don't have line authority. The people with line authority are shown in those boxes with direct lines downward. These people are responsible for results."

"Or their bosses are."

"Sure, because you can't delegate responsibility. But for all practical purposes, if you sit in a line job, you're responsible. If you really blow one, your boss might get into trouble, but you get fired first."

"I see that each executive vice president has a staff too."

"Right. This is a complicated company. It's impossible for any one man to cover all the bases. But staff lower down do different things. For example, the Industrial Executive Vice President has a real estate expert too, but he deals only in industrial properties, like buying factories and getting zoning permits for construction. He does what is necessary for his division. The same guy in our Consumer Durables Division worries a lot about shopping center leases. It depends on what has to be done."

"There's something that bothers me. Suppose that the real estate expert said not to buy a certain tract of land, and he or she gave reasons for that advice. The expert really isn't line, but it would be a strange line manager who would ignore that kind of advice if it was good."

"Of course, and that's the essence of the puzzle. Staff doesn't command ... but staff really *does* command, when something requiring expert opinion is needed. There really is no way to resolve this problem. I suppose that the smart line manager tries to hire the best staff he can. You have to trust someone in the end. Sometimes the line man doesn't, but he usually pays the price in the end."

"If you had more than one boss, things could get confusing," Al said. "Sometimes it seems as if I have five, and they're always messing each other up. Me too, for that matter."

"There's a management principle called unity of command," Joe said. "It merely states that everyone should have one, and only one boss. That's why the org chart looks like a pyramid. Every boss has many subordinates, but every subordinate has only one boss. But watch those staff guys. They can start acting like bosses, and then trouble is certain."

"Boy, this is complicated," Al shook his head. "What's it all for?"

"For? To get the job done efficiently, whatever that is. A company this size just has to have responsibilities carefully spelled out, or things get lost in between cracks, and they don't get done." Joe tapped the chart. "Sure, everything is carefully laid out here. Everyone knows just what they are supposed to do, most of the time."

corporate pyramids - companies are organized so their organization charts look like pyramids -

Boss

Ass. Boss 1.   Ass. Boss 2

worker 1 | worker 2 | worker 3 | worker 4 | worker 5

Going down the pyramid - moving to a lower level person

CEO - Chief executive officer - Top line manager in the company.

span of control - the number of subordinates the manager has.

A narrow span would be few people (say 3 to 10), a broad span would be lots of people (say, 50 to 150).

The larger the span, the less interaction and attention a manager can give each subordinate.

Perennial problem - How large a span for a given situation? If it's too big or too small, it could be inefficient!

Al glanced at Joe. Something was bugging him for sure.

"Getting organized isn't easy, Al. Spans of control have always given us problems."

Al looked puzzled, so Joe told him what a span of control was.

"They range from four or five up to as many as fifty down at the plant level. That's because we always have to consider just how much time a person has to spend with his boss. If the boss and the subordinate need to interact a lot, the span is narrow. But if the job is pretty routine, then you can have broad spans."

Al thought back. "I read somewhere that some churches have huge spans of control, and churchmen aren't exactly like factory workers."

"No, churchmen are usually highly trained professionals, who know exactly what to do in their work. So they don't need constant consultation with their bishops. The same thing happens in our research labs. Some of the chemists and other professionals can work with very broad spans of control for the same reason. They know what to do. The more uncertain and sophisticated the job, the more likely that spans will be small." Joe paused for a moment. "It's a real dilemma here. Big spans mean fewer levels of control."

Joe saw Al's puzzled look and told him about levels. "Study the chart. From the factory worker down in a plant to the CEO, we have about ten levels of control. Suppose some bright guy started at the bottom. If he worked his way up, and took five years in each level, he'd spend fifty years working to the top. No one can do it."

"So how do you solve the problem of finding top people? Your top men aren't ninety years old."

"Oh, you can skip levels sometimes. And you can start higher up. This really is what we do with highly educated people. They rarely start as factory hands. Usually they start well up the pyramid, sometimes in staff. Later, they can move over to line. The poor guys at the bottom never get very far."

"How did you get where you are, Joe?"

"I started close to the top, in a staff planning job for the Vice President of our Retailing Division. I worked there for five years, and then I moved up here."

"I suppose that you went to college?"

"Sure, I'm very well educated for this job. I have an M.B.A. from Chicago. But there is another way to get to the top, namely the crown prince, or maybe princess route."

"How does that work?"

"The company selects a few fast track people and plugs them in well up the pyramid. They give them lots of choice assignments and shift them around a lot close to the top. If they prove out, they'll move into top line jobs before they are forty."

"Like you, right?"

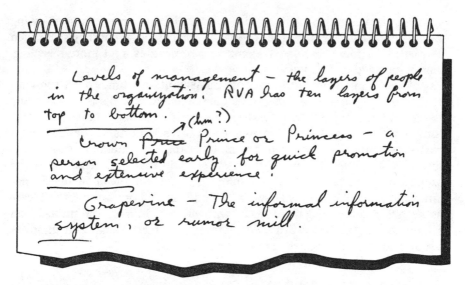

Levels of management — the layers of people in the organization. RVA has ten layers from top to bottom.

↗(hm?)
Crown Prince or Princess — a person selected early for quick promotion and extensive experience.

Grapevine — The informal information system, or rumor mill.

Joe laughed bitterly. "Not like me. No, I'm just one of the loyal troops. I'm not going to make it to the top in this company." Joe lit another cigarette. "How's Vicki? Are you really going out with her?"

"Yeah, sure. How come you know about that?"

"Oh, there's a grapevine in every company. You've caused lots of comment by wandering around here. Did you think no one would notice? They're making book on what kind of stuff you're going to write."

It figured, Al thought. Reporters were seen as bad news if someone had something to hide. "What does Vicki have to do with that?"

"She's a crown princess, among a few crown princes. A really smart cookie, that gal. Some day she's going to be a vice president at least."

"I guess that I'm talking to the right people then, right?"

"Oh, yes, you sure are. No, Vicki's smart. Do you think that you ran into her by accident?"

"Well, she was around when I needed some accounting information."

"Sure, but she volunteered for that job. You could be an important factor in this company, Al. If you get handled right, it could mean a lot to the one who does the handling."

"So Vicki wasn't dazzled by the charming guy I am, huh?"

Joe laughed. "Grow up, Al! For a supposedly smart reporter, you're pretty naive. You run around asking silly questions to high-powered people, and you look pretty dumb. When are you going to wise up?" Joe lit another cigarette and puffed furiously. "You're being set up, man. Don't you see that?"

"Well, you know I really don't know much about the business world," Al replied. "I guess I'll just have to keep on asking silly questions."

"It's your funeral," Joe said, sighing.

Sometimes, Al thought, an idea works. He could run around showing total ignorance and let the other people do the talking. What they said when he played the fool was a lot different, and sometimes a lot more revealing, than if he acted like he knew what he was doing.

"You're into some organizational things that sometimes don't show up in the books," Joe said, drawing a diagram. "See here? This is what's really going on. That organization chart shows the functional subsystem of this company. It tells you who does what work. It's important, but it's only a part of the story. You've seen lots of this other informational subsystem, since you've been listening to Vicki ... she's in that one. It concerns the proper flows and accumulations of information all over the company. Sometimes we show informational flows with dotted lines. For example, the Treasurer's office communicates directly with all the division comptrollers on accounting matters. You can study forever about functional and informational materials. The books are full of them.

JOE'S ORGANIZATIONAL CHART

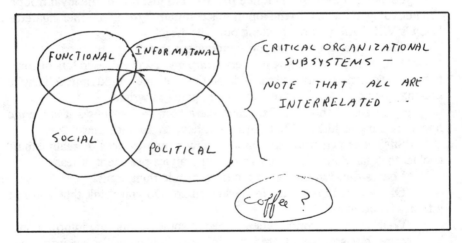

"But here's where things get tricky, with the social subsystem. People relate to each other all over the place, because they like to socialize. Some guys join bowling teams and meet people from other divisions. Some guys date women from the office. Others meet down at the union hall, or happen to be neighbors. And where you sit may determine who you know. I know most of the people in the legal office because it's just down the hall, and we bump into each other a lot. I met my wife that way."

"And then there's the grapevine."

"Sure. I heard about you and Vicki from a legal secretary, who heard it from her boss, who had lunch with Vicki's boss. Information can be very formal, but it also can ramble all over the place."

Joe poked at his diagram. "Then there's the political subsystem. This place is a power game too, and never forget it. Everyone's maneuvering to get more power. You've talked to Beeman ... he's trying to figure out how to move up to the CEO's slot, and he has a good shot at it, too. But Vicki's boss is trying to head him off, because his candidate is Gardner, who heads up the Industrial Division. Your friend Wilson will retire next year, and you wouldn't believe what's going on around here. Incidentally, if Gardner wins, your Vicki will move up very fast. But one reason she volunteered to keep you in line was to pacify Beeman, who's terrified of you."

"Why?"

"Because you could write a story about his defective products that could blow him right out of the presidency. Or maybe you could do one on how his supermarkets rip off customers. If Vicki can handle you, then Beeman will owe her something. That little girl knows her way around. If she can't, then Gardner will move in, and she'll still be in good shape. Of course, Wysocki is a long shot, too, but he's a little old ... sixty-two."

"So power is the name of the game." Boy, attractive spies and all, Al thought. He looked over at Joe, who was lighting another cigarette. It wasn't very smart of Joe to tell him all this, but it was useful. He could see why Joe was a loser. He talked too much to the wrong people, and his bitterness showed.

"You know, Joe, I can't believe that all you do is seize power. I mean, you have to have something else going for you."

"Of course you do. You have to be competent, smart, and pretty good in your functional and informational job. But not too good. If you're a hero in engineering or marketing, and you're the best guy they have, then you may stay where you are. I may be like that. I'm a great long range planner. And you have to have the right social situation too. Your friend Tribble is black, and that means that he'll win big even if he isn't all that great as a computer jock, which he actually is. And Vicki's female, which these days means that she'll be favored over us WASPs. In the old days, you had to have the right Eastern family connections and go to the right Eastern Ivy League schools, but nowadays if you're a minority or female, you move ahead. And you have to be the right age too. Wysocki's a first-rate guy, but he was born five years too soon. He's too close to Wilson, who's just turning sixty-five."

"Is that what bugs you?"

"To win big, you have to have a bit of everything. You have to be pretty good at everything, and outstanding at nothing. I guess that I just don't quite fill the bill."

Al looked at Joe's diagram. "Your subsystem circles overlap. Does that mean that the subsystems are interrelated?"

"Sure. You socialize while you're doing your functional job, and you play politics while you do accounting, like Vicki does. And of course the functional and informational subsystems are closely related. You can't run a production line without good information."

"I see why big organizations have so many committees," Al said. "If you have a problem that affects a bunch of subsystems, then you need representatives from every group."

"Sure. We're always putting together committees for long run planning work. Supposing we're thinking about new products for five or ten years down the road. We need some people from various functional areas, like marketing, finance, and production, because new products involve new plants, finding markets, and getting financing. But we also make darn sure that some of the socially correct people are there, because they help grease the wheels when the decisions are being made. And we surely have the powerful politicos, too, because if they aren't there, nothing much will happen.

"Remember that we report to Beeman? That was a power play all the way. Back then, long range planning was new, and no one really was quite sure what it could do. But Beeman wanted to set up a group, and he fought for a budget and got it. Every once in a while, Wilson tries to pry us loose, but so far, Beeman's headed him off. Beeman's smart. He figures that the group that plans the long term future can control the company."

"Is he right?"

"Check next year, and see who's the new CEO."

Al looked at the organization chart again. "Joe, it would seem that each one of these boxes on your chart really is a place where decisions get made."

"Sure, and the person in the box has to know what to do. One thing we spend a lot of time on is job descriptions. When a guy is the manager of plant #2 of Snap-Kwik, he should know exactly where his duties and responsibilities lie."

"That seems easy. He manages the plant."

"Suppose he has a strike. Is he authorized to make a separate agreement with the union?"

"Well, probably not. That could mess up your labor relations all over the country."

"You see, you have to let people know what to do. A plant manager is not in charge of marketing in Snap-Kwik, although in other divisions he possibly could be. The org chart, plus the job descriptions, really give us the level of centralization or decentralization we want."

"But what do you want? I mean, just how do you figure out who makes what decisions, and at what level?"

"There are quite a few criteria we use. One is communications requirements. By that I mean we simply can't have our top people swamped all the time with memoranda, data, and other stuff. No one can possibly read all the materials we generate in this company."

"That makes sense," Al said. "Mr. Beeman mentioned that he could read for years if he had to cover every daily item his division generates."

"Of course. He can't possibly do it, so lots of things get shoved down the pyramid to lower level managers on this point alone. Then there's firm complexity and size, too. RVA is a very complicated company for its size ... we have thousands of products, hundreds of markets, and all sorts of special situations that only a few experts know about. A top man probably wouldn't know much about the markets for locks in the Midwest, so this marketing problem would be handled by a lower level manager. A top man might not know anything about specialized production processes in our electronics division, so again the problem gets sent down to someone who does."

"I've read about big companies where everything gets decided at the top," Al said.

Joe waved his hands. "Sure, if the company is basically simple, it can be done. Suppose a company has 50,000 employees, but all it produces is a narrow range of auto parts. It's possible that the company could be very centralized. We just can't be that simple, so we're decentralized."

Joe thought for a moment. "Then there's the Al Faber kind of problem."

"The what?"

"You, my friend. The general rule is that if a problem is very important to the firm, it gets centralized. Remember that strike example? In that case, labor relations and union negotiations are very important to the whole company, so they get centralized. The lower level manager doesn't make a key decision about a major labor contract. But you're like that ... you represent a real danger to the whole company."

"Because I could write some devastating stories."

"Sure, and in this case, it isn't trivial, since you could get us investigated by Congress, called into court for some real or imagined offense, or even cause a vice president to resign. That's why everyone is handling you very, very carefully."

"I'll try to be good," Al said. "What else do you worry about in decentralization?"

"Try management's view of man," Joe said.

"What do you mean?"

"Basically, the way top managers feel about people. If you trust them, you're more likely to decentralize. If you think they're a potential bunch of crooks, lazy slobs, and generally no good, then you centralize more. You have to, because you can't trust anyone."

"How does RVA rank on this one?" Al asked.

"Oh, pretty good. They're smart enough to know that they have a highly skilled work force, and the managers are usually professionals. These kinds of people generally work better when they have lots of responsibilities and authority than when you try to tell them what to do."

"Anything else?"

"One more ... this is really the ability of managers to build good PARF loops. If they know what's important, and they can figure out relevant and quantifiable deviations for their loops, then they know what to centralize and what to decentralize."

"On balance, it sounds as if RVA is pretty decentralized."

"It is," Joe agreed. "But don't worry, things like the problem you present get very centralized. All the vice presidents are worrying about what you might do. And finance gets centralized, too. You don't let junior people spend all the money they want. Things that are very crucial, such as labor relations, important government relations, critical tax problems, and overall planning, are also quite centralized. Top management tries to do what is important, and leaves the rest to subordinates."

"Joe, just how do those PARF loops fit in here? I sense that they do, but I don't quite see how or why."

Joe smiled. "Beeman loves those things, but he's right. Others call it management by objective. Here, take a look at this chart Beeman had printed up. Those are the ways of fouling up good management."

MR. BEEMAN'S CHART

Indications of Poor or Inefficient Management

1. Bad Planning
   - A. Lack of realism
   - B. Inadequate quantification
   - C. Poor integration with action system
   - D. Poor integration with information-feedback system
   - E. Inadequate tolerances or no tolerances
   - F. Inadequate monitoring or no monitoring
   - G. Inadequate revisions or no revisions

2. Bad Actions

3. Bad Feedback
   - A. No feedback
   - B. Badly designed feedback
   - C. Too much feedback system noise
   - D. Inadequate feedback system redundancy
   - E. Feedback distortion
   - F. Feedback misdirection

4. Bad Reactions to Correct Feedback

5. Bad Interactions of the Total System

Al looked. "Yes, he talked to me about most of this."

"OK, one thing you're doing with organization is to make sure that none of those horrible things happen. You can't win them all, but you can try. You're really dealing with two basic factors here, human and machine. The machines are easier ... at least you can get them to work precisely and logically, although if you've ever worked with them, you know how tough this can be. The people are tough ... they don't always behave quite the way you would like. And of course you get the two together, and either could foul up. The machine may do something wrong, which is correctable, but the man who is supposed to correct it is out on a coffee break. With proper organization you can avoid the worst disasters."

Al glanced at Mr. Beeman's chart and tucked it in his pocket. "I'll study it later. What else do you have to worry about?"

Joe sighed. "Plenty. For example, we are always fighting about our macro-organizational problems. Take a look at our org chart again. Right now, we're organized by product groups at the top. We have a consumer, industrial and raw materials group. Earlier, we were organized functionally, by marketing, production, engineering, etc. See, that's the way our individual companies are still organized."

Al studied the section on Kwik-Snap. "I see. Down there, the manager is responsible for production, marketing, or whatever. He actually does a functional job."

"It works well when the unit is small and the goal is well focussed. That manager of Plant #2 knows exactly what to do. He has certain production and quality goals, and his job is to get the product out. In the same way, the marketing manager of Snap-Kwik knows what he has to sell. The PARF loops there are pretty well structured, and the goals are clear."

"And in the old days RVA was a small outfit, so it wasn't too hard to run it that way?"

"Right. But we grew up, and it became more difficult to coordinate

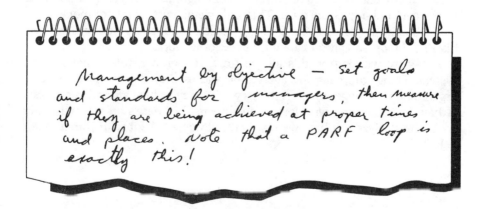

Management by objective — set goals and standards for managers, then measure if they are being achieved at proper times and places. Note that a PARF loop is exactly this!

things across a dozen companies. So we had a geographic organization for a while, where there was an East Coast, Western, and International group. But this got too hard to coordinate. The top managers were fighting all the time. Now we have the product structure you can see on the chart. Each group vice president is responsible for his own products, including international." Joe paused and thought for a minute. "There really is no optimum way to organize anything, since you're always fighting coordination and assignment problems. Things keep getting lost between groups."

"What's the assignment problem?" Al asked.

"Who is assigned which activities. For example, where does this long range planning group belong, or who is responsible for a certain kind of product development."

"From your chart, it looks as if the Vice President for Research and Development would be."

"Sure, but suppose a smart engineer down at Snap-Kwik comes up with a great new idea for a better lock? Should we give him money and skilled people to develop the idea? After all, his company knows more about locks than anyone. Or should we bring him to the central R & D laboratory and have him work it out there? If we do, his boss will scream. Remember that we have to deal with the social and political subsystems too. His boss may be a good friend of the R & D vice president, or they may not even know each other. Or Beeman may see in this new lock a means of getting some more power and push hard to control it. Things aren't quite as logical as the textbooks would suggest."

"I suppose that you get into micro-organizational stuff, too," Al commented. "Who does the janitorial service for that Plant #2? Or which secretaries do letters for which managers?"

"Sure, and that stuff is important. It may seem trivial to worry about who's going to clean the floors, but not if it's a food plant. One time we actually had a plant closed down by the federal sanitation inspector, when it turned out that two different groups were fighting over just this question. In the end, nobody cleaned up. That little detail cost us lots of money."

"So you try to organize 65,000 people so that every one of them gets his PARF loop straight? That could take some work."

"We're working on this all the time. Remember, this is not a static system. Things are changing every day, and as they do, we have to make organizational changes to make things work." He fumbled around in his desk. "I hate to bother you with lots of documents, but here's an internal paper we use to analyze just how we restructure things. Take it with you, it might help."

"Thanks, Joe, I will."

RVA: Organization Analysis

When considering an organizational change, keep in mind the following points. If you cannot answer these questions accurately, you have not done your homework!

It is possible to begin an organizational analysis by following through a series of questions:

1. What kind of organizational problem is this? Most analysis deals with micro-organizational problems, although the other types also present very real problems.

2. What are the goals of the system? The goal of any subsystem will be some output that is to be integrated with other subsystems. Often it is necessary to consider a number of systems simultaneously, since the way one works and the output it generates may affect the manner in which other related subsystems perform.

3. What kinds of inputs are required? Any output requires some inputs, and these must be considered. Such factors as men, machines, materials, information, and other inputs can be itemized. Often there are many ways to get the same job done, and alternatives have to be considered. But it is usually possible to indicate what is needed to perform the job.

4. What are the constraints? Any system is subject to many sorts of constraints that prevent some kinds of systems from operating. A few of these constraints are·

A. Financial: No one has all the money needed to build perfect systems, and this factor must always be considered.

B. Technical: Some systems cannot be built and some organizations will not work because no one knows enough to make them perform properly. It might be nice to have a production system based on the use of atomic fusion, but at present this is impossible.

C. Integration with other systems: A desirable organizational pattern might not be possible because some other subsystems would be unable to operate properly in coordination with this system. Students see this problem all the time. Some professors would prefer an ungraded, unstructured organization, but this cannot be done because any single class (subsystem) has to be integrated with other subsystems.

D. Real input restrictions: Some needed inputs may be unobtainable. If a system needs 125 skilled technicians in nuclear physics in Grants Pass, Oregon, it is unlikely that this requirement can be met. Or if a raw material of unobtainable purity is needed, the system will not operate.

E. Inability to complete the PARF loop: Problems of timing, communication, data storage, or similar factors may prevent the organization from operating properly. Such problems may be related to items A through D above or may be some combination of all of them.

These questions, when answered in some detail, begin to indicate how the organization should be structured. It should be noted by now that there is no easy way to get at the problem, which is one reason why there are so many kinds of organization analysis. No one to date has managed to reduce this complex problem to a series of easy steps to follow.

Joe began to doodle on his note pad. "This is what we do, really. Each subunit has its own PARF loop, and each stores some of its own information. But the output of one group becomes the input of another group. The production group has a bunch of subunits. The unit producing resistors for toasters has to integrate perfectly with the subgroup making toaster bases. You don't want 20,000 resistors and 40,000 bases, if you need one of each for every toaster. So the plans and activities have to mesh. The managers of each unit have to be given goals and plans that are reasonable, too. But then note that these subunits have to mesh with bigger units, like the toaster assembly line group. And this bigger group has to coordinate with the marketing people. You don't want to make 20,000 toasters a week when you can only sell 15,000."

"OK, so each subunit feeds into something at the same level, like production into marketing. But then these units feed up into higher units, who in turn go right on up the organization."

"Sure, it looks easy, but it isn't. Too many things can go wrong."

"Would any of this stuff make sense to a small business? I mean, RVA is huge. How about some small manufacturer with fifty employees?"

"He has the same problems, really, except that they aren't quite as complicated, because he doesn't have as many people or machines to coordinate. But smaller firms make things like toasters, and they can often compete pretty well with us. Remember, coordination costs plenty of money. You don't get those executives for nothing. Smaller companies can often avoid those costs."

"I would think that most of them would be organized functionally, instead of by groups, the way you are."

Joe nodded. "Sure, they usually look about the way that Kwik-Snap looks. They have a marketing department, production, engineering, finance, and so on." Joe looked at his watch. "Hey, let's go get some coffee. It's time for a break."

They walked down the hall to the coffee area. Joe bought Al some coffee and had a big Danish himself. He's a bit overweight, Al thought. Not too many top men he'd seen around RVA were heavy. Was that a part of the corporate image? But maybe Joe didn't give a hoot anymore.

"Hey, Joe, who handles your coffee? It seems to be available and hot at just the right time."

"We have a catering service that handles the whole building. It's a small firm that specializes in such things, and that's cheaper and easier than trying to do it ourselves. I think that someone over in Wilson's staff office actually draws up the contract." Joe finished his Danish and got another. "This catering is an example of a service that runs right across all our organizational lines. Everybody, no matter where they work, needs a coffee break. If we assigned it within the organization, we might have a problem. The group in charge could get all the best rolls and hottest coffee. Such things have been known to happen."

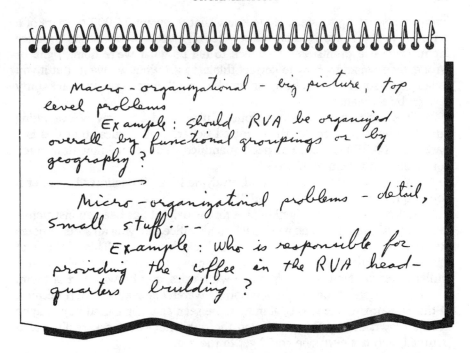

Macro - organizational - big picture, top level problems
    Example: Should RVA be organized overall by functional groupings or by geography?

    Micro - organizational problems - detail, small stuff. --
        Example: Who is responsible for providing the coffee in the RVA head-quarters building?

"After talking to you people, I sometimes wonder why anything gets done right," Al said. "But I suppose that if you work at it long enough, you can organize almost anything."

"You can, Al, if you know what you are trying to accomplish. The usual problem that you find in a badly run operation is that people have forgotten what they were trying to achieve. Then they get all messed up in the internal politics or socializing of the organization, and nothing much comes out the end. But if you really have good goals, you can plan to achieve them, some-how."

"So what are the goals of RVA?" Al asked.

"The main one has to be long run profitability. All this planning we do, all the organizing, and everything else, is considered in terms of net profit contribution, after tax. Oh, we have other goals too, such as being good corporate citizens, paying a bit above the local averages, and making very high quality products. Sales growth is important too. After all, RVA is a growth-oriented company. But in the end, when we set up our objectives for any project, the critical goal has to be long term profitability. It's the only goal we can have that we can measure, and we can also try to figure out what to do by using it. That is, we go in the directions that yield the best return."

"My church has a lot of organizational troubles," Al said. "Maybe It's because saving souls is such a nebulous business."

"How do you know that you've saved one?" Joe asked. "It's a lot different from making toasters. If we know that we want 15,000 toasters of a certain type every week, then we can get organized pretty fast to produce them. If we use profits as a feedback to tell us what we're doing right, or wrong, then we know how to correct things to get what we want. But if you save twenty souls a week, how can you be sure that you couldn't save thirty a week by reorganizing?"

"We can't, and that's our trouble. If we had any way of evaluating ourselves better, we could get organized better. Well, I guess that this is a part of the PARF loop too. You need quantified feedback to know how much you're deviating from your goals."

"You learn very fast," Joe said, studying him. "Sometimes I wonder if you're quite as naive as you sound."

Al left after a while, thanking Joe for his help. It has been an instructive interview, Al thought, as he went back to his office, carrying all sorts of notes and documents. He wondered just what Vicki was up to. This business of internal power struggling was pretty clear now, and he should have seen it earlier. After all, *Newsworld* had its own battles, and he was part of them. Already a couple of the business reporters weren't speaking to him because of this assignment. He was beginning to be seen as a fair-haired boy, maybe even a crown prince. Business, even the publishing business, really was a pyramid, and not everyone could get to the top.

Well, he would be having dinner with Vicki tomorrow evening. It might be fun to find out what she thought about Joe's observations.

DISCUSSION QUESTIONS

1. What is a crown prince ... or princess? How do you get to be one, or can you?

2. The president of a major company was thinking of buying a presumably successful smaller company. His financial staff planner took a close look at the books of this company and recommended strongly that he not buy it because there were some irregularities that couldn't be easily explained.

The president ignored his advice and purchased the company anyhow. After five years of losses and scandal, the big company finally sold off this smaller company for an $8 million loss.

Should this financial expert have been put in line management for this decision, and thus saved his company lots of money? Why or why not?

3. The professor who teaches this class reports to someone, probably a departmental chairman. What is the span of control here? Is it about right, or is it too broad or too narrow? Why?

4. How many levels of control does this class of yours have? Is it about right? Why or why not? How many people are on each level?

5. A very successful English department in a major university had a span of control of 128. There was one chairman and 128 faculty members reported to him. This arrangement worked fine, even though the typical professor only saw his chairman once a month or so.

Why do you think that this arrangement would work out, since such huge spans of control are not usually suggested for efficient organizations?

6. What is a grapevine? Are you linked into any? If so, which ones?

7. Al thinks that Joe talks too much. Does he? Why or why not?

8. Al was surprised to find out that Mr. Beeman was terrified of what he might do. Does this terror make sense? What could a person in Al's position do that would make life difficult for Mr. Beeman?

9. What is the functional subsystem?

10. What is the informational subsystem?

11. What is the social subsystem?

12. What is the political subsystem?

13. Consider any organization you have ever been connected with. Did this organization have those four subsystems noted in questions 9–12? Which one seemed the most important? Why?

14. Most organizations have committees, and typically the bigger the organization, the more committees. Why? What does a committee accomplish that nothing else seems to do?

15. What are four major indicators of poor or inefficient management?

16. What are five major constraints that prevent some systems from operating?

17. Joe said that making toasters is easier than saving souls. Why? What do toasters have that churches don't have?

18. A small businessman, who employs 28 people in his retail store, read this chapter and commented that nothing in it made any sense for his small organization. Do you agree?

Look back over this chapter and list four or five points that this small businessman might use in his own operations.

7

MARKETING

I am very pleased that you took the trouble to visit me," Mr. Suzuki said, as they walked into his plush office near San Francisco, "but I really do not know why."

"There were a couple of reasons," Al said. "I wanted to get away from your corporate headquarters for a while. It seemed to me that I was getting trapped in all the top level thinking. And, then, when I asked who had the best marketing knowledge in RVA, your name kept coming up."

"My colleagues flatter me," Mr. Suzuki murmured.

"There was another reason, Mr. Suzuki. At headquarters, almost everyone seemed to be a white American. I was curious about you because of your name. Are you Japanese by birth?"

"Oh, no, I am Nisei . . . first generation Japanese-American. I was born in San Leandro, just across the Bay from here. My father came from Japan."

There was a framed collection of medals on Mr. Suzuki's wall. "You fought a war, I see," Al said.

"Yes," Mr. Suzuki said. "I fought in World War II, in Italy. Those are the Silver Star, Bronze Star, and Purple Heart, with three clusters. I'm in the picture, there," he pointed to a framed photograph of a military group, most of whom were Japanese-American, "third from the left."

"But I thought all the Japanese in this country were locked up during the war, in camps."

Mr. Suzuki sighed. "You are young, Mr. Faber. They let a lot of us out, if we'd enlist. Then they sent us to fight Nazis, in Europe. They didn't trust us too much. That photograph was taken near Anzio. It's part of our history that most people don't seen to know much about."

"Mr. Suzuki, how did you get to be president of Snap-Kwik? It seems like a long way from a war and this part of the world."

"I was a small businessman. This was my company."

Al sat back in the plush chair. He must have looked puzzled.

"You see, Mr. Faber, I was 19 in 1942, when the war first started. I was a sophomore at Berkeley. My father ran a small farm, where he grew fruits and vegetables for the local market. Japanese parents want their children to succeed, just like American parents. My father insisted that I go to college, even though at that time there were not many jobs available for

Japanese in California. He would say, 'Work hard, Daniel. Study, and you will be an important man some day.' So I studied. But in 1942 we were sent to Manzanar, and I had to leave school in the middle of the semester."

"Manzanar—the concentration camp we set up for Japanese-Americans during the war?"

"They called it a preventive detention camp then, Mr. Faber. But after a while I got bored. I was young and restless. So I joined the Army. After all, I was an American. When I got back after the war, things were still very tight. Besides, I had only one leg, and what could a one-legged Japanese do? I really didn't want to go to school, because I was married. But I noticed that people were still very nervous. Just after the war, some Americans did not trust Japanese very much. I began to sell locks to them. Sometimes it was important to have a good lock on your door in 1946, when you had just returned from Manzanar."

"Did you start your own company then?"

"Not at first. I was an agent for a small lock company in the Midwest. They made very poor locks really, but it was the only company that would deal with me. Any lock is better than no lock, when you need one."

Mr. Suzuki paused and thought for a while. "That was when I learned my first marketing lesson. If you want to sell something, be sure to find an item that people really want. It is so much easier to sell a person something he wants, rather than something he or she does not want."

"So you sold locks and got rich, right?"

Mr. Suzuki smiled. "It was not quite that easy. Another thing you need in successful marketing is a broad market, and I was selling mainly to Japanese people. Locks can last a long time, and after a while, I had saturated my market. I needed to expand."

Al thought of a young Japanese, trying to sell locks to suspicious Anglos a long time ago. It must have been tough.

"Disaster struck, and as is so often the case, it turned out to be a blessing. The company that I bought locks from went bankrupt, and I lost my source of supply. So I decided to make my own. I rented a small building, hired a few people, and began to make my own product in 1949."

"Just as Mr. Ross and Mr. Vogel did a long time ago," Al said.

"Ah, you know something of this company, Mr. Faber. Good! Yes, something like that, but I was not nearly so successful. Sales were slow, because I didn't know much about marketing then, and I had to keep my costs low. I again turned adversity into an advantage. At that time, no mainstream company would hire a minority person in a responsible job, so I did. I found a first-class black machinist, and he became my key man for production. I could pay him much less than an Anglo. I hired Japanese-American girls cheaply to work on the assembly line. I hired several deaf people to work in my office. They were very efficient, because they are not distracted, and they were cheap too."

Al shifted uneasily in his chair.

"But I hired only white Americans for my sales force," Mr. Suzuki went on, "because most of our new customers wanted it that way. You see, I was beginning to find out about selling. You give people what they want, not what you want, and your sales are easy. Now they call this the total marketing concept, but in those days, I just did it to survive."

"But that was racial discrimination," Al blurted awkwardly. "I mean, limiting your sales force to whites—that would be illegal now. And the cheap labor you hired was really the result of discrimination too, against minorities and handicapped people."

"I know, I know. I have been discriminated against myself. But in those days, I was thinking only of survival, and the cheap labor I hired was glad to have a job. We use all kinds of people in sales now, but of course, our customers accept our minority salespeople much more willingly now than they used to.

"You would be surprised at how many people and companies do what they want to do, rather than what the customers want them to do. It is more fun that way. But I learned early that if I asked myself just what the customers would want, and then tried to manufacture that product, sales would be easy. Unfortunately, production was not that easy, since customers want a lot for little money. But we managed, and by 1950, our total sales were over $88,000."

Mr. Suzuki leaned forward in his big chair. "It is not always so easy to figure out what customers want, because sometimes they do not know themselves. They may not be aware of new ideas, so they do not want them. The real trick is not to satisfy what the buyer needs now, but rather what he or she will need in the future, and that is not easy."

"Mr. Suzuki, I would think that making locks and related items would have been a growth market since 1950. I mean, crime is going up."

"You are right. Crime rates were rising, and people wanted more security. Even more importantly, there was a long term building boom, and every new building needs lots of locks. You see, moving into a rising market is very nice because it makes sales easy."

"I can see that. Then you branched out into other kinds of security devices, such as burglar alarms and smoke detectors."

"Correct. Our business kept growing very nicely all through the 1950's and 1960's. By 1967, I did $5.7 million in sales, and I made a profit of $585,000. I had a very nice, profitable little company."

"So you sold out? Why?"

"Did you ever achieve something you really wanted, Mr. Faber? I mean, something that you thought was totally impossible?"

Al shook his head. "Not anything really important, I guess."

Mr. Suzuki leaned back. "I did. It seemed very funny, but I had achieved the American dream. I was rich, successful, and perhaps even happy. My children were not interested in the business." He pushed a picture folder over to Al. "My son is a successful surgeon in Los Angeles, and my daughter teaches English at San Pablo Junior College. There was no point in thinking about turning the company over to my family. Besides, I was a failure in many ways."

Al laughed. "You, a failure! It doesn't seem likely."

"Oh, yes. I had 430 employees by 1967, and I cannot delegate at all. I had great trouble getting organized. I could see that somehow all the really good young managers I hired were chased away very soon, even the Japanese ones. I suppose that I took too much authority. The company was getting away from me." Mr. Suzuki began to sketch a diagram. "Then I had some tax problems. If I died, my heirs would face very tough taxes. So when RVA wanted to buy my company, I sold out for stock. Five million dollars worth of RVA stock at $6 per share."

"So you took your capital gains?" Al remembered what Mr. Robertson had said. RVA was selling for about $25 per share now, so Mr. Suzuki, even after capital gains taxes, was many times a millionaire.

"Yes, I did. Then RVA asked me to stay on and manage my own company for a while. I did not want to, but they made it very attractive for me. I believe that I make as much money as some of the vice presidents, and it is still enjoyable to be a manager."

"It makes sense. You know more about your company than anyone in the world."

"Yes, but now I am about to retire. RVA was able to recruit some very good young people, and next year an efficient young man will replace me. I have seen my little business become a well organized corporation. But I still do all the market planning."

"That's why I came to see you. We're supposed to talk about marketing."

Mr. Suzuki pushed the diagram he had been drawing across to Al. "I know, and here it is. You see, the physical flows of the goods are shown in solid lines, while the information flows are shown in dotted lines. I have shown the information flows with arrows going both ways, since we not only give information to our distributors, retailers, and customers, but we also get much information from them. A lot of marketing is nothing more than knowing what is going on."

Al studied the diagram. "It looks like goods can move through various channels."

"Oh yes, and there is a big field in marketing called channel theory, which deals with exactly that question. What is good for one company might not be efficient for another. Some companies sell direct to retailers, others have distributors that they sell to. Some even sell direct to the final user."

"What does Snap-Kwik do?"

"We sell mainly to distributors, who in turn sell to hardware stores and

MR. SUZUKI'S MARKETING DIAGRAM

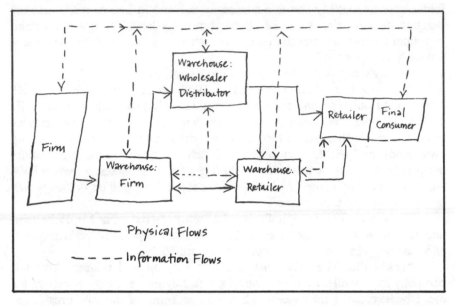

other sales outlets. Smaller contractors sometimes buy direct from the distributors. But we also sometimes sell direct to the retailers, particularly big retailers. In some government sales, and for major items such as bank vaults, we even sell direct to the final customer. Right now we have a big contract with the Defense Department for thousands of special alarm systems which will be shipped direct to them."

"Using distributors must be expensive. After all, they have to have a markup."

"Distribution is always expensive. But consider a small hardware store in the Midwest, that sells perhaps a few hundred locks per year, divided into dozens of different models. Such a dealer cannot buy many locks at once. His costs would be high, because it costs us much money to handle small orders. Besides, he might not have the right assortment of models. A regional distributor can carry a large assortment for hundreds of such stores. He can fill small orders from his large stock much more easily than we can. He will know his region much better than we do as well. He charges for his inventory costs and his knowledge, but this is often cheaper than a small company trying to do it all by itself."

"I can see that," Al said. "I suppose that distributors give you lots of information too?"

"Of course. We are constantly in touch with them. Styles in locks are quite different around the country, and abroad they are even more different. We constantly listen to our distributors, because they can help us so much with our market forecasts."

"A friend of mine once bought half a million dollars' worth of new auto parts for ten thousand dollars. It turned out that they were not the parts people needed."

"One major cost of distribution is a mistake like that," Mr. Suzuki said. "Unfortunately, we also make such mistakes, although hopefully not too often. I just scrapped thousands of dollars worth of obsolete inventory, an old model lock that really did not sell very well. We manufactured too many of them, which was our mistake. But our customers have to pay for such mistakes. If we make too many mistakes, we will not be around for long."

"Those warehouses really act like buffers, don't they? I mean, it's like a dam holding water for the dry season. I suppose that you can't just change production overnight if you need some other model."

"Right, Mr. Faber. We are always trying to balance out our production manager's desire to have a long production run against our sales manager's desire to have fifty different models to sell all the time. The way we do this is to try to build up reasonable stocks of various models and hold them in inventory. But you see, we have a problem. We save money on long production runs, but then it costs a lot of money to hold inventory. We try to do a balancing act. It is not easy, since there are so many factors involved."

"Like what?"

"Oh, it costs money to build warehouses. We have some, but our distributors have more. Their capital costs have to be covered, and interest rates are very high these days. So are building costs. Then they have to hire warehousemen and clerks to keep track of shipments received and orders shipped out. There are obsolescence costs, and insurance and taxes to pay. The more inventory you have, the higher your costs. But then we can produce 50,000 locks in one production run at a cost per lock of perhaps one-third of producing 5,000 in a run. It costs money to set up machinery, get people trained to assemble one kind of lock, and order the right components for each lock. It is an interesting job, to try to decide just how to do all of this."

"Mr. Suzuki, your diagram tells me what is, but it doesn't say much about the future. How do you figure out what to do next?"

"You are talking about marketing planning, Mr. Faber, and you are right. My drawing does not tell you what kinds of new things we might be doing. Snap-Kwik is quite good at figuring out what should be done next. It is one reason why we have been growing so nicely."

"So what do you do?"

"We worry a lot about trends in our business. As I mentioned, we talk to lots of people who know what is going on in the lock and alarm business. We also spend a lot of time looking at new technical developments. If I can find some new technology in another field and apply it to our business for a product that might be attractive to customers, we can do very well. Our new electronic smoke alarms are an example. The technology came from the aerospace industry, and a bit from television. At first, the lock and alarm companies did not realize that such technology could be used successfully in our business, so we got on the market first with our sensitive smoke detector."

"You seem to be putting pieces of a puzzle together all the time."

"The trick is to get all the pieces to fit," Mr. Suzuki commented. "And always we have to figure out just what consumers really want. Remember, we start from there. But often, buyers do not really know what they want, and we have to show them. People have worried about home fires for a long time, but it took quite a while to convince most buyers that spending some money for a smoke detector was worthwhile."

"I've run into some problems about demand forecasting already," Al said, thinking back to Vicki's comments about baby cribs. "I suppose that you do that too?"

"Oh, all those numbers and equations? Of course. I am not very mathematical, Mr. Faber, but fortunately we do have some people who are. We use the New Jersey computer facility quite regularly, I can assure you." He jotted down some notes and handed them to Al.

"You see, like any other product, there are lots of variables that influence our product sales. Unfortunately it is not always so easy to get good data on some of them. But we do pay careful attention to housing starts and other demographic data. And we spend much time talking to architects and

MR. SUZUKI'S NOTES

Demand Variables: What determines Snap-Kwik's sales volume?

For locks:
1. Housing starts.
2. Other construction (apartments, office buildings, factories, etc.)
3. Price (our price relative to our competitors.
4. Government policy and laws.
5. Crime rates (for crimes involving breaking and entering?)
6. New technology - ours and competitors.
7. Trends -- the way people feel about security.

other technicians in the building industry. Often they give us excellent ideas about security systems."

"And you take those and go out and create new products?"

"We use those ideas to help us, but we are not going to invest perhaps half a million dollars in tooling just because a few housing experts tell us it is necessary, Mr. Faber. No, we do a lot more demand forecasting than that."

"One of your variables is trends. Do you watch the market?"

"People change their minds about security. A sudden crime wave in a city can send our sales way up. Police publicity about avoiding robberies by having better locks and alarms can also help us out. Actually, we work quite closely with the police in many cities, since they have a lot of experience in how locks can be broken. We had one model we thought was theft proof, but it turned out that it had one fatal flaw, and robbers were easily able to break the lock once they learned about it. We changed the design, and we stressed in our advertising that this new model had been developed with police cooperation. It sold very well, and it still does."

"I guess that people in the security business would know a lot about breaking and entering."

"Oh, yes. We also work with private security agencies, for the same reason. If someone has something valuable to guard, these agents and companies know exactly how to do it. We also have worked with ex-convicts. One of our best consultants, who now works for us, was an expert safe cracker. He really knew what was wrong with locks!"

"I see that you also worry about government activities."

"Of course. Actually, our smoke alarm systems are often sold for us by government. Many localities now have building codes that require such systems in all new buildings. This means that Snap-Kwik, or one of its competitors, is going to make a sale. We have to be able to offer a good, approved system at a proper price, however."

"So you take a look at all factors affecting your sales, work out a sales forecast, and then go tool up and make the locks and alarms. Then you sell them and make a profit." Al thought about that. "It sounds easy, but I suppose that it isn't, just like most things in RVA."

Mr. Suzuki smiled. "Young reporters are always running around accusing companies of doing nasty things. You don't sound like that kind of person."

"Oh, I've found a few skeletons in RVA's closets, Mr. Suzuki, but I'm beginning to appreciate the problems anyone has in making things work."

"It certainly is not easy, Mr. Faber. A houseowner in Syracuse decides to buy a new lock for his house, usually after he has had some trouble with a burglar. Or he may decide to buy a smoke alarm. So he goes to his local hardware store, or perhaps his suburban department store, and he finds what he wants, at a price he can afford to pay. Somehow, most of the time, the smoke alarm is there in the store, and we hope that it is a Snap-Kwik model.

He pays for it, takes it home, and we have done our job. But months or years before he made his decision, we had to figure out what he, and thousands of others, might want. We had to design the product, test it, find distributors and dealers for it, and make sure that the store's inventory was adequate. If everything works out, we make a profit. If it doesn't, then we disappear and no one cares."

"I did some shopping before I came in, Mr. Suzuki, and I noticed that your products were pretty high-priced, compared to some of the competition. Does that mean that you are inefficient?"

Mr. Suzuki sighed. "I hope not. You should learn about market segmentation, Mr. Faber. We are not a huge company, at least in my division. We are not even interested in selling all types of locks and alarm systems to everyone. To do so would take a much larger company than this, and quite a few segments of the market are too competitive. What we do is try to cover a few segments of the market very well."

"Then a segment is nothing more than one part of the total possible market?"

"Right. The lock market is huge. It ranges from very cheap little padlocks and bicycle locks to very expensive door locks and safes. Again, consider the way a customer might see his problem. If you own a cheap bicycle, you might be willing to pay a few dollars for a small bit of protection. I could make and sell a two-hundred-dollar, absolutely theft proof lock for you, but if your bicycle is worth only forty dollars, I doubt that you would buy one."

"That makes sense," Al said.

"But supposing you need a lock for a door which encloses some high explosives on a building site. Theft here could be very dangerous and expensive. Or perhaps you are guarding an inventory of silver, as a photo film making company might do? You would be willing to pay two or three hundred dollars for a very good lock, wouldn't you?"

"I suppose so. What you're saying is that you try to get at the Cadillac part of the business."

"Exactly. Remember when I began, I sold locks only to Japanese-Americans. That market segment was very good for a while, and no one else really competed against me. Later, we tried for a while to broaden our business to everyone, but I soon found that in some segments, we could do very well, while in others, my competition ruined me. So gradually we built up a market segmentation strategy based on selling only in areas where we were better than our competitors. I suppose that they in turn found other niches."

"So now you sell only high-quality products at high prices to people who want the best?"

"Right." Mr. Suzuki toyed with his pencil. "We cannot compete, for example, at the very cheap end of the lock line. Foreigners from Taiwan or India can make good cheap locks better than we can. But if you really want protection, then you come to us. Note, Mr. Faber, how production ability and marketing come together. Our metallurgists are very good. They can harden steel better than anyone. But it costs money to do it. To cut the hasp on our eighty-five-dollar padlock would take too much effort for almost any thief. Our smoke alarms are the best by far in the business, but they are the most expensive, too. No, we stress quality above all, and price is really not too important."

"Does the rest of RVA follow this advice, Mr. Suzuki?"

"I hope so, although I am not sure. Actually, I make many speeches about this all over the company, since many managers too often are blinded by sheer sales volume, or by what the production people can do, not what the market is. But my boss has me do the talking because Snap-Kwik is, by both percentage of sales and capital invested, the most profitable single company in RVA."

"Can you please explain that, Mr. Suzuki?"

He did, and Al made a note of it for future reference.

"You know, Mr. Suzuki, I really can't say that I know your company very well. I don't recall seeing much of your advertising."

"You would not, unless you read banking journals or the trade magazines dealing with industrial security. Remember that we really are not in the mass market. We do not advertise on television, nor do we use mass circulation magazines, because our market segment is a specialized one. It would make no sense to spend lots of money talking to people who would not be buyers."

"So you stress security to people who really are willing to pay for it?"

Profits as a percentage of sales —

$$= \frac{Profits}{Sales}$$

So, if profits as $10,000 and sales $100,000,

then $\frac{10,000}{100,000} = 0.1$, or 10%

(per year, month, or some stated time period)

Profits as rate of return on net capital

$$= \frac{Profits}{Net\ Investment}$$

"Yes. Our advertising is focussed on our segment, just as our product is." Mr. Suzuki flipped the pages of a slick paper magazine which was on his desk and showed Al an ad. "You see? This magazine is directed at bankers. We have a line of locks for safety deposit boxes which we promote here. This ad is very sober and informative. Smart bankers are not impressed with puff talk."

Al read through the ad. "I see what you mean. What is heat treated, acid pickled, chrome molybdenum steel, anyhow?"

"The toughest steel known. We use it in these locks. Note that we do not even mention prices. For this purpose, price is not too important."

"It is for me, but then I don't need maximum security on anything I own, either."

"You would not be a good customer for us, Mr. Faber. But then, most consumers would not be."

There was a brief pause, then Al struck off in a new direction. "You know, it sounds like there are some things you can control and do something about, and others you just have to live with."

"Correct. We can control our product lines and qualities, and we can set our prices. We can advertise and let our customers know what we have. We can choose our retailers, distributors, and other personnel. If we control these activities wisely and efficiently, we may even make some money."

"But you can't control crime rates."

"Only in part, since we can help keep them down by providing better means of security. You are right, however. We cannot be responsible for the criminal elements. If the number of these people goes up, our business prospers. We cannot really control the fire rate, and if it goes up, our smoke alarm systems sell well. We certainly cannot control how many new houses and offices are built, or how much income our customers have. And we cannot control what our competitors might do. Right now there is a new and very clever company in Indianapolis introducing some new products that hit us directly. They are very good, very good indeed. We certainly cannot control laws governing smoke alarm systems, although we try to influence legislation."

"How?"

"Oh, we make sure that legislators get information about how many people lose their lives needlessly in fires. We work with fire chiefs and insurance companies to lobby for new legislation."

"I don't suppose that you pay people off," Al observed dryly.

Mr. Suzuki smiled. "If I did, I wouldn't tell you! And if I deny it, you might not believe me. But no, we do not. It's not worth it. After all, pushing for safer houses and apartments is something like selling motherhood. We do not get much opposition to our lobbying efforts, when we point to children who died needlessly because their house didn't have a smoke alarm. Persuading legislators to do something about fire safety is not too hard, if we can get their attention."

"I would think it would be very easy."

"No, because so much is wrong with this world, Mr. Faber, that it is hard to get anyone's attention even for an important safety idea. Our legislators have very much on their minds. Besides, if everyone had to buy a smoke alarm unit, it would cost a lot of money, and consumers want other things. But if a legislator knows personally of a fire tragedy, he or she is often willing to help. And we do get lots of help from insurance companies and fire departments, who do a lot of advertising for us free."

"How about consumerism, Mr. Suzuki?" Al asked. "Government can help you a lot, but they also can control you, can't they?"

Mr. Suzuki sighed. "Oh, yes. In the past ten years there have been many new laws which attempt to protect consumers. One which we have had much difficulty with is the one covering warranties. We now must be very careful about what we promise our customers. We also have to do what we promise to do."

Mr. Suzuki thought for a moment. "Another set of laws which affect us are consumer safety rules. We cannot produce locks that are unsafe."

"What could be safer than a lock?"

"Well, strange things can happen. We had a safe which had an electric interlock for a timer. Our wiring was not very well designed, I am afraid, and once in a while it shorted out. When the clerk started to pull the opening handle, he received a painful electric shock. If the floor had been damp, and if the person had had a weak heart, such an incident could actually have been fatal. We had to redesign this circuitry to meet new safety standards, although we would have done it anyhow. Shocking your customers doesn't do much for your sales."

"In this case, I suppose you would have done something quickly, as you say," Al commented. "Why have new laws?"

"Because our legislators think that some companies at least might not be too anxious to spend money to redesign products. Of course food companies and drug manufacturers have very complex laws regulating the safety of their products, and many others, such as automobile manufacturers, also have special safety rules. The trend until recently has been to have more such legislation. It raises costs, but it also may protect consumers."

"If costs go up, I suppose that prices go up too," Al said.

"Of course, but I think that many people would rather pay more for something safe than save money on something dangerous, don't you agree?"

"I wonder," Al said. "I haven't got all the money in the world."

"Some of those rules are very costly, and we have great difficulty trying to observe them," Mr. Suzuki said. "But we try to observe the law. However, in the 1980's, there has been some easing of such rules. As you say, some of them can be very expensive, and apparently people are not willing to spend so much money. They take their chances."

Mr. Suzuki drew a graph. "Here is another marketing concept for you, Mr. Faber. You see that we are now in the stage of early adoption for some

MR. SUZUKI'S ADOPTION GRAPH

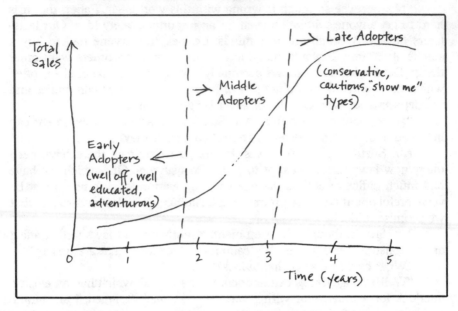

products, such as our smoke detectors, down here on the curve. Most consumer products behave like this. Somewhere between one and five percent of consumers are very adventurous, very interested in new things, and quite affluent. They will try anything, even if it does not work out too well."

"I have a friend like that," Al said. "She'll buy anything new as soon as it hits the market. She stays broke buying all sorts of stuff."

"Exactly. But if the product is useful and desired, the next group begins to buy, and you move rapidly into a mass market. Smoke alarm systems are just beginning to reach this second stage, actually. We think that the late adopters learn from the early adopters. Finally, the product moves up in sales until the market is saturated, at the top here on the graph."

"How high is saturated?"

"It depends on the product. If it is something like a television set, it may be as high as 98 percent of the total possible market. If it is a car, it is around 80 percent. If it is a set of silver goblets, it might be ten percent. For smoke alarms, we think that it might go as high as 80 percent of the total possible market. But it will take many years to get there."

"That means that you can look forward to rapidly rising sales then," Al observed. "After all, you're only at about ten percent now."

"It also means very rapidly increasing competition. Remember, as the market expands rapidly, it becomes more and more attractive for new firms to enter. Right now, we are a bit out of balance. Too many companies have jumped in, and competition is fierce. This often happens."

"So I suppose that your strategy is to take the best segment again?"

"Of course. Our smoke alarm system is premium priced, but it is also by far the best. We will be satisfied with a five percent market share."

"You seem to have worked out a logical marketing strategy, Mr. Suzuki."

"It works, in that it is profitable. At least, up to now it has been profitable. But remember that nothing stays the same for very long. My successor may have to change our plans, simply because conditions in the market keep changing. In marketing, you cannot sit still for very long."

"I begin to see why."

"Another area which you will probably discover in marketing, Mr. Faber, is buyer behavior. You see, we can produce excellent products, and we can get them distributed, but in the end, a sale occurs because a customer decides to buy the product. Now, the question is, why? This is a problem in applied psychology, I think, and many scholars have done excellent work in attempting to determine exactly how consumers behave. That adoption curve is one manifestation of behavior, but a deeper question is, just why do some people buy early, while others buy later?"

"It sounds as if you could use a lot of psychology there," Al said. "Half the time, I don't even know myself why I buy things."

"You may not consciously know, but many marketing people spend much time trying to develop usable theories to explain what you do. Obviously, what a consumer does depends on many factors. Perhaps the color of the box is appealing. Perhaps the odor of the product brings pleasant memories. Perhaps even the product's location in the store is important. This is a complex field, but a critical one."

Mr. Suzuki paused. "Some marketers sum up the critical elements in marketing with four P's. Product policy, place decisions, price mechanisms, and promotional activities. You can see that we have been talking about those four P's in our discussion. Our product policy is to produce the finest locks, which automatically puts us in only a few market segments. Place decisions for us involve what areas to service, and which distribution channels to use. Again, these decisions strongly affect how we can sell, and how much.

"Our promotional activities are strongly influenced by our product policies. You have seen that we are not interested in mass marketing, but that we promote our products to our premium clients quite strongly. Our price mechanisms are in part determined by the market, since we cannot price too differently from our competitors, and in part by our product quality."

Al wrote down those four P's. "This seems to be a good way of looking at all sorts of marketing decisions," he said.

"Structure is useful for any problem, Mr. Faber. When I was young, I often tried to operate without knowing the structure of the problem I faced. I almost always had difficulties, unless I got lucky. As I grew older, I realized

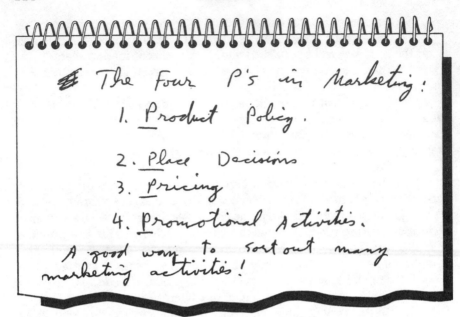

The Four P's in Marketing:

1. <u>P</u>roduct Policy.

2. <u>Plac</u>e Decisions

3. <u>P</u>ricing

4. <u>P</u>romotional Activities.

A good way to sort out many marketing activities!

that what so many business scholars were trying to do was help practitioners by developing structures for problem-solving. Then I began to use them, and I did much better."

"I'll be talking about marketing to lots of other people, Mr. Suzuki, but what else is there to it? I've read that distribution accounts for over half of all costs. The things you mentioned are obviously important, but this isn't all of marketing, is it?"

Mr. Suzuki wrote out a list in his precise hand. "No, not at all. Here are some other things that marketing people do, and all are very important. Remember, when you pick up that item you want in a store, literally hundreds of experts have done their jobs well. Otherwise, it would not be there."

Al glanced at his list. "Most of this we've talked about a little, but what exactly do you do in after-sales service?"

"Our products are often quite complicated, and our customers need spare parts and advice about how to keep them in good condition. Sometimes they do not work right. We have a staff of experts to help our customers."

"That's expensive, isn't it?"

"Of course, but a satisfied customer is our best next customer. Besides, people talk to each other. If we satisfy one banker, he may tell his banking friends about us." Mr. Suzuki paused. "Every business has different problems. One of ours is to open locks where keys have been lost, or where no one knows the combination. It is surprising how often smart people forget

MR. SUZUKI'S LIST OF MARKETING ACTIVITIES

1. Channel planning
2. Market segmentation
3. Advertising and ad planning: includes ad campaigns, working with distributors and retailers, media coordination, etc.
4. Information feedback planning: figuring out your information system in marketing. Also information processing.
5. Wholesale and distribution.
6. Retailing
7. Logistics — physical movements of products, plus warehousing and other functions related to physical product.
8. Sales work: the actual job of selling the product. Also sales promotion — see advertising.
9. Merchandise management: controlling inventories, financing them, planning, etc.
10. Pricing and price policy.
11. After-sales service.
12. Technical sales service.
13. Marketing finance: interrelating marketing and finance.

numbers or lose keys. We are famous for sending men immediately to help out, and this is good for future sales. Just last week, one of our technicians had to get up at three in the morning and rush to an office to open a top secret file. The top man was in Europe, and certain information was badly needed. It cost us some overtime, but that customer will remember us."

"I wish that the guy who sold me my car would get up at three," Al said, "but he doesn't."

"If you paid enough for your car, he might," Mr. Suzuki said. "But our after-sales work ties very closely together with our technical sales work.

Many of our best salesmen are engineers or other experts. They work closely with clients in developing new products, or in adapting our products to the customers' needs. If they do their job well, then we will get many new sales. But it is not uncommon for one of our technical salesmen to talk a customer out of buying something, because he or she knows that it will not fit the customer's needs."

"Then just what are you selling? I mean, you obviously make locks and such, but if sometimes you're not even interested in sales, what's the point?"

"We really sell various types of security systems, Mr. Faber. Many companies make the mistake of getting involved in their product too much. They have some hardware, and they think that that's what they are selling. But no one really wants hardware. They want something else. Our customers do not want locks—they want security. If a lock happens to be the best way to provide security at the level they desire, then we sell them a lock. But perhaps what they really need is a guard, or possibly a camera, or perhaps an electronic surveillance system. We try to sell them security, not hardware."

"And that idea has led you away from locks as such?"

"Yes, it has. We are now working on a completely new system of computer security. You see, if a person could crack the access codes of your computer system, and if he knew what to do, he could steal millions. It has happened. So what the company needs is a new kind of security concerning computer access. We are now getting into this field, and most of our sales will consist of expert services, not hardware. It's logical for us to move in this direction, since we sell security."

"But that has nothing to do with locks. You could end up being some sort of computer service company."

Mr. Suzuki nodded. "But if our market takes us there, we will go. Perhaps in the future, few will want to lock up files and documents with hardware. Rather, files will be stored in computer memory banks. Those banks cannot be protected with locks. Hence we have to change."

Al shook his head. "If you follow the logic of the market, you may end up in a strange place."

"Certainly. I feel sorry for some companies, because they are technology bound. Poor Amtrak! Its public charter requires it to run passenger trains. Its manager will probably fail, because the company is forced to use only one technology to produce its product."

"So what would you do if you were running Amtrak, Mr. Suzuki?"

"I would try to obtain permission to sell passenger transportation, no matter how it was done. For all I know, leasing autos might be the proper way to fill customer needs. Perhaps I could fly airplanes, or run buses, or even rent bicycles.

"Remember the total marketing concept we talked about a while back, Mr. Faber? The correct way to do marketing is to start from the market and work backwards. Poor Amtrak starts from the production technology and works down to the market. If no one wants to ride trains, then they cannot compete. If Snap-Kwik wants to sell computer security systems, no one objects to our using whatever technology is necessary to do the job properly. I have a much easier job as a result."

"Amtrak was started in the early 1970's," Al mused. "Yet the Congress stuck it with that philosophy of doing it only one way."

"I think that most companies, and probably most individuals, are still stuck with a production orientation, Mr. Faber. It is fortunate for us, since we can compete so much better if our competitors do not think properly." He glanced at his expensive-looking watch.

"I guess that our time is up, more than up. Thanks, Mr. Suzuki, for taking the trouble to talk to me." Al rose to go.

Mr. Suzuki nodded. "No trouble, Mr. Faber."

Al paused for a last look at the medals and the fading pictures on the wall. "We white Americans didn't treat you very well, Mr. Suzuki. Was Manzanar very tough?"

Mr. Suzuki gazed at his medals. "No, not too tough. But it was not much fun. I am an American, Mr. Faber, and I always have been. I do not even speak Japanese very well, and I cannot read or write it. My father was a landless peasant in Japan, and like so many other immigrants, he came to the land of opportunity. He worked hard all his life, and he earned very little. But he had a great faith in America. When we were at Manzanar together, I would chide him for his faith. 'Look,' I said, 'see what these Americans do to you, a naturalized American. They put you in jail.' But he still kept the faith. He said to me, 'You forget this. You join the Army, fight for our country, show them that you are a patriot too. In the end, you will show them, and you will win.' So I joined the Army. That was a lot tougher than Manzanar. We fought pretty hard, and lots of us got killed. My best friend, Kobayashi, he was killed by the same shell that took my leg. He never left Italy ... a long way from San Francisco, and farther from Japan.

"But I followed my father's advice, and he was right. In the end, I won. You do not win easy games with much satisfaction, Mr. Faber. I suppose that my game was tougher than yours, but others have more trouble."

"What happened to your father?"

"He died in 1958. I sold his farm to a real estate developer, and my father got rich too in the end. Indeed, the eighty thousand dollars I received helped save this company during the late 1950's. He is a part of it too."

"He must have been a fine man," Al said.

"He was. But I bore you with old war stories. Young people never like to listen to old soldiers. My own children would never listen. Thank you for being so patient."

They shook hands, and Al left. You find some interesting people around this world, Al thought, as he found his car in the lot. Maybe sometimes we should listen to the old war stories, because they might tell us more about ourselves today than most of us think.

DISCUSSION QUESTIONS

1. What is the total marketing concept?

2. A small university now realizes that in the 1980's the college-age population will decline, because of lower birthrates 18 to 20 years ago. If the percentage of this population it traditionally has enrolled as students remains the same, its enrollments will decline.

What might this school do to keep enrollments growing? What other market segments might it tap to keep growing? Would the same kind of programs that attract 18-year-old freshmen work for these new segments? Why or why not?

3. Take a close look at your own college. What is it really selling? Why?

4. What is after-sales service? For what kinds of products do you think that good after-sales service might be very important? Why?

5. What is market segmentation?

6. One auto dealer sells antique autos at high prices. Another has a Cadillac agency for new and cream puff used cars. A third sells five- to ten-year-old transportation cars at low prices to lower income workers and students. A fourth sells new Datsuns. A fifth sells new and used four-wheel-drive Jeeps.

All these people sell cars, so they obviously should be selling their cars in the same way, right? Or wrong?

Consider the kinds of customers each of these dealers might logically attract. What kind of segmentation do you see here? Why?

The dealer selling low-cost used transportation cars thinks he should expand. He has been very successful selling cars to his present customers. He has a chance to obtain the local Rolls Royce agency. Do you think that he would know all about potential Rolls Royce customers? Why or why not?

The Cadillac dealer normally resells his used car trade-ins. These are typically luxury cars that are a few years old. They usually have been perfectly maintained by upper-income buyers, and they can be sold guaranteed at premium prices.

From time to time, this dealer gets an old dog of a trade-in, such as an eight-year-old medium-priced car, with lots of rust and mechanical problems. He immediately wholesales such cars at low prices at a local auction and makes no effort to resell them in his used car lot.

Why would he do such a thing, when he could easily put them in his lot at a big discount and make some money?

The Jeep dealer has a chance to get a Kenworth truck agency. These Kenworths are very heavy duty, premium-priced large trucks for use in over the road commercial hauling. They can cost over $100,000 each. Do you think that his known skills in selling four-wheel-drive light trucks would be useful in selling these big commercial type trucks? Why or why not?

7. Mr. Suzuki knows what key variables determine lock sales. Consider what key variables determine the sale of textbooks for this course you are taking. Are any of these similar to Mr. Suzuki's list? Why or why not?

8. What are profits as a percentage of sales? Who uses this information, and how?

9. Mr. Suzuki hired minority and handicapped workers long before most companies would do so. He also paid them much lower wages than mainstream workers received. Was Mr. Suzuki ethical in doing this? Why or why not?

10. Mr. Suzuki used minority and handicapped workers, but he made sure that his salesmen were white Americans. Was this ethical? Why or why not?

11. Mr. Suzuki used an ex-convict to give him advice on how to build better sales. Your business school is interested in finding out how to do a better job in business education. What kinds of experts could the school consult? Why?

12. Mr. Suzuki noted that it makes sense to advertise in magazines that are read by his target buyers. Suppose that your local student bookstore wants to do some advertising. What are the best ways to do it? What magazines, newspapers, TV stations, or other media should be used? Why?

13. Snap-Kwik can increase sales if it can persuade state legislatures to pass laws requiring smoke alarms to be placed in every house and apartment. A good unit will cost at least $100 installed.

Do you think that Snap-Kwik should really push its lobbying effort to try to get these laws passed? Why or why not?

If Snap-Kwik spends about $300,000 in one state on certain "favors" for key legislators, such a law will be passed. If it is, Snap-Kwik should increase sales enough to earn an extra $500,000 per year in net profits for at least the next ten years.

Should Snap-Kwik make this "investment"? Why or why not?

In this same state, fire experts estimate that over 900 people die needlessly each year in fires. Proper smoke alarms could save over 600 of these people. Is your answer to B above still the same? Why or why not?

14. Auto makers in the United States once carried out a major campaign to buy up and scrap old cars. Why would these manufacturers waste time and money doing this, when they are in the business of making new cars?

15. You are asked to advise a very poor country about doing a better job of consumer marketing within the country. The country has a per capita income of about $200 per year, and it is conservatively estimated that half the population goes to bed hungry every night.

Do you think that modern American methods of sale persuasion for food products would work well here? Why or why not? What would work in modern marketing, if anything? Why?

16. You are asked to help out with the federal passenger train service now being operated. Passenger miles by rail have declined by 80 percent since 1945, and the downward trend is continuing slowly. Many marketing people have argued that all this field needs is some good sales promotion.

Is there any sales promotion that will do any good in this type of declining market? What might it be?

Write down five good reasons for taking a 500-mile trip by rail. By air. By car. Who has the advantage here? Why?

8

RETAILING

It was early summer, and Al had been on his RVA project for several months. He decided to take a semi-vacation through the Midwest, driving slowly through that industrial heartland. He could justify it by visiting a number of RVA's plants in the area, and his notebooks were full of jottings about what he had seen and whom he had talked to.

After three weeks on the road, he limped into Bloomington, Indiana, tired, hot, and grateful that his car had run at least that far. Vicki's parents lived in Bloomington, where her father worked as store manager for Limelight Stores, Inc., a major regional food chain. Vicki was spending her vacation there. The vacation part of the trip was to spend a few days visiting them and her. But his well-worn '76 Delta 88 was dribbling a steady stream of transmission fluid, and he was lucky to make it to Bloomington.

"Vicki's talked a lot about you, Al," Mr. Masters said, as they sat in his air-conditioned study. "You seem to have made quite an impression on her. Odd . . . few young men have."

"Well, she impresses me too, Mr. Masters."

Mr. Masters sighed. "I always wanted a son, because I thought that only a son could get into business successfully. You know, follow the father's footsteps and all that. Funny how Vicki turned out to be more successful than I'll ever be."

"Oh, I don't know. After all, you are a pretty high-level executive."

"Just a middle manager, Al, that's all. And that's about as far as I'll get. But Vicki could go all the way to the top. She's a shrewd one, that girl. Takes after her mother, I suspect." Mr. Masters poured himself some coffee. "She's tough, Al, tough minded. Maybe even a bit too shrewd, from what I hear. But I suppose that you know all about that."

"Oh, I've heard a few things. But then really competent people tend to get sniped at."

"Yes, they do. Say, Al, what's the trouble with your car? Anything serious?"

"I don't know. Something's wrong with the transmission. It leaks badly. Do you know any good mechanics around here? I don't know anything about transmissions."

"Now there's a business with a bad reputation, isn't it? Lots of crooks doing things that don't need doing, and overcharging even when they do the work." Mr. Masters fumbled around for some papers in his desk.

"I've read that car repairs and warranty work have the highest percentage of consumer complaints in the whole country," Al replied, "And I can believe it. The last time I had my car checked out, the guy said that it needed a wheel alignment. He said he did it, and charged me twenty-five dollars. Later I found out that it hadn't even been done. Now this transmission goes bad, and I hear that a replacement can cost over five hundred dollars."

"It can, but how do you know that you need one?" Mr. Masters asked.

"I don't, and that's what bothers me. I hope that you can recommend a reliable shop to take a look at it. I'm really a stranger here myself."

Mr. Masters tossed a document over to Al. "These fellows are my mechanics. You might be interested in reading this."

Al sipped his coffee and read the sales pitch. "It sounds odd. Who are Farmer and Lombardi?"

"A couple of professors here in town. They started this thing as a sort of hobby. I think that they're honest, but they're not too cheap. At least they do a better job than the last mechanic I used, which really isn't saying very much."

"These fellows don't even have a shop, do they? I mean a place of business, where they hang out a sign?"

CEDARWOOD PRESS
1115 E. Wylie Street
BLOOMINGTON, INDIANA 47401

J & J Auto Repair
Farmer's Garage

SCHEDULED PREVENTIVE MAINTENANCE PROGRAM
FOR YOUR OLD BUT FAITHFUL CAR

Objective: They really don't make cars like they used to, mainly
because of various governmental mandated safety and pollution controls.
Mileage requirements don't help either. So if you own an American made
car manufactured between 1960 (or even earlier) and 1975, you may be
interested in keeping the beast alive. Our program is intended to do
just this, with minimum cost and inconvenience. Nothing is free, including our program, but we think that you may find this program a lot less
expensive than anything else you can do. It can be fun, too.

Costs, Costs, Costs: To replace a 1970 car these days will run
between $4,000 and $9,000, if you purchase a new vehicle of similar size
(assuming that you can even get one). Your new car depreciation alone
will run from $1,000 to $2,500 per year, or perhaps $2.75 to $6.90 per
day. The new car may get 18 to 20 miles per gallon of gas, while a 1970
gets 10 to 12. You save perhaps $300 per year in gas, while losing a
thousand or more in depreciation alone. Routine maintenance costs for
more modern cars will run somewhat higher than for older vehicles, because
their various safety and anti-pollution systems are so complicated.

For those worried about extra energy use and pollution, remember
that if you use an existing car, we avoid all the energy needed to make
a new one, which more than offsets the extra energy you use by burning
a bit more gas.

In short, it pays to keep a car. You want it to be reliable, which
is what our program is all about. Cars can last forever if they are
treated right, and the cost of doing so is surprisingly small.

And finally, we know from experience what driving a neat slightly
obsolete (hell, real obsolete) car can do for one. It is fun. The old
babies attract more attention than new ones, and they often are more
comfortable. They give everyone a nostalgia kick too. And this really
is why we bother.

How to keep any car alive: The difference between a $100 junker and
a brand new car is about two pounds of metal and plastic. Unfortunately
the material is scattered all over the car--a thousandth of an inch off
this bearing, a hundredth of an inch off that hose, and a bit of rot here
and there in various hoses, cables, and rust spots. If you take care to
minimize wear, the thing will last a long, long, time. A really well
maintained car can last over 300,000 miles before major repairs, but boy,
this maintenance has got to be good.

This gets to preventive maintenance. Most cars at about the three
year old mark begin to fall apart because the second owner is rarely careful about maintenance. Oil doesn't get changed, and worse, filters don't
either. Some little gismo breaks which is not critical to operations
(like a door lock on the right hand side), so it doesn't get fixed. Lubrication doesn't get done, so those bearings begin to go. And rust is
beginning to take its toll in this snow bound part of the world.

In short, preventive maintenance (PM) gets neglected, and the car
falls apart. When something big blows, like the engine or transmission,
off to the junkyard the car goes, typically in its 5th to 9th year.

The way to keep your car alive is to do everything you are supposed
to continuously. Few of us really bother, particularly for older cars,
and lots of what we are supposed to do is invisible and doesn't seem
important at the time. But it's your money. As the ad says, you pay me
now, or you pay more later. This is absolutely correct.

Another problem most of us run into is ignorance. A car is a complicated gadget, and all sorts of specialties are involved in even knowing
what might be wrong. Repair men have on occasion even been dishonest,
and most of us know that sinking feeling when some greasy minion comes up
for air from under our car, shakes his head, and says, "The frammus is
off center. Looks like an $850 job." When the car is worth (in good
shape) maybe $900, forget it. And not one owner in a hundred really
knows exactly what kinds of maintenance he or she should be doing. You
have to trust somebody out there, and it might as well be us. With no
modesty at all, we can only point out that we are virtuous, skilled,
sincere, honest, and we only beat our wives on Thursdays.

The PM Program: Our plan is this:

1. We sign you up as a continuous customer. We only want about
100 people, because this is all we can handle in our available time. If
you don't behave, we'll find some one else who will and exile you.

2. We analyze your car totally at the beginning. See the attached
list of things we will check out. This analysis costs you $25. If we
find your brakes are shot, your engine is about to die and needs expensive
repairs, we will inform you about it, but don't expect us to do $200
worth of work for free.

3. Once we find out what's the matter, we'll tell you about it in
writing. We'll also start a file on your car, with all this information
enclosed. If you want the defects corrected, we'll do it for you for
a decent price. That includes anything on the attached checklist sheet,
plus anything else that turns up.

4. We fix all sorts of weird things, but some items we don't handle, either because we don't have the equipment, or because we're too lazy. Such items as fixing air conditioning, changing tires (and balancing and finding the right ones), automatic transmission overhaul, and some others will be farmed out if you want. We know pretty much who is honest and capable and who isn't around town, so we should be able to get you quality work at reasonable prices. Our charge here is only for the time spent in lining up the job, which normally is pretty small.

5. Now that we know what's wrong with your car (and you do too), we'll sit down with you and figure out just what you want done and when. Some things (like bad brakes) you fix up NOW, or we'll send flowers for your funeral; other items, like a bit of rust in the rear fender, can wait for quite a while. It's up to you. We'll happily give you all the cost estimates you need.

Right here is where people often run into big trouble. Say your heater isn't working, and you want it fixed. Fixing a heater, if you're lucky, can be an hour's work. But if you're not lucky, it may mean 8 to 12 hours of labor taking the thing out of the car and getting it back in right. The cautious repairman may give you a huge estimate, just to be on the safe side, and you either sigh and pay the $150 bill or forget it. If the repairman lucks out and gets the job done in an hour, he wins this time around. He is not dishonest, just cautious, since he doesn't want to work for a buck an hour if he can help it.

We'll try to level with you in such circumstances. You'll just have to trust us, but if we run into something like this, we'll explain why the estimate is variable. If we get it done in an hour, you pay for the hour; if it takes a week, sorry about that.

The reason for the confusion is that often you have to start the job and try things before you can diagnose correctly. In that heater problem above, the first thing to do is to pull your heater hoses and flush the heater core. You don't know if this is the problem until you do it. One hour gone, and if that doesn't work, we go on to other tests. There is no way to avoid this--but then doctors do exploratory surgery too.

6. OK, we now have your car in fairly good shape. About once every three months, we'll call you to bring it in (usually on weekends) for routine preventive maintenance. As we learned long ago, oil is cheaper than engines, and new clean filters are the cheapest things you can buy. We'll handle the programmed PM routinely, and if you don't show up, we'll chase you down. This is important. In addition to doing routine things, we'll look closely at everything again, and tell you if anything else needs work. If you want it done, we'll do it.

This routine stuff, which is mainly oil and filter changing, plus some other lubrication and tuneups, will cost you about $150 to $200 per year. For three to ten year old cars, figure an extra $200 per year, since rubber belts wear out and parts do eventually need replacement just because they are worn.

7. If you quit the program, your folder is yours. It will help if you try to sell your car.

So what you get is a programmed PM program to keep your car running forever. You also get repairs made before anything horrible happens, which increases reliability. You may find us recommending that you replace all the hoses in your ten year old car, as one example. This is cheap insurance, since it is no fun to have your engine boil over in Northern Michigan or Central Wyoming on your next vacation just because you didn't pay us four or five dollars to replace a rotted heater hose.

If you stick with us, your car should run forever. It will cost some money, but it should cost less than anything else you can do. Please, please remember that old things do rot, wear, and rust, so there will be some repair costs above the basic minimum. But lots of these things only get done about once every five years or 30,000 miles, and once done, they shouldn't cause trouble again. If your car has just run for five years or more, with nothing much done to it, you may want to make some investment in bringing things up to par, and this will cost some money.

All our work is guaranteed, so if it doesn't work, we'll do it again.

Conclusion: If you're interested, sign up. We'll be happy to expound endlessly on this deal. Our main interest, oddly enough, is to keep those lovely old beasts running, and running right, since we really do enjoy them. We hope that you do too, since you can save much, much money, energy, and maybe even achieve happiness by running around in something exotic and special that really isn't.

John Lombardi

Dick Farmer

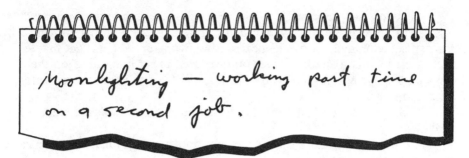

Moonlighting — working part time on a second job.

"No, it's a subscription service. They have a couple of mechanics working for them part-time, I think. The guys probably moonlight. They also pick up and deliver cars. They have a couple of college students do that. It's convenient, at least."

"Will they work on my car?"

"I don't know, but I'll call Farmer and find out."

"On Saturday afternoon?"

"Sure, they work a lot on weekends." Mr. Masters dialed a number and explained who Al was and what his problem was. "OK, you can drive it over. They're working on a car now, but they'll take a look. Here. I'll draw you a map on how to get there."

"No pickup service, huh?"

"No, you're not a regular customer. Their deal is more like going to a dentist, by appointment only. Remember, the basic idea is to avoid major repairs, and they can only do that if they can regularly contact their customers."

"How about paying? Do they accept credit cards?"

"Cash or personal checks only. But if it gets expensive, just tell them not to do it, and they'll only charge you for the consultation."

"It sounds like a couple of doctors."

"They have Ph.D.'s, not medical degrees, but I guess you're right. They do act like doctors. You should see their equipment, too, more electronic stuff than you would imagine."

Al drove over to the shop and found it in the basement of a small house across town. A polite young man jacked up his car and crawled under it. He messed around for a while and came up for air. "Mr. Faber, I think that one of the O rings on the vacuum shifting mech is leaking."

"How much is that in money?" Al asked.

"Not too much, maybe twenty dollars." The young fellow wiped his hands. "We don't do it, but Monday I can take it over for you and get it taken care of. We know the best man in town on automatic transmissions."

"OK, do it," Al said, and gave him his motel address.

"I'll put in some transmission fluid, it's way low," the young man said. "It should last until Monday, if you don't drive too far."

"I'm not going anyplace," Al said. "How did you get into this business?"

"I'm an M.A. in History. My dad ran a gas station all his life, and I learned something about mechanical work growing up. When I got my degree, I tried to get a job, but have you ever tried to get a teaching job these days in History? Medieval History? Dr. Lombardi knew about me as a mechanic, and here I am."

"You fellows have got to be the most educated mechanics around," Al said.

"It helps to verbalize the customer's problems," another man said as he came up behind Al's car.

The young man introduced Al to Dr. Farmer.

Al explained who he was and why he was here. "Oh, Sam will fix you up Monday, I think," Dr. Farmer said. "Unless you're really unlucky, it shouldn't be much of a deal. Joe, our pickup man, will get it for you and bring it back." He looked the car over. "That's a good car, Al. You shouldn't let it get run down. Talk to Mr. Masters. His car was a basket case a while back and now his maintenance cost is pretty low."

"Say, Dr. Farmer, this is a pretty odd retailing setup you have here. Why did you do it this way?"

"It sounds like you're doing more research for your RVA project, Al."

"How did you know about that?"

"Oh, Vicki Masters was in the other day for a tune-up on her Chevvy. Couldn't stop talking about you. Now what was your question?"

"People I've talked to about marketing have stressed the idea of market segmentation. It looks like you people have tried to practice what they were preaching."

Dr. Farmer laughed. "Oh, we try to practice what we teach, but it's hard sometimes. But you're right. We tried to figure out a little segment of the market that we could handle, and here we are. We don't want, and can't be bothered with, a general trade. We know our customers, and we try to give them good service. Lord knows, that's hard enough in this business. Cars are very complicated gadgets, and very few people can either fix them or understand them."

"How did you forecast sales? I mean, I've seen the demand equations for RVA, and I've seen the computer work, but I can't see you people doing that sort of thing for a small operation like this."

"We don't. If you ever took my managerial economics course, you would learn a lot about econometric modelling of demand functions, but when we started last year, we simply figured out that we needed about a hundred customers. We knew that there were over 30,000 cars in the county, so we figured that it would be easy to get at least a hundred of them. You've probably learned that small businessmen don't have the staff or money to do much complicated forecasting."

"So you found your hundred customers?"

"Almost, but it took a year of growth to get them. You have to build a reputation first, and our reputations don't have much to do with fixing cars."

"Mr. Masters told me that you only have cash accounts. Isn't that a bit odd?"

"If you were after the mass market, it would be crazy. But we're not. We only want a handful of quality customers, who don't mind paying a bit more for superior service. Lots of garages will give you credit and lower prices, but sometimes the work is not the best, and you have to take your car in and wait yourself. Our customers are typically professional people, and for them time really is money. They would prefer to pay us ten dollars to pick up and deliver their cars and take care of all the details, rather than waste an afternoon hanging around waiting for their car to get fixed."

"So your prices are high, right?"

"Well, not that high. Tell me, what are we selling here?"

Al thought for a while. "Repair services for sure. Parts, I guess. Pick up and delivery services. What else?"

"Try knowledge. We know something that you don't know. You knew your transmission was acting up, but you didn't know why. We could have shaken our heads, psyched you out, and tried to sell you a five hundred dollar transmission replacement. If we were good salesmen, we might have even done it."

"You sure could have. I was braced for it!"

"But we didn't. There isn't a job comes in here that couldn't be built into something bigger than it is. We know lots of guys around who might try to sell you something that you really don't need. But we try not to do that. On the other hand, that transmission O ring replacement will cost us about eight dollars. We'll charge you fifteen for knowing where to go and what to say, and taking your car over. Now, are you being overcharged?"

Al thought about that. "It will take you about a half hour to do that?"

"Right."

"So you charge me twenty dollars an hour. Well, I . . . I'm not sure. On the one hand, that's a lot of money for just an hour's work. But on the other, if I didn't buy your knowledge, it might cost me a lot more."

"We charge eighteen to twenty dollars an hour, plus parts. Sam here, our mechanic, makes seven fifty an hour. If we do our job right, and your car runs well, it's cheap. If we foul up the job, it's terribly expensive. It depends on how you look at it, doesn't it?"

"I suppose so. But your pricing is really based on what you can get away with, isn't it?"

"More or less. That happens to be the rate charged by shops in this area, so it's a competitive rate. When you toss in the pickup and delivery, which is a premium service, it costs a bit more. And when you figure that we chase our customers down and make them come in for routine maintenance, it's even more expensive. But somehow our customers' cars run virtually all the time, and they rarely have trouble on the road. You pay us maybe a hundred dollars a year extra to get more assurance that your car will run right. One long road tow will cost more than that, and if your engine blows in 40,000 miles instead of 150,000, our prices are very cheap indeed."

"Say, isn't that what they do with airplanes? I mean, I've read that airplanes are way overmaintained."

"You're right, it's exactly the same concept. The cost of being wrong on maintenance with airplanes is so high that they get overmaintained by a factor of several hundred percent. We try to overmaintain our customers' cars by a factor of perhaps thirty percent. If your car breaks down, the cost is not quite so high. But we throw away a lot of perfectly usable parts simply because it's more reliable to have new ones when there is some question about whether it will work or not."

"So you have a hundred subscription customers. How do you handle your selling and sales promotion?"

"Just the way you got here. Word of mouth, plus the brochure you saw. Actually, you're a poor customer for us, since you're not living here. But if we do our job right, our problem is usually turning people away, not getting more customers."

"So why don't you expand?"

"This is a part-time business with us. We just don't have the time to get into it full time. Besides, we're beginning to think that we're running out of premium, cash paying customers. We don't want the other kinds."

"Why not?"

"Too much hassle. A friend of ours ran a typical repair service out of his gas station for years. When he retired, he had over $20,000 of accounts receivable he couldn't collect. He also had a bunch of customers that couldn't understand what he was trying to do, who were always mad at him for charging too much. He also had to work on a bunch of wrecks that had been neglected so badly it was a wonder that they would run at all. And he was forever arguing with nasty people who were trying to cut corners."

"So you duck all that by just doing this little service?"

"Right. We like to think of ourselves as preventive maintenance/knowledge specialists, not mechanics. It's rather like being a dentist. It's better to practice prevention, rather than pay huge bills that come about with neglect. One of our big costs is keeping proper records so that we can get our customers in when they are due. If we don't do that, there could be trouble."

"It sounds like a good marketing niche," Al commented. "You should be making money."

"Oh, we make a little, but not as much as you might expect."

"Even with eleven or twelve dollar an hour overheads?"

"Even then. There are a few expenses to worry about, like those accounting costs. Then we have some wild tax problems, and that costs plenty. We're too small to get hassled much by various government agencies, and that's one major reason for not expanding, but we still have a lot of paper-work to do. And then there are tools to buy and utility bills to pay, and plenty of insurance to purchase. This small shop costs money in rent and taxes, too. We need a pickup truck to run around chasing parts in, and that's a big expense. And we guarantee our work, and believe me, nobody's perfect in this game. We spend a lot of time redoing our stupid mistakes."

"You don't seem to have much inventory," Al said, looking around.

"We don't, just some items that we know turn over fast, like oil and filters. That runs up our expenses too, in several ways. We buy our parts wholesale from local parts houses, but they charge enough to cover their carrying costs, which are high. And we have to go get them all the time, which takes both manpower and money."

"Why don't you buy your own inventory? You should be able to get low prices."

"We could, but do you realize just how many parts there are in the auto business? Right now, we have 97 customers, and only four cars are the same make and model. Most are the only one of their type for us. There are about 5,000 major parts in a modern car. Any one could be bad at any time. There is no way we could plan properly for any large inventory in this business."

Al looked around, noticing a few battered old parts. "Do you always use new parts, Dr. Farmer? I've heard that they can get very expensive."

"They sure can, and we don't. Suppose that one of our customers has a wreck ... and that happened just last week. Smashed his grill and broke the windshield. We go over to Auto Heaven and get some used parts, if we can find them."

"You go where?"

"Auto Heaven. It's a local junkyard, though the young man who runs it calls it a recycling facility."

"Cute name. Did you get your parts?"

Dr. Farmer nodded. "We were lucky, but then Chuck Forney, the owner, used to teach for me in my W100 Introduction to Business class. A very bright guy, and he treats us right. We found a grill and the windshield. It would have cost over $600 new for those parts, but we got them for $125. A body man we know got the car back on the road for less than $700, which is a lot less than it would have cost if we had bought new parts. We use recycled parts whenever we can with safety, and that usually means for body parts. Once in a while, when we can't find a new part for an odd car, we'll use Chuck's parts. It makes good economic and business sense."

"I guess your location really doesn't matter much, given the kinds of customers you have," Al said, looking around at the small garage.

"Not really. Retailers looking for the mass market have to locate prop-erly, since they rely on location to get business. Mr. Masters' company spent over twenty thousand dollars on site analysis here in Bloomington before they placed their supermarket, and it was money well spent. But if you look at the real estate market here, or anyplace else, you'll discover that choice consumer store locations have very high rents. Retailers are willing to spend big money for the right location, because that means big sales. But in our case, we looked for a low-cost location, since we're not even interested in attracting people off the street. Look around, and you'll notice that lots of retail outlets are stuck away in odd places. Some are there because they need low rents, like a hobby shop or a pet shop. They just don't normally have enough volume to justify a really prime location. Others, like department stores, mass market auto supply stores, and supermarkets, need prime locations. It all depends on what you're trying to do."

"It makes sense," Al said. "I've been looking too closely at RVA, I guess, and I just haven't thought much about how you operate a small business."

"Well, I teach about big ones, but small ones are probably more fun, at least personally," Dr. Farmer said. "You can see everything in a small operation like this. I can also test out a few pet business theories I have."

"Do they work?"

"Usually not. This business makes an academic face reality a bit more than he otherwise might."

"How many people work for you, Dr. Farmer?"

"John Lombardi and I are partners, and we do some of the work. Sam here works part-time for us, as we need him, and we have another part-time mechanic on call once in a while. My teenage son does the bookkeeping for us. There's not much specialization around here, I can assure you." Dr. Farmer glanced over at the car Sam was working on. "We have a couple of students that do pickup and deliveries for us also, and that's it."

"So it's all part-time labor?"

"Right. It's simpler from a legal and tax angle, and we really don't have the space or volume to need more."

"So how do you motivate people?"

"Beats me. We try to pay them a bit more than anyone else, and that sometimes works. I threaten my son a lot, and John is a working fool anyhow. Besides, in a small operation like this, motivation is more a problem of people liking each other and being willing to work together than any formal system. RVA has thousands of employees, and key managers can't possibly know all of them. We've known, respected, and liked each other for a long time. That makes motivation pretty simple. If someone doesn't fit in, he or she doesn't last long."

"One more question. Vicki Masters is an accountant, and I've been learning a lot from her. But again, RVA's accounting systems are really complex and computerized. How do you keep track of expenses?"

"With great difficulty," Dr. Farmer said. "John costs out each job, and we try to keep good paperwork on every customer's car. It's real easy to forget to write down things when you're under the car working on it. Just last week, I forgot to include a forty dollar part in a bill. There went the profit for the job."

"But you can keep track."

"Sure. We work on a job cost basis, since we can get data easily and quickly for each one. Our bookkeeping and accounting are very simple, but the hard part is doing it. You see, most small businessmen get into business on the technical side. They rarely know much about finance, marketing, and accounting, and typically this is where they get into trouble. We try to keep out of trouble. In theory, I know exactly what to do, but it's hard when a customer is yelling at you."

"If it's tough for you, it must be murder for a person who never studied business," Al commented.

"It is. Most small businesses that fail do so because of managerial or control failures, not technical ones." Dr. Farmer thought for a while. "You know, the hardest part of this business is keeping a handle on reality. We get a big payment, and we have lots of cash. But we also have lots of expenses. It's really easy to start spending money on tools we need, or something we feel we should have. Then, after a while, we discover that we're taking in a few thousand a month and spending twice that. Lots of small business people just never quite understand this."

"I don't think that I ever would," Al said. "Dr. Farmer, you're really small. But how would a larger company behave? I mean a firm that's bigger than yours, but still small?"

"You mean something like an auto agency?" Dr. Farmer asked.

"Yes, about that size. I still think of such operations as small, but they'd be a lot bigger than this."

"For one thing, a business that size could be both small and large. Even a small new car dealership that sold about 500 cars a year would be a multimillion dollar business."

Al thought about that. "I see what you mean. A new car these days might cost over $6,000. If you sold 500, your total sales would be over $2.5 million per year."

"Right. Dealers get discounts of course, but even so the average wholesale price of a new car is probably over $5,000 these days. But a dealer does more than just buy and sell cars." Dr. Farmer started writing down some things on his note pad.

"Take a look at the functions that a typical dealer would have to worry about. One of these would be all of what we do, namely maintenance and after-sales service. Dealers are expected to service what they sell. It's in their franchise agreement."

"Their what?"

Dr. Farmer explained what a franchise was, and Al wrote it down. "I see what you mean, Dr. Farmer. The manufacturer wouldn't be too happy

DR. FARMER'S LIST OF AUTO AGENCY PROBLEM AREAS

Sales:
New car marketing
Used car marketing
Other (Trucks, parts, etc)

Service:
Repairs
Parts availabilities
After sales

Finance:
Internal -- Budgets, cash flow, credit, etc.
Credit management for customers
Capital requirements

Location of sales offices, car lots, etc.

Control:
Accounting
Inventories

Personnel:
Hiring
Training
Compensation
Legal requirements, etc.

Franchise agreement --
Settling disputes with manufactures
and so on! In short, all the problems any
firms have, big or small!

[pick up fender from auto Heaven]

with a dealer that sold cars and then never fixed them. It could give the
company a bad name."

"But new car dealers also sell parts," Dr. Farmer continued. "We buy
from them every so often."

"Why not always?" Al asked. "I would think that the company that
sold the car would make the best parts."

Franchise — permission granted by a manufacturer
or service company to a distributor or retailer
to sell his products.

      E.G., Coca Cola, Chevrolet,
Seven UP, McDonald's, etc.
Franchises can be exclusive or not.
Franchisers give advice, know how, national
advertising, etc. to local firms.
Good way (sometimes) for a small company to
get national expertise.

"Sometimes an independent parts house offers a better price," Dr. Farmer said. "And there's a competitive problem for the dealer, which he has to worry about. Anyone can make a bearing for a Ford, since it's not a proprietary part. But the dealer clearly has to worry a lot about his parts and maintenance services if he is going to be successful. And remember those used parts we buy every once in a while, too."

Al looked at Dr. Farmer's list. "OK, how about marketing? Doesn't the manufacturer do most of the advertising and promotion?"

"On the national level, sure. But here we are in Bloomington. Now, I'm thinking of buying a new car. Suppose I know that a dealer is sloppy wih his maintenance, and that he doesn't give very good finance terms, if I'm buying the car on credit. I'm likely to go to a competing dealer, right?"

"Sure. How do you know that the dealer is sloppy?"

"I've lived here quite a while. I can ask my friends and check around a bit."

"My dad did exactly that when he bought his last new car," Al said. "I can see that the dealer's local reputation can make a difference."

"If you talk to marketing people from the big auto manufacturers, you would find out that these local factors can make a tremendous difference. Here in Bloomington, the local Olds dealer sells about twice as many cars per capita as the average dealer around the country. He's a very capable manager and marketer. Other makes sell far less than the national average. They just have weak local dealers."

"How about personnel problems?" Al asked, looking down Dr. Farmer's list.

"We don't have any full-time employees, but a dealer would have salesmen, probably a secretary or two, an accountant or at least a bookkeeper, mechanics, a sales manager, some clean up people, perhaps a used car salesman or two, and so on. If you're running a multi-million dollar business, you need people, and immediately you have all the personnel problems that any firm with hired people has. You have to figure out how to motivate them, worry about how much to pay them, and meet all the government tax and reporting rules."

"Say, why would you need used car salesmen in a new car agency?"

"Because some people trade in their old cars. Dealers may wholesale older cars, but they often run used car operations to sell the good used cars they get as trade ins. Now we're back to retailing and marketing skills. I've often wondered how a Dodge dealer talks up the virtues of a nice, two year old Ford he is trying to sell, but somehow they manage."

Al studied Dr. Farmer's list. "You know, I see a lot of problems here that RVA has too, but I suppose that they aren't quite as complicated."

"RVA has thousands of employees, while an auto dealer may have from five to fifty," Dr. Farmer said. "Smaller companies have exactly the same problems big ones have, except that they tend to be somewhat simpler. There are just not as many people involved, and the dollar figures are a lot smaller. But an auto dealership that is a small business might look pretty similar to a single store that RVA has in its retailing division. In RVA's case, a hired manager operates the store, while the auto dealer could be an owner/manager. But they would have a lot to talk about if they met."

Al slipped Dr. Farmer's list in his pocket. "Thanks, Dr. Farmer. I keep running into problems I never thought existed, and this is just one more of those."

"So you know Vicki Masters? She was a student of mine a few years back. She also taught in Intro to Business for me. A very nice young lady."

"She did?" Vicki hadn't mentioned that. A teacher too. "Was she good?"

"The best, Al. But then a lot of these modern young women who take our M.B.A. program make terrific teachers. I just wish that I could have kept her."

Al grinned. "Well, she seems to be on the fast track at RVA now."

"She's very smart. I would expect her to do well. The people who teach for me in W100 usually do. If you can teach something to freshmen, you can surely talk persuasively in business. Well, I've got to be going. Great meeting you, and good luck with RVA." He smiled and extended his hand.

That night on their date, Vicki drove Al to the movies in her car. On Monday a young man showed up and took his car away. He was back in two hours with the transmission fixed and a bill for $28.64. Al paid it on the spot, and he had no more trouble with his transmission for a few years.

But he never did get his car maintained really well, in spite of what Dr. Farmer had said. There were more important things on his mind than a beat up Delta 88.

DISCUSSION QUESTIONS

1. Do you think that this maintenance idea of Farmer and Lombardi is a good or bad one? Why?

2. Did Al pay too much for his transmission repair? Why or why not?

3. Look around the area near your college campus. What kinds of retail shops seem to be in excellent locations? Why? What kinds are stuck in odd corners, where the rent is probably low? Why?

4. Why do you think that consumers complain more about auto repairs than any other single thing they buy? Are American mechanics and repair shops often incompetent?

5. Suppose that you want to start an auto repair shop that caters to a mass market. You want to attract as many customers as you can. What kind of structure would you develop, as compared to the one Farmer and Lombardi built? Why? What key things would you do to attract volume?

6. Take another look at the area near your home. How many food markets are there? What kinds of business are they interested in, such as volume, specialty, or whatever? List three things that are different in each of the food markets.

7. After doing question 6, which one of these markets would you do your own shopping in? Why?

8. Consider some specialty product you buy, such as pets, models, odd magazines, specialty phonograph records, electronic equipment, knitting supplies, etc.
Where is the retail store located where you do your shopping? Is it in a major, prime location?
Does this store do a huge volume of business, or is it much smaller? Why?
Do the clerks (or owners) who wait on you seem better or worse informed about this specialty product than clerks in high volume, mass market stores such as supermarkets? Why?

9. Take another look at the Farmer/Lombardi sales brochure. In your judgement, is this a good piece of sales promotion literature? Why? What's right with it? What's wrong with it?

10. Consider the possibility of setting up a small shop to sell something you like and enjoy.

If you did set this shop up, could you do a good demand forecast? Why or why not?

What kinds of sales promotion would you think might work well in your shop? Why?

Where would be a good location near where you now are for such a shop? Why?

11. List five key factors about business that a small retail shop has to worry about.

12. Dr. Farmer said that most small businessmen enter business from the technical side. Find a small businessman or woman near you and ask about this point. Is it true in the case you are considering?

13. A person trained in finance and accounting has read this Farmer/Lombardi sales brochure, and she thinks that this would be a good business for her to enter. What kinds of specialized knowledge would a person have to learn before she could expect to make a reasonable success of this venture?

14. A new book company is considering setting up a shop near your college campus. This company will sell both textbooks and general trade books. Find a good location in your area for this store. Why is it good?

15. A bicycle nut thinks that it would be a great idea to set up a small bicycle sales and repair shop near your campus. He would sell very expensive ten speed racing type bicycles, and he would also repair and service them.

Would you advise this person to set up such a business near your campus, given what is now going on there? Why or why not?

9

INSURANCE AND RESEARCH AND DEVELOPMENT

W hat's bugging Joe Chapman?" Al asked Vicki. They had ordered lunch in a pretty plush place near the RVA main office building. Vicki was picking up the check on her expense account. Al wondered if this was really proper. Was he being bribed? But he hadn't seen Vicki for a few weeks, and he really did want to talk to her.

"Why?" Vicki responded guardedly. "What did he say?"

"Oh, I ran into him this morning. I was up in the planning area, and he made a nasty crack."

"About me?"

"Well, yes."

Vicki sighed. "Lots of things are wrong with Joe. First, he married the wrong woman."

"He did? She seemed nice enough to me. I met her a while back."

"Oh, she's very nice. She was a legal secretary before she married Joe. But, well, she just doesn't fit in. She has a bad habit of trying to push Joe hard at all the parties, with his bosses. She's convinced that Joe is God's gift to the business world, and she says so, too often."

"I thought that those days were gone for good," Al said. "I mean, having the right wife and moving in the right social circles. Companies these days really don't pay much attention to that stuff, do they?"

Vicki toyed with her glass. "Not really, but it does matter, if a wife calls her husband's boss on a Sunday afternoon and tries to push her husband. Things like that. But Joe is bitter about not being promoted last year, too. He's mad at me because I was."

"He did make a pretty sexist comment, and he used some language even I wouldn't use in mixed company."

"Yes, Joe talks too much. Actually he's a very capable guy. Brilliant, really. Some of his work in long term planning is the best I've ever seen. But he really doesn't relate too well to lots of people, including me, I guess, and he feels that RVA isn't appreciating his talents. It's a people game, Al, and Joe doesn't relate too well, too often."

Al remembered Joe himself talking about the social subsystem of a complex organization. Apparently he didn't practice what he preached. "I can see that, even after talking to him for just a little while."

"I suppose he told you that I volunteered to meet you and show you around?"

"Well, yes he did. He also said some things about your being, well . . ."

"The crown princess and all that? Well, I did volunteer to show you around. Why not? If I could do a good job with you, well . . ."

"You'd get promoted, your boss would get to be CEO, and you could move up in the company, right, Vicki?"

"Sure, but maybe I've spent more time showing you around because I like you, and, anyway, is there something wrong with wanting to get ahead? Why did you accept this RVA assignment from *Newsworld*?"

Al groaned. "To get ahead, of course. Some people, like my mother, who's pretty smart, think that I'm a real overachiever. Sure, I want to win. I guess that I'm just not used to seeing the same thing in women." Al looked carefully at Vicki. She was slender, attractive, dressed in one of those women's business suits that made her look a lot harder and more capable than Al thought she was. No, she was capable, but not hard. Not hard at all.

"Al, do you have any idea of what I have to put up with at RVA?"

"I can guess, Vicki. Amorous males, sexists, guys who can't stand the thought of a female boss, committee meetings where nobody knows how to behave, because the men never had a woman in a meeting before, and all their tasteless off-color jokes somehow don't fit."

"That, and lots more. Lots of comments behind my back, too. Very few women have made it to the top in American business, and I think that I can. It gets tough sometimes. Guys like Joe are typical, and they make it tougher."

Their lunch was served, and they ate silently for a while.

"My father always really wanted a boy," Vicki said finally. "I think he still has the electric train and baseball glove he bought for me when mom was pregnant. He never really got over his hurt that I turned out female. Mom is a professional, too, a nurse, and I learned early that if I was going to please my parents, I had better get ready for a man's world. Al, they're great people, really, and I wanted to please them. So I studied business, and my timing was perfect. In the early 1970's things really began to open up for women. I've been with RVA for four years, and last year it suddenly dawned on me that I just might go all the way to the top, if I played my cards right. No more sitting in a corner, no more being number two, or ten, or thirty, but maybe even number one."

"So you're going for it?"

"Wouldn't you? It's really sort of exciting. You know how few women have made it to the top, and lots of the ones who did had inherited something when their fathers or husbands died. I can make it on my own."

Al sighed. "So you pay the price. You cut your hair short, wear suits, and generally try to conceal your feminine charms, which are quite ample, I can assure you."

Vicki giggled. "You already have, quite a few times."

"Yeah, I guess I have. And I know you can cook. That last meal you fed me . . . wow!"

"Is that what you want, Al, a nice pretty little wife who stays home, has babies, and knows how to cook?"

"I don't know. I guess I was programmed that way. My mom stayed home, and dad earned the family income. But no, not really. Girls like you are too attractive and interesting."

"Like me?"

"OK, you. I must say that I'm not sure Joe isn't right. Maybe I am being set up. But I think that my objective reporter's instinct can survive even you. Maybe."

"So the crown prince and the crown princess got married and lived happily ever after, right, Al?"

"Who's the crown prince?"

"You, my friend. Your grapevine works too, you know. Your boss has his eye on you. Plenty of your co-workers are pretty mad about your getting this plush assignment."

Al tried to think of an answer to that one, but he really couldn't.

"Hi, Vicki." A tall, middle-aged man came up to the table.

"Hello, Vince." Vicki introduced Al to Vince Marston, from the insurance section.

"I'm supposed to meet with you just after lunch," Al said.

"I know, and I figured that you might be a little late, seeing how lunch was going, so I dropped by."

"You're here, so have some coffee," Vicki said, smiling.

Vince sat down. "Actually I wanted to talk to you for a moment, too, Vicki. Do you have that pension calculation yet?"

"It'll be ready tomorrow."

"Now, what's that about?" Al asked. "Does Vicki do insurance, too?"

"No, but she does some long term profit and cash flow forecasts for us, and these do matter for our employees' pension program," Vince said.

"How does that work out?" Al asked.

"We have a big pension program for all RVA employees," Vicki replied. "After ten years' service, an employee qualifies. The employee pays half the cost, and RVA picks up the other half. The size of the pension payment goes up with years of service."

"We have something like that at *Newsworld*," Al said. "But what do accounting and cash flow have to do with it?"

"We invest the employees' pension money in stocks and bonds and government securities," Vince said. "Actually, a special section over in finance does this. And we have a pension reserve, which we pay into each year. But we just can't pay in enough to cover all our future liabilities. So we have to rely on current income to cover some of the pension costs. Vicki was giving me a ten year forecast of these so I could see what kind of financial position we were in."

"Let's see," Al said. "You're getting a long term financial forecast. But it seems to me that what you pay would depend on whom you pay."

"Right," Vince said, and took a sip of his coffee. "What we pay really depends on how many pensioners we have, how long they worked for us, what they earned, and how long they live. So we've done an actuarial calculation on this, and we came up with some dollar figures."

"What's an actuarial calculation?" Al asked.

Vince explained. "What we're after is to see if we can cover our obligations. People are living longer, and they're earning more than they used to. Both factors raise our payments, and frankly, we're a bit worried about what might happen. There are also some tough new federal regulations on private pension plans, and I need the data to complete our report to the government."

"So that's a part of your insurance operation."

"One small part." Vince glanced at his watch. "Let's get the bill, and walk back to the office."

The waiter brought the bill at Vicki's signal. He handed it to Al, who passed it across to Vicki. I guess we do live in a sexist society, Al thought, watching the waiter eye him strangely as Vicki signed. He was wondering

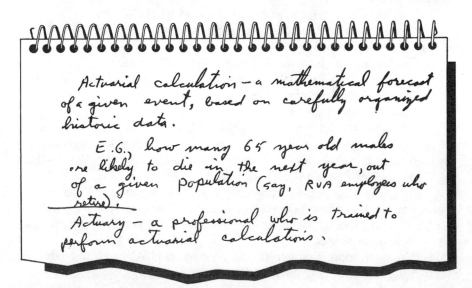

Actuarial calculation – a mathematical forecast of a given event, based on carefully organized historic data.

E.G., how many 65 year old males are likely to die in the next year, out of a given population (say, RVA employees who retire).

Actuary – a professional who is trained to perform actuarial calculations.

what kind of setup Al had, for sure. Well, if their positions were reversed, Al might wonder too.

"You see, Al," Vince said as they walked along, "a company as big as RVA has a lot of insurance problems. We need a special section to do our insurance planning."

"Let's see," Al mused. "I have auto insurance, theft and fire insurance on my property, a life insurance policy for my parents, and of course my pension plan. I have trouble keeping track of just those few."

"We really don't have too much to do with life insurance," Vince said, "although we do have a group life policy on all RVA employees. But we do worry a lot about casualty. Most of our troubles come from that side."

They reached the RVA building, and Al waved goodbye to Vicki as they left the elevator to go to Vince's office. The higher up you were in the building, the more important you were, and while Vince was two-thirds up, Vicki was eight floors above him. It made you wonder.

When they were settled in Vince's office, Al asked, "Just what can you insure? I keep reading about all sorts of wild things, like a singer insuring her voice, or a pianist his hands. Is that common?"

"If you pay enough, I suppose you can insure anything. But there is one fundamental principle to keep in mind. What's a risk?"

"Why, a, a probability that something will happen, I guess."

Vince nodded. "Technically, a risk is the likelihood that some future event will occur that you can predict with considerable accuracy."

"OK, how about your pension plan? Where's the risk in that?"

"You can forecast with very close accuracy, from a given large population, just how many will die each year. That is a risk."

"But you can't predict when a given person will die."

"Of course not, but if we have perhaps 6,400 65-year-old males, we can predict that, say next year, 225 will die. Of course, there will be fluctuations from year to year, but the overall forecast can be surprisingly accurate. Note that if these 225 do die, we do not have to pay out pension money. The next year, perhaps 318 are expected to die, and so on. By age 95 or so, all will be gone."

"Then these are risks because you can forecast them pretty well?"

"Right, Al. We can do the same things for marine losses of our shipments. We have no idea which shipments by sea might be lost or damaged, but we do know, from long years of experience, that about 0.34 percent of our shipments, by value, will be subject to loss or damage claims. The same applies to fire insurance, personal injuries in our plant, or, for that matter, playing certain slot machines in Las Vegas."

"OK, you have a very good idea of what's going to happen, so you can insure against losses, right?"

"Correct, Al. We buy policies from different companies for various risks. They of course have their own actuaries, so they are well aware of the risks involved, too. Their prices cover the risk; plus their own administrative costs, plus their profits."

"Vince, why don't you do it yourself, if you know the odds?"

"Because the odds may apply to much larger groups than RVA, and only a huge insurance company which can form a big protection pool can carry the occasional huge loss. One of our plants might be worth $100 million. If it burns to the ground, even RVA could ill afford such a loss. But an insurance company carrying tens of billions of fire insurance for tens of thousands of companies and individuals could carry the loss, if it happened."

"OK, that makes sense. So you can insure anything."

"No, there is another kind of event that is uncertain. What will RVA's profits be next year?"

"I have no idea, but I suppose that Vicki's group is doing some forecasts."

"They are, but the essential part about profits is that they are uncertain. You cannot forecast them the way you might forecast the deaths of certain unknown people out of a group. Too many intervening variables are involved ... possibly wars, riots, acts of God, government actions, unexpected windfalls, and so on. Profits involve uncertainty, and no one will insure an uncertain event."

Al thought for a moment. "Will you insure me against the chance of my getting promoted at Newsworld next year?"

"No, that's uncertainty again. I will sell you a life insurance policy, or rather an insurance company will. The policy price will cover their costs, plus the benefits they will have to pay out. And this price depends on your age, possibly your occupation, and perhaps even where you live."

"I remember our correspondent in the Middle East had to pay extra for his life insurance when he was out there."

"And if you were a skydiver, or worked with high explosives, you might pay more, too. But in any case, the event can be forecast in general, so it is a risk, and hence insurable."

"I recall seeing those words, acts of God, and war, in a couple of my policies. Now I see why they were there. Such things are essentially uncertainties, and hence uninsurable, right?"

"Correct, Al, although governments may offer such insurance as a public service. But a private, profit making company cannot."

"You must have lots of insurance policies for RVA."

"We literally have thousands. Just to keep track of company owned cars and trucks keeps two people busy full time. Remember, when we sell or buy a vehicle, the policy has to be changed. Every shipment we make by air or sea internationally has to be insured separately. If the shipment arrives safely, the policy dies. We issue hundreds of these every week."

"How about inside the U.S.?"

"Under American law, most, but not quite all, domestic shipments are insured automatically by the carrier. But if we do get damage or losses, we have to deal with the carrier's claim agent. This takes more time and effort, even though our transportation people help us a lot in this area. You see, the freight rates we pay include an insurance charge."

"And I suppose that some of your policies are government controlled?"

"Oh, yes, by law we are involved in the Social Security system, which covers all our employees, and we also are required to pay for industrial accident compensation and unemployment insurance. These programs take a lot of time and money, I can assure you."

"My dad used to tell me about being unemployed in the 1930's, with no money coming in," Al said. "And grandad just did get into the Social Security system before he retired. If he hadn't, he would have starved."

"If you examine our insurance concepts and thinking, and how they have changed in the past sixty years or so, you would find that lots of risks that were considered personal fifty years ago are now considered socially important. Hence government requires insurance, or sets up its own system. We at RVA of course have to live with whatever the law requires."

"Which means lots of paperwork, I suppose."

"And lots of costs, too. But the other side of this is the effect on people like your grandfather. I suppose that everything has its costs ... and its benefits."

"Vince, what it seems to boil down to is that RVA insures whatever is a risk and takes its chance with uncertainties."

"Not quite, Al. One of our activities in this office is to analyze payments for premiums very carefully. Sometimes we self-insure, if we feel that the premium costs are too high. For example, right now we are self-insuring against quite a few product liability possibilities. There have been some very large claims paid for defective product accidents, so premiums are very high. But, after considerable analysis, we have decided that it is better to self-insure."

"That means paying yourself if you get claims. That could wipe you out, couldn't it?"

Vince smiled sadly. "It could, but we are quite confident that if we do our production job right, we will not be faced with huge claims. So far, we have been right. This is a typical cost-benefit analysis, Al. Total coverage would cost us well over $125 million per year. So far, in the past four years, we have paid an average of $1.3 million in claims on defective or dangerous products. We are far ahead, but who knows about next year?"

"A billion dollar lawsuit, maybe?"

"It could happen. But we can't pay out all our income in premiums." Vince glanced at his watch. "I'm afraid I have another appointment, Al."

"Actually, I'm due to see Dr. Freeman, up in Research and Development, in about ten minutes."

Vince saw Al out of his office in a cordial manner. R & D was two floors up, and on the elevator Al wondered just who had sat down and figured out these floor assignments. Was R & D really more important than insurance?

"I gather that you're doing some R & D yourself, Mr. Faber," Dr. Mark Freeman commented after they had introduced themselves. "Although your type of research is not typically seen as R & D."

"Well, I'm trying to find out some facts and interpret them," Al said.

"Research refers to the activities involved in the discovery of some new process of scientific development, so you really aren't doing that," Dr. Freeman said, "whereas development refers to the evolution of something already known, so perhaps that is what you are doing."

"Dr. Robertson told me a lot about the old Ross and Vogel company. It seems to me that the modern RVA is pretty much founded on some good R & D work."

Dr. Freeman looked like a scientist to Al. He was a slender middle-aged man with rimless glasses, who seemed in constant motion, moving his arms or legs or his body all the time. He poured Al and himself cups of coffee from an urn in the corner of his office. "Yes, this company has had a long tradition of well thought out R & D. We have purchased companies, like the Snap-Kwik Lock Company, that also were good at new ideas, and when we acquire a company that isn't, we can usually use our knowledge to get it running better."

"You do have this central R & D office. Do you do most of your work here?"

"Oh, no, we only plan and coordinate here. We have several laboratories and development groups scattered around the country, and we even have one in Europe. Various divisions also do a lot of research. Our problem here is to make sure that there are no duplications of efforts. We also try to keep our scientists and engineers thinking along commercial lines. It is very easy to spend a lot of money developing something that won't sell and never will. We try to inform everyone of what's going on elsewhere in the company, since often a good idea has unexpected possibilities in other divisions, and we try to figure out what we might need, so that we can work on it in the future."

"It sounds odd that you can think of what you might need commercially, and then go out and discover it. I always thought that scientific discoveries were accidental, or the result of sudden inspiration, or something like that."

Dr. Freeman shook his head. "No, we can and do come up with ideas and then go out and develop them, but we don't succeed all the time. It still is true that an occasional insight or flash of brilliance can lead to something big, but a lot of our work is not quite so dramatic."

"I think I see what you mean. My boss tells me to write a story on, oh, say crime in Baltimore. I have no idea of what's going on in Baltimore, but I do some research and develop a story. That's what I'm trained to do."

"That is not much different from our telling a group of smart electrical engineers to design a better circuit for our new cassette TV, is it? You know that there is crime in Baltimore, and you know how to ask questions and read materials to get the information. You also know, as a writer, how to organize this data. Our engineers are trained in electronics, and we know that a better circuit can be designed and built. So they know how to proceed."

"This process begs the key question," Al commented. "Just why bother with crime in Baltimore, or why bother to design a better TV circuit? Why not do something else?"

"You've hit the critical problem. My job is to help RVA develop better products and processes, cut costs, and so on. But I only have so much talent. I have to select my priorities."

"And I suppose that your priorities are determined by profit, or potential profit?"

"They have to be. RVA spends over $145 million a year on R & D, and we can justify such expenditures only if the payoffs can be shown."

"Suppose that you hit on something that looks great from a scientific standpoint, but doesn't look like it will pay off in the market?"

"Then we drop it. Other institutions, such as government labs and universities, have the responsibility for such work. Remember, most American R & D is paid for by non-profit organizations. We have a more limited role."

Al thought of Dr. Farmer out in Bloomington, with his three-man repair shop. "Dr. Freeman, small companies must have a lot of difficulty with R & D. I mean, they really can't afford much, can they?"

"Normally, no. But a surprisingly large percentage of commercially viable innovation comes from smaller companies. Not the one or two man companies, really, but firms with sales of under $20 million annually. Really this is how RVA got started, remember? Mr. Ross tinkered in his garage with new machines, and Mr. Vogel backed him. This process still goes on, except the tinkerer these days is more likely to be a professor of physics, or an engineer with advanced degrees. Technology and science are much more complicated these days than in the 1920's. But such a person may have great knowledge about some product or process with commercial potential, and he or she may obtain backing from venture capitalists, just as Mr. Ross did."

"It doesn't sound very easy. I'm sure I wouldn't know where to begin."

"It never was easy. But there are very few really good ideas around, a lot fewer than developers and inventors think. But tell me, would you know how to get a book published?"

"Well, yes, I suppose so. I know a lot of people in the publishing business." Al thought for a minute. "Oh, I see what you mean. I know publishers because I write. I suppose that smart engineers and scientists might know people who could help them out, too."

"They well might. In the past, tinkerers might by chance find a backer. Indeed, this still happens. Lots of R & D really isn't the kind of super science people think about when they see white coated scientists in spotless labs, surrounded by mysterious gadgets. Someone might invent a slightly cheaper way to cut meat in a supermarket, or to align wheels on cars. These developments are not too dramatic, but they could lead to excellent profits. We still see this happening all the time."

"But Dr. Freeman, most patents are obtained by big companies, and most major developments are started by those same big firms."

"Certainly." Dr. Freeman got up and began to pace back and forth. "A small company cannot afford a twenty million dollar project the way we can. Few small companies do much long range planning, so they don't think through the implications of what might be needed or useful ten years from now. RVA does, and we have projects that will not mature for years. We can afford such things. It gives us a major advantage in the market."

"So you smash the little guys, right?"

"I only wish that we could. No, we get surprises all the time. Snap-Kwik is well known for its innovations. Mr. Suzuki really built that company well, and he is brilliant at sensing what the market needs next year. But this year a little Midwestern company developed a new steel hardening process which is much cheaper and better than the one we use. This company doesn't have sales of ten million dollars a year, and yet they are giving us fits. They can produce quality locks much cheaper than we can."

"Why don't you buy them out?"

"Do you remember the antitrust laws? We really can't buy them. They also have a patent on their process, so for the next seventeen years they are protected. We cannot copy their process."

"Patents run seventeen years, I remember that. But you must have quite a few yourself."

"We have thousands, Mr. Faber, and some of them are worth millions of dollars. But we by no means have them all."

"It seems funny that our government has antitrust laws, and then gives a company a seventeen-year monopoly at the same time."

"Ah, the idea is to encourage innovation, and our patent laws certainly have done that. Indeed, much of what we do with R & D involves patent considerations. If we can somehow come up with a patentable idea, we can develop it with this legal monopoly."

"I've also read that the rate of innovation in the U.S. is slowing down. Is that true, Dr. Freeman?"

"In some senses, yes. Remember, every discovery or development, once done, cannot be repeated. As we know more, and as we become more sophisticated, it gets harder to find new things. Sometimes government regulations are troublesome, as with various medical and medicinal patents. Before a company can sell a drug, it has to go through a very complex testing procedure, which can take many years. In recent years, this process has become very burdensome, which tends to make companies less interested in developments."

"But such tests are necessary for human safety, aren't they?"

"Of course. No one objects to reasonable standards. But twenty years ago, we developed a new drug for certain burns. It took us five years and $12.8 million to develop it, and another $1.3 million to get it through the government test program, which took two years. Macer & Van Ormand, our drug company, developed Xenathin in 1972. It cost $14.4 million to develop, and seven years and $28.5 million to get approval from the Food and Drug Administration. Since our costs were so high, this product sells for a high price, too. Moreover, we are having serious reservations about further extensive drug development, since our best forecast is that it could take up to ten or even fifteen years to get approval of new products in the future, and possibly $30 to $80 million in costs."

"Which gets to a critical point, doctor. You have lots of things you could do, and one thing I've learned in looking at RVA is that you can't do everything at once. So exactly how do you decide what to do next? What do you postpone?"

"You've hit the very essence of R & D management, Mr. Faber. All we can do is look over our prospects, try to estimate where the maximum benefits are, and then match these up with the best research possibilities. Obviously, we can only make good estimates about the future, but we have some smart people around to make those best guesses. We miss a few, but we win some also."

"From what you said, I guess that your competition also forces your hand."

"It does. Right now, we are doing a lot of work involving better steels and better locks. We want Snap-Kwik to stay very profitable, and as you say, the competition forced our hand. The same thing happened a number of times in the development of our cassette TV recorder. At least four times that I can remember, we were about to finalize production plans when we realized that a competitor had made an improvement we had to match. So, back to the drawing boards, as they say."

"I understand that you bought some licenses to use other firms' processes and patents on that one too, Dr. Freeman."

"Yes, we're using several things developed in Japan. Buying and selling licenses for patents, production processes, and various know-how is quite common. But we also license many others to use our materials. Actually, we receive about $122 million in such payments, while we pay out about $65 million each year. There is no particular monopoly on new ideas, and one way to make money is to sell the idea, not the product."

"Does it bother you to buy Japanese licenses?"

"Should it? Some Japanese firms are brilliant in electronics. We try to use the best technology we can."

"It does seem strange that foreigners can sell us know-how. It wasn't always this way," Al said thoughtfully.

"It was, but few paid much attention. Actually, the U.S. sells more patents and know-how abroad than it buys. But we have always used foreign ideas, and I suppose that we always will. As I said, Mr. Faber, no one country has a monopoly on brilliance, hard work, or discovery."

It had been an interesting day, Al thought on the way home. Joe Chapman had blown his cork, and Vicki had said a few things worth thinking about. He had discovered the usual thing these days, that fields such as insurance and R & D were pretty complicated. All that would go into his notes, too, and he wondered how he would ever sort all of this out and write the story he was supposed to do.

DISCUSSION QUESTIONS

1. As an under-twenty-five driver, you pay very high auto insurance rates, since your age group has lots of wrecks. A thirty-five year old married man with two children pays rates perhaps one-fourth as high as you do.

Is this fair? Why or why not? What other systems of insurance might be used to get the same results without penalizing younger persons, who don't have much money anyhow?

2. If possible, visit the person on your campus who handles insurance for your college or university. Find out:

What kinds of risks are covered.

What kinds of risks are not covered.

How this individual analyzes insurance before s/he buys it. That is, what key points does s/he see as important when s/he shops for a policy? Why?

Examine carefully the workers' compensation system your school has. Is this a good system? Why or why not?

3. Check the *Wall Street Journal* for some mention of a new R & D development that some firm expects to pay off. What is it? Why does the firm think that it will pay off? Do you agree?

4. A medium-size and very successful firm has a policy of never spending any money on R & D. The firm's managers merely keep a close eye out for new developments in government research and in universities. If something comes up that is useful

to their basic business (house paints), they buy the item; otherwise they just work with existing line managers and technicians in informal development.

Is this a good R & D strategy? Why or why not?

5. What is risk?

6. What is uncertainty?

7. What is research?

8. What is development?

9. RVA only does R & D in areas that make a profit. Do you think that this is a good strategy? Why or why not?

10

FINANCIAL MANAGEMENT

Al was back in RVA headquarters in New York, right down the hall from Vicki's office, seeing about finance. He had learned in talking to Vicki that if anything was going to be centralized in a big or even a small company, it would be finance. Money is far too important a matter to decentralize down to the divisions.

Lamont Baxter, the controller, had just as plush an office as the other key managers, but he was considerably more aloof than most. Still, he politely offered Al whatever he needed. Al figured that a man who controlled the cash would probably have to be a bit more removed from the people under him than some other managers, and he asked Mr. Baxter about this.

Mr. Baxter smiled thinly. "I suppose that I say no to more people every day than anyone else in RVA, Mr. Faber. Remember that I am responsible for budgets in this company. Everyone can easily figure out new ways of spending money, but there is only so much to go around. I spend much of my time patiently explaining to eager people why they can't have more money than they actually get. Which, unfortunately, I am going to have to go and do now. Can I give you a rain check?"

"But I had an appointment to ask about finance," Al replied.

"I am aware of that, but unfortunately a very critical matter has just come up. You will have to excuse me." Mr. Baxter handed Al a small pamphlet. "This is the booklet we give to our junior executives, which gives a brief coverage of basic financial problems. Perhaps you can read it and return soon. I am really sorry."

He did look upset, Al thought, but he supposed that he had been lucky so far. Few major executives at RVA had brushed him off. He promised to make another appointment, which Mr. Baxter urged him to do, and he took the pamphlet home to study. It made for some interesting reading.

FINANCIAL MANAGEMENT

Money is the universal asset, so all successful firms pay great attention to financial management. If this function is not handled properly, the company is in deep trouble all the time. Without cash, all other problems become irrelevant. Moreover, money is used to measure profits as well, so owners and stockholders pay special attention to how well this function is performed. If a firm knows how to manage cash, it is likely to perform quite well.

Finance, like other firm functions, is constantly preoccupied with time. Perhaps our notorious reputation abroad as clock watchers and time-conscious persons stems from such considerations, since in professional management of all sorts, time is critical. In finance, time *is* money, literally, since interest payments are time-related. But other time considerations, such as how fast sales are going for a given product, are also critical. Slow sales may mean higher costs of carrying inventories, which in turn means cash tied up, which can mean more capital needed—and steep interest charges.

Time is also money on the cost side. The delay in getting a new plant into full operation can cost millions because fixed capital is tied up without returns. Men are also being paid by the hour or month, and such outpayments without incoming cash can be rough on any firm.

Hence one can hardly speak of internal financial management without constant reference to time. Time slips away, and costs always seem to mount. If anything can be done faster, then we are ahead of the game. With millions of Americans being involved in games like this, it is not surprising that we are a very time-conscious people.

As with all firm functions, finance consists of the various managerial functions (particularly planning, organization, and control) used on the firm function. A manager plans and controls his finance functions, and he organizes his interrelationships in the firm so that this planning-control system works as efficiently as possible. He also has problems of staffing and directing his personnel, but these points were covered earlier.

This paper follows the above pattern. We will consider financial planning and control problems first, then work back through financial organization questions by considering such problems as uses of funds and financial problems involving sales credit policies. As usual, the question is how financial managers build relevant and efficient PARF loops to handle their numerous and complex problems.

Internal Finance Functions

Figure 1 shows the typical pattern of cash flows through any firm. Initial

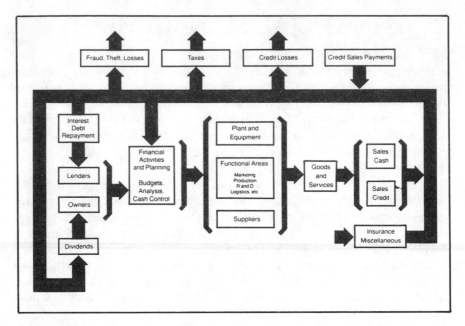

Figure 1. Financial Flows Through a Firm.

cash comes basically from two sources. The first is owners, who directly invest or buy stock in the company. The second cash source is lenders, who may be any of the institutions or individuals.

Once the firm is in business, its other major source of cash is from sales of goods and services. This cash, along with the other initial cash, is fed back into the system for reuse, and if the firm is successful, it cycles along.

Firms use cash in a variety of ways, as Figure 1 suggests. Uses can be taxonomized as follows:

1. For purchases of supplies, electric power, services, and so on. Note that here, as in every other use, some analysis must be made, typically in cooperation with managers of other functions, of what should be done. Thus a decision to spend cash on a given component, rather than spend cash to make it, would involve production managers, and others in some cases.

2. In various functional areas, such as production, marketing, research and development, logistics, insurance, and the like. Here we can further subdivide expenditures into labor, equipment, and so on.

3. For capital items, such as machinery, plants, transportation, and other equipment. Since most of this equipment is long-lived, special capital budgeting problems arise here, along with much longer-term

risks involved in cash commitments over years instead of days or months.

4. For working capital purposes, such as financing inventory or sales on credit. Note that inventory financing would show up in expenditures on production, noted in item 2. Credit sales would also show up in payments to the functional areas. But in both these cases, cash is being converted to product, and cash is not being received immediately after these payments. Hence these problems merit very close financial attention.

Three leakage points for cash are also shown in Figure 1. These include tax payments, credit losses, and losses because of thefts or frauds. Firms always have considerable outpayments for all of these, particularly taxes. But the other two can also be large.

A final set of outpayments are loan and interest repayments to creditors and dividend payments to owners.

Since we have both inpayments and outpayments of varying sizes, it is possible for any firm to generate various sizes of surpluses and deficits in its cash position. If respectable firms get into cash binds, they can normally borrow money to cover their position. "Respectable" here means a firm in which lenders have confidence, knowing that whatever is happening can be later converted to surplus cash to repay loans and interest. If firms tend to generate surplus cash, they usually either increase payments to owners (e.g., increase dividends) or try to expand operations to make still more cash by having more functional activity (production, marketing, etc.).

If a private firm finds that its own cycle results in permanent cash deficits, it will eventually go broke and be liquidated. More firms have had this experience by the millions than the relatively few that manage consistently to generate large cash surpluses.

Throughout this flow chart is the implicit notion that money can be converted to such things as materials, components, power, labor hours, and so on, and be reconverted back to cash. Good firms know how to do this rather well, but it is not a self-evident proposition. Many firms have gone broke with well-stocked warehouses full of unsalable products. Having any old assets does not mean that cash conversion can be accomplished.

The financial manager is the person who is responsible for monitoring this cash flow through the firm. Others will coordinate their activities with his. Top management or owners may overrule him, but generally the financial manager handles these flows.

Financial Planning

The most important part of planning for any firm is in finance. If planning is not done properly here, nothing else will work well either. More firms have gone broke because of poor financial planning than for almost any other reason.

Because this is one of the more important problems firms and all other organizations face, there is a long history of careful work in this area. Various tools and techniques have been developed over the centuries, and most of them are still being refined. This section will cover briefly some of the more important of them.

BUDGETS

One of the early financial planning tools, dating back centuries, is the budget. It is a detailed list of expenditures that the organization proposes to make. There are about as many ways of making a budget as there are organizations, but a common pattern is to lay out for the total organization various financial constraints (such as, "We will not spend over $6 million this quarter"). Then, various subdivisions of the operation prepare their parts of the budget, indicating how they are going to spend funds, and in what amounts. Typical subdivisions would compute direct labor costs, materials costs, utilities costs, and so on. Here, the pattern is to price out various expected inputs. Another common practice is to budget for departments (production, marketing, etc.), with each unit then further subdividing its allocation.

The budget normally allows for some possible actions if expectations are not realized. Thus if sales are higher than forecast, leading to a need for more output, the production department may be permitted to spend more than authorized to pay overtime wages or higher materials cost bills. One variation in modern budgeting is variable cost budgeting, where the budgeted amounts slide upward or downward along an agreed-upon scale as product rises or falls.

A common problem in budgeting is slack, or attempts by subordinates to build in a bit more than they really need. If a man wants two new secretaries and thinks that he can justify them, he may ask for five. In a good year, he may get three. Now he has a bit of slack in his system. When times get tough and he needs to cut, he can get rid of one and look good. It is common in successful firms to have slack build up slowly and steadily for years in this way. When the crunch comes, outsiders are amazed at how quickly and how much costs can be cut. Since no one at the top really knows how many secretaries are absolutely essential, the subordinate may be able to get things built in that no one really needs.

Another common budget problem is overcategorization. A subordinate may find that he has plenty of manpower money left to spend for the quarter, but he has depleted his equipment budget. If transfers cannot be made, he may end up hiring typists to copy items at high cost that a low-cost copier could do better. But if subordinates have too much leeway, they can get into trouble by spending too much on some items and not nearly enough on others. Firms and other organizations have wrestled with this problem for decades, without really resolving it.

Budgets are the financial plans for the various PARF loops in the firm. Note that almost any PARF loop can be reduced to money terms, which would be a budget. As activities proceed, normally there are feedback loops that tell managers and subordinates what is happening to money flows. If they begin to go astray (as when the manager discovers that a four months' labor budget has been spent in two months), then replanning is common and necessary.

FORECASTING

Budgets deal with costs, and some forecasts can be expressed as cost forecasts in budget form. But there are also forecasts of revenues, which require an analysis of demand. How much will the firm sell next week, month, or year? If the firm can forecast this correctly, or with small error, then money managers know that cost budgets will have to be less than these revenue estimates, or the firm will quickly get into deep trouble.

Demand analysis is a complex problem that we will return to in our chapters on marketing. Note again the interrelationships here. Financial managers must consult with marketing managers to determine sales forecasts; they must also consult with production and logistics managers to get cost forecasts. When the forecasts are in place, it is possible to prepare a complete *pro forma* profit-and-loss statement for the next time period, showing all estimated costs and all forecast revenues.

No one forecasts with perfect accuracy, either on the cost or revenue side, but it is common to find cost forecasts within a few percentage points of perfection, while demand or revenue forecasts can often be made within a range of plus or minus 3 to 5 percent. Firms that can make forecasts as closely as this on cash flows tend to do well, since they are always in a position to modify cash flow, particularly on the cost side, if it appears that there will be cash problems.

Most firms don't bother with such sophistication. Remember that there are about 5 million firms in the United States, of which perhaps half have no employees other than the owner and his family. Another 2 million have under ten employees. Most of these firms have virtually no cash planning at all, except what goes on in their owners' heads. And of course these are the firms that always get into major problems with cash. Most of them have no forecasting techniques either, except the wisdom (if any) and experience of their owners.

It is hard to believe that many firms somehow stumble on, taking what comes and trying to react to it, but this is common. When cash pressure comes, with luck the firm can borrow a bit and stagger on some more. But without these critical PARF loops, the possibility of rational management is quite small.

Hence what was described above under both budgets and forecasting was something done by most larger firms, along with a small minority of smaller ones. When done well, the combination of planning and forecasting can lead to excellent results for any firm.

Good forecasting and budgeting take skills not possessed by many persons. One not commonly noted is discipline. Most of us spend money as fast as we can get it. It takes a special kind of person to hold off, knowing that next month things will be a bit different, and cash will be tight. It also takes the ability to peer into the murky future and foresee things others may not care to see, which is an extremely rare skill.

FINANCIAL STRUCTURE

Publicly held corporations have many options about their financial structures. Under American law, various kinds of securities can be purchased by investors. Some of the more common are:

Common Stock. Here the investor actually owns a fractional part of the corporation. Such shares have limited liability. If the company goes under, the shareholder is liable only for his shares. This notion is expressed in Great Britain by the term "limited" after the name of the corporation and in the United States by "incorporated."

The corporation is not obligated to pay dividends on its stock, although the owners of stock are the owners of the corporation, and they can vote in the directors they prefer. One share is one vote, so those holding the most shares control the company. The board of directors appoints the managers, is responsible for the general affairs of the corporation, and can be sued or sue in the name of the company.

Preferred Stock. This class of stock normally carries a fixed annual dividend and is an ownership share also. As with common stock, liability is usually limited to the owner's purchase price. Preferred owners normally do not vote for directors or otherwise run the corporation, although exceptions can be found. If dividends are in arrears, the preferred owners may take over and operate the firm, since a precise payment obligation has not been met.

Bonds. These are loans to the corporation, and as such, they receive their interest and repayment when due before shareholders get anything. Under American law, interest payments are considered costs and hence deducted from income before paying taxes. Stock dividends are earnings distributions after taxes.

Bonds normally are issued in thousand-dollar denominations, and they can be bought and sold on various markets. Indeed, various prices of all securities mentioned here are quoted daily in *The Wall Street Journal*, and anyone with money can buy any of them at going market prices at any time.

Convertible Debentures. Often corporations issue bonds of some sort that may be converted to common stock under given circumstances. Note that a bond is a fixed-interest issue (say 6 percent per year). If the firm does very well and earns much money, stockholders will obtain all of the gains, while bondholders continue to receive their 6 percent. Hence in order to make a bond issue more attractive to investors, a conversion privilege may be added to it.

If the firm does not do well, the stockholders are stuck with little or no gains. In such a case, the bondholders come first and continue to receive the interest. A convertible debenture thus offers pretty good upside-and-downside protection.

If there are too many bonds in the corporate financial structure, then fixed-interest charges may eat up too many available funds. But if there are too many common shares, dividend payments (remember the stockholders can force these, since they own the company) may take too much. And the preferred and convertibles have to be carefully plugged in so that capital is easily raised, without seriously upsetting the capital structure.

Like everything else in this book, this problem can invoke a lifetime of study and activity. There is a vast literature on this problem alone, and many very capable persons spend their careers trying to figure out optimum capital structure mixes in a complex and ever-changing world.

This is also a very interesting area to outsiders and investors, since the way firms operate will influence the price of various securities. Hence one who really understands what is going on can make his living buying low and selling high. *The Wall Street Journal*, if read daily, suggests that quite a few clever people try just this. Some succeed, most fail. But it is a fascinating game that one can play at any time.

CONTROL

Financial matters are always subject to very careful control procedures, since we are talking about money here, which everyone wants, and which quite a few unscrupulous people would happily steal. More scrupulous, but not too perceptive junior managers might not steal it, but they very well might waste a lot of it, if not carefully controlled.

The financial PARF loops tend to be highly centralized. Many firms decentralize many things, but fiscal responsibility and control are invariably directed from the top. And various expenditures at any level are audited constantly to determine if they were made according to plans and budgets.

Here is one place where PARF loops are quite precisely defined. A junior manager may have a budget of $85,000 for the quarter. If he spends $86,000, this deviation will be noted soon, and he will be called to account. Note here how close the interrelationship is between financial planning and accounting. The accountants will be those who keep close track of expenditures, while the financial managers will be those who use these data to spot and correct deviations.

This is one area where no firm can afford to be sloppy. Most post mortems on failed enterprises suggest that one significant reason for failure was the inability to get cash planning and control procedures right. Because these critical activities were not properly structured, the cash leaked away in many ways, and no one knew it or could do anything about it until it was too late.

Control basically involves the return feedback loop of the PARF loop, along with whatever replanning is necessary to make relevant corrections. Well-managed firms not only have the feedback loops extremely well-organized, so that such information is returned to key managers very quickly, but they also have the kinds of technical and managerial information needed to get the new plans structured to correct the situation. Neither of these is obvious or easy, but firms that are confused here are typically in very deep trouble very soon.

USES OF FUNDS

As with everything else in finance, this begins as a part of planning. Funds are scarce. Who will use them most efficiently? In the end, top management has to decide, but the financial managers will play a major role in working out this complex decision.

Every part of the firm is typically convinced that it needs more money. Hence at budget-making time, every subordinate manager will be pressing for more funds to carry out critical projects that clearly are to the great benefit of the firm. The marketing manager is convinced that more money spent on promotion will have a big payoff; the production manager points to needs for new cost-reducing machinery; the research and development director is firmly convinced that only a 10 percent budget increase will bring the new breakthrough that will lead quickly to vast new sales; and so on. Who is right? Unfortunately, only so much cash is available, and allocations have to be made.

Even after these operating cash decisions have been made, various capital structure problems remain. What level should dividends be?

High dividends use up cash but may later attract more investment and make future capital raising easier. But low dividends and a healthy cash position now can lead to bigger bank loans later, as bankers become convinced of the basic soundness of the firm. And if these cash strategies are followed, how about the timing of expenditures on the new plant, which will cost millions and put a squeeze on the firm? Delaying construction for six months might mean that cash can be applied to critical operating needs, yet building costs may be rising, and starting now will save much money in the future.

The usual problem is that any viable firm has more good uses for any cash it can get or already has than are feasible. Allocations have to be made, which is another way of saying that someone will be caught short. This is one of the toughest areas in business, since it is very difficult to say no to perfectly valid requests for just a bit more money. Managers, knowing full well that funds are short, will make every effort to justify their proposals, which makes it worse. Instead of saying no to some idiot, the financial managers have to say no to capable persons sincerely convinced that their causes are just.

Here we find a classic suboptimization problem. Everyone can improve, but the costs of such improvement may well be large enough to make the total system less efficient. Someone has to analyze all requests from the global view, trying to see how each fund allocation will help the whole. Essentially, you get your funds if the expected payoff is greater than the cost and if in the process no other part of the firm is made less efficient. A cost-benefit calculation is employed. If you spend this much, what are the payoffs? If the manager can demonstrate that the payoffs are greater than the costs, he may well get his funds.

Thus if our production man demonstrates that if he buys $50,000 worth of new cutting tools and as a result direct labor costs decline by $80,000, he is in a better position than if he merely argues that better cutting tools make work easier. If our sales manager proves that his $35,000 of new sales promotion money will generate sales of $1.2 million and that profits from these sales are much greater than $35,000, his case is strong. If our research and development director can convince us that the extra $100,000 he wants will yield $300,000 next year in cost savings or new product sales, he may be able to get his funds.

The same principle applies to capital projects. If the new plant investment will pay off at 20 percent, whereas we now are working with an old plant that is expensive to operate and generates only 2 percent profits, the idea is more attractive than if we are unsure about potential benefits.

These cost-benefit calculations can be made more precisely in some cases than others. Note in the above examples that the production manager's calculation was perhaps the most accurate, since he was dealing with hard numbers and close production-engineering estimates. Our sales manager has to forecast revenues, and how do we know he is correct? If he has a reputation of being very accurate, we might listen with more attention, but we know he has missed on occasion. And our research and development director's estimates were also based on some forecasting that is very difficult to do. Anyone can claim to win big, but not everyone does. Hence in this area we find a great deal of cross-checking, recalculation, and careful examination of forecasting claims. Just because a manager says it is so does not necessarily mean that it is.

SALES FINANCE

As sales are made, various financial problems arise. A basic one is inventory financing. A firm may be cranking out products steadily, when sales dip slightly. Immediately inventories begin to rise, and more cash is locked into financing them. Funds must be found for this purpose. If the dip is temporary, this can be a minor matter, but how do we know? Here again, careful coordination must be accomplished. The sales manager may give his best estimate of the situation, and he may point out that he feels sales will be down for the quarter by 10 percent. Now production has to be consulted. Should production levels stay up, or should cutbacks be made? If they are made, what are the costs of slowing down? Such costs must be weighed against higher inventory costs. If the product may deteriorate (as with some foods) or is expensive to store (requires refrigeration), still further calculations must be made. Possibly warehouse leasing costs have to be compared to the costs of cutting back production and taking the risk that getting back into volume production later will be quite expensive. First-rate financial managers can spend much time on such questions. Note that forecasting is at the root of the problem. *If* sales stay low, then drastic budgetary cuts will have to be made, and perhaps the entire cost structure of the firm will be altered; but *if* this dip is very temporary, then only minor budget changes may be sufficient. We all hope that bad news is temporary, but here a manager has to be very cold-blooded indeed, and very realistically assess the situation. If he does not, trouble is certain.

Another key sales problem is in credit policy. A firm can typically expand sales rapidly by granting more credit, but if it does, someone will have to carry the accounts. If the firm does, funds will have to be found to do so. If a bank or other financial agency is willing to carry the accounts (and thus earn income from interest on them), various arrangements will have to be made to turn over the accounts to them.

A real and perpetual problem here is that as more credit is given, buyer financial stability and soundness tend to deteriorate. Really good credit risks are always scarce. The other kind will typically buy anything as long as they don't have to pay for it just yet. And many firms have found that they carry on their books large assets of accounts receivable that never get paid. If they don't get paid, the firm has given away its goods or services.

One's perception of the problem depends upon where he stands. Buyers, even those with very poor credit records, usually think that they will eventually pay off. Sales managers, who tend to be judged on sales volume, may also take a benign view of credit. This client may be a bit shaky, but his business is picking up.

A prudent financial manager is much more dubious. He has seen doubtful credit risks come and go—mainly go—into default and bankruptcy. He knows that some credit has to be given, but why to this fellow, who has a long record of late payments, defaults, and all the rest?

The result is a perpetual balancing act between prudence and the desire to expand sales. Moreover, as some firms have discovered, there can be good earnings in credit. Firms can charge their customers interest on unpaid balances. Thus as long as they repay promptly, money can be made on lending money. But if repayments lag, or if significant numbers of customers fail to pay at all, trouble is certain.

All firms have bad-debt reserves, and like most other things in business, a good PARF loop can be built to check this point. Thus a firm may check its overdue accounts receivable monthly. If this amount is over 1 percent of sales, it is a deviation signal that credit policies are getting too loose. If it falls below one-half of 1 percent, it can be a sign that credit policies are too tight. By using such a PARF loop, some feel for what should be done in this area is developed.

Conclusion

This brief review of internal financial management can only begin to scratch the surface of a very complex area. Here we identified some of the more common financial management problems, and we tried to suggest how they interact with other parts of the firm. Since financial problems run clear through the firm, this is one area that interrelates all others.

Financial planning and control systems are critical. Unless the firm gets these PARF loops straight, everything else will be out of control most of the time. Because financial problems are so complicated, as well as so critical, they tend to be highly centralized at the top of firms. Other things may get decentralized, but financial matters rarely do.

Financial questions also lead to careful coordination efforts among all parts of the firm. Since activities anywhere affect other activities up and down the line, the financial manager has to make sure that all interrelationships are worked out in enough detail to determine total money effects as various subsystems work through their problems. Even apparently minor shifts in financial allocations can percolate through any firm with disastrous results. Here we find a business activity that necessarily must consider the firm as a whole, even as each subsystem spends its funds in its own way.

Al did get back to see Mr. Baxter about a week later.

"Thanks for the pamphlet, Mr. Baxter. Actually, it answered most of my questions."

"We feel that it is quite useful. The ignorance of younger people on financial matters is really quite abysmal these days, I'm afraid. Many of them act as if money were everywhere. They fail to perceive that as a private, profit seeking corporation, we can only spend something less than we take in."

"But you can and do borrow money?"

"Oh yes, and if you look at our balance sheet you will note that we have $818.91 million in long term debt. The bulk of this is in bonds. We have gone to the money market on a number of occasions. But remember that we can only sell bonds if our credit is excellent. It is, mainly because we are so very cautious about our financial planning and budgets."

"You don't have preferred stock, though."

"No, we never had occasion to resort to that type of financing. You see, we try to get our money as cheaply as possible, and while preferred issues have been attractive to investors from time to time, we have always found that bonds were better for us."

"Those numbers seem huge to me," Al commented. "The idea of even trying to raise $800 million just staggers me."

"It staggers me too. Remember, there really are only a few ways for a private company to raise money. Three, actually. We can generate cash from our own internal operations. If you have looked at our Consolidated Statement of Sources and Uses of Funds, you will note that we managed to generate about $549.3 million from this source last year. Second, we can borrow money from creditors, and those bonds we sold are a good example. Finally, we can get owner investments, that is, sell more stock. But all of these are really contingent upon profitable operations through time."

"OK, suppose that I am thinking about buying some RVA stock, or maybe some bonds. What should I be looking at?"

"Well, the most common measure of success is the rate of return on your investment. ROI, it is sometimes called. You would not be very interested in investing in an RVA bond which pays eight percent, when you could buy a similar bond from another company which pays twelve percent."

"How about stocks? There I don't get a fixed return."

"Correct, Mr. Faber. You might receive dividends, but they are not guaranteed. And of course if the company does very well, you might receive

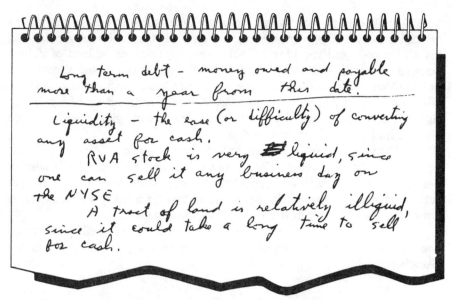

Long term debt - money owed and payable more than a year from this date.

Liquidity - the ease (or difficulty) of converting any asset for cash.

RVA stock is very ~~B~~ liquid, since one can sell it any business day on the NYSE

A tract of land is relatively illiquid, since it could take a long time to sell for cash.

capital gains as the stock appreciated in value on the market. This, I suppose, is really the attraction for many investors. It is quite nice to buy RVA at $48 per share and have it rise to $96 per share within a year or two."

"But there's no guarantee of that either, is there, Mr. Baxter?"

"Of course not. The stock could just as easily go down to $25 per share, unless it is RVA. But even we could have a bad year, as indeed we have had on occasion in the past. Remember, as a stockholder, you are an owner, and you share in both gains and losses. But remember also that limited liability. You can only lose the value of your shares, and nothing more, even if the company goes bankrupt."

"So if I buy your stocks or bonds, what I really should do is consider the alternatives?"

"Of course. We cannot offer a worse proposition than other companies. Investors want security, earnings, liquidity, and reasonable safety consistent with the risks they take. We have to remain competitive."

"Who can give me all this information?"

"The most likely source would be a broker or dealer in stocks and other securities." Mr. Baxter walked over to the neat coffee table in the corner of his office and found another pamphlet. "I hope that you take a look at this, Mr. Faber. It was prepared by the Wall Street firm of Ricks and Goldberg, a very prestigious and reputable firm. It describes major financial markets."

Al tucked it in his pocket. "Thanks. I did plan to visit a company like that later on."

"I'll be happy to give you an introduction to Mr. Goldberg. He is a personal friend of mine."

Al talked with Mr. Baxter for some time, going over some of the financial issues the RVA pamphlet had covered. Al often had trouble balancing his checkbook, and the idea of really keeping track of billions of dollars boggled his mind. The recording and developing of the financial data was done in Vicki's accounting department, but Mr. Baxter actually had to figure out how to spend all that money. Mr. Baxter mentioned that he had just signed a check for $88,376,345.78, and Al tried to imagine what he would do if he had to handle sums like that.

"What happens if you're wrong?" he finally asked.

"Very simple. I resign. This is not a job for a person who is faint of heart, Mr. Faber. It requires considerable skills, considerable faith in your subordinates, and most of all, the ability to take prudent risks." Mr. Baxter wiped his glasses. "But in the end, it is absorbing work."

It might have been absorbing, and it certainly was well paid, but Al was not too sure that he would be the one for the job. His interests ran elsewhere.

DISCUSSION QUESTIONS

1. Prepare a budget for yourself for the next three months. Indicate exactly what you are going to spend money on, in detail. Show weekly expectations.

Now, check for the next three weeks to see how close you came to the expected sums. Note that this involves keeping track of expenditures also. How close were you? Of what use is this kind of PARF loop?

2. Find out in your own college who prepares budgets for your school. Now find out who approves them. Is this a centralized or decentralized function? Why do you think that it is organized the way it is?

3. You know the fees students must pay per quarter or semester at your school. Prepare a forecast of revenues expected from this source for the next quarter or semester.

What might go wrong with your forecast? What factors might change that would make this cash inflow significantly different from what you expected?

4. A sales manager of a clothing store near a major college campus has noted that when credit is extended to students, sales increase by more than thirty percent. He suggested to his boss that the store change its credit policy to provide that any student who wanted credit could get it by showing his college ID card. The sales manager figures that this step would increase sales enormously, and increase profits as well. Do you think that

his suggestion would be a good idea? What's right with it? What's wrong with it?

5. Visit a nearby dealer for durable consumer goods (autos, TV sets, furniture, etc.) and ask about the store's credit policies. What would you need to do to obtain credit? Why? Do you feel that these credit policies are sound? Why or why not?

6. Take another look at the *Wall Street Journal*. Note any announced sale of new securities (stocks, bonds, etc.). Study this announcement. What is going on here? Why would the company want to offer such securities? Why do you suppose they choose this method of raising cash as compared to other methods?

7. A production manager and sales manager were asked for budgets by the financial vice president. The sales manager said, "I can't give you the budget until I know what the costs of goods will be. When I know this, I can get my selling prices, and this will tell me how many units I can sell. This will give me my cash inflow, and from this I can work out the rest of my budget."

The production manager said, "I can't give you a budget until I know how much to produce. My costs are very sensitive to production volume, so until you tell me how many items to make, it is impossible to tell you how much each one will cost."

How would you resolve this suboptimization problem? What is the next step the financial vice president should take to get good budgets from each of these subordinate managers?

8. An office manager needed to have some documents copied, but his old copier had broken down. He had no funds in his current quarterly budget for repairs ($200) or the purchase of a new machine ($2,500), but he did have $10,000 in his labor budget still available. He hired some part-time typists to copy type his documents, at an average cost of sixty cents per page. In this way he produced 6,000 pages of copied materials and got his work out. The copier could have done the job for two cents a page.

What is the matter with this kind of budgeting? What could the financial planners do to avoid the office manager's wasteful dilemma?

9. A production hotshot was brought in to cut costs and get his budget down. This firm had been having much trouble with production, and not only were costs high, but sales were sometimes lost because production could not get the work out on time. Last quarter the department produced 10,000 items at a unit cost of $14 each, and all were sold for $18 each. With inventories totally depleted and customers screaming for the product, something had to be done.

The new production manager produced 19,000 units in this quarter at a unit cost of $10 each. However, 14,000 are now in inventory, and marketing is screaming for blood. The production department is producing only a single model in two colors, whereas before it produced twelve models in nineteen colors.

At a managerial meeting, the sales manager wanted the production manager fired. But the production manager argued that he deserved a bonus. "You told me to get production up and budgeted costs down, and I did it," he said. "What more do you want?"

What more *do* you want? How could you solve this suboptimization problem with better budgeting?

10. What are three ways that a private company can raise money?

11. What is long term debt?

12. What is liquidity in an investment?

11

PHYSICAL DISTRIBUTION

George Brown, Vicki's secretary, was getting married, so his friends threw a party for him, and Al was invited with Vicki. It was surprising, Al thought, just how many RVA people he knew by now. He almost was a part of the executive floors. George was a favorite of Al's, since George had helped him a lot in getting appointments and generally steering him through the intricacies of RVA's executive suite. His fiancée was a charming girl from accounting, and Al knew her too.

The party was well under way when Al found himself talking over the punch bowl with Frank Safranski, a pleasant man, slightly younger than Al, whom Al hadn't met before.

"I'm in Physical Distribution Planning," Frank was saying, "I've heard about you. You seem to have everyone in a tizzy all over the executive suites. They're making book on what you're going to write."

"What are the odds?"

"Six to five that you expose us as a bunch of crooks and rapacious monopolists," Frank replied. "But the odds change every time you talk to someone new. Some of our guys, and gals, are very, very persuasive. How's Vicki these days?"

"Fine, I came with her. She's over there someplace."

A young fellow from Don Beeman's office wandered over. "Hey, watch out, Al ... you're talking to fanatic Frank. You're in trouble!"

"Gee, he doesn't look fanatic to me," Al said. "What are you fanatic about, Frank?"

"Pay no attention to him," Frank said. "Those guys are just jealous because I have the best job in the company."

"He thinks that it's the best job in the company, but no one else does. He's a transportation nut."

"I know all kinds of people who like things a lot," Al said, "so tell me about transportation."

"You'll be sorry, Al," Sam muttered, as he wandered off.

Frank pushed Al into a corner. "You've been talking to all kinds of people in the company. How come you haven't hit our office yet?"

"I'm not even sure where you are. Besides, is transportation so important?"

"We're under Jason Cabot, the Executive Vice President. We have a small group that does logistics and physical distribution planning."

"Now, what's that?"

Frank told him, and Al sighed, dug an envelope out of his pocket, and started scribbling. "It's a lot more than just transportation, although that's where I got into this thing. You see, everything moves, sooner or later, and moving it cheaply, rapidly, and well is a part of our job. Actually, the various companies have their own traffic managers to do the job, but we plan better systems. We also give lots of advice on how to organize for transportation and storage."

WRITTEN BY AL ON THE BACK OF AN OLD LETTER

> Physical Distribution — deals with movement and storage of goods within a firm, plus related functions, such as in plant movement, terminals, loading and unloading facilities, and packing. Sometimes called _logistics_.

"That sounds pretty straightforward to me."

Frank waved his arms. "Yeah, but transportation runs right across everything. You've seen the organization chart, haven't you?"

"Sure."

"Well, the organization is vertical. Things go up and down channels. But transportation is horizontal. It runs across all groups."

"Let's see. You start with some raw materials or components, and I suppose that they go into the factory."

"Right. Now production has them. Then they get turned into product, and marketing has them. Then they get shipped out to distributors, or into warehouses, and physical distribution has them, or maybe marketing still. Then they get moved again to retail stores. Every functional area has something to do with it, including finance, who pays the bills, and accounting, who keeps track of all that movement."

"So who's in charge?"

"That's the point . . . no one really is, which is why we have a physical distribution group to try to coordinate the whole thing. See, it looks like this." Frank grabbed Al's envelope and scribbled a diagram on the back of it.

"It's a system, see? Everything depends on everything else. In the old days, we had nothing but traffic managers, who usually reported to a marketing boss, and warehouse managers, who often reported to production.

FRANK'S BACK OF AN ENVELOPE DIAGRAM

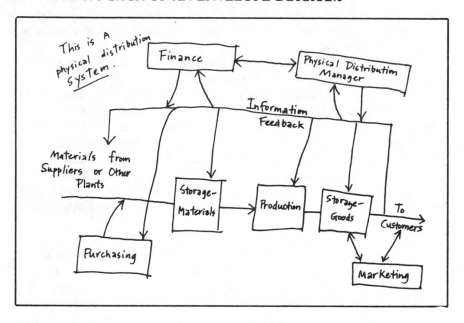

The traffic men were experts on transportation, and they tried to buy cheap movement. The warehouse people were specialists in storage, and they tried to get low cost storage. They rarely talked to each other, and they didn't even report to the same people."

"So what? I suppose that you don't really need to worry much about that problem."

"OK, so suppose that the cheapest movement for some of the raw materials is by river barge. The only trouble is that it takes six weeks to get delivery, and you have to have lots of inventory, because sometimes the river ices up."

"So?"

"So in the old days, we congratulated ourselves for getting real cheap transportation. But meanwhile, we were spending a fortune for inventory costs and storage. When you look at the whole picture, it could make sense to ship by rail, which costs more, but cuts inventories sharply. If you add up all the costs, what seems reasonable may not be."

"So your office tries to see the whole picture, right?"

"Right. But that's not all. Suppose that we're shipping some consumer goods to warehouses, and then out to retail stores. The marketing guys are terrified of being out of stock, since they lose sales if this happens. You can't sell one of our TV cassette recorders if you don't have them in the store. So they tend to pile up too much inventory, just to make sure that they'll never be out of stock. But that costs a fortune in high quality warehouse space. Now, how do you maximize profits—by never being out of stock, and spending a fortune in inventories, or by being out of stock once in a while and saving a ton of money in warehousing?"

"Beats me," Al replied. "That sounds like one of those cute problems for your computer boys down in New Jersey."

"You do get around, Al. That's exactly where the problem goes, because it's quantifiable, or at least most of it is. We can figure pretty closely the costs, in terms of lost sales, of being out of stock, and the rest of the problem is just numbers. It turns out that being out of stock about one percent of the time, and losing a few sales, can save millions in inventory costs."

"I begin to see what you're up to. You take a look at all the elements that go into movement and storage, and you try to put the pieces together. If you do your job right, you end up making more money and living happily ever after."

"We used to suboptimize terribly," Frank mused. "Even now, it's a hassle. Everyone wants to control everything. I guess it's because if something goes wrong in the logistical system, then some poor manager gets yelled at. The production people want huge inventories to protect them from strikes, bad weather, and other delivery foul ups. The marketing people want to have enough stock to cover all possible sales. If you let them loose, they'll run costs right out of sight."

Al remembered an article he had read recently. "Say, isn't that what Japanese car makers are doing, I mean keeping inventories way down? It seems to save money."

"Yes. Some Japanese plants work with less than a half hour of inventory of parts on the assembly line. The trucks drive right up to the work stations and unload. Ford recently studied this system, and they really began to cut inventories. They took about a half billion dollars' worth out of the system. Remember, Al, that's a half billion dollars of working capital they used to need, but now they don't. At twenty percent interest, Ford saves a cool one hundred million bucks a year!"

"So why didn't they do it earlier?"

"It takes terrifically good management to pull it off. One truck delayed, and the whole assembly line stops, and that can cost, oh, a hundred thousand dollars an hour in a big auto plant. And it takes a lot of people who know what we know in physical distribution to make the new system work."

"It makes sense," Al said, looking around for Vicki.

"But there's more. Consider packing, Al. Some things we fly around, and the guys used to put those items in heavy wooden crates that weighed a ton. We finally got around to having some items, like women's clothing, just carried by air on aluminum pipe racks. No packing at all, and we saved big money there. Then some export shipments were packed so flimsily that the cases fell apart before they got off the boat. Boy, some ports can really knock things around! We got some engineers in to design some low cost, durable containers, and again our costs went down, even though they went up. That is, we gained more in loss and damage reduction than the new cases cost us."

"You know, *Newsworld* just ran a long article on the plight of the railroads. I gather that they're regulated pretty closely."

"They are, but not as much as they used to be. The whole transportation regulation game has changed a lot since 1979, when a lot of air transport was deregulated. Since then, there have been rail and truck deregulation laws passed, too. But there still is plenty of regulation, and we, and the carriers, have to know the law." Frank dug a piece of paper out of a pocket and wrote things down as he talked. "All common carriers are regulated, as are most contract carriers. A good physical distribution person has to know a lot about transportation regulation, and with all these new laws, we have to unlearn a lot of what we learned just a few years ago."

"Wait a sec, Frank. How did you get into this business? Did you learn it working?"

"Lots of it, but some schools do have good transportation programs. I

FRANK'S SCRATCH NOTES

COMMON CARRIER - A TRANSPORTATION COMPANY THAT OFFERS IT SERVICES TO THE GENERAL PUBLIC - SERVES EVERYONE

CLOSELY REGULATED BY THE ICC (INTERSTATE COMMERCE COMMISSION) FEDERALLY, AND USUALLY BY STATE REGULATORY COMMISSIONS FOR IN-STATE (INTRA STATE SHIPMENTS.

CONTRACT CARRIER - SERVES A FEW CLIENTS ON A SPECIFIC CONTRACT BASIS. LESS REGULATION. VERY COMMON IN TRUCKING.

PRIVATE CARRIER - CARRIES ONLY ITS OWN GOODS. LITTLE REGULATION (I.E., RVA's OWN TRUCKS)

TRANSPORT MODES - TECHNOLOGIES FOR MOVEMENT - E.G., RAIL, AIR, MOTOR, PIPELINE, WATER.

went to Indiana University ... they have a really good program there. I studied under George Smerk. Ever hear of him?"

"No, not really."

"He's a great guy ... he loves transport history, and he's always talking about abandoned electric railways."

It takes all kinds, Al thought, as Frank scribbled on. But antique trains really were not his bag.

"Take this, Al, and drop around at the office later."

Al took a look at the stuff Frank had written down. "As usual, something that seemed simple wasn't. "How do you decide between different kinds of carriers?" he asked. "Let's say that you have some of those TV cassettes to ship. What do you look at?"

"Well, we could fly them by air freight, ship by truck, or go by rail," Frank said. "The rates are likely to be different, the shipping times are sure to be different, and the volume minima will be different too."

"Now, what's that?" Al asked, and Frank told him.

"You see, Al, it depends on how much, to where, and what other physical distribution factors are involved. Your choice of mode isn't just a matter of picking the lowest rate. Remember that value counts a lot, too. Those TV cassettes are worth thirty dollars a pound or more. A truckload could be worth over a million dollars. If you're paying fifteen percent interest on your money, that's about $410 per day in interest costs alone. Suppose you can ship by rail in eight days, or by truck in three days." Frank did some

AL'S NOTE ON THE BACK OF A NAPKIN

Volume minima — lowest weight accepted for a given rate.
E.g., rate = $8.50 per hundred pounds, with a minimum of 100 lbs. —
You ship 65 lbs., but pay for 100 — which is why traffic people pay close attention!

(V's birthday soon — present?)
↳ how much?
 etc ...

figuring in his head. "You save five days of carrying costs by going by truck. That's $2,050 alone. Only if the rail rate were that much cheaper would it make sense to go by rail. That's one main reason why rail these days handles mainly low value, bulk items, like coal and wheat. Trucks usually are faster, so they handle most of the high value stuff."

"Once again, this sounds like something that you could put on a computer."

"Oh, we do a lot of it that way, but it still takes some smart traffic people to make the key decisions. One thing we can computerize pretty well, though, is plant and warehouse location."

"OK, I can see that. You take a look at all these cost and marketing factors, and you try to minimize your costs."

"Not quite. We try to maximize our profits."

"There's a difference?" Al asked.

Frank drew another diagram on the back of another napkin. "Sure, take a look. You might want to spend ten thousand dollars to make fifty thousand, right?"

"Sure."

"Well, that's what we try to do. We might put a warehouse in a fairly high cost location, because by doing this, we can serve our customers faster and better. If we do, sales go way up, and we come out ahead. For example, we just put a new warehouse in Atlanta to serve our southern electronics

FRANK'S BACK-OF-THE-NAPKIN DIAGRAM

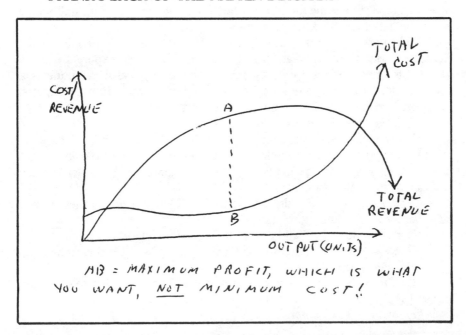

customers. The price of land there was out of this world! Remember, we can't just stick our warehouse in any old place. They have to have rail spurs, good highways, and sometimes easy access to water transportation and airports. But the point is that by sticking a big distribution warehouse in Atlanta, we can deliver our merchandise to anyplace in the whole southeast within two to three days. We ship the stuff in by truckload or carload, and we deliver it out in small bits and pieces, usually by truck. When you work out all the financial, marketing, and production angles, it makes sense, even though it's an expensive proposition."

Vicki had finally wandered over. "How's Frank treating you?"

Vicki looked pretty special tonight, Al thought. "Oh, he's been lecturing me on physical distribution. It's not quite the right time or place, but it's interesting, I guess."

Vicki laughed. "Frank will talk about his job any time and any place."

"You're just jealous," Frank said. "You people just don't realize the important work we do."

"Well, I do," Vicki said. "I figured last week that you've saved RVA $2.7 million this past year in freight charges alone. You saved another $1.8 million in warehouse relocation ... shall I go on? The accountants are right on your trail, Frank."

"It figures," Frank said. "I wonder sometimes, though. We show you how to save millions, and you turn us down cold."

Al remembered something Beeman had said about suboptimization and bright young managers. "I think I know what your trouble is. You may save a million, but someone else in the company can save two million, so he or she gets the cash and the approvals."

Vicki nodded. "You're learning. Frank's big trouble is people, really. He comes up with these great ideas, but the highly skilled experts he needs to get this thing done are just too much for us. Physical distribution is a complex field, and you wouldn't believe the engineers, computer experts, transport specialists, and whatnot they use in that area."

"After hearing Frank talk, I'll believe it," Al said.

"What you've just heard is only the tip of the iceberg," Frank said. "You should go talk to Dr. Smerk. He could really tell you what's going on!"

"I'll leave that to the experts," Al said. "Come on, Vicki, let's dance and talk to the future bride."

"Hey, Al, be sure and drop by the office," Frank said, as they moved off. "I can give you lots more information then."

"Sure, Frank," Al called back as they began to dance.

"Frank's pretty wrapped up in his work, isn't he?" Vicki commented.

"He seems to be."

"It's funny, how some young people can't figure out what to do, while some of them, like Frank, are totally committed."

"How'd he get that way?"

"Oh, he just liked transportation … he's quite a rail fan, you know. So he found out that you could study transportation and physical distribution in college, and that's what he did. He started out in history at Indiana, but he took Dr. Farmer's Intro to Business course, where you have to write a career planning paper. Dr. Farmer mentioned transportation, and sent him to Dr. Smerk. He talked to Dr. Smerk once, and he never looked back."

"How do you know all of this?"

"Oh, when I was getting my M.B.A. at Indiana, I was an Assistant Instructor in that course. I helped earn my way through the program that way."

"Did they pay much?"

Vicki laughed. "You could starve on that stipend, but the work was fun. I learned how to talk to people by teaching elementary business in W100."

"Talk is what you can do, Vicki."

"It was fun. I actually taught a bit of physical distribution, even though I know almost nothing about it. But when you teach, you learn."

"I bet the guys in your class never knew what you said, given your other charms. It must have been a shock, having a lovely lady give them physical distribution diagrams."

"They survived," Vicki said dryly. "And a few of the girls realized that they could have business careers in this generation. I think that I earned my pathetic pay."

A PAGE FROM AL'S NOTEBOOK (Made much, much later!)

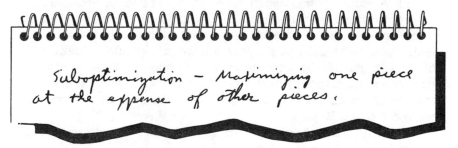

Suboptimization — Maximizing one piece at the expense of other pieces.

"I'll drink to that," Al said. "You I would like in class, even though I might not learn much."

"Well, Frank learned a lot and he's enjoying life."

"Once in a while I like to forget work and just enjoy life too," Al said. Which they did for quite a while thereafter.

DISCUSSION QUESTIONS

1. What is physical distribution management?

2. Take a look around your own college or university. Lots of things move into a college, such as food, paper, books, etc. Who handles all this material? Where are the storage facilities for most of it? What kinds of transportation are typically used to get the materials in?

3. Lots of materials leave a campus too, such as garbage, sewage, more books, manuscripts, etc. Who handles the physical movement of this material? Where are the storage facilities?

4. You have probably run into an out of stock problem when you tried to buy something. The store did not have the item at that time. What do you normally do then? Who loses a sale when this happens?

5. What does a marketing manager have to do with physical distribution? Why?

6. What does a production manager have to do with physical distribution? Why?

7. What does a finance manager have to do with physical distribution? Why?

8. What is suboptimization?

9. What is a common carrier in transportation?

10. What is a transport mode?

11. A student once nearly flunked out of school because he had great difficulty with math. He would study for ten to twenty hours for his math class each week, and then barely get a D. Meanwhile, he would not study much for his English, Spanish, and Speech classes, because he was quite good in these subjects. But because he didn't study, he received C-'s and D's in these too, even though with a bit of time spent studying, he could have received A's and B's.

Was this student suboptimizing? Was there a better strategy for maximization he might have followed?

12. What is a private carrier in transportation?

13. Suppose that you have 228 pounds of new textbooks to ship from where you are to a bookstore in Washington, D.C. Check around a bit locally and find out just how you might do this.

What mode offers you the cheapest price? The best service?

14. What is a volume minima?

15. A young engineer in a company just dreamed up a brilliant idea for automating the warehouse he works in. He

figures that the company could invest $800,000 in equipment, hire one highly trained technician, and build an automatic routing distributor for all the various shipments that pass through the warehouse. He figures that this change would save the company $10,000 per year net.

When he presented his idea to his boss, he was politely but firmly turned down. He was bitter, and he figured that the company just didn't want to be innovative.

What is wrong with this engineer's proposal, assuming that his figures are correct? Why would a profit seeking company turn down a perfectly good money saving idea?

12

PURCHASING

Al picked a bad day to be visiting with Mark Brandon, head purchasing agent for the Ace Engineering Company. An unexpected problem had come up, and Mark had excused himself for the second time, leaving Al in his office. Al passed the time by studying the purchasing function chart on the wall.

Mark came back 45 minutes later. "Gee, I'm sorry, but I just had to cover that panic. For a while there, I was afraid that the new Arizona plant would have to close down."

"What happened?" Mark was quite young, and Al liked him as soon as they met. He was a serious fellow, with thick horn-rimmed glasses.

"You know that we're building a new truck braking system out there ... boy, these days, those systems are complicated! It takes about 900 parts just for the rear end alone, including a bunch of electronic assemblies. Well, someone forgot to get enough 3/4" lock washers. Without the washers, no production. They cost about five cents each, but down time for the plant is over twelve thousand dollars a day. If we're responsible for closing, the union contract says that the workers get a full day's pay."

"How many washers do you need for an assembly?"

"Twelve. Silly. For want of a nail ..."

"The horse was lost. And so on. Did you find them?"

"Yeah, a hardware wholesaler in Tucson had a zillion of them, and he was happy to unload them on us for only twenty cents apiece. There goes an extra fifty dollars, plus all that wasted time."

"I thought that RVA made things. Why the fuss about getting washers?"

"Take another look at our annual report, the Income Statement," Mark replied. "We buy almost $2.5 billion worth of stuff outside, from over 60,000 vendors."

"Why?"

Mark leaned back in his chair and put his feet on the desk. His office wasn't plush, with coffee tables and all the rest, but it was a comfortable place. "Take those washers. We use maybe $50,000 worth a year, which is a lot of washers. But it surely wouldn't pay for us to set up our own plant to make them. I suppose that the smallest feasible lock washer plant would produce at least five million per year. If we made them, we'd be in the washer business. No, it makes sense to find an expert and buy from them."

Mark stared out his window. "It's funny. Here we buy about 56 percent of our total costs. Typically more than half of costs in most big companies are purchased items, and yet you can hardly find any systematic study of purchasing in colleges. Most schools don't even have a course in it."

"So how do you learn the business?"

"Oh, you get in it and learn as you go. I did have a business degree, but I never thought much about purchasing. Then I went to work for Ace, and they eventually put me in here. I like it fine, but I wish that I had had a chance to study more before I got the job."

"That chart of yours seems to lay it out pretty well," Al said. "I've been looking at it pretty closely. I never even thought much about purchasing, but like lots of things around this company, it looks a lot more complicated than I would have guessed."

"Oh, it's nothing complicated. All you have to do is figure out how to buy maybe 160,000 items a year, and always make sure that you get the best price and service consistent with quality. That was what went wrong with those lousy washers. One of our younger buyers tried a new supplier, who offered us a very low price. The only trouble was that he couldn't come up to quality specifications. The guys on the assembly line would tighten the bolt, and the washer would crack. So we had to junk a whole shipment. She saved a few hundred dollars, but we spent a few thousand chasing around."

"What do you do? Fire the buyer?"

Mark laughed. "Of course not. I'll have a few words with her later. She's a fine prospect, and this is part of learning. When I was in her spot, I once spent $90,000 buying bolts, and every one was the wrong size. My boss told me that if you didn't make mistakes, you never learned, only it's smart not to make too many mistakes. But note that Janet was trying to save us some money, which is one reason she's here."

Mark's phone rang, and while he was handling what seemed to be another panic situation, Al wandered over to his bookcase and picked up a volume. It was a supplier's catalog for electronic sensors, and most of it was like Greek to Al. Mark settled his business and hung up.

"OK, Mark, suppose that you do want something. I assume that the production people tell you what's needed?"

"Take another look at that chart. Production and engineering are involved, but finance, marketing, and in this case, our legal department were all involved too."

"Why the legal department?"

Mark sighed. "Because truck brakes are subject to very precise Department of Transportation safety standards these days, and we wanted to make very sure that we were well within the law."

THE FIGURE ON THE WALL
AT ACE ENGINEERING COMPANY

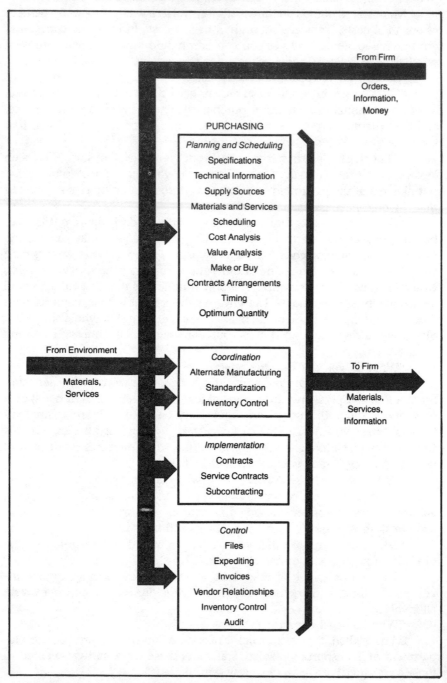

"We ran an article in *Newsworld* about product liability, too," Al said. "Aren't you liable if something goes wrong with your product later on?"

"We sure are, and do you have any idea of how big a lawsuit could be if a truck lost its brakes? It could be for hundreds of millions of dollars!"

"So the lawyers get in the act. Finance I can see. I suppose that they are worried about budgets and costs."

"Right. And marketing wants to know what we are up to so they can go around to truck manufacturers and tell them about all the new features we have."

"You don't make trucks, do you, Mark?"

"No, we sell brake systems to manufacturers."

"So then you get at the other end. Their purchasing agents look at your product."

"You know, lots of business is a chain. We buy the bits and pieces, make some more, and come up with a system, or really a subsystem. Then we sell that to someone else, who puts it in another vehicle and sells it to someone else. Incidentally, lots of times a heavy truck isn't finished. It still needs a body or other items, such as winches or special lights, so there is still one more link in the chain. And all the way up and down the line, there are purchasing people."

"OK, so now you know about what you want. These catalogs will tell you where to get it, right?"

"Sometimes. But we get lots of visits from salespeople, too. When the word got out that we were developing a new truck braking system, I had dozens of visits from various people in electronics. We sent them to our own engineers at first. It pays to know what is available off the shelf. It can save you a lot of money if you can buy some standard item. Actually, we saved several hundred dollars a system because we discovered that someone had an electronic sensor fully developed for some maritime use that we could easily adopt. By doing it this way, we avoided having to pay extra for special tooling and development."

"So what is important when you buy something?"

"Price of course, but this is only one factor. Quality is critical, but we don't want to pay for too much quality, and we don't want shoddy parts and materials either. And delivery speed and reliability are very important. We fouled up that washer deal on two counts. We didn't get proper deliveries, and the quality was bad. We won on price, but it really didn't matter."

"Why don't you just store items and make sure that you don't run out?"

"Because it costs money to store things. You pay interest on borrowed money, or if it's your own money, you lose the use of it for other things. And you have to build warehouse space. We figure that it costs at least thirty percent per year of total value to hold inventory. We do, sometimes, anyhow, particularly for low cost, routine items. We should have done that with those washers. But for big items, it usually doesn't pay."

Al looked over at the chart. "I can see that coordination function all over the place. And we've talked a bit about planning and scheduling. But what's cost analysis and value analysis?"

Mark smiled. "Engineers, bless their hearts, tend to get carried away from time to time. They always want the best, and I suppose they can't be blamed, because if something goes wrong, they get blamed. But consider an ordinary bolt."

"I never did before," Al said.

"Well, there are literally thousands of different kinds of bolts, and I don't mean only sizes. Some are designed to take terrific heat and stress, and others are soft steel, just to hold a couple of parts together. You can find that kind down on the rack in any hardware store. If you want to bolt your bicycle rack together, those soft bolts are fine, and they're cheap."

"I bought a package for 69 cents just last week," Al said. "I needed to replace a bolt on my kitchen table leg."

"Fine. But suppose that we're putting one of those bolts in our truck braking system? It might take thousands of pounds per square inch of stretching pressure. If it fails, the brakes could fail."

"So you buy the best you can find, right?"

"Wrong. The best bolts you can find might cost twenty dollars each, and we need fifty of them in this system. The best are for aerospace and aircraft jet engine use, where a failure can really be deadly. No, we try to find a quality bolt that is better than we really need, but not perfect."

"How much would these cost?"

"Maybe fifty cents each. But our engineers had twenty dollar bolts in the prototype. No way were they going to fail."

"I can understand that."

"We have a value committee. It has finance, production, and engineering people on it, along with me," Mark said. "We go over every item to see where we can cut costs without compromising the product. In this case, the engineers agreed that the fifty cent bolts were fine. Actually, they are about twice as strong as we need. So this little item saves us maybe $975 on the final product. But if we had used twenty cent, less durable bolts in the system, we would have had failures. They just wouldn't stand up."

"I begin to see what you do," Al said. "You buy items that are correct for the application, even if they cost more than the cheapest. But you don't buy the best, because that would gold plate the system. You'd end up having costs way out of sight."

"You can do this in a lot of ways. For example, we just shifted from a zinc die casting for a part to a plastic one. The plastic does the job better in this situation, and we saved a few cents a unit, too. We made a wire part to replace a stamping, and once again we saved some money and got the job done better. In this case, our own engineers redesigned the part, and we make it ourselves instead of buying it."

"That sounds like that 'Make or Buy' item on the chart," Al said.

"Right. We make some things, and we buy others. The trick is to know what to do for each item. For those washers, buying is the only realistic answer. But for many items, the actual answer is pretty tricky, and we have to do some close figuring to decide what to do."

"It sounds like the accountants get in the act at this point," Al said.

"They do. Vicki's group does some cost accounting for us. It's surprising how you can forget to add in costs, if you're working on the back of an envelope."

Mark waved to another bookshelf. "These days, we have to spend a lot of time with the legal angles, too. We just got into a make or buy decision because of a law."

"Explain, Mark. What does the law have to do with make or buy?"

"Well, there are some very tough clean air standards now coming into force, and the foundry business is about as dirty an industry as you can imagine. Lots of old iron foundries are closing, or have closed, because it costs them too much to meet the clean air standards. We discovered that our casting costs were going up very fast, and worse, our suppliers were getting fewer every year. It got so bad a few years back that we built our own modern, and very clean, iron foundry in Ohio. It serves all of the RVA divisions, including ours. Now we make, although we would prefer to buy."

"What happened to the people that worked at those closed foundries?" Al asked.

"How should I know? All I do know is that we had lots of trouble getting grey iron casting for a long time."

"Now we get to optimum quantity," Al said, looking at the chart.

"More marketing. This time, we need sales forecasts to know what we might need. Suppose we assemble and sell a hundred of our braking systems a week. That means that we need 5,000 of those bolts we talked about. But if we're selling two hundred, then I have to buy 10,000 a week. Remember, we usually can get quantity discounts, so it makes a big difference to me what use rates are. And remember too that I don't want to pile up big inventories, because of costs. It can be a tricky problem to figure out just what quantities to order. A couple of my people are working on this all the time." Mark thought for a moment. "We worry about inflation, too. Sometimes, if we know prices are going up, we order more, because it pays. But in our business, prices can go down once in a while, too, so we worry a bit about that."

"Prices go down? I never heard of that before."

"Sure ... for example, things made of copper can go down because the price of copper floats around on world markets. A few years back, copper was a dollar a pound, and now it's about 65 cents. We watch prices of commodities that we buy, and sometimes we even try to guess what's going to happen. We even consult with a couple of expert brokers about copper and tin, because we use a lot of both metals."

"So when prices went down, how'd you come out?"

"Pretty good. We kept our inventories small, and we saved over a half million dollars in 1981 on this one item. A friend of mine in another company got stuck for over two million bucks, because he was betting that the copper price would stay up, and he had excess inventory. But you can't win them all."

"You get into all sorts of things," Al mused. "What else?"

"Well, there's transportation."

"Yes, Frank Safranski told me all about it."

"You've talked to fanatic Frank, eh? He's real good, and we work with him a lot. Remember those carload and truckload lot discounts? We worry about that too, because often we can cut the per pound rate by forty percent or more if we order in truckload lots. This can offset the extra costs of storing bigger inventories."

"To say nothing of saving on capital."

Mark grinned. "You're learning, Al. Oh, we have to worry sometimes about another problem. We carry a pretty big silver inventory for our truck braking systems."

"What for? Silver, in a truck?"

"A lot of key wire joints are silver soldered. It's very strong. It only takes a fraction of an ounce per system, but it adds up, and silver is worth from six to twenty dollars an ounce. Come to think of it, that's another price that goes all over the place. But no matter what the price, it's attractive to thieves. A worker can walk out with five hundred dollars' worth of silver a day, if we don't watch it."

"So your storage costs go up again, right?"

"Sure, and so do our security costs. We were losing silver, not much, but more than we could account for with normal wastage. So we hired a private detective and put her in the plant as a worker. She caught the thief within two weeks, but at a hundred bucks a day, it wasn't cheap."

"What did you do with the crook?"

"Oh, we fired him. We didn't prosecute, because it would take too much time and money. But we did change our security routines in silver storage, and we haven't lost any since. Hot items, and lots of things are hot, need extra security, and hence extra cost."

"Name a few."

"Try spark plugs, cigarettes from the vending machines, candy bars, ignition parts for our own cars and light trucks, and anything that people can sell quickly."

"I see. Now we get to standardization," Al said.

"That one is a headache, but what it involves is trying to use as few items as possible. We discovered, in doing value analysis on the truck braking system, that we were using seven different kinds of bolts. We took a close look, and got it down to three. By doing this, we were able to order in bigger quantities, and we saved money. But we also made it easier for the production guys. They didn't get stuck when some odd item wasn't available."

"Mark, it sounds like you could standardize all the way across RVA, instead of just at Ace."

"We do, for some items. Light bulbs are one odd example. You have no idea about how many different kinds of bulbs we used to use. Then someone at headquarters got interested, and it turned out that we only need about twenty basic types. We were buying over 1,100 different kinds. The result was that now central purchasing buys that item, and we order from them. It seems crazy, but we save over $300,000 per year on light bulbs because we're standardized."

"You report to Mr. Garland, the head of Ace, right?"

"Yeah, but there's a purchasing advisory group at headquarters for all of RVA. We have a committee that meets every month, and all the major purchasing agents are on it. There's a finance person, and an auditor, too. The idea is to get together and see what we can save. Sometimes standardization across divisions really doesn't pay, but we can win big on other items."

"You sell all over the world. How about metric versus U.S. standards?" *Newsworld* had run an article on that recently.

Mark groaned. "Boy, don't remind me of that one! The U.S. is the only major country not on the metric system, and yet to convert now would cost literally hundreds of millions of dollars, just for RVA. We do a lot of metric work in Europe, and we even do some in the U.S., but not too much. Right now, we metricize all our engineering drawings, but even that costs millions of dollars per year. I really don't know how this will turn out, since it does cause us lots of trouble. We're damned if we do and damned if we don't."

"Hasn't the Congress been considering a law to put the U.S. on metric?" Al asked.

"It has, but it hasn't acted yet. Given the static they get from the home folks whenever it gets discussed, it isn't likely to move soon. Right now we have a double standard, and we have to live with it. It's funny ... back in 1891, someone sat down and set some standard, say for a light bulb socket, or the voltage of the telephone system. Now we're stuck with his standard, like it or not. Do you realize how much it might cost to change every light bulb socket in the country? Wow! We have to live with a lot of historic accidents."

"I believe you. Now, how about implementation?"

"Simple in theory, and terribly complex in practice, Al. We sign purchase contracts with people all the time, and of course our lawyers, and the vendors' lawyers, are checking to make sure things are legal. Every so often something goes wrong, and either we're in court, or we have to work out satisfactory arrangements out of court. Contract disputes are pretty cut and dried, but still you get some surprises."

"I've had a few disputes myself with people I bought things from," Al said. "Like the time my hi fi turned out to be defective. The seller wanted me to pay, and I wanted him to fix or replace it. We had a great battle."

"We get into the same kinds of arguments, but really not too often. Most vendors are reasonably honest, and they don't like to make us too mad. We pay them too much money. But once in a while we do get into problems."

"With all the money you do spend, it would seem that you could really put the screws on vendors," Al said.

"We could, and once in a while, if we feel that we are being taken, we do. But most of the time, we're anxious to avoid fights, and we're willing to be reasonable. Oh, we shout a lot at vendors, and they yell at us, but basically, we try to get along."

"Who cares if you do or don't, Mark?"

"It's really simple. If you squeeze your vendors too hard, they get resentful. Sooner or later, you need a favor from them, and somehow, they can't comply. Just a few months back, there was a big shortage of a special kind of stainless steel. A plant had been closed down for months because of a flood in Pennsylvania. The price went sky high, but our supplier managed to get us enough to keep us going, at the old low price. You see, we had helped him out a year or so ago with a prepaid order, when we knew he was in a bit of a financial bind. He remembered. A competitor had to close down for two weeks because of this shortage. Somehow his supplier remembered how nasty he had been on some deal before."

"That makes sense."

"Now we get to control, Al. I personally am responsible for spending over $50 million per year, and my boss makes darn sure that it's well spent. So do the auditors."

"You're buying all kinds of weird stuff that no one knows much about. Wouldn't it be easy to ... well, get in on the take?"

Mark laughed. "You wouldn't believe all the creeps that come in here and make me offers. Maybe you would, since you're a reporter. Sure, I could start cutting corners, and sooner or later the auditors would catch me, if the engineers didn't. And I'd be fired. If I stole enough, or took big enough bribes, I'd probably be prosecuted, too. I'd end up blacklisted. No one would ever hire a purchasing person who had been on the take."

"So you stay honest."

"If I were a crook, I wouldn't tell you, Al, but sure, I have to. Remember, it is pretty easy, as you suggested, for me to approve a slightly higher price than I should, or to cut quality just a bit, and let the vendor pay me off. Actually, anyone in purchasing is constantly being offered things. Some are trivial, like when the seller picks up the lunch tab. I've been offered booze, blondes, trips to Europe, and you name it. But our auditors weren't born yesterday. They keep a real close eye on us, believe me. I even get checked out in my personal life once in a while. If I started living as if I made twice as much as I do, I'm pretty sure that our auditors would be very, very suspicious and meticulous."

"Say, Mark, how do you handle this business? I mean, suppose that a vendor does pick up your lunch tab. Is that OK?"

"We actually have a company policy for buyers that explains, in great detail, what we can or cannot accept. Lunch is OK, unless you make a habit of it, like twice a week for months. Gifts under twenty-five bucks for Christmas are OK, but not more. No cash payments of any kind are allowed. The list goes on and on. I guess that it's necessary. Every once in a while, I have to dismiss one of my people, because he or she is getting a bit careless."

"You've convinced me that you're important. But I still can't figure out just how you handle all the variables."

"We probably don't, but we keep trying. I guess the biggest difference between a professional buyer and the typical consumer is that we try to be professional, informed buyers. If we have to buy some tires, we don't just read the sale ads and buy something. We make a systematic study of tires. If we don't know the answers, we'll consult with some expert who does. It's pretty hard to sell us a product just because you say it's good. We try to be rational about the whole process. The difference between good and bad purchasing in a company this size can be hundreds of millions of dollars every year."

"I'm convinced, Mark, really!" But Al wondered just how he could write up a dynamic news report about purchasing. Unless someone were accused of taking a big payoff, it was hardly exciting stuff, unless, of course, like Mark, you really enjoyed doing the job.

DISCUSSION QUESTIONS

1. Consider the problem of buying something used around your school, such as paper clips, erasers, chalk, or whatever. Look around and find out who does this purchasing. Do you think that this purchasing is done well? Why or why not?

2. Find someone who was in on the purchase of a building, or some similar large item (possibilities: local firms, a university building, a school building, etc.).

What kinds of purchasing problems were involved here? How much lead time was required (time from first firm plans to the actual completion of the project)? What legal problems were important? How did the contractor get paid, and when?

3. A professor reaches back for the chalk and finds none. "Darned fool supply department!" he mutters.

What kinds of coordination are required to buy chalk efficiently? Trace the purchasing scheme, and indicate all persons who might get involved in this simple purchase.

4. A local rancher is retiring, and he has offered your

college his whole operation, which includes 2,000 head of beef
cattle. Since a lot of meat gets eaten around the college, in
cafeterias, the faculty club, and so on, this seems like a good deal.
Instead of buying a critical item, you can now make it yourself.

What advantages would a college have if it ran its own beef
growing operation? Why? What new kinds of problems would a
college have if it got into such a business, instead of going to
outside suppliers for this item? Why?

Do you think that this ranch operation would be a good idea?
Why or why not?

5. A paper salesman just visited your college purchasing
officer and made him an offer. He can supply all the paper the
college needs for the next three years for exactly 50 percent
of the going price. Someone has a huge inventory and is interested
in getting rid of it, even at a loss.

Do you think that this would be a good deal? Why or why
not? If possible, visit your purchasing officer and find out how
many dollars and tons are involved here.

Consider that interest costs on money are twelve percent. If
you use your money to buy paper, you will be forfeiting the
interest it would have earned.

Is your answer still the same? Why or why not?

6. In one college each of twenty-six departments insists on
having its own letterhead. Since none is very large, this means
that no department can buy more than two gross at one time.
Total demand is 103 gross per year.

Visit a local printer and price out letterheads. Would there be
any advantage to standardization here? What kind?

7. A very expert purchasing clerk is being considered for
promotion to head purchasing agent in a small firm. He is
technically very well qualified, but you know that he likes to play
the horses (he usually wins) and that he is cheating a bit on his
wife.

If this were your company and your money, would you
promote this man? Why or why not?

8. We've just started a new small firm, and we need six
electric typewriters. I ask you to buy them, getting the best deal
you can.

Take a look at the phone book, catalogs, or other sources of
information, and give me a list of potential sources of supply.
Indicate which of these you think are best and why.

9. Every college has to publish a schedule of classes each
quarter or semester. If a college missed its deadline on this key
item, the result would be chaos.

Find out in your school whether the schedule is a make or buy item. In either case, also find out what lead times are required to get the schedule out on time. Check on who the expeditor is on this job. What does he or she do if there is a delay?

10. Ace Engine Company checks up on Mark Brandon's personal life once in a while, just to make sure that he isn't living a lifestyle beyond his means. Is it ethical to check up on employees this way? Why or why not?

11. Mark Brandon hired a detective to work around the plant and find out who was stealing silver. Is this proper? Would you like to work in a place where a private detective might be investigating things?

12. Take a look in the *Wall Street Journal* on the commodities page and find out what has been happening to the price of soy beans. A major food processor buys over $10 million per month of them for use in various products such as cooking oil. What do you think the purchasing agent should be doing right now— building up inventories, or cutting back? Why?

13

PRODUCTION

John Jefferson, Snap-Kwik's plant manager for Plant Two, was pleasant enough as he showed Al around. It was funny, Al thought, that he had been studying RVA for almost four months, and this was the first time he had been in a plant. People at RVA had all sorts of offices, and they did various things with paper, but actually very few of them seemed to be making anything. Al knew that only about 15 million of the 95 million American workers actually were in production, and his experience at RVA must be typical. People thought, planned, controlled, audited, designed, or maybe even managed. But in the end, someone had to produce *something*, *somewhere*. Al had read about the Industrial Revolution, and he had looked at pictures of machines that had revolutionized the world. Somewhere along the line, though, the paperwork and the thinking had somehow become more important than the doing.

Plant Two was a modern facility near San Jose, California. It had been built in 1971, and it looked more like a big warehouse or low-lying office building than a factory. There were some noisy operations, but they occurred in well insulated rooms. Al supposed that some of what he saw was pretty dirty, too, but the plant was spotlessly clean. He had read a lot about mindless assembly line workers doing endless repetitive tasks, and indeed, some of the operations he saw were pretty repetitive. But there were no moving assembly lines, and workers seemed to wander around doing mysterious and apparently aimless things. Mr. Jefferson pointed out that the biggest single department was quality control, which was full of electronic testing gadgets and neatly dressed inspectors performing various tests on finished locks and safes.

They ambled around the plant for several hours, and Al watched Mr. Jefferson chat with workers and foremen, examine a process, talk to an engineer about a heat treating problem, and check over some production reports. He was slow spoken, short, fat, and black. If anyone cared about that, it wasn't evident. He obviously knew his business, and the workers knew it.

"How did you get into this business?" Al asked, when they returned to Mr. Jefferson's neat, small office. Not as plush here as at headquarters, Al thought, but it was nice and neat. He had had an image of harassed production people messing through papers in untidy, grubby offices. One more image shot, he thought.

"Oh, I started as a machinist, back before the war. Actually I started as a laborer in a shipyard. No one gave training to colored people in those days. I learned by observing and reading, and by doing. I always wanted to be a machinist. When I was growing up, in the depression, machinists always seemed to have jobs, and their pay was real good. But there weren't any black machinists, and most people figured I was crazy. But I watched and learned."

"Did Mr. Suzuki hire you just after the war?"

"He did. He was struggling to start Snap-Kwik then, and he didn't have much money. So he figured that he could get a Negro cheaper than a white man. He was right. I couldn't get a job anywhere, after the shipyard closed. During the war, when manpower was tight, I got a bit of a chance, but as soon as the soldiers came back, it was all over."

"So you stuck with Mr. Suzuki."

Mr. Jefferson laughed. "Sure. What else was there? He was paying me half of what I was worth, but I stuck it out. After a few years, when he began to make some money, he got my pay up to about 80 percent of what it should have been. A tight man with money Mr. Suzuki was. But he was fair. He paid *everybody* less than they were worth. That's one reason Snap-Kwik had such low costs. He'd avoid the hot shots and mainstream types, and he'd come up with all sorts of characters. I was a foreman on the assembly line once, and he got me a bunch of people from the mental hospital. No one would hire them. Funny thing, most of them were great workers. Some of them are still with us, and that was over twenty years ago."

"Why? I mean, why were they good?"

"Some weren't too smart, and they found repetitive work challenging. I'd go nuts myself on an assembly line, but a person with few brains doesn't. Some were plenty smart, but they had been mentally unstable, and who would hire them? They were grateful for the chance, I guess, and they worked hard and well. One of them is in New York now, at RVA headquarters. He really moved up fast. One of them is my best quality control engineer, and another is the plant auditor. Mr. Suzuki was funny. He'd take chances with people, and most of the time it paid off. Sure, I stayed, and finally, after Mr. Suzuki sold out to RVA, I got promoted to plant manager. Mr. Suzuki never would have done that, I think. He's still a bit of a racist. But I know more about this plant than anyone. It's a good plant, too. We have the lowest costs in the industry, and we don't pay low wages any more, not with the tough union we've got now. We pay premiums, but we produce more per person than anyone else. People forget that you don't get high pay unless you do a lot of work. Productivity is the secret."

"You're the plant manager, but you sound like a production man."

"I am. I'm responsible for getting production out here, and while I do have some accountants and others under me, basically I'm a production manager. That's what I always wanted to be, and that's what I'll be when I retire. I get the goods produced." Mr. Jefferson looked thoughtful. "I don't handle marketing or finance, or all the other company functions. In the Soviet Union, I'd be called a company director or president, because their state owned companies just produce according to plan, too. I'm told what I'm supposed to produce, and then it's my job to produce it."

"And they tell you to produce good locks and safes."

"Right, Mr. Faber. This plant manufactures all of those items for Snap-Kwik. It's not quite that simple, of course. We have over sixty types of locks and twenty-two safes. I have to figure out just how to get the right product mix running down the lines."

"Do you have much flexibility?"

"Not as much as I'd like. Those marketing guys always want me to produce one of everything every day! I have some flexibility in production runs, though. I try to get them to give me reasonably long term forecasts of what they're going to sell, so I can plan my production runs as far ahead as possible. Lots of times, though, they change their minds, and I have to change my production plans. I guess that the market talks. It doesn't make sense to produce what you can't sell." Mr. Jefferson toyed with his pencil. "I have a budget, of course, and what I spend depends on what we're doing. We have a flexible budget for production. If we get a sudden surge in orders, my budget automatically goes up to take into account the extra labor, materials, and power I have to buy. If production goes down, the budget shrinks, too. I do a lot of fighting for more money, and sometimes I even win. Right now, I'm trying to get approval for a couple of new machines that will save the company plenty of money. I can shout and argue a lot with my boss, and I suppose that's flexibility. And I talk a lot and plan a lot with the transportation and purchasing people. They're reasonable enough, when they know

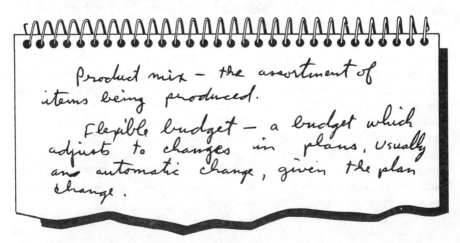

Product mix — the assortment of items being produced.

Flexible budget — a budget which adjusts to changes in plans, usually an automatic change, given the plan change.

the facts. Some of them are very smart, too. They can help out in a pinch. Sure, I guess that I have flexibility."

"OK, Mr. Jefferson, just what exactly do you do? I mean, you've told me about a few things that you work with, and I've seen your plant and observed you working. But what do you do, really?"

"Oh, you're a theoretical one, aren't you? You're really asking a poor black machinist what's production management, right?"

"Oh, come off it, Mr. Jefferson. I'm just doing my job."

"I know. I'm sorry, but every once in a while some reporter comes in here and asks me all sorts of questions. You see, there aren't many black production managers around. Why, I even got my picture in *Ebony* once. You know ... the black success story. Most folks want to know how I relate to my people, or what it's like to be a black executive in a white man's world. You're funny. You ask me about my job." Mr. Jefferson leaned back in his chair. "You know, I think you paid me a nice compliment. You seem to think that I know something, not that I'm some sort of symbol."

"You do know plenty. That's why I'm here."

"All right, Mr. Faber, I'll tell you about production. You see, I never went to college, and I never took the right courses, but I learned a big secret a long time ago. Anybody can read the books, because they're color blind. Anybody can watch a man work, and anybody can ask him questions about what he's doing. Sometimes they even answer you. These young folks, they always think that going to school is going to be magic, but it isn't. You still have to read the books and the magazines, and even the newspapers, and you still have to ask questions. You still have to work hard, too."

"So, tell me about production. I noticed that you gave a paper at the last meeting of the American Security Association on protective devices and how they're made. You're right, you don't learn everything in school. Now, tell me."

"Production is really a transformation system. It takes inputs, which are things like labor, materials, and energy, and transforms them into usable outputs. That's the highest level of abstraction. To convert inputs to outputs, you have to perform all kinds of functions. You bend metal, stamp it, forge it, melt it, cast it, cut it with high speed lathes and milling machines, drill holes, combine elements using chemical knowledge, boil things, freeze them, change them from liquids to solids and back again, and on and on. You use all sorts of machines and all kinds of labor skills. Here at this plant, we are working largely with metals, with a bit of plastics tossed in. We buy steel and brass and aluminum of various sorts, then we bend and stamp and cut and drill, and when we're done making parts, we put them together. We buy a lot of items and make more. I suppose the fellows at the steel mill do pretty much the same thing, except that they start with scrap iron or ore and melt it and work with it to produce the bars and rods and plates that we buy from them."

"Fine. Now, how do you do this transformation process? I thought that I'd see some sort of endless assembly line, but it doesn't look that way at all, except in a few places."

"You're thinking of the usual system where thousands, or even millions of items are to be put together. We have a bit of that here. You saw our lock tumbler assembly line. We use the same tumblers in dozens of different locks, so our production runs are long enough to mass produce them. In this system, a flow of components comes to the assembly line, where everything gets put together."

"But most of your plant isn't like that."

"No, it isn't. First, consider some things we don't do here at all. You see, I can give you a lecture on this production system. Oil refineries and some chemical plants use continuous flow processes, where materials move along in pipes, tanks, and vats, and where they are combined automatically, often under heat or pressure, to make the final product. Plants of this sort are usually very capital intensive. That is, they use a lot of capital equipment per worker. We have about $85,000 in capital per person in our plant, but an oil refinery might have $500,000 or more per worker.

"Then there is batch processing, where things are mixed in batches to get a product. A steel mill often uses this process. Many bakeries do, too. It is not continuous. We don't have either of these processes here."

"So what do you have?"

"We do a lot of job lot work. This is where we make only a few items at once. You saw our safe division, where they were making just two big room safes for a bank. You don't mass produce two items."

"I would think that job lotting would be pretty expensive," Al commented.

"It's a lot more expensive than mass production, but how many room safes are we going to sell in a year? Maybe twenty to thirty, and we build them to order. With demand that small, there is no way anyone can mass produce them. But we do mass produce some of the components. That safe requires over 8,000 special rivets, and we crank them out on a machine in big quantities. We also make one-offs all the time. You saw that double doored safe being made?"

"I guess so. It didn't look like much to me."

"We're just getting under way. It is for the main office of a bond broker. He will be storing literally hundreds of millions of dollars' worth of bonds in it. It requires some very special security features, and it is being built as a unique unit. We do quite a bit of this special work. Of course, we try to mass produce such things as bolts and rivets that go into the final safe."

"Your marketing people sold that safe, right?"

"Yes, although my chief engineer was in on the discussion quite early. The customer knew what he wanted, but we had to make sure that we could do the job properly."

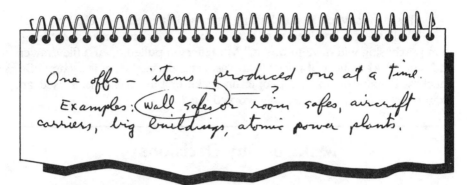

One offs — items produced one at a time.
Examples: (Wall safes or room safes), aircraft
carriers, big buildings, atomic power plants.

"So who is most important? You, or the people who sold the product?"

Mr. Jefferson toyed with his gold watch chain. "Which link of this chain is most important, Mr. Faber? If those marketing people could not sell the customer, we would have nothing to do. If our finance people could not find funds for working capital while we built the product, we could not proceed. If our transportation people could not figure out how to transport that 23-ton safe to an office building in Los Angeles and get it up ten stories, the job could not be done. If our insurance people could not arrange for liability insurance, we could not function. Each of us is a link in a complex chain, and if there is a weak link, the chain breaks."

"And there's no real point in having a strong link either, is there? I mean, if you make too good a safe, or if you have too much money, it really is unnecessary. Each link should be strong enough, but not too strong."

"The folks back east said you were a fast learner. I see they're right. I really like production. One of the hardest things I had to learn was not to be too good. Once, long ago, Mr. Suzuki nearly fired me. I was making a lock that was to be sold cheaply that would last a hundred years. It was a great lock really, but it was too good. It hurt me to cheapen it. Yet it made sense. We are always discovering that something we do is really too good and too expensive for the product. Why design a car frame to last fifty years, when the useful life of the vehicle is about ten years? It means extra cost for no good purpose."

"Mark Brandon, over at Ace Engineering, told me about gold plating," Al said, "But it's annoying when something doesn't hold up for the life of the product."

"That is poor design, poor materials, or shoddy construction, Mr. Faber. That we try to avoid. But how many times have you discarded some product that was still very good, except for some small component that didn't work?

"Lots of times."

"A weak link then. We try to avoid that."

"OK, what else do you do?"

"Have you heard of make or buy decisions?"

"Yes, Mark, who's in purchasing, discussed them extensively with me."

"Well, we get involved very heavily too. If we don't make something, then purchasing will have to buy it." Mr. Jefferson pulled open a file drawer and handed Al a sheet of paper in a plasticene sleeve. "Here is a copy of a checklist I made up for my people on make or buy decisions. I used an example of bolts that we actually worked out."

Make or Buy Decisions

The decision on whether to make a particular component needed in production or to buy it from an outside supplier is a critical one involving both purchasing and production. If the firm does the job itself, it must make the investments in machinery, plant, equipment, and often human skills needed to do the job. If it buys the item, someone else does all of this, but the price is higher. Which should be done?

Thus we may discover that certain bolts we need for our product cost five dollars per thousand, while the steel stock we could use to make our own costs the equivalent of two dollars per thousand. The value added by the bolts is thus three dollars per thousand. Now, should we buy them or make them? Here are some of the practical considerations we have to think about:

1. What new capital investments would be required, and how much per thousand would they cost? Note that the decision might be quite different if we already had some idle screw machines that could do this job and spare plant space instead of having to buy new machinery and build or expand the plant.

2. Do we have, or can we get, the kinds of skilled technical and managerial labor to do this job?

3. How many of these bolts will be required each week, month, or year? There may well be scale economies in producing them. If we use ten thousand a year, it might not pay to make them, but if we use ten million, it might be worth considering.

4. How consistent are use patterns? If we use these bolts steadily and regularly, then we can plan a steady, regular production subsystem for them. But if we use many this week, then none for five weeks, then many more the following week, we may have serious production and inventory problems. Carrying inventories can be very expensive.

5. How complex is the managerial pattern in this production? Few firms have an abundant supply of first-rate managers to supervise new activities. If this process is simple, straightforward, and uses little management, it may cost less than if it requires much skilled management.

6. What are the costs of raw materials? We are now going to buy steel stock, instead of finished bolts. Costs of bolts have to be compared to costs of less finished materials.

7. What are other production costs? Such new use items as electric power, lubricating oils, storage space, and whatever else may be needed have to be added in.

8. What are the estimated total costs of production? Given all of the above, it is possible to work out these costs. They have to be less than the three dollar per thousand margin to make the deal even worth considering, but even if this is so, we are not yet ready to make our decision.

9. What else could we do with our scarce resources that would pay off better? Here is a tricky concept known as opportunity cost. Suppose that we can make 10 percent on our money by making bolts. But in the process we use up most of our spare cash, managerial talent, or skilled labor. Another project proposed in accounting will pay off 20 percent. So, top management tells us to forget the bolts and keep on buying them.

Al glanced at the list and put it into his briefcase. His files of things that various people in RVA had given him were bulging, and he wondered if he would ever get time to look them all over.

"One thing that doesn't come through on that checklist is the cost of getting information," Mr. Jefferson said. "It took me a long time before I realized just how expensive it is to get good information. I always was reading books and not getting paid for it. But if I need a tight, well reasoned and factual analysis of whether to buy or make a special bolt, it costs Snap-Kwik a fortune to get it. We have to pay very highly trained people to get such information. Lots of times we have to rely more on intuition than analysis, just because we don't have the money, time, or talent to figure out the right answer."

"Is that partly what you're paid for? You really exercise judgement, don't you?"

"I suppose you're right. Young men can do the figuring, but older people have the experience. I just know sometimes what the answer is. When the numbers and facts are in, I'm usually right. I've been there before, sometime in the past thirty years. I suppose that it takes a while to develop that instinct."

"All right, what else, Mr. Jefferson?"

"Try procurement timing, which is when to obtain key components and raw materials. A big part of my job, which is done by subordinates, is to make sure that we have everything we need to produce the item. Remember, when we are making a certain type of lock with 124 parts, every-thing stops if we don't have one part."

"So once again you keep closely in touch with purchasing, right?"

"And also with my own production people. Remember, we make lots of parts, too. But remember also that if we stockpile too much inventory, the finance people will be after me hard."

Mr. Jefferson thought a moment. "This gets to another key problem, which is average inventory levels. I have to balance my need to avoid being out of stock with the high cost of carrying excess inventories. This is one place where I have lots of long discussions with finance people. They always want me to run on no inventory." He sighed. "But we have to consider possibilities of strikes in suppliers' plants, fires, lost shipments, occasional poor-quality components that have to be rejected, and transportation de-lays."

"I see that you tie in with just about everyone," Al commented. "You've mentioned marketing, purchasing, insurance, transportation, finance, and a few others."

"Why not? Everyone gets into the act. It's a team effort. But of course there is more. One thing I do worry a lot about is degree of production stabilization. This is the problem of trying to keep my production system moving at a steady and smooth pace. It is a lot cheaper to have nice long production runs. I can set up more complex machinery, and my people can learn to do the job right. But long production runs conflict with marketing's desire to have all kinds of products available. They want ten of this and forty of that, while I want to run off five hundred or maybe ten thousand of the item. If the run is short, the costs are high."

"So how do you resolve the issue?" Al asked.

"We argue a lot." Mr. Jefferson smiled. "But usually marketing wins. Remember that this is a market oriented company. However, once in a while I can point to big cost savings, and this means lower prices, and I win. It is a problem we never really resolve."

"It sounds like the marketing people do a better job if they can plan ahead far enough to keep you producing steadily," Al said.

"That is exactly what I tell them. The better they can forecast demand, the easier my job is. They are very good on some items. For a few types of locks, I can produce steadily all year long. Sales peak in October, for some reason that I don't understand, and they are over twice as high then as they are in January. But I produce a steady run at very low cost, and our surplus in January is neatly sold off later on. Of course, it costs something to hold inventories, but not as much as it would to be constantly stopping production and then starting it again."

"I keep seeing the same problem all over RVA," Al said. "Something costs money. So managers ask the same question, namely what are the benefits? If the benefits exceed the costs, then RVA goes ahead. If they don't, they stop."

"This is exactly what we are doing with this production stabilization problem. It costs something in inventory holding, but we save more in stable production. It costs a lot to do good market forecasting, but these costs are offset by better production planning. In the end, if the payoff is good, we proceed. And of course, part of my job is to point out to all concerned what the costs and gains are in production."

"Mr. Jefferson, one thing that surprised me in the plant was so much hand labor. I rather thought that modern factories had everything done by machines. But you have people doing all sorts of jobs by hand."

"You're looking at a classical economic problem, Mr. Faber. How do you choose your inputs, that is, how much labor, how much capital, how much energy, and how much space, or land? I could get machines to replace a lot of that labor you saw, but if I can hire a man or woman at six dollars an hour to do a job which only needs doing perhaps twenty days a year, why should I buy a $200,000 machine to do it? It makes no economic sense. But you may have noticed that on the mass production jobs, we have some pretty complex machines to do most of the work. There, it pays to automate."

"Some looked like robots to me. I keep reading that they are the coming thing."

"They may be, and the machine manufacturers keep coming up with better systems all the time. Now we have many computer controlled tools, and we will have more. The price keeps getting cheaper all the time, thanks to the chip revolution." ·

Al remembered some things Jack Tribble had said when he was in New Jersey. "Do you compute here, too?"

"Not only compute, Mr. Faber, but also use computers to run machines, do drawings, design parts, and much more. We may even have a robot soon, although the definition *robot* is still not settled. But this new machine, which is a painter, will be able to move around, figure out how to select colors, spray only certain areas, and much more."

"Driving some people out of work, I suppose?"

"Perhaps. But more properly, it will restructure work. Painting is often dirty, hard work, and it can even be harmful to your health. We have to move slowly with people, because we can't have the paint room too hot. But our new robot doesn't care, and the job will be speeded up enormously. Those painters will be out of a job, but the people who design and build that machine, plus those who will maintain it, are new. I doubt that there is any balance between the old losses and the new gains, but all the changes are not losses. One thing is sure: the people who have these new skills will do well, while the less educated will fall behind."

Mr. Jefferson shook his head sadly. "I often get invited to speak at ghetto high schools about careers. I try to tell those young people that the only way they can win is to get as much education of the right type as they can. But many do not believe me. They still think that they will have a good job on some assembly line at high pay, even if they never study. They are wrong. Those types of jobs are the ones robots will replace. But if you know how to service and maintain a robot, you will do very well."

Al was just glad that he had taken the trouble to get a good education. What would he be doing, if he had never finished college?

"Mr. Jefferson, I have read that capital costs are going up very fast."

"Right, and since 1974, energy costs have gone up over tenfold. One result, which lots of Americans still don't believe, is that often labor is the cheap input, relatively. Labor costs have gone up about 70 percent since 1970, but energy costs are way up, while capital costs have more than doubled. Many people seem to think that there is only one way to do a job. Actually, there can be many. You may have noticed that in those two special safes, we have to drill a few thousand rivet holes. I could get a special machine to drill them all at once, but it would cost more than the safes are worth. I could have a man with a hand drill laboriously drill out each one, but this would be so slow and costly that it wouldn't pay. What we do in this case is take the middle ground. The worker has a four hundred dollar, high speed, high powered drill, along with some fourteen dollar apiece drill bits. If you went to your hardware store, you might buy a good electric drill for twenty dollars, and a bit for a dollar or so. These are special."

"Why?"

"The bits are special high speed steel, and they can cut fast and long before you need to sharpen them. If our man has to stop and change bits, he isn't drilling holes, and time is money. The high powered drill also means that he can drill much faster, so more holes get drilled in the same time. Productivity is up. Incidentally, each hole costs about sixty cents to drill. If we bought the machine, they would cost over ten dollars each. If I used a slower electric drill and routine bits, it would be six dollars each."

"So you try to choose your inputs to get the best results."

"Exactly, Mr. Faber. Actually, we never get it quite right. I propose new capital items all the time, and only occasionally does the company approve my purchases. I suppose that capital is scarce, and only when I can make an ironclad case for big savings does my boss listen to me. Right now, if I don't show a thirty percent return on new capital after tax, I'm not likely to get the money."

"As I recall, this is because the other parts of RVA can make more than this," Al said.

"I suppose so, but it is frustrating to work with processes that aren't efficient. But then, I'm not running the company, just this small corner of it."

"You don't seem to have too many unskilled workers here."

"No, not in this business. The job lot and the special orders we handle mean that our people have to be pretty flexible. They have to know a lot. You might think drilling those holes in a straight line is easy, but go try it. It isn't. Besides, the man who does that for this week or so will be doing other kinds of work later on. Remember, we often produce just a few items, or even one. If we do this, people have to be able to read blueprints, plan their work, lay out patterns, and a lot more. We need highly skilled maintenance people to keep our equipment running, and so on. About the only unskilled people we have are a few assemblers and some clean up workers."

Mr. Jefferson stared at Al. "Mr. Faber, you will be writing about your study of RVA. Please, tell about this fact. Young people are so naive, and they think that they know everything. The unskilled labor jobs are disappearing fast, and if the young people, particularly the minorities and girls, don't learn the proper skills, they will never get ahead."

"I'll see what I can do, Mr. Jefferson." Al didn't know what he might be writing, but this might make a good article.

"Some plants still have production lines and work that requires unskilled workers, but we just can't use such people. Incidentally, skilled people are quite scarce in this area, and they are rather costly too. This gets back to our factor inputs. If we can figure out ways of using skilled people more productively, we go ahead." Mr. Jefferson thought for a moment. "Another problem that most people never think about is that some capital not only saves labor, but it saves capital, too."

"Now, how can that be?"

"Take the pocket calculator. That's capital, right?"

"Sure. You buy one and use it for years, if you don't lose it. Capital is a long lived asset, so I suppose that a calculator is capital."

"In the old days, we had a bunch of mechanical calculators, and they cost over a thousand dollars each. They were very slow, too. Now, we buy sophisticated electronic calculators for under fifty dollars each. Sometimes we buy a micro-computer for under a thousand dollars. Hence we save capital. But because they are so cheap and fast, we use them much more than we used the old mechanical calculators. So we save labor too."

"And sales of those things have skyrocketed for years. Micro-computers have only been around for a few years, and already sales are many billions of dollars per year. It figures."

"This point also illustrates the economies of scale in mass production. As calculator sales went up, it became cheaper and cheaper to produce each one. As they became cheaper, sales went up some more, production expanded rapidly, and it became still cheaper to produce them."

Al asked Mr. Jefferson to explain what economies of scale were, which took a while, so he took careful notes.

"Most computers and related equipment are like this, which is why they sell so well. You're saving both capital and labor if you buy them. Actually, they save energy too, which is a real gain these days. Those old mechanical calculators were a thousand times slower than a modern job, and they used five hundred times as much electricity." Mr. Jefferson shook his head. "I keep forgetting that we were using those things as recently as 1970. Times have really changed."

"So it comes down to technological change, doesn't it?"

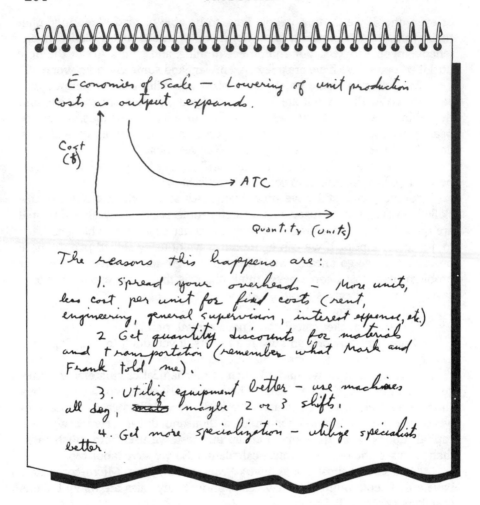

Economies of Scale — Lowering of unit production costs as output expands.

Cost ($)

ATC

Quantity (units)

The reasons this happens are:

1. Spread your overheads — More units, less cost per unit for fixed costs (rent, engineering, general supervision, interest expense, etc.)

2. Get quantity discounts for materials and transportation (remember what Mark and Frank told me).

3. Utilize equipment better — use machines all day, ~~scale~~ maybe 2 or 3 shifts.

4. Get more specialization — utilize specialists better.

"Certainly. We do a lot of our own technical work with our own products, in our R & D work. Remember, our locks and safes are really inputs for a job done by someone else. A bank buys a safe from us in order to accomplish other things, not because it loves safes. But we follow up on the R & D work of others who make machines and develop various technology which we use in our own production. I'm always talking to salesmen who have a new product that will save us money. Sometimes they're right, and often they are not. You have to watch those marketing types!"

"What do they try to sell you?"

"Everything from a complete new production system to a specialized machine to a new kind of floor cleaner. R & D comes in all sorts of sizes and shapes, and once again, we get back to inputs. If someone can show me how to save labor, capital, energy, or all three, I'm interested, if it doesn't cost too much. I even look at things designed to save space, and I sometimes buy. Last year, we installed a new storage system which allowed us to stack a product one layer higher than before."

"That doesn't sound too exciting to me."

"Oh? Well, one extra layer meant that we could store thirty percent more product in the same inventory space. We avoided building a $250,000 warehouse extension by doing this, and the new system only cost $30,000."

"So you put a bit more capital in to save some space and still more capital?"

"Right, Mr. Faber, you're getting the idea. You see, a big part of my job is to figure out how to put all those pieces together correctly. I never finish, because new ideas, products, and services keep popping up. I have to watch technical journals, talk to salesmen, and keep my eyes open all the time. Once in a while, I find something that makes our product better, or makes it cheaper to produce. I'm constantly shifting things around a bit to come up with a better system. My personnel are always encouraged to do the same, and lots of our men and women have developed something better. Who knows more about a problem than the one who's working on it all the time? Do you have a suggestion box?"

"Of a sort. It's more informal than that, but we spend a lot of time talking about how to improve things."

"You know, Mr. Jefferson, this part of RVA seems a lot more precise than many things I've seen. In marketing, if they have a forecast that is within five percent of being right, they're happy. In finance, a budget that's within two percent of being correct makes them feel good. But you're working with problems at a pretty accurate level, aren't you?"

"Sometimes if a part isn't correct to a ten thousandth of an inch, it is scrap. Yes, we do precision work. Our numbers have to be correct. You can't assemble a lock with 623 parts, when you only have 622 of them. If one part doesn't fit precisely, you can't put the lock together. We do a lot of computer work as a result, and we also spend a lot of time on tolerances."

"Meaning what?"

"Nothing is perfect. All things have some variation in them. And the closer you get to perfection, the more it costs. I can machine a safe bolt to plus or minus a thousandth of an inch for perhaps three dollars. To get the same bolt accurate to plus or minus a ten thousandth of an inch would cost us perhaps fifty dollars. Now, what do you need? If the accurate part is necessary for long product life, or a superior product, we might do it. But if we don't need such close tolerances, we can save lots of money by being sloppy."

Al remembered what Mark Brandon had said about purchasing bolts that were too strong. This sounded much the same, except that now RVA was making the item. "A thousandth of an inch doesn't sound sloppy to me," he said.

"It would to a machinist or engineer. Right now, we have a few safe mechanism parts that are machined to a hundred thousandth, and a very, very expensive job it is. But it is necessary to get the reliability we want for that safe. Customers are willing to pay for it, because it does lead to a superior product. You know, Mr. Faber, production is perhaps the most precise part of a company, but in one sense, it's the easiest. There is little slop, carelessness, or blustering through here. My machinists cannot claim a part fits when it doesn't. We can measure an item and if it doesn't meet specified tolerances, it is scrap, no matter what the maker says."

"You can't think up a good excuse when the thing just doesn't work," Al mused. "But if a marketing person misses a sale, maybe he can. If a lawyer loses a case, he might have a really good reason. I see what you mean. If things have to be precise, and if the people who make them are judged by this precision, then typically things do fit, and the product does work."

"And that's what makes this job fun for me. I like to be judged by what I do, and I always have. As a black man, it was easy to judge me because I was black, not because of what I could do. But when I was young, I discovered that if I machined parts correctly, then no one really cared what color I was. It didn't matter. In this job, being able to do the job right is what counts. Companies that forget this do not last very long."

"OK, Mr. Jefferson, what else do you do?"

"I suppose that I worry a lot about basic production processes. Should I cast a part, stamp it, or make it out of wire? Each process has a different labor/capital ratio, and each uses different materials. In something as complicated as a good lock or wall safe, there are lots of these choices to make."

"And that gets back to factor inputs, too, doesn't it?" Al asked. "I mean, if you make a part out of wire, then you must use different mixes of capital and labor."

"We do, and this kind of choice does get back to capital and worker prices. Sometimes we look for a new process because the old one has gone up in cost so far. Last year stainless steel prices went up fast, so we decided to shift our production a bit and use some new plastic parts in place of some stainless ones. The result was that we started using different machines, less labor, and a quite different kind of labor."

"And to do this seemingly simple thing, I suppose that you had to talk to people in purchasing, finance, production, and marketing?" By now, Al was beginning to see that everything depended on everything else.

Mr. Jefferson smiled. "Not to mention transportation, law, and insurance. Sure, we can't make major decisions without consulting with everybody."

Al thought for a moment. "Mr. Jefferson, just who is your boss? I mean, in this simple case, any one of those other departments could have said no, and you would have stayed with stainless steel. It sounds like you have five or six bosses, not just one."

"Maybe I do. The textbooks say that there is a chain of command, and that every person has only one boss. This is technically correct. I report to Mr. Suzuki. But when you're considering some technical point, like that stainless steel problem, you necessarily consult with all sorts of experts. They really have a sort of veto power. If the marketing people said that stainless was absolutely necessary for successful sales, we would have taken their advice. But the marketing director was not my boss. If the finance person had said that the project was too costly, or that funds were unavailable, we would have taken her advice. Every expert takes part, but in the end, only one boss tells me what to do."

"Still, it sounds like a committee to me. But I guess that it's the only way to get everyone who matters in on the act."

"This is a complex product in a complex company. You can't fly as much by the seat of your pants any more. Such a policy would only lead to disaster."

"Another thing I've noticed here is that your plant is so visible. Most of RVA seems to happen way off in some office or another. It's hard to get excited about a planning problem, which is just on a piece of paper. But your machines and products are *here*."

Mr. Jefferson laughed. "You've hit on a problem which bothers lots of people in poorer countries, where all this machinery and factories aren't yet in place. I'm interested in African development, and every so often some Africans visit our plant. They are very impressed, and often they want to build a replica back home. I try to explain to them all our relationships with marketing, finance, and all the rest, but all they can see are those beautiful machines in action, generating wealth. Production is visible, and it's part of business that everyone thinks about who hasn't been through the total development process. But the production process is just one link in the chain, although the most visible one. If a country just builds plants, it doesn't get very far."

"Lots of people I know right here think the same way," Al said, "and lots of them think that production is easy."

"Strangely enough, it *is* easy, Mr. Faber. You have to have highly skilled people, and you have to have plants and equipment. But the very precision of production makes it easier to do than any other business function. It is tough to figure out what a new market might be, or what the effects of a new law are. Marketers and lawyers work with much uncertainty. But I know that part C has to fit into part D. My problem is not uncertain. It just requires high levels of skill to do. If I can get those skills and machines, everything falls in place. If we make a mistake, we know about it right away. Things won't go together, and we have to correct our errors. Our feedback loops are very accurate and very precise."

"So you have PARF loops too?"

"Of course. The difference is that they are so carefully planned and the tolerances are so precise. The really hard part is trying to figure out what to do with the product once you produce it, or worse, trying to figure out what to produce in the first place."

It was time to go, and Mr. Jefferson walked with Al to the front door. "Say, Mr. Jefferson, what you said wasn't true, about your being able to earn as much as anyone if you did precise work. You told me that you were underpaid for years, working for Mr. Suzuki. How come, if your work was so good?"

Mr. Jefferson smiled sadly. "A wise old man once told me that something is always better than nothing. While lots of black folk were unskilled laborers, or unemployed, I always earned good money. Not as much as I should have, but pretty good. I was able to do this because I could prove myself, every day. I had something, while lots of people had nothing."

"What do you think of Mr. Suzuki, really, Mr. Jefferson?"

He sighed. "I've worked for him for almost thirty years. Doesn't that tell you?"

"Not really."

"He's a smart man."

"Sure."

"He's a rich man, too."

"Sure, and you helped make him rich."

"I respect him, I guess. He gave me a chance when no one else would."

"And he underpaid you for it, too. He took advantage of you."

Mr. Jefferson patted Al on the back. "You reporters! What do you want me to say? There's no black or white in a man, Al. Sometimes, in the same man, you find lots of good, and lots of evil. You people want to find something nice and clear cut, like a good bribery case, or a homicide. Then everything is clear and black and white. The guys in the white hats win, or something. The world's not like that. Mr. Suzuki is a fine man, a brilliant man, a person that I've tried to work hard and well for for a long time. Sure, he gave me the business. But he gave me a chance, too. I hate him, respect him, admire him ... and in the end, I may even love him. But I'm damned if I know why."

Which was, Al reflected as he went to pick up his car, about what he was beginning to think about RVA. It was all kinds of things, good, bad, and indifferent, and it was pretty hard to figure out just what he felt about it at any given time.

DISCUSSION QUESTIONS

1. Consider the class you are taking in business as a production subsystem (which it is). Answer the following questions about it.

How is the one class linked up with the total production subsystem in the business school? In the college or university? What feedback loops are around to tell managers and administrators what to do?

What is the internal feedback loop within the class between you and the rest of the subsystem? How are you told how well you are doing?

What kinds of labor are used for production of this educational service by your school?

What kinds of capital equipment are used by your school to get this production job done?

Do you feel that the capital/labor mix in the class is correct in economic terms? Why or why not?

Professors are supposed to control their grades totally. Grades, of course, are a major feedback device to show how students are progressing. Do you think that this production subsystem would be untouched by higher management if everyone in the class got F's? If they all got A's? Why?

2. Find a food service operation run by your university that you may use (a cafeteria, dormitory eating place, etc.), and run through all the questions of question 1, except the last. What differences do you see here as compared to a class? What accounts for the difference?

3. Now go over to the library and answer all the questions posed in question 1, except the last. What is the difference here? What is the output of a college library? What key production PARF loops do you suppose the library has to figure out to determine whether it is doing its job efficiently?

4. One university with extensive dormitories and over 5,000 students living on campus contracts out all its food services to a private contractor. In effect, it has decided to buy this service from an outside supplier. A similar school in another state operates all of its own food services. This activity is one of the largest on campus. In both places, students are always complaining about the lousy food.

Analyze this make or buy decision. Indicate what key factors should be considered to make this choice. Why do you suppose that one school would make, while the other would buy? What are the key market linkages here?

Why do you suppose that the customers in both cases are always complaining? What might be done in either case to make a better market linkage than now apparently exists?

5. If possible, visit the reproduction or printing center of your school or college. This is the place where memos are printed or copied, exams prepared, and various data reproduced. In some places this is a central office; in other places various smaller units may operate around the campus. After seeing what goes on in this operation, answer these questions:

How is this center linked up to customers? Is it doing a good job in satisfying them?

What are the production processes used? Describe briefly the physical transformations that are taking place.

What kinds of financial linkages does this reproduction center have with the finance function? Who makes budgets? Who approves them?

What are the transportation linkages? Who or what carries the stuff to and from the users? Do you think that this is a good system?

How is the procurement function handled here? Who buys supplies and equipment? Who approves such purchases? Who justifies various items?

Such operations often have budget overruns. What happens in such a case? Who has authority to approve excess expenditures? Is this a good system? Why?

6. A visitor from a relatively poor and underdeveloped country is visiting you. His country has recently discovered some oil, so it now has lots of ready cash and is ready to industrialize. After visiting the United States, this person is convinced that all his country needs to do is to buy some plants and begin production. Within a few years the country will be as rich as the United States. The first plant he thinks worth buying is a cement plant.

Explain to this visitor what else he might need besides physical capital and equipment before he can operate a cement plant successfully in his country, where literacy rates are about twenty percent. What other kinds of business and managerial functions might be useful to know about and link up with the physical plant?

7. Mr. Jefferson used lots of skilled labor instead of machines for many of his production processes. Why didn't he replace all of this labor with machines, since everyone knows that machines could easily do all of this work?

8. What is gold plating? How can a company avoid it?

9. Why do you think that the marketing people win most of the arguments with Mr. Jefferson about the length of production runs? Isn't production more important than marketing?

10. Mr. Jefferson has to fight hard for his budget, and often he doesn't get the money he wants. Why? Is RVA being short-sighted in not giving their production people the capital equipment they need?

11. What is a tolerance limit?

14

PERSONNEL

Jim Garland, Assistant to Michael McComb, Vice President for Labor and External Relations at RVA, chatted easily with Al for a while before they got down to business. Al wondered about these assistant-to's that he kept meeting around RVA headquarters. They seemed to be all rather the same ... very bright, well educated, usually with law or M.B.A. degrees, and extremely efficient. Clearly they were staff, since their bosses had the line authority. Al wondered if being an assistant-to was the way to the top. These people were usually rather young, too. Jim was in his early thirties. Maybe this was the way the top people sorted out potential crown princes and princesses.

Jim's office wasn't quite as imposing as the vice presidents had, but it was more than adequate. And it was way up on the 30th floor, which, in the RVA pecking order, seemed to suggest someone close to the top. Jim himself was an engaging man, and he certainly didn't look haggard or harassed. But Al did pick up from time to time an offbeat note. Something was bothering Jim a bit. Well, perhaps he could explore that later.

"You know, Al, we have over 65,000 employees at RVA. Most of the routine stuff regarding personnel is handled at the plant or local office level, by personnel people. Here at headquarters, we worry about a few key things, such as major labor negotiations. But I suppose that the most important thing we do is worry a lot about personnel policy and planning. It may sound trite, but it's true that people are a company's most important asset. RVA needs literally thousands of hard working, highly skilled people. Our problem is to make sure that we have them, and that we continue to get them."

"So what really are the key personnel issues?" Al asked. "If you could sum up the big picture, what would it be?"

"Just three things. First, we have the problem of motivation. The difference between the well motivated employee and someone who doesn't care is profound. It's not uncommon to find that productivity goes up two or three hundred percent, when you find the right motivation keys."

"Why not just pay people more?"

"Money's important, but it's not the only thing, particularly with highly skilled people. Consider yourself. Are you working just for money?"

"I like my work."

"Yes, but even if I doubled your salary, would you do things that bored you, or that you felt weren't proper?"

"Well, probably not."

"How's your status over at *Newsworld*?"

"Oh, up and down." Al thought for a while. "I think I see what you're driving at. I have a thousand-dollar electric typewriter and a good secretarial staff to help me out. Other guys don't."

"Exactly. Now, why do you have these perquisites?"

"Well, they come with the job. I mean, once you get a certain reputation, it's a way to reward you."

"Suppose they took away your nice typewriter and your good staff?"

"I'd be pretty mad, I guess."

"And suppose, Al, that they raised your pay at the same time. Would that make up for losing the other things?"

"Not really. OK, you've made your point. I get some things that tell the world and my co-workers that I'm somebody. I suppose that RVA does the same."

"Sure, and it's a part of the motivational package. You've seen the big offices, and you've heard of the expense accounts and other perks. These things matter to most people. You may not have seen the special lab equipment we buy for key scientists, or the medical facilities we have for our in-house nurses in the plants. Professionals like such perks. They tell the world that you're important, and sometimes these things work better than money for motivation. But some of our people would just as soon take the money and run. It depends on who it is, and how that person thinks. You don't just plug in any old motivation and hope it works."

"OK, Jim, what's the second thing?"

"Well, there's the question of leadership. Again, it may sound trite, but we really need leaders, lots of them, all over the company. Just doing what you did yesterday doesn't cut it these days. We need men with vision. You

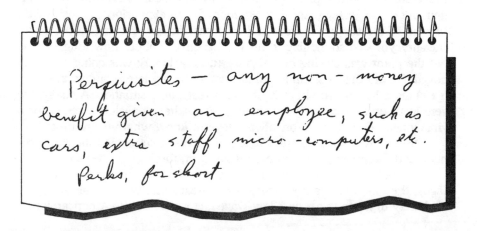

Perquisites — any non-money benefit given an employee, such as cars, extra staff, micro-computers, etc. Perks, for short

can't really go out and hire leaders, as you can hire assembly line operators, but you can try to create conditions where people with leadership ability can flourish."

"That sounds right," Al said, "although for the life of me, I can't imagine how a creative, leader type person could flourish under all the rules you have."

"How does a creative guy like you flourish at *Newsworld* under the rules *you* have?"

Al grinned. "With great difficulty, but I manage. I guess your people can be pretty creative, too."

"Some can, but we keep trying to create the proper balance between discipline and creativity and leadership. It isn't easy, I can tell you. Remember, one thing any good person can do any time is quit. Lots of companies have lost their best people because they couldn't get this balance right. After a while, those companies stagnate."

"So making room for creativity and leadership within the company structure is number two. What's number three?"

"You could call it communication," Jim said. "People like to know what's going on. We can never talk individually to 65,000 people, and the rumors and distortions about what's actually going on are amazing. Just last week, someone got the idea that we were going to close down one of our New Jersey plants. The rumor spread through our grapevine like wildfire, first from people in the plant, and later from reporters and others outside the company. The productivity loss was terrific, and we even got calls from the governor's office asking us what we were doing in abandoning New Jersey and putting 800 people out of work."

"I heard that rumor, too, over at *Newsworld*. I was going to ask you about it. What actually happened?"

"We sent in some equipment surveyors to figure out how to remove some special machine tools we weren't using at the plant. We're going to ship them to another plant in another division near Cleveland. We want them out of the Jersey plant to make room for an expansion, for gosh sakes. But one of the surveying crew had a brother-in-law working in the plant. The surveyor said something to his brother-in-law about how tough it was that the plant was closing down, since the machinery was going to be removed. He did this at a family Sunday gathering. By late Monday, everyone in Hoboken had heard about it. It was a real panic situation. Actually, we were in trouble, because we wanted to keep the expansion a secret for a while longer. Our competitors always love to know what we are up to."

"I can see your problem. Panicky workers, a concerned local government, and I suppose that the union was upset, too."

"Upset? They were furious! By the time I sat down and talked to Ed Bagby, the union local's president, he had heard that we were shipping the machinery to Japan to set up a low-wage factory to cut into American jobs."

"Wages in Japan aren't exactly low."

"You know that, and I know that, but Ed Bagby didn't know it. I talked to him for hours before be began to see that we really weren't doing anything that would hurt his people. Actually, we plan to hire about 200 more workers over there shortly. You see, Al, this was a communications failure. We should have had enough sense to realize that when you send a crew of outsiders into a plant to figure out how to take out machinery, someone is likely to get very curious and very nervous. We made a mistake there."

"I've run into a few communications failures myself at *Newsworld*," Al said. "You'd think that a magazine would know something about communications, but every once in a while some rumor starts that sounds terrible. Then everyone panics."

"What we try to do is to let people know as soon as possible what's going on. Obviously you can't go around blabbing top company secrets, say about a new product line, or a revolutionary new development in manufacturing. But we can post stuff on bulletin boards, and we can and do have a company magazine, and we do have lots of local plant papers. We can pass on the word to foremen and supervisors to tell their people. We can always do a better job than we've been doing, but I suppose that it's impossible to do the job perfectly."

Jim leaned back in his chair and thought a moment. "Good communications also involve teaching your subordinates to do what they are supposed to do without confusion. It involves letting people know what's going on on the job. It involves working well with your peers in other fields, so that those guys in marketing and finance know what you're up to in pro-

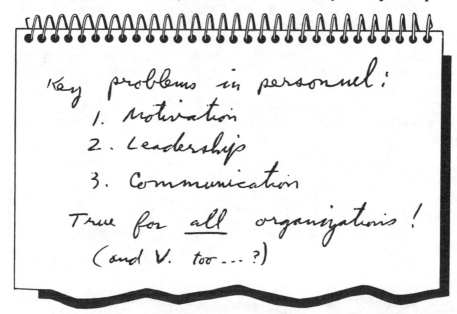

Key problems in personnel:
1. Motivation
2. Leadership
3. Communication
True for _all_ organizations!
(and V. too ... ?)

duction. In short, it involves keeping everyone well informed, so that the work doesn't get all fouled up."

"People are pretty complicated, and I suppose you're right. But you do handle people. What else do you do?"

"We have to plan our whole employment function, Al. As I said, the actual hiring is done by divisions and plants, but we're responsible for the big picture. For example, we have to do all of RVA's manpower planning and recruiting."

"How do you do that?"

"The various divisions have long range plans for their future activities. We ask them to state their expected manpower needs based on their expansion plans. Or, if they are shifting production, or going into new fields, we need to know what people they will be needing. In a few divisions, we actually are cutting back. In such cases we can usually transfer people to other divisions, or see if they might want early retirement. But when we get the division reports about manpower needs, we have to do two things: first, figure out if we will have people ready internally, when they're needed."

"You mean finding younger people who can be promoted?"

"Right. Often we need to think about extra training or experience for them, too. Then, second, we figure out who we might be hiring, and at what skill levels. Skilled and experienced manpower is pretty hard to find, and we have to go and recruit them."

"That should be personpower, shouldn't it?"

"You're so right, Al. Actually, one of the really critical things about our function these days is affirmative action programs. I've had to lay out a ten year plan for us and for government, showing exactly what we're doing to make sure that females and minorities not only will get hired in fair numbers, but also will get promoted if they're good. This company is pretty WASPish right now, and it's run mostly by men, particularly at the top. You probably know that next to Mrs. Cool, who's on the board of directors, and Mrs.

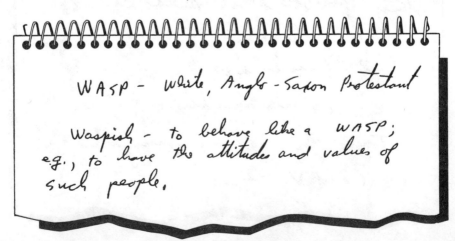

WASP - White, Anglo-Saxon Protestant

Waspish - to behave like a WASP; e.g., to have the attitudes and values of such people.

Bryant, who's our corporate secretary, your friend Vicki is the highest ranking woman in all of RVA."

"That sort of sets her up for some fast promotions, doesn't it?" Al knew that Vicki was already making half again as much as he was, and that she had just received a twenty percent raise.

"Maybe, if she's very good. We have quite a few younger women who look good, both as managers and as high level technicians and professionals. We have quite a few good minority people too."

Al thought about Joe Chapman, who probably was born at the wrong time, in the wrong place, and into the wrong sex. "Trying to change makes it tough on some of the WASPs, doesn't it? I mean, if the women and the minorities get the good jobs, then those guys won't."

"Maybe." Jim looked troubled. "You know, one of the real problems we have in RVA is that we are so confounded efficient."

"Why is efficiency a problem?"

"We're growing in real terms at about eight percent per year—more in money, given inflation—but I'm talking about actual real production increases, without taking account of inflation. We get an average productivity gain per person in RVA of about nine percent per year. We have an annual turnover rate of about six percent per year. Now, put all those numbers together. To get nine percent real gain, we would actually need fewer employees than we now have, except that we do have turnover. People die, retire, and quit. But it nets out to a five percent gain in employment. That's about 3,250 people a year we need to hire, and almost half of those are in other countries. So we're planning on hiring about 1,800 Americans this coming year. And that's for all of RVA's divisions in the U.S."

"I begin to see. How can you get, say ten percent minorities, which would be about 6,500, and half women, say 32,500, into a company that's 90 percent WASP?"

"You can't. That's one of my problems. Al, you get into all sorts of ethical problems here. We can't just fire a group of men who have worked for us well for over twenty years. They have some rights, too. But we got into just that problem when we had to cut back one of our work forces recently. We had a seniority agreement with the union, and it turned out that when we cut back, everyone with less than five years' seniority got laid off. That included virtually all the women and minority workers. So they sued us. In this case, the union and we are in the same camp."

"So what's going to happen?"

"We're not sure. The courts will tell us. A few decisions have been made, but so far, nothing totally conclusive." Jim groaned. "What a mess!"

"We also have a selection and placement problem to worry about," Jim went on, "and a part of it is the sort of thing we've already discussed. But there's more. We try to figure out what kinds of personpower we are going to need, and then we try to find out where it is."

"Which explains, I guess, why Vicki got her job here, after getting an

M.B.A. degree. Someone, maybe you, figured out that people with M.B.A.'s can make good managers."

Jim smiled. "It wasn't me, because RVA had figured that out long before I came on board, but sure, and we do the same for engineers, welders, biochemists, and a thousand job specialties. We spend quite a bit of time trying to figure out where good people are, and then we spend lots of money trying to recruit them. This leads to some other things we do, including employee testing."

"Even when you find the good people, you still test them?"

"That's one way we find out if they're good. Suppose that we need a highly skilled welder for one of our plants, or a secretary. It makes sense to have tests for prospects to see if they can do what they say. If that welder says he's good, it's easy enough to find out, and you wouldn't believe what people will say they can do, if it leads to a good job."

"Oh, I believe it," Al said. "A few weeks back, we were approached by a fellow who claimed to have graduated from Harvard and worked for a number of very good magazines. The whole record was phony. He made it all up."

"I'm glad someone else has those problems," Jim said. "We run into phony credentials all the time. But we also test for aptitudes. We don't want a person who hates math and can't add in a job where those abilities are important. But that person may have good verbal and writing skills, and we can use him or her in a place where he or she will be productive."

"How do you know that your tests are any good?" Al asked. "I've been taking tests all my life, and I'm never sure what they prove."

"That can be a real problem. We spend a lot of time and money validating tests. You're right. We don't want to get a test result that shows a person is poor at math, and then find out later that the test was invalid, and the person really is misplaced. There is a very big and complex literature on test validation, and a personnel professional has to know a lot about this."

Al sighed. This was just one more place where expertise he had never heard of turned out to be important. He wondered how any company could keep track of all of its experts.

"Jim, you mentioned that your average productivity rate gain was nine percent a year. I recall that the national average is about three percent, and even that has been falling since the early seventies. How come you're so good?"

"Probably because we have great people. We have modern machines too, which helps. And we have managers who know how to put the pieces together properly. You'll find that most fast growing, highly successful corporations are quite a bit above the national average on productivity. That's why they're good companies." Jim thought for a moment. "Actually, American productivity gains have been about one percent per year since 1971. That's one main reason why we've been having so many economic and social problems. If you don't grow, you have to split the fixed pie, which means if you win, I lose. We can fight a lot. But if we get three percent per year productivity gains, we can all have more pie, which is a lot easier to arrange."

"I can see that." Al said. "When *Newsworld* makes a profit, we get good bonuses. When we have a bad year, well, tough. No one can get what isn't there."

"Under this general heading of employment functions, I'd add counseling and personnel records and research. Most of this work is done in the divisions, but we work with some of it here. For example, we've been trying to figure out where our most successful people came from. In effect, we've been making profiles of such people. What schools they went to, what kinds of attitudes they have, what sorts of family lives they had, and have, and so on. If we can figure out who's been successful, maybe we can find more good people like them."

"There's a bit of a conflict here, isn't there? I mean, if your past successes were all WASPs from the Ivy League universities, and if you have to hire minorities and women from now on, won't the new profiles be different?"

"How about a black fellow from an Ivy League school? Or maybe women with educations and backgrounds similar to those of our successful men? Your Vicki is like that. She came out of a family background that suggests good success (in men) as executives. She has an M.B.A. from a good school, Indiana. Did you know that their B-school is in the top ten in M.B.A. programs in the U.S., out of over 450? Its undergraduate program is even better, about third out of over a thousand programs. And maybe Vicki even has the kind of highly competitive, aggressive personality that makes for executive success."

Al didn't know that Indiana was that good, but with characters like Dr. Farmer there, it certainly was, ah, unusual. He recalled a few times when Vicki was not too aggressive, but he was, and a few when she wasn't too competitive. "Well, maybe you're right."

Jim shrugged. "What else is there? We have to try to find the best people we can, and doing research on various personnel types is one way to get insight into the problem."

"How about counseling? What do you do there?"

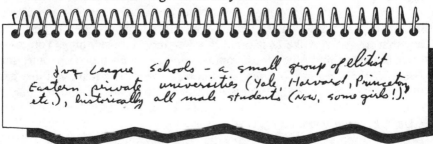

Ivy League schools - a small group of elitist Eastern private universities (Yale, Harvard, Princeton, etc.), historically all male students (now, some girls!).

"Lots of things, although again most of the actual work is done in the field. But as one example, we have a drug and alcohol unit working right here in this building, and we have a psychologist who works full time on it."

"So you have alcoholics and addicts, even here?"

"Sure. This is a tough, competitive life, and every so often a person goes over the edge. Often this is a first rate person. We could take the easy way out and fire him, but it makes more sense, and I think that I could justify it in dollars, to try to rehabilitate instead. We even do some family counseling. If a man is all messed up with a divorce, or wild kids, or some other family problem that's too much for him, it can affect his job performance."

"I can see that, but do you have to justify it in dollars? I mean, if you're partially responsible for screwing up a guy's life, don't you owe him something?"

"Maybe, Al, but it's easier to sell the board of directors on it if we can justify it in terms of benefits exceeding costs." Jim looked troubled. "It's funny, but I came to RVA in personnel about ten years ago. I had a degree in psychology myself, and I got it because I liked the idea of working with and helping people. In the old days, and it wasn't too long ago, personnel was like that. You did clerical work, kept payroll records, and every once in a while tried to help someone out." Jim sighed. "Now, you notice that I work for a key vice president. We handle legal problems, and everyone is mad at us for something. We get sued all the time for discrimination or reverse discrimination. I find myself being a hard-nosed cost accountant about some poor person's problem with alcohol or drugs. I also find myself becoming a computer expert, because we need so much data that you wouldn't believe it, both for our own internal purposes, and for our government reporting. I play with paper all the time, and some days I never even talk to anybody, except a few close colleagues. In the old days, no one much cared what happened in personnel, as long as we got the checks out on time and found some decent new people. But now we're almost in the driver's seat."

"It sounds like your job got away from you, Jim." Lots of people, Al thought, discovered, sometimes too late, that what they thought a job would be wasn't quite what it was. Jim obviously didn't like what had happened to him.

"Yeah, it did. I was happy enough messing around as personnel director for one of our plants. Then I get here, which is a big promotion, and I find out that my boss, Mike McComb, is a key man in everything. You know, there is a little thing which most young people, even most older people, don't realize. To win big in this world, you don't have to be a hero, you just have to be a bit better than the next guy. Our managers are good. They may be one percent better than our competitors' managers. But that one percent edge, taken ten years along, leads to a widening gap in our favor. Young people see some real hero, a superstar, and they think that because they're not like that, they can't win. But Al, did you ever see a 100 meter Olympic race?"

"Sure."

"Who came in fourth?"

"Who cares?"

"Exactly. The guy who came in third gets up on the winner's stand with the first and second place fellows, and they hang a bronze medal on him. Five hundred million people all over the world watch him on TV. But the poor fellow who came in fourth gets nothing. Yet he missed third by perhaps an inch. You see what I mean? Just get in there an inch or two ahead of the next person, and you win. Maybe you don't win big, like getting first place, but third place sure beats fourth and obscurity."

"Jim, what's this got to do with personnel?"

"Don't you see? That's exactly what we're trying to do. We can't expect to get the grand champion every time, but what we try to do is put together a team that can be just a bit better than the competition. They may be so close at first that you can't tell the difference, but after a while, our people begin to pull away. I didn't realize this when I started. I didn't want to pick superior people, I just wanted to help the average guy. And then all these government rules and regulations come in, and suddenly I had to be a lawyer too. I didn't want to be a lawyer!"

"So the game isn't what you thought it was."

Jim nodded. "It was when I started, and I guess that in some places it still is. But I'm not doing what I thought I would be, and I guess that it bothers me."

I'm not sure I am either, Jim," Al said, "but so far it hasn't bothered me too much."

"We do some other things here that are pretty important," Jim said. "Take training and development. It's not enough just to find good people. You have to make them better. Remember that things change pretty fast, like my job. We break it down into three parts: worker training, management development, and professional development."

"Where do you fit in, Jim?"

"I'm a hybrid, between management and professional. But for example, I just got back from a week-long seminar on the legal aspects of modern personnel work. This was a professional conference, and the participants were all personnel specialists. What we did was to get up to date on the various government rules and laws governing discrimination. We listened to lawyers, labor relations experts, a representative of a minority group, two government people who enforce the rules, and so on. The idea was to train us so that we wouldn't get our companies into serious legal problems." Jim thought for a moment. "You know, none of this material was taught when I was in college, over ten years ago. It cost the company over two thousand dollars to send me to the conference, but they obviously felt that it paid."

"How about the management part?"

"Last year I went to a conference on office management. I have eight people under me here, and I never took a management course in my life. My boss figured that it would do me some good to find out how professional managers manage things."

"Did it?"

"I think so. At least I got my own turnover rate down. And Al, one of the nicest parts of going to these conferences is talking to professionals from other companies who are there. I find that other people have the same problems I do, and sometimes they have figured out good solutions."

"Same here. I learn more from talking to other journalists than from anything else I do."

"The conference also had lots of material on modern computer based information systems that's proved very useful to me. RVA spends millions of dollars a year on such training. And we spend millions more on worker training. Remember, our technology changes all the time, and skilled, and even unskilled workers have to learn new stuff too. Right now, one of our electronics plants is shifting production to totally integrated circuitry, from our old transistor technology. We've had to run four different training programs for various workers to teach them their new jobs, or how their old ones will be modified."

"I would think that schools and vocational colleges could teach those courses," Al said.

"They can do a lot with basics, but when it comes to specific company activities, we have to do it ourselves. For example, most of the people involved in this electronics training have been trained in the basics at various schools. We have everything from specialist technicians who completed vocational courses in basic electronics repair up to electronic engineers, who completed tough four-year engineering degrees. But our circuitry is special and unique for us, as are the special machines we use, the assembly techniques, and lots more. If the job is to be done right, we have to do it ourselves. It's easier, though, when our personnel are well trained in fundamentals."

"So you run training programs. It sounds almost like a school."

"A lot of what we do is like school, Al. Some people think that they graduate and stop learning. In a fast moving company like RVA they usually have barely begun to learn, and they'll keep on learning all their working lives."

Jim leaned back in his plush chair. "But we do a lot of other things in personnel. Consider wages and salaries. We have to structure our wage and salary policies so that they are fair, and so that they retain the people we want."

"That sounds like a nice can of worms," Al said. "I've been here a few months, and already I've heard plenty of griping about how unfair your salary policies are. Younger people get too much, until you talk to a younger person, who claims that he or she gets too little. Supervisors gripe that they get less than some of the people who work for them, and the secretaries in the legal department complain that they make less than the secretaries in the accounting department."

"If you've heard it after a short time, just think how much we hear it! Sure, salaries are always fouled up, because by the time we figure out what is equitable, something happens to mess up the works."

"What's so difficult about it? I mean, can't you just set salaries at some sensible levels and go home?"

"We try, but consider this: this year we need about twenty really top level engineers, in mechanical and electronic fields. OK, so say we're paying last year's engineering graduates $22,000 per year. They started at about $20,000, and if they're any good, they've already got a nice raise. So we plan to hire some new people. But there's a shortage of new engineers, so the market has pushed the price up. To hire good people this year, right out of college, we have to pay $23,000 to $25,000 per year. We haven't done anything, but now we have an inequality. People who have been doing a good job for a year are getting less money than brand new, untested people. Naturally, they're mad."

"So, raise their salaries."

"Sure, and where do we find the millions of dollars we would need to do this? We'd have to restructure budgets, raise prices, and do all sorts of nasty things. What we try to do is to pay higher salaries to the people we really want to keep and raise the others a bit. If they get mad and leave, perhaps it won't be so tough. But we hope that they don't."

"But you still have to pay more, and if you really do get a lot of people leaving, you'll pay more still."

"Of course. But in the meantime, we have inequities. We get into another one with older people who have been around for ten or fifteen years. They may have started at a low salary, which was pretty good at the time, and they have gotten raises. But most of our people aren't superstars. They're good, solid men and women, but not great. So they really don't justify fast merit boosts. Then we find out that they're making perhaps $19,000 a year now, while those young people are making more. But in this case, we just can't raise their salaries too much, since we can't justify it. The result is that the pay differentials get badly squeezed. Even if the older workers are ahead of the younger, it is by very little."

"So why don't these people quit?"

"Often they can't do any better than we're paying them, and sometimes they can only do worse. So they stay, but they're plenty mad about it."

Jim sighed. "This is really a tough part of my job. I like people, remember? Now I find that 90 percent of all the RVA personnel dislike me intensely because in some way I'm unfair. And there's not much I can do about it."

"*You* could quit."

Jim laughed bitterly. "I'm one of those people who now holds the best paying job he can get. Companies pay something for seniority and experience, and I've been here ten years. My wife is pregnant, my oldest child needs some very expensive dental work, and I have to help support my widowed mother. It sounds like soap opera, doesn't it? But unfortunately it happens to be true. I can get plenty of jobs, but a lot of the knowledge I have, and get paid for, is useless to anyone but RVA. I'm pretty locked in. Are you?"

Al thought about that. "I don't know. I've been with *Newsworld* for four years now, and the pay is pretty good. The assignments are great, too, and so are the perks. I haven't thought of a job change recently. Maybe it's because journalism jobs are very, very tough to get. I don't even know if I could get a new one, let alone one as good as I now have."

"And you're not married, so you don't have a family to worry about. But your time will come, Al."

"Maybe." Al began to see why Jim was a bit unhappy. His world hadn't quite worked out the way he thought it might, and he felt trapped. Well, so did lots of other people.

"We work a lot on wage administration too. Like most companies, we have two kinds of workers—those on salary, usually paid by the month, and those who get paid wages by the hour. The wage people mostly belong to unions, so when we start talking wages, we usually end up in a bargaining session."

"Are wage problems as messy as salary problems?"

"They're not quite as bad, but we do have lots of differential problems. Sometimes even the union has troubles. One thing we're always disagreeing about is the differential between skilled and unskilled people. Some of our unions want this differential to be pretty small, and we usually want it big."

"Why? Big differentials could cost you money."

Jim nodded. "Sure, but they also could help us get the very best skilled people. For example, in one of our plants we need about twenty skilled tool and die workers. We have 300 semiskilled or unskilled workers in that plant. We pay the lowest ranked people $5.42 per hour, while a toolmaker, who is really skilled, and in short supply, gets $7.85. At that rate, we can't hire any good toolmakers. We'd like to pay them maybe $11.00 per hour, but the plant union is nervous. They want the differentials small, because it's fair. It may be fair, but we can't get our toolmaking done."

"I see what you mean. If the differentials are pretty high, then some of the younger people might be interested in getting additional training."

"Exactly. It takes at least four or five years of tough training to become even a junior toolmaker, so why bother for an extra few cents an hour? But if you can make really good money, you just might sign up for the training."

"Well, somehow people get paid, and somehow the system goes on. But I suppose that no one will ever be really happy about it."

Jim nodded. "You're right. Actually, if nearly everyone were happy about their pay, I'd get very nervous. It would probably mean that we're overpaying most people."

"So why worry about pay? How about those perks and benefits?"

"That's a whole other story. We do worry about them, and we try to plan logical and attractive benefits. Lots of times the unions push us, too. We have a pretty good pension plan now, we've got an excellent medical insurance plan, and we have supplementary unemployment benefits for most of our workers in most plants. The union pushed us on that one. We are just planning a new dental program for all workers, and boy, is that one going to be expensive!"

"What do you do it for? Just because the unions push you?"

"No, actually a good benefits package helps us keep our good people. A guy may be mad about his pay, but his wife may need some very expensive medical care. Under our health plan, she gets it almost free. He might hesitate before quitting as a result. He might even like RVA because of this benefit. They call these benefits fringes, but they amount to over 25 percent of our total payroll."

"I have quite a few myself over at *Newsworld*," Al said. "And you're right. When I get restless, I think about all those nice benefits I'd lose by leaving."

"Most bigger companies, lots of small ones, and most government and educational organizations have fringes just for that purpose. But fringes are just one small part of our total territory. We also get involved heavily in employee health and safety. One fringe we have is an annual physical checkup for almost all our employees. It's nice for the employee to get a free physical, but it pays off for us too. If something is wrong, we might find it and correct it before it gets too serious."

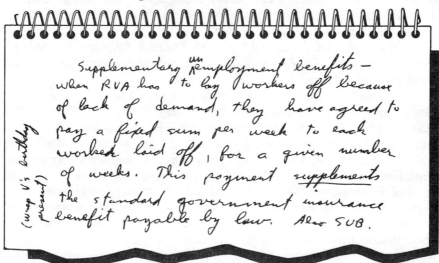

Supplementary unemployment benefits — when RVA has to lay workers off because of lack of demand, they have agreed to pay a fixed sum per week to each worker laid off, for a given number of weeks. This payment supplements the standard government insurance benefit payable by law. Also SUB.

(wrap V's birthday present)

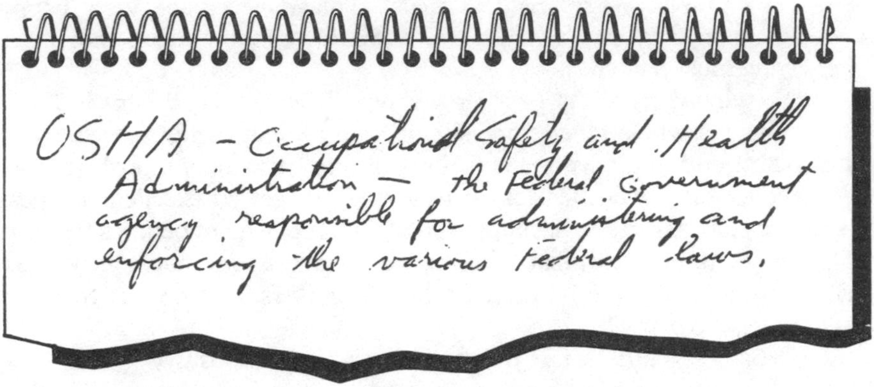

"Safety means dealing with OSHA, doesn't it?"

Jim groaned. "It sure does. We've had some government safety legislation for a long time, but only in the 1970's did the rules get really tough. And OSHA inspectors enforce the law. Right now we've got about 55 serious citations all over the country to correct, or else."

"Are those guys really as bad as they say? I mean, I've heard some pretty wild stories about OSHA."

"Oh, they're tough enough. For a while, in the late 1970's, they really got wild. It was a classic case of confrontation. . . . OSHA officials apparently felt that we in business were moral monsters who got our kicks from seeing employees chewed up in the machinery, or something. It got so bad that many companies began to stonewall, to refuse to let an OSHA inspector on the premises without a legal warrant. Anything an OSHA inspector did or said was met with a court case. A lot of it was petty, like the company that almost got closed down because its fire extinguishers were hung 32 inches from the floor, instead of the legal 36, stuff like that. But in recent years, OSHA has been a lot more reasonable."

"I've read a lot about that," Al said. "Apparently, some OSHA guys were so convinced of the evils of capitalism that they were trying to close down most of industry."

"Maybe," Jim said, "but RVA really never had too much trouble with them, simply because we've had a long history of safe operations. You've heard of Mr. Tavis, who built this company. He was a real safety nut. I understand that he once saw a man killed in a stupid industrial accident, which was caused by the company not taking rudimentary safety precautions. Forever after, he insisted that the highest safety standards be observed in all of RVA's plants. We had, long ago, the best safety engineering group in the country. I do know that we spend more money on employee safety than almost anyone. And our industrial accident record runs consistently lower than the national averages in virtually all of the industries in which we operate. It makes sense, since you don't want good employees injured or killed just because you tried to save a few dollars by omitting a guard rail, or because you didn't paint stairs properly. Safety costs big money, but it saves lives and money too."

"But OSHA is on your back anyhow?"

"Al, in recent years OSHA's been more concerned with saving lives and preventing injuries than with baiting companies, as it did some years ago. These days, the agency is concentrating on high-risk situations, and if you run a mine, or some activity where accident rates have been very high, they'll be on your back. They don't bother us much, since we're not in too many high-risk situations, plus the fact that our record is so good."

"If the value of human life is infinity, then the costs are infinity, too," Al murmured.

"What do you mean?"

"I was talking to an old professor once for a story. He pointed out that one thing we really can't handle in the U.S. is the cold-blooded cost calculation about what a human life is worth. Philosophically, we believe that every human life is infinitely precious. But then, suppose we discover that people are going to get killed in auto accidents. We can save perhaps two lives a year by spending ten million dollars on some safety devices. Is it worth it? Of course. But then we discover that people get killed in airplanes, and we can save another life for fifty million dollars. We say yes to that cost, too, but pretty soon, long before we eliminate all risks, we run out of money and resources, and people are still doing unsafe things. We just can't keep everyone alive forever, because we don't have infinite resources."

"You know, Al, I think that may be the problem with the laws OSHA is trying to enforce. They in effect say that any cost is acceptable, if the result is to make a plant or office safer. But RVA, or anyone else, just doesn't have the resources to provide a totally safe environment for everyone. One of those citations is for the use of an allegedly cancer-causing chemical in one of our processes. There are no good substitutes, and the next best chemical would run costs up so high that we just couldn't compete. We're fighting this one, and if we lose, we'll just close the plant. Our technical people have spent several years looking for a good substitute, at a pretty high cost, but so far, they haven't come up with anything we can use. Neither has any other company, any place in the world."

"But every other company has to do the same, right?"

"The American ones do. We'll just import the item from abroad if we're forced to close."

"But Jim, it's quite possible that the government is right. Your workers could die of cancer if they work there."

Jim threw up his hands. "I happen to think that they are right. I've read the lab reports that they're using as a basis for their decision. A worker handling those chemicals is twice as likely to develop throat cancer as the average citizen, after thirty years. But we'd have to raise the price of the product by 800 percent if we change the chemicals. That merely means that we can't sell the product."

"A nice mess. So some foreigners will make it, and they will die."

Jim smiled ruefully. "I'm the guy who liked people, remember? Now I find myself being a lawyer and a doctor and a moralist all at once. I'm even, I think, on the wrong side of this one."

"What do the workers think about this?" Al asked.

"No one's quit yet, although the union wants us to switch to some less toxic stuff. But they're nervous about a possible shutdown. Al, we always seem to want it both ways. We want the jobs and income, and we want utopia, too. I really don't know how to get both."

"Neither does OSHA or anyone else."

"Let's move on to something nice and easy, like union-management relations, OK?"

"That's easy?"

"Compared to philosophizing about life and death it is. Most of our plants are unionized, and we have union contracts covering the workers. The usual labor contract runs for three years, but since various plants have different expiration dates, we're almost always involved in negotiations about a new contract someplace. These sessions can be tough!"

"How are your unions? I mean, are they real tough, irrational, and all the other things I read about?"

"Oh, once in a while they get pretty wild, but basically the union people are doing their job, which is to get a better deal for their members. Some companies try to fight off unions, but we've had a long history of accepting them and trying to work with them. We also try to pay close attention to grievances and grievance procedures, so that we don't have a whole bunch of problems suddenly come up on us at contract time."

"And once again, you have lots of laws controlling you, right?"

"Lots. The federal laws and regulations are very extensive, and the government keeps us pretty much in line. But once again, our productivity gives us a big advantage."

"Explain, Jim."

"Remember, we're increasing productivity a lot faster than the average. This means that we can offer bigger pay packages and better fringes to our people, simply because they get much more productive each year. If, on the average, each worker is nine percent more productive this year than he or she was last year, we can offer him or her nine percent more without having to increase prices."

"If you're above average, somebody's got to be below average." Al thought about that. "I see what you mean. Suppose the industry bargaining settlement pattern is, say, eight percent pay increase this year. With a nine percent productivity increase, your costs actually go down a bit, but a company with no productivity increase is in real trouble. They get squeezed a lot, while you don't."

"You're on the right track, but it's a little more complicated than you think. Our costs don't go up a full eight percent, because labor costs are only part of our total costs. If labor costs are 50 percent of the total, and we have an eight percent wage increase, then total costs go up by only four percent, or in our case, the unit labor costs actually decrease by about five percent."

"I never was good at math," Al said. "but I can see that the more productive your people get, the more you can pay them."

"Sure, and that's the main reason why RVA is a company that ranks high in average earnings per employee. But you can look at industry data, and you see that the industries that are most productive are invariably the highest paying too."

"You mentioned grievance procedures. What's that all about?"

"Our typical union contract has all sorts of provisions in it about working conditions, pay, overtime work, even how hot or cold certain buildings should be. If we violate a worker's rights under the contract, then he or she might bring a grievance against us. The contract also provides for such procedures. One example we're arbitrating now concerns a seniority list. We laid off some people in one plant because of temporary lack of demand, and one worker feels that she was unjustly laid off. She thinks that her seniority was computed wrong. So she brought a grievance. We disagreed, and now we have the case before an arbitrator."

"Who's the arbitrator?"

"He's a professor of personnel at Georgia State University, name of Crane. We and the union have agreed that we will abide by his decision. He does this a lot, since he's supposed to be neutral in the game. He'll look at the facts and give us a decision shortly."

"Are there lots of arbitrators around?"

"Plenty, because there are plenty of disputes. But we write this arbitration clause into our contract, because it's a useful way to settle disputes. We try to get impartial arbitrators, since they have to be acceptable to both sides. We won't accept a person who has a long history of always supporting the union, regardless of the facts, and the union won't accept anyone who comes out the opposite way."

"So how do you come out in arbitration?"

"Pretty good, because we only arbitrate when we feel we really have a strong case. If we don't, we usually concede the point and go back to work."

Jim took a sheet of paper from a file lying on his desk. "I made this list a while back of the items that we've negotiated with our various unions about. It may give you some idea of how broad union-management relations can be."

Al stuck the paper in his notebook. "Boy, people are complicated! How do you manage to get all this stuff done? Everything you mentioned could take forever to resolve."

Items for Union-Management Negotiations.

Wage rates
Wage differentials
Incentive wage plans
Transfers, demotions, promotions
Special wage situations: hazards, hardships, etc.
Contract reopening conditions
Wage payment provisions (when paid, how often)
Guaranteed wages
Time off (when, how, for whom)
Paid vacations
Disciplinary actions
Pensions, pension rates, pension funds
Fringe benefits (insurance, sick pay, etc.)
Treatment of temporary employees
Supplementary unemployment benefits
Piecework rates
Seniority
Working conditions
Amenities (restrooms, smoking rooms, recreation, etc.)
Union recognition and security
Union agents (recognition, duties, etc.)
Grievance procedures
Arbitration
Organizing activities
Basic wages
Absences allowed (for whom, when, conditions)
Overtime pay rates
Regular hours; pay for odd hours
Dues collection
Union shop recognition
Strikes and lockouts
Bulletin boards
Management prerogatives
Manning scales (workers needed for given jobs)

"We never get bored. We never get done, either. There are always plenty of problems cropping up." Jim leaned forward. "I do think that we do a pretty good personnel job at RVA, all things considered. Nobody's perfect, but we're better than average. This bothers me."

"Why? I'd think that you'd be proud of it."

"I am, in spite of my fussing about all the things we should be doing. But in a funny way, we've created an enclave."

"Why? You're part of the country too."

"Do you know what's going to happen when we advertise for those 200 new jobs in New Jersey?"

"Lots of people will apply, I suppose."

"About 25,000 will apply, and most of them will be unskilled. We have perhaps 30 jobs for unskilled workers out of the 200. We'll fill most of the jobs for skilled people, but it'll be a scramble to get a few, maybe 20 to 30, really highly skilled people. But why should there be 25,000 people outside, who want in? We can only accommodate a relative handful of the work force. Organizations like the Federal Government, that also pay well, have the same problem. If you're lucky, you get into one of these great organizations, where the pay is good and the perks and working conditions are better. But if you're not lucky, you scrounge around at some minimum wage job with some fly-by-night employer. It's not very fair, and I'm not sure I like it."

"But you can't do anything about it, can you?"

"Of course not. Still, I like to think that I'm a nice, humanitarian guy. Then I spend most of my time making sure that a handful of superior people get a good deal. The rest are someone else's problem. It bugs me."

"For a guy who started out liking people, you sure got yourself into some odd things, Jim."

"Sure, but what else is there?"

Al thought about that for quite a while after this conversation. What else was there, really? You take a job, thinking that it's one thing, and after a while you, or the company, or the technology, or the world changes, and you suddenly find out that what you thought was there is not. But about all you can do is to plug ahead and try to do what you can. You can change jobs, but you can't change the whole world.

"Jim, you said that good jobs are hard to find."

"They are. There are a lot out there, but most people don't really know how to find one."

"I have a cousin who's just graduating from high school. He asked me to come to his class and talk about getting a good job, or starting a good career. Do you have anything I could use? It's nice to know that the company will pay you well and give you fringe benefits after you're hired, but these young people don't really know how to get hired in the first place. Neither do I, really. I just stumbled into this neat job I have now."

Jim walked over to his bookcase and found a slim paperback. "Try reading this. Two Toledo guys wrote it, Beeman and Rump. They really get down to cases. It's a terrific job."

"Beeman? No relative to your vice president, I hope."

"Boy, I hope not! But it's good, Al. Young people, and lots of older ones, could really use this advice."

DISCUSSION QUESTIONS

1. What is OSHA? What does it do?

2. What is a perquisite?

3. What is a fringe benefit? Give an example of one.

4. RVA has a problem with dangerous chemicals in one of its plants. Suppose that the facts given in this chapter are true—that employees working with these chemicals are incurring a significant cancer risk, and that it is economically infeasible to substitute something safe. The result, if the plant is closed down, is that the American workers will lose their jobs, and they will not be exposed to risk. But some foreigners will do the work and be exposed.

Should the federal government force RVA out of this business? Why or why not? Are foreign workers less valuable than Americans?

5. What are the three strategic key problems in personnel?

6. What is a WASP?

7. Suppose that new laws insist that RVA bring its minority and female representation up to the national averages. This would mean that RVA needs about 12 percent minorities and 50 percent females in its work force. This should take place within one year.

RVA now has about 23 percent women and 5 percent minorities in its American work force of 42,000 U.S. employees. Given the turnover and productivity factors noted in this chapter, what would RVA have to do to bring its work force in line with these female/minority requirements? Who might lose their jobs? Is this fair?

8. RVA has employee counseling for alcoholic and drug addicted workers. Are these problems really a company responsibility? Counseling costs lots of money, and RVA's customers must pay for it. Is this fair?

9. Jim noted that if someone was just a little bit better than the average in something, he or she could win in the long haul. What are you just a little bit better than the average in, if anything? Do you think that it might make a difference in your work success?

10. Your college campus is undoubtedly unsafe, since accidents do happen once in a while. We want to avoid such risks or accidents as much as possible.

Find out who is responsible on your campus for safety. See if you can determine one obvious risk, which has caused accidents in the past (look for unsafe intersections, icy paths, poorly lighted stairwells, inadequate electrical circuits in buildings, poorly laid out and marked bike paths, and similar hazards).

How much would it cost to reduce this risky situation you discovered? Why doesn't your college immediately spend the money and correct this situation, since clearly all human life has infinite value?

11. Colleges have difficulty in increasing professorial productivity because their only strategy for doing so is to increase class size, which is not too popular with professors or students. But professors like pay increases anyhow, and they sometimes get them. Consider a pay increase this year of seven percent, when productivity goes up zero percent. What does this do to the costs of operating your college? Remember that not all costs are payroll costs!

What is the difference between your college in this situation and RVA? Which organization can more easily absorb the additional payroll costs?

15

INTERNATIONAL BUSINESS

T he Pan American flight to London was pleasant, but it was a long trip. Al was finally going abroad, to examine the overseas part of RVA's empire. He had a good meal, then settled back to read the paper Dr. Farmer had given him when he was in Bloomington. Farmer's academic specialty was international business, and when Al had explained his assignment, he had handed over the paper with a comment that it might prove useful. Al had been far too busy to read up on future problems at that time, but he had stuck it away for further reference. He fished the paper out of his briefcase and began to read . . .

International Constraints

by Richard N. Farmer
Indiana University

Until several years ago, international activities of American firms could be covered, if at all, by a brief description of export and import practices. The United States is a large nation with major local resources, and while international trade always has been large in absolute terms, it has been small as a percentage of total income. Exports were seen as nice marginal business to be picked up if foreigners really wanted a firm's goods; imports tended to be products like coffee and bananas from subtropical climates.

But a lot has happened in the past forty years. Instead of being a marginal part of a large firm's activities, international business now often reaches 30 to 50 percent of the company's total sales. The portion of profits coming from abroad is frequently still larger. Instead of merely exporting products, over 3,000 American firms have direct investments in foreign countries, including many major manufacturing plants and extensive marketing systems. International business is now so important to most major American firms that anyone working for one of them can expect to be directly involved in this phase of the business at some time during his career, directly or indirectly.

We define international business as including any business transactions that take place across national frontiers. Besides traditional export and import activities, it takes many new forms, such as:

1. Direct investment in manufacturing, mining, marketing, and so on.

2. "Turnkey" projects, where a firm builds a complete facility to turn over to a foreign firm or country.

3. International contracting, where an American firm works on construction projects in another country.

4. The sale of financial services, such as banking, by establishing branches abroad.

5. Licensing arrangements with foreign firms, where an American company sells patents, trade processes, and the like.

6. Indirect investments, where an American firm or investor buys bonds or other nonvoting securities of foreign firms or governments.

7. Service contracts, where an American firm provides technical expertise for a foreign firm, an American firm abroad, or a foreign government for a fee.

8. Sales of international services, such as insurance and transportation, for international transactions.

These activities work both ways. Over 3,000 American firms have direct investments abroad, but over 400 European and Japanese firms have direct investments in the United States as well. Many foreigners fly Pan American Airlines, but many Americans use BOAC or Japan Air Lines in return. Many foreigners use the facilities of branches of Chase Manhattan or the Bank of America in their countries, but many Californians use similar facilities provided by Japanese banks there. To date, the American penetration abroad is the larger, but foreign expansion into the United States is growing rapidly, as the whole Western world moves toward more economic integration.

It was possible, not too long ago, for a perceptive and well-trained manager or technician to ignore completely what was going on abroad. There was plenty to do at home. This is still possible, and we still have more provincials than cosmopolitans among our top people, but every year such local attitudes become less relevant. The entire postwar period since 1945 has seen a massive outward push by Americans, countered by equally massive inward pressure from foreigners, to the point where any reasonably well-educated manager or technician now should know something about the whole world, not just his own little piece of it.

And that is what this paper is all about. The international dimension is important to most firms, and this brief survey is intended to provide some background and analysis for this new trend.

Imports and Exports

The traditional form of international business was exports and imports, and this dimension of the American economy has grown steadily for over 40 years. In 1950, perhaps five percent of our total income stemmed from this source; now, over 18 percent does, and the U.S. is much more interrelated with other countries than it ever was in the past. Certain critical materials, most notably oil, now come in part from foreign countries, and autos, electronic equipment, toys, steel, textiles, and thousands of other products now are imported. Older Americans felt, correctly, that the American could go it alone. Now this strategy is impossible, and our daily papers talk about OPEC and oil and auto import competition and many other international problems connected with foreign trade.

The balance of payments is continually being discussed these days. If a country wants to buy from abroad, it must earn the money to pay for these imports by selling something abroad. Foreigners usually do not want your money—they prefer their own. But while Americans can create dollars, they cannot create English pounds or Japanese yen. These currencies must be earned, or borrowed, and a country's borrowing capacity, or credit, is limited, just as yours is. The analogy to your personal finances relative to dollars is correct. You cannot print dollars to spend, without going to jail. You have to earn or borrow them. Hence the U.S. now is very concerned about exporting enough to pay for critical imports, and government agencies now talk about export promotion and international competitiveness of American goods. Such items as agricultural products, trucks, diesel engines, electrical equipment, aircraft, and many others now are sold to foreigners so that we can buy from them. If we can't sell enough, we have financial problems. If you can't somehow earn enough dollars to finance your standard of living, you are also in trouble.

Any country can control its trade in any way it sees fit, subject always to retaliation by annoyed trading partners. Thus, if we choose, the U.S. can raise import duties (taxes) on Japanese cars, making them more expensive in the U.S. Presumably, fewer Americans would buy them and American auto producers would be better off. The usual popular analysis goes about this far.

But suppose that the Japanese, now unable to earn dollars, decide to raise import duties on American transport jet aircraft? Now we find that some more auto workers are employed, while some aerospace workers are out of jobs. Since the aerospace workers were internationally competitive, they were very efficient people, while the auto workers were probably less productive. We have traded off more productive jobs for less productive work, and for some reason it is harder for you to find a good job paying lots of money. Note that what actually happens depends on how the Japanese react; on how American car buyers behave; and on whether or not aerospace firms can find new customers elsewhere, so this issue is never very clear cut before the duties are raised. Every country in the world has inefficient industries with problems, and powerful producer groups will happily push for their own advantage regardless of what it does to the whole economy. Hence this debate about how to control foreign trade goes on continuously and always will. It has been going on since Genesis, when Joseph worried about selling Egyptian wheat to foreigners, and it will be going on as long as there are countries participating in an international marketplace.

Americans are new to this debate, thanks to our historic self-sufficiency in so many critical products. But now, and particularly in oil, we find ourselves joining the world and worrying about things that countries like England, Japan, and France have worried about for hundreds of years. Not until the late 1960s did we really get involved in this debate, so it is all very new and unsettling to many Americans. Many still believe that this new world doesn't exist, or that if it does, it doesn't much matter. But it does.

Behavioral Factors

International constraints also have a somewhat different behavioral flavor. If we debate a change in a local constraint, such as expanding a certain type of education, we all know that our fellow citizens are involved, and whatever happens will affect all of us. But if we are concerned about changing a given international constraint, we rarely worry about what might happen to foreigners. Thus a proposal for a new tariff on foreign textiles in the United States is generally argued in terms of what will happen to Americans. We leave it to the foreigners to figure out solutions to their own problems. For example, if the tariff is raised, and one result is massive unemployment and misery in South Korea, we rarely are concerned.

This is a common phenomenon in the modern world. What we are doing is suboptimizing. If America does better, fine, and it does not matter if others do worse. Our horizon extends only to the nearest political frontier. Of course, foreigners are trying to do the same thing to us, so we may justify our feelings by noting that if those South Koreans could figure out a way to get a trade advantage over us they would. Such attitudes are not very conducive to brotherly love and international understanding, but they must realistically be recognized.

It is ironic that many liberal and humanistic persons in the United States (usually quite antibusiness) often take positions that create real problems for foreigners. Most liberals fought hard and long to keep Mexican laborers out of the low-paying (by American standards) agricultural field by seeking to cancel the bracero work contracts. These contracts between the United States and Mexico provided that Mexican laborers could enter the United States to work under specified conditions. In the end, they succeeded, and these contracts were sharply reduced, so that very few Mexicans can now work in American agriculture. From an American point of view, a poor man making perhaps $1.25 per hour was being exploited—but from a Mexican field hand's point of view, the loss of his American job meant that he now had to work for $1.00 a day in Mexican fields. A few Americans were made better off by the termination of these labor agreements; many Mexicans were made worse off. From our point of view as Americans, this is desirable. Or is it?

But indignation won't help. Most citizens of any country suboptimize this way, which gives the whole international field an aura of suspicion, mistrust, and doubt that the domestic arena lacks. It is likely to remain this way for many years to come. Hopefully, attitudes toward foreigners will continue to change favorably, as they have since World War II, but it is a slow, long-term process.

International constraints interact in many ways with local constraints. An English price inflation not only will affect local firms directly but, by encouraging imports from countries with less inflation, will create still more competition. If English prices and costs go up, foreign markets will also be lost to others whose costs have not gone up so much. If American business schools turn out thousands of well-trained managers, then American firms may find an international advantage in countries where business education is undeveloped. And so on. The possible interactions are endless, and we are always finding both pleasant and unpleasant international repercussions of things we did for purely domestic reasons.

Why Go Abroad?

With all the local business complexities to worry about, why should any American firm take on the added problems of international operations? It would seem that managers could keep very busy just minding the local store.

Consider the kinds of success symbols Americans appreciate. If the American economy is moving ahead at about 3 percent per year, then the average firm or manager can also expect to gain about that much in sales each year. Most bigger firms find it easy enough to stay close to the average.

But we expect more from our stars. No one pays much attention to the average football player—the man who beats the average is the one we watch. And the manager who beats the average is the one who gets promoted, receives appointments to Presidential commissions, and generally gains the most prestige. He also gets rich, which is a further spur.

Hence Wall Street and many others reward the firm that grows at 10 percent or more per year in the 3 percent economy. And a small firm with aggressive, talented managers can do this. (So can an aggressive, talented administrator of a university, hospital, or government agency. We all play the same game.) If a firm has $10 million in sales, it is easy to move to $11 million the next year in a trillion-dollar economy.

But how about a $1 billion firm? Finding domestically another $100 million in sales is pretty difficult, given that all your competitors are trying to do the same, and your local market is not growing too fast. Bigger firms typically find it very difficult to get sales and profits gains much larger than the local average.

One option for expansion is to buy other firms. But American anti-trust laws prevent big firms from doing this. Two $3 million companies may be able to merge, but two $1 billion companies never would. One related strategy followed by some firms in the past decade has been to become a conglomerate. A steel mill buys an airframe manufacturer, or vice versa, and then in turn buys a food processing plant. If the pieces are dissimilar enough, the government may not bring antitrust action against the conglomerate.

This strategy might work, although the managerial problems created by merging such dissimilar groups are great. In retrospect, few major conglomerates have demonstrated an ability to do well with very diverse divisions. In recent years very large conglomerates have been running into major antitrust trouble, so further expansion by this means is difficult.

Managers in 1955 or 1960, pondering their expansion path, worked through this thinking. Domestic options seemed blocked. But what about overseas expansion? The idea of American firms going overseas in a direct investment way is not new. The Ford Motor Company had assembly plants in Argentina and England as early as 1914, and United Fruit had banana plantations in Central America in 1910. Many bigger firms had minor operations here and there, often in Canada. These were built after 1930, when very high American tariffs caused Canada to retaliate with equally high duties. Many firms built a plant or two across the border to evade such duties. And by 1960, such odd operations were doing very well. Returns on investment amounting to 30 or 40 percent were not uncommon.

Of course, the international bias noted earlier was strong. How could we trust foreign governments, when at any time they could nationalize the plant, tax us out of existence, or pass strange new labor laws?

But in the late 1950s, European growth rates were 6 to 10 percent per year, depending on the country. In 1958, most West European countries returned to fully convertible currencies, which meant the pound, mark, or franc profits could be converted to dollars without official approval. And further, Western Europe had traditionally been a production-oriented business system, with little or no marketing expertise. If a company made a product, it was assumed it could be sold. As production expanded and as incomes rose, it was becoming clear that this marketing activity would become increasingly important. What did American firms have, if not tremendous marketing expertise?

Also in 1958, the European Economic Community (EEC) was formed by France, West Germany, Italy, Belgium, the Netherlands, and Luxembourg. Through the next twenty years, these countries agreed to move toward a customs union, with all import duties eliminated among them. Instead of six minor markets, protected from outside competition by tariffs and quotas, there would be one market perhaps two-thirds as big as the United States market. Few European firms had much operating experience in such a major market, but most American firms did. Given rapid economic growth, relatively thin local competitive strength, and freely convertible currencies, the stage was set for major American penetration.

And penetrate they did. In 1950, direct foreign investment by American firms was $11.8 billion; by 1968, this figure had reached $65 billion; and by 1980, it had risen to over $300 billion. As firm after firm began to move overseas, others that historically would have nothing to do with anything foreign also got involved. Remember again how important peer group pressure can be. The managers having all the fun, making more money, doing new things, and attracting most of the attention seemed to be those whose firms were involved in major international activities.

Note also the interrelationships here. Firms too timid to move found themselves prime targets for takeovers, since in most cases their expansion rate was slow. Managers of such firms made less money, as their stockholders expressed dissatisfaction with slow gains. And a man who was a big wheel in Kokomo as a major firm manager found that no one else cared what he did locally—the action was elsewhere.

After twenty years of intensive international expansion, we now find that the vast majority of major American firms have extensive overseas operations. Their managers now must become cosmopolitans, and they must understand how to manage in very diverse environments.

Another question is why foreign countries have allowed these Americans into their countries to make such fat profits. What do they gain?

They gain wealth, among other things. If IBM builds a new computer manufacturing facility in northern France, perhaps several thousand Frenchmen will have new, better-paying jobs. And just as an American city gains when a new plant is built, the French city will get new taxes, more local small shop investments, and profits for their owners.

The French will also acquire new skills. If no French company ever built this factory, then few if any Frenchmen would ever acquire managerial and technical skills in computers. At least in this case they will. And they may also learn much about really good management, which IBM has in abundance. Indeed, one French writer has stated flatly that American management expertise is the most important single factor to come to Europe in a thousand years. Given this expertise, it is wise to try to learn how the Americans do it.

So French income goes up, French skill levels go up, and many Frenchmen get into activities that were beyond their wildest dreams even a decade ago. Is this not a pretty good trade for a few million in profits to be sent home to America? Indeed, more often than not the profits will be reinvested rather than remitted, which means further French industrial expansion, further skill improvements, and further income increases.

All in all, it is a pretty good bargain on both sides.

This pattern now works both ways. An aggressive French firm, analyzing its potential markets all over the world, discovers that the United States offers new opportunities. So it invests in Ohio or Indiana, and it builds a plant to manufacture its products. American workers and technicians are hired to produce this product, and American marketing personnel sell it in the American market and sometimes even in export markets. This time, the Americans gain new jobs and new skills. This is called reverse investment, which is defined as a direct investment in the U.S. by a foreign firm. By 1980, over $100 billion of such investments had been made in the U.S.

As foreign-owned corporations become competitive worldwide, this pattern of becoming multinational companies evolves all around the world. All of the strategic factors and problems noted in this chapter for American firms could equally be applied to foreign-owned companies as well, except that the foreigner will be observing the U.S. much as an American company would observe any other foreign company.

Foreign Investment Locations

American firms are everywhere in the world, although we have so far talked mainly about Western Europe. But once a firm sees the world as its beat, rather than just its own country, how does it pick its spots?

We are referring here to the relatively new phenomenon of the multinational firm, which may have an American historical base but sees itself as a world, rather than provincial, citizen. It can go anywhere—but where is best?

It is useful to taxonomize firms to see where is best, since different kinds of companies may go to various countries for quite different reasons. Here are some of the major kinds of companies, along with their fairly obvious overseas choices:

The Market-Oriented Firm

This company has its major strength in its marketing abilities. Of course, it produces things too, and often very well, but its expansion problem is largely a market problem. Ford can make cars far in excess of the ability of any market to absorb them; therefore it must find good markets. Refrigerator firms can do the same, but where can the product be sold? Most consumer goods firms are in this position if they are large and capable.

The locational problem here is to find a good market. And a good market is one where incomes are high and the economy growing rapidly. If the country is affluent, the market will exist. For such firms, Western

Europe, Australia, and Canada are the logical expansion points. If it is profitable to build production facilities in these countries, they will be built, but they are there to serve the new, affluent markets.

Japan would be another very logical choice, but here we encounter constraints. Under Japanese law, it is often impossible or very difficult to make direct investments in consumption goods factories. This market is reserved for Japanese firms. Hence few American companies have managed to move into this market. And the affluent communist countries would also offer very tempting targets (selling autos to Russians would be about the easiest marketing job ever tried), but rarely would any communist country allow an American firm to enter, and then only on a basis which would insure state ownership and control of the investment.

The Raw Materials-Oriented Firm

Here is a firm which needs raw materials, such as petroleum, ores, or a key agricultural commodity such as bananas. In this case, the locational decision is simple—gold is where you find it, and the firm goes where the minerals are, even though the other local environmental or international constraints may be many.

Hence we find major American raw materials investments and firms in such improbable places as Liberia (iron ore), Abu Dhabi, Kuwait, Saudi Arabia, and Iraq (oil). Copper firms wrestle with Peruvian and Chilean problems, and U.S. Steel mines ore in Venezuela. If a company is very lucky, it may find its raw materials in a more favorable situation.

There are still many firms exploiting raw materials all over the world, but in the past decade, many countries have nationalized these activities. Raw materials, more than any other asset, are seen to be the property of the nation, not private companies. Hence most foreign oil production now comes from publicly-owned national companies, not multinational firms.

Cost Reducers

Some firms, which may also belong in the marketing category, move overseas to reduce production costs. Americans often think that labor costs in Western Europe and Japan are low, but this is increasingly less true than it was historically. In a few highly productive Japanese industries (e.g., steel, shipbuilding), total wage costs are almost as high as those in the United States.

If one is marketing on a world basis something like transistor radios or TV sets, which require much production labor input, what kinds of countries are useful? The answer is those with open economies, which allow easy export and import of materials, products, and capital, to say nothing of profits. If well-disciplined, excellent quality workers are available at low cost, other senior managers and a few key technicians can be imported to meet all labor requirements.

These firms gravitate to such countries as Hong Kong, Taiwan, and South Korea, where the open economy requirements are met. The product is assembled and then reshipped to American, Japanese, or European markets.

It often is critical that the country be willing to allow easy import of various bits and pieces, since frequently the country may not have the skills or capability to produce every component. Thus a key condenser or tuner might have to be made in England or America to get the final product right. Unless such items can be brought in duty-free, the advantages of overseas production may be lost.

What do the countries get out of this? Hong Kong, Taiwan, and South Korea are among the most rapidly growing economies in the world, averaging from 5 to 10 percent gains per year in recent years. It is nice to double one's income in six years—and these governments agree. Workers get jobs, contractors build new plants, new skills are acquired, and foreign exchange is acquired in increasing amounts for imports of still more income-expanding items.

This is a new development, which even now is barely ten years old for most countries. The danger is that the country locks its future into the world economy. If the United States raises its tariffs on imported TV sets, down the drain the local economy goes. But the gains are seen to outweigh the risks, particularly when one observes that small, poor countries that try to isolate themselves from the rest of the world are lucky to get 3 or 4 percent income growth per year.

American firms are somewhat reluctant to discuss this activity. After all, they may well be accused of taking jobs away from Americans. But again, everything is relative. Few Americans would work for 60 cents an hour, but if the next best option you have is working as a farm laborer for 30 cents a day, the deal may be very attractive.

Brain Renters

Some American firms basically sell nothing but the services of their talented staffs. In effect, they rent brains to their clients. Advertising agencies, management consultants, architects, accounting firms, and many similar companies are in this position.

What kinds of foreigners might be interested in such service? The likely markets are among the most sophisticated and largest foreign companies. Most of these companies are in affluent, sophisticated countries, so the pattern here is to go to Western Europe and other highly developed areas.

The No-Goes

A final category might be firms who will always stay home. Perhaps 6.9 million of the 7 million American companies have one or no employees, and they typically are far too bogged down with local problems to consider moving to the next town, let alone abroad. In this category would be millions of small retail establishments and small service firms, such as barber shops. Note, however, that many of these firms do get involved in international affairs when they sell imported items. And some very small manufacturers also do a bit of exporting. But direct investment is out for most of these firms.

Another group of firms cannot easily go abroad because they are culture-bound. A local doctor, lawyer, or optometrist is licensed to practice in one state, and there is no incentive to move or expand. Law in particular is very difficult to practice in another country, given wide variations in legal custom and philosophy among countries.

Still another group of firms unlikely to go abroad soon are successful smaller firms who have plenty of expansion possibilities at home. The man who starts a good, successful restaurant in Cleveland, makes a lot of money, and considers new possibilities, is likely to move into other Ohio and Midwestern cities first. He will know how to operate well there, and possibilities are virtually unlimited for a shrewd operator. Small manufacturing companies, service firms, and marketing operations are likely to be in the same position.

But even smaller firms get internationally involved. As suggested above, many retailers sell imported products. For example, many American auto dealers have done very well with European and Japanese car franchises, and small manufacturers both export and occasionally sell manufacturing and patent rights to foreign firms. The strategy they follow rarely involves direct investment abroad.

Firms tend to follow the above patterns, although one can find many exceptions to the general rules. One often seen is the case where a firm oriented toward major markets goes into minor markets, such as Iraq, Mexico, or Argentina. Why do they bother?

The answer gets at the order of priorities question. Examination of such companies usually shows that fifteen or twenty years ago, they were involved in developing their major European markets. But by now these markets are pretty much saturated, much as the American market was twenty-five or more years ago. Some sales increases are possible, but the 10 to 20 percent per year gains are no longer easy.

A company in this position will begin to move steadily into less desirable markets, starting with the best of a poor lot. Thus after Europe, rapidly growing Brazil may offer the best possibilities; after that, Nigeria; and so on. It is logical for a major firm to proceed this way, to the end of the line. But firms just beginning their overseas thrust will logically begin at the best spot.

As firms do move abroad, they must consider all of the international constraints. Our next step is to take each set in turn and see how these affect the efficiency of a firm's operations. If the company can work out the best way of overcoming the innumerable constraints it faces in relevant foreign countries, it will profit accordingly.

INTERNATIONAL BEHAVIORAL CONSTRAINTS

We have noted already that most persons perceive foreigners differently than they do their fellow citizens. The first set of international constraints considers what effects such attitudes have.

Note that there are no international educational constraints. While many students may study in foreign countries, a person always is in some country while he studies. Hence the things he learns will be culture-bound, and there will be no international educational constraints.

National Ideology

The general ideology of any country has much to do with foreign firms. In some countries, business is seen as degrading and low status, something to be done by crooks and rogues and not suitable for people of refinement and taste. When an American manager gets into the country, he may be surprised to find that he and his firm are seen in this light.

Being seen this way may be disturbing to the manager, but to find that key building permits cannot be obtained or that he cannot recruit the best-trained young people for his company shows how such attitudes can directly affect the firm's efficiency. A common complaint in such a culture is that somehow things can't get done right. The firm seems to wade through glue all the time.

Other countries may have socialist political parties that are dubious about any private, profit-making firm. If these parties gain power, their actions against all private firms, and particularly foreign ones, can be disastrous. They may try to take over such firms for ideological reasons. Many governments view multinational companies as exploiters, and they often try to keep them out, or get rid of them if they are already in. As a result, companies spend a great deal of time analyzing the general political climate. Countries that show very negative attitudes are not likely to get much foreign investment.

View Toward Foreigners

We have already considered this constraint at some length earlier. If the view of foreigners is very negative, the usual result is no entry for American firms. And if you can't get in, everything else becomes irrelevant. Thus it is extremely difficult to get into any communist country, since their view of foreign capitalist firms is extremely negative.

All things change, however. Yugoslavia now allows foreign firms to invest in joint ventures with state-owned firms, and even in odd places like Bulgaria and Rumania, the welcome mat is out for selected American firms with technology or marketing skills to offer the local economy. Many joint ventures or cooperation agreements now exist between Western companies and East European communist governments.

There is a paradox here for many countries. They are very proud of their local culture, and they want it to remain pure. But the prestige and power these days is on the side of the productive countries, and one result of isolation is to miss the innovations foreigners bring. Western Europe these days is bubbling with new ideas, new energies, and rapid change, largely brought about by activities of American firms and management. Eastern Europe, instead of presenting a dynamic, exciting image, is seen as a stagnant backwater. Instead of dynamic industrial expansion, the countries have great difficulty even holding existing industrial export markets.

How to get back on the track? One way is to try to attract foreign investors, despite their improbable philosophies, to gain from their tremendous industrial potential. But to accept this change will also involve very real dangers of capitalistic contamination.

Many poorer countries also face this dilemma. American and European materialistic capitalist philosophies may be repugnant to local leaders and elites. Yet, if your own people are desperately poor, what else is there? Note the interactions—looking to Eastern Europe and communism does not exactly offer an exciting alternative. So many overcome their repugnance and let the foreigners in.

Americans in particular are not popular in many parts of the world. Marching on American embassies to protest is a classic play in many countries, and the image of the American as rich, arrogant, insensitive to local values, and unwilling to learn anything about local language or culture is common. Moreover, the dominance of American physical power worldwide makes lots of foreigners nervous.

Events in Iran in 1980 show this point very clearly. Iranians apparently desperately want their own culture, at any cost. If one result of their actions is to reduce wealth and production, then this is a small price to pay for cultural independence.

Note also that feelings about different kinds of foreigners vary widely. In some countries, Americans may be detested, but Swedes or Swiss may be respected and liked. In others, a Muslim foreigner may be welcomed as a brother, while a Jew may be detested. In still others, a black person is viewed with suspicion, while in many African states he often is welcomed. Rarely does any country show uniform feelings toward all types of foreigners. One very operational result of such differences is that American firms take some care in selecting the managers who represent them abroad. It may be useful to have a black manager in Nigeria, a man named O'Hara in Dublin, or a Jew in Haifa. Given the diversity of American types, such matches can often be made, sometimes with excellent results.

Nature and Extent of Nationalism

This is a nationalistic world, and every nation jealously guards its sovereignty. Newer nations in particular seem very anxious to prove to the world that they are independent, and they may take action accordingly—such as restricting certain economic sectors to local firms or expropriating plants run by some feared foreign giant.

This constraint interacts with the previous two. If a country has strong nationalistic sentiments, while at the same time it distrusts foreigners, foreign firms are likely to be in trouble—if they can even get in. And if its ideology is also unique, further trouble is certain. One example of very negative constraints is Albania. No one gets in, even from the rest of the communist world. But note that Albania pays the price—it may well be that no one wants in!

LEGAL-POLITICAL INTERNATIONAL CONSTRAINTS

This is the longest international set, since these are the ones that directly affect foreign firms, as well as local firms with interests abroad. While the behavioral constraints consist of feelings and attitudes, the legal-political constraints tell firms precisely what they must or must not do.

Political Ideology

The main reference here is to the continuum of political systems, from pure communism to pure capitalism. In general, the more to the socialist or communist side a country is, the less interested it is in foreign enterprise, and the more difficult it will be to get into the country.

Relevant Legal Rules for Foreign Business

It is common for countries to have special laws and rules for foreign firms. Thus in France, any American company must get special permission to enter or expand activities. Often such special treatment is necessary in the interest of fairness. The United States and most Western European countries have special tax laws applying to foreign firms, so that a firm operating in two countries will not be double-taxed. Many poorer countries have much special legislation pertaining to foreign operations. Such legislation ranges from special rules about foreign concessions for raw materials to land ownership restrictions to special labor legislation. Often such countries feel discriminated against by foreign companies that are larger than the country, and this special legislation is an effort to equalize the contest.

International Organization and Treaty Obligations

All countries have treaty agreements with other nations, and many are members of various international conventions dealing with important technical matters. A publisher would be most interested to know if a country observes international copyright conventions; a pharmaceutical firm would want to know about international patent agreements; and an airline might be interested in whether the country is a member of international organizations dealing with air navigation and safety. Such agreements can be critical to given firms, since a country's obligations under them can determine whether or not business can profitably be carried on there.

Many countries have agreements with the United States about fair treatment of nationals and firms, including clauses relating to expropriation and nationalization. Most Western countries are also signatories to the General Agreement on Trade and Tariffs (GATT), which binds them to certain actions about tariff changes.

Any country can abrogate an agreement at any time, and there have been plenty of such instances in the past few decades. But most countries, including some that often talk rather wildly for foreign consumption, are reluctant to risk damaging their reputation by abrogating an agreement.

Power or Economic Bloc Grouping

Many countries also belong to formal coalitions for economic, social, or defense purposes. We have already mentioned the EEC, which is one major economic bloc. The European Free Trade Association (EFTA) is a similar, but looser, economic group. Two others are the Central American Customs Union and the Latin American Free Trade Association.

Such economic blocs are extremely important to American firms, since they may offer much larger markets than any single country. If a plant built in Austria can also supply markets in Sweden, Portugal, and Norway without tariff penalties, it can be bigger and potentially more efficient.

Countries are also grouped into military blocs, and most Western countries are a part of the North Atlantic Treaty Organization (NATO), which is charged with the defense of Western Europe from Soviet aggression. The Eastern European countries and the Soviet Union have a countering political-military bloc to meet feared Western threats.

Such a military bloc could have major implications for some firms. The NATO countries might wish to buy compatible aircraft; a firm that can get the American or West German order might accordingly get many more from other NATO countries. Or NATO might jointly agree on key trade restrictions against various communist countries. The Arab bloc will try to boycott and force out of Arab countries any American firm that invests in Israel, which can be a major determinant of some investment decisions. Normally, any firm contemplating major investments studies and considers the implications of such bloc groupings for countries it is interested in.

Import-Export Restrictions;
International Investment Restrictions;
Profit Remission Restrictions;
Exchange Control Restrictions

These four constraints are considered as a unit, since they all deal with restrictions on moving goods or money into or out of a given country. The internationally oriented firm necessarily is concerned with free (or relatively free) flows of people, money, and materials, and wherever major blockages or restrictions exist, serious problems arise.

Such restrictions may also force investment and activity. Many years ago, Brazil decided to force the development of an automobile industry. By raising import duties sharply for foreign vehicles, while at the same time encouraging foreign investment in plants and equipment, it literally forced foreign makers to build plants in Brazil. If they did not, they lost the market to other foreign firms who would invest. Similarly, a high duty on a complete car and a low duty on parts could force assembly in the country—and many countries have tried such tactics, often with success.

Every country has its own currency, which is used domestically. Each currency is linked to all others by an exchange rate, which defines the local money in terms of gold or dollars. Since 1971, most major currencies have not had par values. They are allowed to go up or down in terms of other currencies depending on supply and demand in world markets. There exists a huge trade in foreign currencies in all major countries, including the United States, and literally billions of dollars in English pounds, French francs, German marks, Japanese yen, and American dollars change hands every day. A country's currency is worth exactly what the market thinks it is worth, in a manner very similar to stock or commodity trading.

These daily fluctuations in foreign currencies can make life very difficult for firms trading internationally. Suppose that an American company sells a jet transport aircraft to West Germany for $30 million, to be delivered next year. It can receive payment in German marks or American dollars. Which is better? If it accepts dollars, and the German mark rises 30 percent next year in terms of the dollar, then the company has lost about $9 million. If it accepts marks, and the mark falls by 30 percent, then it will lose about $9 million. In effect, the company is forced to speculate in foreign exchange.

This company could buy marks or dollars for delivery next year to protect itself, but such transactions are expensive. One critical financial decision that all major multinational firms (and those just exporting and importing) must make is how to deal with these foreign currency fluctuations. Since currencies can fluctuate for many reasons, including trade imbalances, wars, revolutions, and local inflation, among others, trying to figure out what a given currency might be worth in three months or a year is never easy.

A currency is said to be convertible when it is freely transferable to any other currency or gold. But many are not, and firms or individuals wanting to obtain foreign currencies must have official permits or licenses. It may be fun to earn millions of Indian rupees, but if the profits cannot be brought back home, the effort may be wasted.

Foreign currencies, unlike the domestic variety, must be earned or borrowed. They cannot be created. The American government can create all the dollars it wants, but it cannot create pounds or francs. Hence most countries worry a lot (just as you do as an individual with dollars) about how their international balance of payments is going. If they are paying out more than they are taking in, the country is apt to have some new restrictions on currency transfers. Foreign and domestic firms pay very close attention to such developments, since all foreign activities, including exports and imports, are affected by them.

If a country has foreign exchange controls, firms face extra problems in getting licenses to import components, get profits out, and generally carry on any international transactions. Where such conditions exist, it is not uncommon to find managers spending more time worrying about exchange problems than running the business. Most American companies are extremely wary about investing in such countries. But the oil may be there, or the firm may have invested years ago when currency controls did not exist.

These four constraints are among the most important and practical that any international firm has to face. They get right to the gut issue of profit and loss, and they determine very directly many activities and how they are carried out. Any international firm will necessarily be involved in all of them.

INTERNATIONAL ECONOMIC CONSTRAINTS

We have just discussed briefly some problems of monetary controls, and these constraints relate to similar problems at the country level.

General Balance of Payments Position

The balance of payments of any country is a statement of all international transactions in the given time period. It includes on the credit side all earnings from exports, sales of services, and tourism, along with capital inflows from investments or loans. On the debit side, it includes all expenditures abroad for imports, tourism, and services, along with capital outflows for investment or loans abroad.

After all transactions are stated, there usually is something left over on one side. If it is a credit, the balance of payments shows a surplus; if it is a debit, the balance of payments is in deficit. Note that if all international transactions were recorded in every country correctly, with no errors, for every balance of payment deficit there would be a surplus someplace else.

The balance of payments is exactly similar to any individual's position in his country. Since he cannot create money, he must earn or borrow what he spends. You could create your own balance of payments statement with the rest of the United States by lining up items as suggested above. Do you show a surplus or deficit for the past week?

Countries that get into balance of payments troubles these days find that the value of their currency sinks on the international markets. Imports become more expensive, while exports get cheaper for foreigners. This is because foreigners can now buy this country's money more cheaply than before, and if local prices are about the same, then the price to a foreigner is lower. Higher import prices mean less sales, so imports decline. Lower export prices mean more sales, so exports increase. In the end, the country can come into balance again.

The usual problem is that it may take years to work out these adjustments, while a country's creditors have to be paid next month. Hence it is common to find countries borrowing foreign currencies from major international banks, just as a local firm might borrow to meet current needs. Countries have credit ratings, just as individuals do, and some are seen as good risks while others are not. At present, over $100 billion of loans are out to various countries all over the world; international lending to countries is one of the largest credit operations around. All sorts of countries borrow, ranging from communist states like Poland to poor countries like Zaire to developing countries such as Brazil and Mexico. The major international banks that extend the loans are typically from the wealthier countries in North America, Europe, and Japan.

Firms involved in international trading study balance of payments figures very carefully, since a big deficit or surplus can cause the value of a country's currency to change rapidly on world markets. Remember the discussion of that aircraft manufacturer a few pages back. If West Germany's balance of payments looked as though it would improve dramatically next year, the German mark would go up in value. Knowing this, or being able to forecast it, could lead to multimillion dollar gains on this one sale.

Some American multinational firms are so perceptive at forecasting exchange rate shifts that they make almost as much money by moving money around as they do by producing products. But some are not so perceptive, and the added foreign exchange risk cuts into profits. The above discussion suggests why it is so important to consider the balance of payments position of any country you are interested in, including the United States.

International Trade Patterns

Countries have quite different patterns of foreign trade, which may affect their balance of payments position from time to time. A country like the United States, with a complex and diversified export pattern, is not likely to get stung too hard if one or two markets get into trouble. But many countries export only one or two crops in markets where prices fluctuate erratically. For example, the coffee crop may be good, but if foreign prices decline by 50 percent, export earnings will drop off very fast. The country then gets into balance of payments trouble, and all of the above discussion applies. Or a country may have most of its trade with countries with inconvertible currencies. On the books it looks good, but it cannot transfer monies around to pay its bills. Countries with big Soviet trade can get into this position, since the ruble is totally inconvertible.

All of these considerations go back to the balance of payments, which firms pay attention to. If trade patterns are risky and erratic, so might be the currency.

One can see how important these trading patterns are by considering U.S. oil imports. Until the 1970's, the U.S. imported relatively little oil; now it imports about half its needs from OPEC producers and others. If the U.S. cannot obtain oil, its whole economy falls apart. Hence there is continuing concern and debate about what to do next. Instead of being a provincial and relatively uninteresting problem, the oil business these days is a major multinational problem for most countries, including the United States. American oil companies, oil users, and distributors must now track carefully the supply and demand for petroleum all over the world. Even small shifts in supply or demand can create shortages or gluts in the center of this country.

Membership and Obligations in International Financial Organizations

These institutions are another constraint that in the end works back to the balance of payments and how a country might meet a crisis. The most important of them is the International Monetary Fund, which is an international bank. When a country becomes a member, it puts up funds in its local currency and in gold, the exact amount depending on the country's size and economic importance. If the country needs help for balance of payments reasons, it can borrow short-term funds from the IMF. If the problem is temporary, a loan of this sort can prevent devaluation.

Member countries, which include most Western nations, also commit themselves in various ways to maintaining the international value of their money. While countries can renege on these agreements, they are reluctant to do so, since they might lose some borrowing privileges. Hence interested firms pay special attention to such details.

The IMF has moved toward being a true international central bank, since it now has currency-creating powers of its own. By agreement of all members, the bank now creates specific amounts of Special Drawing Rights (SDRs), which are used as money by the member nations to settle international bills. This is not currency, but rather bookkeeping money— one country merely credits another through the IMF. But the whole story of this new development in international finance, with its potentially far-reaching effects on many private multinational firms, will have to wait for much more detailed and specialized treatment. If you want to work for a large American firm, this is the sort of specialized knowledge you may have to acquire.

Conclusion

In the good old days, it was hard enough to figure out what was going on at home, and any good manager could spend his life involved in the infinitely complicated domestic scene. He still can, but now we have the new complexities and opportunities presented by the new multinational corporations.

Few basic books on business deal with this international dimension in any detail. The field is so new that even the advanced texts are still largely unwritten, and few scholars in the United States have been able to catch up to the firms they are studying. A big, solid company that only ten years ago merely engaged in some minor export activity may now be deriving a third or more of its revenues from overseas.

One result of this new development is that business people are far ahead of their governments in advancing international understanding. While governments are still engaged in the types of petty nationalistic concerns that predate the twentieth century, business managers are making a new world in which mutual economic interests transcend national boundaries. In contrast to the wariness of statesmen, who may take many months or years to reach any sort of agreement, business people can meet amicably over a drink and work out a complicated transaction that may involve four or five countries. Somehow agreement is reached because, as in every trading deal, there is something in it for everyone. As a means of resolving international differences, this approach is certainly far preferable to war.

Curiously, no critics of American business seem to have caught this point. They point to big firms exploiting the poor countries of Latin America or talk about world monopolies of big American companies, but they never realize that it is much better to trade with one's enemies than to fight them. Right-wing conservatives suffer from the same myopia. They become hysterical if someone sells a computer to the Russians, not seeing the advantages to the United States in having a thousand IBM or Ford managers and technicians building something inside the Soviet Union and working and interacting with the Russians.

Two days later, having got over his jet lag somewhat, Al was talking to Loren Vickers, general manager of Ace Engineering Company, United Kingdom. Mr. Vickers was English, and he spoke with a delightful Oxford accent. Al thought that he sounded like Basil Rathbone, or perhaps Sir Laurence Olivier. Mr. Vickers had also read Dr. Farmer's paper, so Al began by asking, "What do you think of it?"

"Oh, for an academic work, it's not bad. But of course he omits many of the interesting problems."

"Such as?"

"There is not much about international management, things like marketing, finance, and so forth. Academics know very little about such things, so it is understandable that Dr. Farmer left them out. But of course another possible reason is that we manage here in Britain just about the same as you do in the States. The big difference is that the answers come out differently."

"Now, explain that please. I would think that if you did the same things, you'd come up with the same answers."

Mr. Vickers smiled. "No, because of those constraints that Dr. Farmer was talking about. Suppose that we analyze a market here in Britain. We would use the same marketing techniques that we use in the States, or for that matter, in Thailand or Japan. We look at such things as personal income, market size, prices, and so forth."

"I've talked to some American marketing people, so I have an idea of how that's done," Al said.

"But in Britain, personal income is lower than in the States. If that is a critical factor in sales, we get fewer sales per capita here. You see, we use the same analysis, but our numbers are different."

Al thought about that for a moment. "I suppose that the crime rate here is lower than in the U.S.?"

"Certainly, much lower."

"With lower incomes and lower crime rates, I'll bet that your Snap-Kwik locks don't do too well here."

"They don't, Mr. Faber. This is not a good market for such premium quality locks. We can only sell a few."

"And I'd guess that your interest rates are different than in the States, too."

"They are different in almost every European country, and that means that any financial calculation, made of course with the very best analytical techniques, will come out differently in each country."

"So Mr. Vickers, management and managers do about the same things everywhere, but they have to remember what environment they're in."

"Dr. Farmer might give you an A for that statement," Mr. Vickers said. "Also remember that all of those international constraints make a big difference. Before 1971, Britain was not a member of the EEC, and the EEC tariff on the braking system we manufacture was over thirty percent. So we could never compete on the continent. But after 1971, when Britain was an EEC member, the tariff was zero, and so we were able to sell successfully in West Germany and France. An international constraint changed, and as a result we completely restructured our marketing effort, our financial structure, and our production system. Now we are over four times as large as we were in 1970." Mr. Vickers paused. "Of course it works both ways. When the EEC tariff went to zero, the British tariff also went to zero, and we had some difficult new competition in Britain from German and Italian firms. But we managed to hold our own."

"So you're sitting here minding your own business, and then your government changes a law, and all of sudden it's a new ball game. It makes you wonder. Relatively few Americans have even heard of the EEC."

"It is actually worse, Mr. Faber. Some other government could change its laws, and suddenly you have a very sticky wicket."

"A what?"

Mr. Vickers smiled. "A new ball game, as you would say. A sticky wicket is a British term for a difficult situation. Comes from cricket, you know."

Al didn't know, but he liked the phrase.

"The EEC recently dropped the tariff on frozen chicken, and one result was a rapid increase in sales of American frozen chicken in Europe. You Americans are the most efficient poultry growers in the world, you know. Growers in Mississippi suddenly had new markets, which they may not have even thought about before this new tariff was put into effect."

"I begin to see now why *Newsworld* and the *Wall Street Journal* use so much space describing international events and meetings," Al said.

"Over here, the *Financial Times* and *The Economist* do the same, and we read them very carefully. You see, Mr. Faber, our internal management system is interlocked with our environment, both domestic and foreign. When something in the environment changes, it is quite possible that something internal will have to change."

"Mr. Vickers, just how does the international part of Ace Engineering fit into RVA? Who do you report to?"

"Mr. Martin, the European head of Ace. He in turn reports to Mr. Schollhammer, the Ace president. You see, we really don't have a purely international structure, or one for each country. Ace's organization runs across the world, since our business does as well."

"You manage the same everywhere, except that those local environmental differences trip you up. That makes sense." Al paused. "You're English yourself, aren't you?"

"Yes, although RVA is an American company, I doubt that they have over ten Americans here in Europe, out of a work force of over 7,500."

"The way to avoid those political risks, I guess, is to have local people working for you."

"Correct. In the States, English, German, and Japanese firms do the same. Their work forces are Americans, except for a few key people."

"Come to think of it, we do the same thing at *Newsworld*. Our foreign offices are almost totally local people. It's pretty hard to get an overseas assignment."

They chatted on about various Ace problems, and Mr. Vickers noted when Al left that he hoped Al would have a chance to see a lot of RVA's European operations.

Al did. He stayed in Europe for three weeks. He saw endless RVA factories, all of which looked much like the ones back home, except that the workers might be speaking Italian or French instead of English. He talked to many executives, and they all seemed to operate about the same way that those in the U.S. did. He did notice, however, that everywhere things were just a bit different. When he probed a bit, it turned out that the usual reason was environmental. An Italian labor law made the workers perform slightly differently, or personnel work came out differently in Germany because of their laws. Overtime policies varied widely because both unions and labor laws were different. Discussions with marketing people suggested that product lines often varied quite a bit because of local laws and rules, as well as customs. Ace braking systems were made under European, not American, rules, and they weren't quite the same. They were all built to metric standards, for one thing. Managers were talking all the time about currency values, since so many of their sales were in other countries. An increase or decrease of four or five percent in a currency's value could double or halve profits. The EEC countries had a customs union, but they all had different monies, and Al was forever trying to get some currency changed, and usually losing money at it. Like many Americans, he never could quite get the hang of all of those different rates.

On the plane home, he reflected that no one would ever believe him. He had seen Europe, but in a way that most vacationers never quite would. Factories, offices, night shifts, marketing discussions, financial people showing him equations, and much more had been his beat. He never even had time to go to the night spots. It was all work and hectic travel. Vicki had been to Europe a few times on business, and Al had envied her, but when he left she had just looked oddly at him and said, "You'll see what it's like!"

Now he knew, and to his dismay, he had discovered what so many other expatriate workers had discovered. It was a lot more work than play. Too bad, because Europe looked like fun.

DISCUSSION QUESTIONS

1. Find the latest annual report of any major American corporation. Observe what the company says about its international activities. How important are they?

2. Find a local firm that sells a foreign product, such as a Toyota or Sony dealer. What does the manager of this firm feel about international trade? Why?

3. Many Americans are worried about foreign competition in many fields. If a foreign firm sells textile products, Americans will lose their jobs, and we will all be poorer.

What's wrong with this argument? What's right with it?

4. Royal Dutch Shell is a major multinational foreign company (Dutch and British owned) with extensive operations in the United States. Visit your local Shell dealer and see how he operates. Does the place look very foreign? Now visit an American-owned gas station. What's the difference, if any? Do you care that Shell happens to be a foreign company? Why or why not?

5. Find someone who owns a Toyota or other foreign car. Ask him about it to see what he says about its quality, economy, bad points, and so on. What view of foreigners do you see in his or her comments? Why?

6. Consider a fellow student from each of these countries: England, Japan, and Italy. Write a paragraph describing the general characteristics you expect in each person. Are there any differences in your expectations? Why?

7. At present, the United States has many trade controls in dealings with the Soviet Union. It is argued that we should not trade with potential enemies.

Is this a good argument? Why or why not? Write a short argument in favor of present policy. Now, write an argument against it.

8. *Time* and other news magazines carry many articles about foreign business. Look for one such article in any recent issue. Why do you think that anyone in the United States would care about this item?

9. The *Wall Street Journal* carries daily currency quotations in terms of dollars for many countries. Find these quotations for Great Britain, France, and West Germany. Suppose this textbook sells for 71 French francs, 39 German marks, and five English pounds. In which country would students get the best buy?

10. Many Canadian bonds are also quoted in the *Wall Street Journal*. Assuming that these quotations are in Canadian dollars, and using the current exchange rate, quoted, give the American dollar price for any Canadian issue.

11. The United States is a member of the International Monetary Fund (IMF). Go to the library and find out what its obligations and rights are under the membership terms. Do you think that membership is a good idea for the country? Why or why not?

12. Some Americans feel it is unpatriotic to own a foreign-made car. Millions of others obviously disagree, since they have purchased one.

Do you think that we are better or worse off for getting so involved in international trade in autos? Why?

13. If American textile tariffs are increased, a few thousand American workers will hang on to their jobs, but many more thousands of foreign workers in South Korea, Hong Kong, and Taiwan will be unemployed. Are these foreigners any concern of yours, or any other Americans? Why or why not?

14. Is it patriotic and proper for an American electronics firm to set up a cheap labor operation in Taiwan to produce products for export to Australia and Japan? Why or why not? Would your answer be the same if you knew that if the firm could not produce in this way it would close down its American operation anyhow and give up this foreign business?

15. Many American market-oriented firms, such as Coca Cola and Procter & Gamble, have done extremely well in Western Europe. What advantages do you think that their managements might have in marketing that European firms might not have?

16

CAPITAL MARKETS

$\mathbf{A}$l had a lot of trouble recovering from jet lag. For a week, it seemed like he was working at two in the morning, instead of four in the afternoon. But he finally got back in stride, took a look at his extensive notes, and tried to figure out what else he should be considering. He found a copy of the pamphlet that Ricks and Goldberg had published on the capital markets, and it occurred to him that it would be a good idea to talk to them about money in general and RVA in particular. He made a date with Mr. Goldberg, and he sat down to read their material the night before his appointment.

MONEY MARKET ESSENTIALS FOR THE AVERAGE INVESTOR

Ricks and Goldberg, Inc.

Money capital is the lifeblood of all firms, for without money the firm ceases to function. All companies have some investments to make in various equipment, machines, and inventories. Hence they are always interested in how much capital they can obtain and on what terms they can obtain it.

This is not just a capitalistic problem. Although it may obtain its capital from different sources, a publicly owned firm, such as the Chicago Transit Authority, has exactly the same problems as a privately owned one, such as IBM. Public firms in Marxist countries have capital problems as severe as those of private firms in capitalist economies. Changing the ownership of resources doesn't change this basic problem at all, although it may well change many of the institutions involved in the capital accumulation and disbursement system.

Here we are interested in the actual input of capital, not in the way firms use it once they have it. Within the firm, financial managers and planners must decide how money is to be most efficiently utilized;

but before they can do this, they must obtain the money. This paper deals with the outside world, where the money is. Except for the occasional big and profitable firm that can generate all of its capital from its own operations, all firms must go outside to obtain capital. Where they go and what they have to do to get money is the topic of this paper.

Here we study the interface between the firm that wants money and the various individuals and institutions that have it. Note that as usual where the firm interfaces with the environment, we find a bargaining situation. Someone out there has capital; some firm needs it. The owner will not give his money up without extracting his price; the user wants to pay as little as possible. This bargaining situation is at the core of most capital problems and is responsible for most debate, discussion, and argument about what should be going on. Users will always claim that the price is too high or that not enough capital is available. Lenders will normally say less but will hold back from lending to various persons and firms if they feel that the deal is not a good one.

Younger persons, seeing all around them fantastic affluence (which normally belongs to someone else), often conclude that capital is being withheld from good uses simply because lenders are nasty people. Hence one easy reform is to change the rules so that presently deserving persons can get all they want.

But examination of any input problem suggests one basic fact in all economics—resources, including money capital, are limited. There are not enough to go around, and there never will be. If this is true, then every society must figure out how to ration scarce resources, and when we examine the capital supply problem, we are doing nothing more than observing how the United States rations money capital.

One can grasp this basic point about the scarcity of resources by noting that to rebuild New York City alone, in terms of buildings, sewers, etc., would cost perhaps $1 trillion. Why don't we just make the money available and do this next year? After all, few would argue that it would not be desirable to replace rotting, ancient buildings with modern, comfortable structures. We all would be better off if this could be done.

But we just don't have the resources. Note that money capital must be translated into real resources, including in this case plumbers, building materials, steel, and everything else that would go into a city rebuilding program. It just isn't here. National income, which measures the flow of all productive effort, was about $1 trillion in 1970. If we tried to rebuild New York City next year, we would all starve to death. And of course if we tried this, we could not rebuild Chicago, Cincinnati, or Los Angeles, all of which have equally serious problems requiring expensive solutions.

It is well worth repeating that all societies have this fundamental problem. They may well ration resources in different ways, but anyone who takes a quick look at any country and concludes that there is always enough capital to go around, and hence everyone has all he needs, is shortsighted. Moreover, he will get exactly nowhere with any practical business or economic problem.

One may observe that the present rationing system is faulty on moral grounds. For example, a distiller may get $40 million to expand. Does this mean our system is corrupt or blind? Any system must make tricky moral judgments in its rationing system. Should certain stable, but "dubious," users get capital? We all have private judgments on such matters.

No matter what a country does, this mix of ethics and economics is always present. Soviet planners have decided not to allocate capital to building autos, while they do allocate large sums to railroads. Soviet citizens thus cannot buy cars, but they can ride comfortable trains. Such judgments were in part economic but were also moral. Citizens should not have cars!

The American rationing system, on the other hand, has made much capital available to auto makers and highway builders for seventy years. Hence Americans can ride cars, but they have trouble finding any passenger trains. Which decision is "correct"?

These points about the necessity of both rationing scarce resources and making moral judgments about the eventual results are included here because many critics of American business too hastily conclude that this or that reform would eliminate both problems. No reform will ever do this. It would just shift the situation to somewhat different grounds. Curiously, with the exception of some institutions involved in capital rationing in the United States, this entire chapter applies equally well to Great Britain, Rumania, India, Albania, and the Soviet Union. All countries and all cultures have the same problems. It is just the way they solve them that is different.

Basic Structures

The American capital rationing problem is shown diagrammatically in Figure 1. Some persons and institutions have funds that are in excess of their immediate requirements. These are the savers in the economy. Thus a firm may find that it holds cash balances in excess of its needs. It turns the funds over to others for safekeeping and interest earnings. Or an individual may put his surplus funds in a savings bank or buy a government bond. Such acts create savings for him, and he normally regards them as such. Government agencies at all levels may have temporary surpluses of funds, as when a county collects in one month its property taxes for six months. The county government may save by

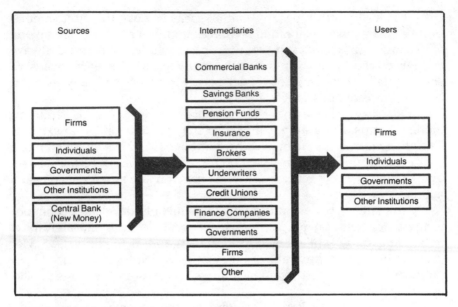

Figure 1. Capital Sources and Flows.

buying federal government bonds or interest-bearing certificates of deposit from local banks.

One supplier of savings is the Central Bank (Federal Reserve System). This one bank of issue creates new money in the form of new checking accounts of banknotes. No one else can do this.[1] The rest of us have to earn our money the hard way.

This money creation (or destruction) problem leads directly to macro-economics and the analysis of the total economic system. It partially determines what level of income, employment, and inflation the whole economic system has, which properly belongs in a course on macro-economics. But many perceptive businessmen and managers will spend much time studying this key point, since what these economic factors are, and how they are changing, will determine a firm's sales in the near future.

Funds saved by these persons and institutions normally flow into financial intermediaries, which are shown in Figure 1. These intermediaries, among other things, have the job of reallocating savings into

[1]It is possible to create new money through the pyramid of credit in the commercial banking system. This creation occurs as a result of fractional reserve banking practices and is described and analyzed in most basic economics texts. See Paul Samuelson, *Economics*, 3rd ed. (New York: McGraw-Hill, 1955), pp. 26–85, for one such explanation.

other uses. While some persons and firms are piling up surplus funds, many others are in need of them. One company may have a temporary surplus, but across town, another firm needs working capital to expand its inventories for the Christmas season. The commercial bank can take in savings from the first firm and make a loan to the second. Or a builder may need capital to construct a new apartment house. He goes to the local savings and loan association and borrows the funds that other individual savers have put in their accounts.

A financial intermediary is thus an institution that allocates capital. In the complex American economy, such intermediaries have evolved for two centuries, and they now present a richly complex pattern in themselves. The list in Figure 1 suggests only the major categories. There are intermediaries with very general business, such as commercial banks; there are others, such as savings and loan associations, that have quite limited and specific purposes; and there are even government agencies that perform this function, typically with narrow assigned purposes.

Most intermediaries are also private firms, and they have efficiency problems as well. They must try to be as efficient as possible, subject to the risks involved. Their profits come from the difference between the interest rates they pay and those they charge. Note also that risks are extremely important to such companies. It will not do to make a loan at 10 percent interest that never gets repaid. Hence intermediaries spend much time and effort evaluating loan requests. If they are not right most of the time, they go broke. This has happened many times and will happen again.

Each intermediary block in Figure 1 is a richly complex subject in itself, and one can find dozens or hundreds of books analyzing their operations. Such examinations range from diatribes about system corruption to very detailed managerial analyses of how to do the job right, given the legal and economic constraints under which such firms operate.

The final set in Figure 1 is the user block. All the savers are also borrowers—although not necessarily the same ones, as suggested above. Individuals borrow for both working and fixed capital needs; governments borrow to carry out their various functions, often including such investments as schools and roads; and other institutions, such as hospitals, private schools, and charitable organizations, also borrow occasionally, for many purposes. The uses to which such borrowed funds are put can be divided into consumption expenditures and capital. Our major interest is capital borrowing for firms, which includes many government firms.

Who gets the scarce funds? It depends. Firms with good records of financial solvency and the proven ability to repay loans tend to get funds at relatively low interest rates. The federal government, which controls the money supply (and hence can *always* repay loans) gets the lowest interest rates of all, because such loans are virtually risk-free. Consumers sometimes get loans, but they have to prove their ability to repay, as many of you may have already discoverd.

One bias the capital market always has is that potential borrowers always think that they can repay. The only exceptions are a few crooks who plan to borrow and skip. But intermediaries know from long and sad experience that thinking doesn't necessarily make it so. Hence they tend to be very careful about how they place funds. Since any borrower is totally convinced that his cause is just, and since many potential borrowers get turned down, much, much noise is always present in this subsystem. Cries about discrimination, about the "interests" who prevent proper lending, and so on, have been heard for 5,000 years. Capital *is* scarce, which means that somebody won't get his share.

Financial Markets

Of considerable interest to larger firms are the major financial markets in the United States. These markets grew in response to the needs for a mechanism to allocate funds to firms; they continue to grow as firms grow.

The complexity of such markets can be seen any day in the *Wall Street Journal*, or any major metropolitan newspaper that carries pages of fine print noting stock and bond transactions. Here several thousand of the largest firms offer, through the market, various stock and bond issues, along with various delightful mixes of convertible debentures, preferred stock, commercial paper, and many other esoteric items that show who owes what to whom. The purpose of such markets is to allow both lenders and borrowers, to say nothing of speculators, a chance to take part in this whole capital market.

Most quotations on any given day for stocks and bonds are for old issues. Here there is no new investment, but rather a transfer of ownership from one person or institution to another. If you buy ten shares of General Motors, you are giving up cash to obtain an earning asset. The seller gets your cash, and the broker pockets a commission for bringing buyer and seller together. Or if you decide to buy a local government school bond, the same principle applies. Nothing new has been added.

But on occasion, an underwriter offers a new issue. Here new stocks, bonds, or other securities are sold to investors. These investors give up cash for an earning asset, while the firm receiving the funds takes the cash for investment. As before, the underwriter takes a commission for bringing buyers and sellers together.

Such national securities markets help make the whole system more efficient, since buyers and sellers all over the world are brought together to allocate scarce money most efficiently. A little old lady in Pasadena may have ample funds and want income. New York Telephone may need funds but be unaware of where they might be. Through the market, the Pasadena lady gets her income, while the New York Telephone Company gets its funds. Hopefully, if it does its job right, the ultimate result may be better phone service in Syracuse at lower costs. Without the securities markets, such investment would be extremely difficult.

Stock and bond markets also have another delightful aspect, which is speculation. Since prices do vary depending on expectations of investors, it is possible to buy low and sell high. Many stories abound about the man who bought Xerox in 1954 at $10 per share and sold out in 1968 at perhaps $5,000 per share. Even the man who buys a good bond when interest rates are 8 percent and sells it when rates have fallen to 4 percent can double his money. Stock prices bounce around as firms show good or poor results, and wise investors can make money just in the buying and selling of such issues. Many do—and of course many go broke also, since this market works both ways.

Societies since at least 1600 have been hit from time to time by speculative manias, and modern America is no exception. Somehow, to most people, the idea of buying at 10 and selling a week or so later at 500 represents the ultimate dream of something for nothing. If enough people get carried away, the result can be a bull market, with prices rising daily, with millionaires being made everywhere—until finally sobriety and realism rear their ugly heads, and collapse occurs. Moralists then speak ominously about ethical decay and moral lapse, and sadder but wiser (and poorer) investors and speculators count their losses. Inevitably, a few sharp operators come out of the game way ahead, but such individuals usually say little.

This speculative activity interweaves with the serious business of getting scarce capital allocated and providing opportunities for all investors to get into whatever kinds of assets (including cash) they prefer. Persons who dislike gambling tend to view the whole affair as something morally depraved. Those who like to play numbers and the ponies tend to enjoy the game as soon as they accumulate a small surplus to begin activities. As with most human institutions, there is much good and bad in the situation.

Capital Market Controls

Any time there is a chance to make easy money, we encounter the sharp operators, confidence men, and crooks. Dealings in the ultimate asset—cash—always attract such dubious individuals. Since no one person can know enough about a given investment or financial intermediary to

Intermediary	Regulating Institution
Commercial Banks	General Law, Federal Reserve System, Federal Deposit Insurance Corporation, State Banking Laws
Savings Banks	Same as Commercial Banks
Savings & Loan	Federal and State Regulatory Laws
Pension Funds	Trustee Laws
Insurance Companies	State Insurance Legislation, State Regulatory Agencies
Brokers	General Contract Law, Securities and Exchange Commission (SEC)
Underwriters	Same as Brokers
Credit Unions	Special Federal and State Law
Finance Companies	Special State Legislation
Governments	Various Specific Acts, State and Federal
Firms	General Contract Law

Figure 2. Regulation of Capital Markets.

avoid fraud, and since we have had many instances over the years of major and minor frauds in these markets, we now have very complex legislation to regulate all parties in such transactions. Figure 2 shows the general pattern of regulation for intermediaries.

Such laws take three basic forms:

General Legislation. This may apply to all buyers and sellers, as well as trustees. Neither party can defraud the other by giving false information or attempting systematically to defraud. A trustee is, by law, given certain obligations and responsibilities, such as always attempting to maximize the interests of the party for whom he is trustee. Hence if a trustee knowingly sold securities at lower than market prices, he is in deep trouble.

Regulatory Law. Here intermediaries are prevented from doing certain things. A savings and loan institution cannot lend its funds to borrowers other than those involved in the housing and construction markets; a commercial bank may be unable to lend any one customer more than a given percentage of its deposits; an insurance company may be able to hold only specific types of securities; or a government agency may be able to lend only to customers of a given type.

Informational Law. The idea is to force intermediaries and borrowers to disclose all information about the proposed loan. A prospectus is issued, which explains carefully what is to be done and what the expected risks are. Until the prospectus is approved, the issue cannot legally be offered.

As with all law, these noted above are extremely complex, and a good lawyer can spend a lifetime working with one small part of them. But the basic idea is clear. If we are to have complex, large, and anonymous markets where millions of persons place their funds with limited knowledge, then a variety of controls must be used.

Of course crooks and thieves work along as usual, law or no law. If a man just might, with a bit of thought and ingenuity, convince a banker or broker to lend him a million dollars, which he can then skip with and spend in Brazil, such activities will be tried. And even a reputable firm in need of cash may hedge a bit in giving information about its new issue of commercial paper. On occasion, we read about a small bank that went broke because its largest borrower skipped, or a salad oil firm that borrowed money on the basis of falsified invoices showing more oil than it possessed, or a broker who illegally used his customers' money to speculate unsuccessfully on the market. Occasionally, blondes and ponies are involved, but more often it appears that the basic reason was the eternal optimism of such persons, who "knew" that the market would rise tomorrow, or that some poor investment would turn out right in the end.

International Money Markets

To this point, we have discussed only American markets. But like most things in this steadily shrinking world, we find that nowadays both Americans and foreigners jump national frontiers in lending and borrowing.

Thus an American firm may have extensive operations in France, and it may feel that it can successfully borrow needed capital in the French money market. Here the Americans go abroad, often with considerable success, to tap sources of savings in another country. Or a French firm, having surplus funds, may decide to buy American bonds for investment purposes. Daily, literally billions of dollars flow back and forth across national boundaries as firms, individuals, and countries seek optimum advantage.

To borrow money in France, a firm would have to study carefully all French legal and economic constraints, as well as the pattern of French monetary institutions. We would have to rework Figure 1 to reflect French patterns, since very possibly some of the intermediaries noted would not exist, while other uniquely French institutions might be extremely important.

Similarly, a Frenchman buying shares on the New York Stock Exchange would have to know something about American institutional patterns. Since many foreigners do invest, information about American markets is demanded, and books with titles such as *Know the Stock Market* are sold in Paris and London as well as San Francisco and Seattle.

Capital flows across national borders also are subject to many separate international constraints. Some countries do not let their nationals buy or sell foreign currencies; others allow transactions under special rules. Such rules work both ways—if an American buys a British stock, he must pay high special taxes on the transaction.

Many large American firms, and many foreign firms, use the major international market in dollars. This Eurodollar market is supplied by foreign savers who have accumulated American dollars. The dollars pass through various intermediaries (mainly commercial banks) and are lent to others to be repaid in dollars. Here the dollar becomes an international currency, since a British firm may borrow dollars, use them to make machinery sold to Iran, and use the proceeds in dollars to repay the loan. With Americans not remotely involved in the transaction, the dollar gains an international flavor.

Such international markets bother domestic regulators, who feel correctly that they are very hard to control. When a firm is wheeling and dealing across twenty countries, borrowing and lending in perhaps twelve currencies, working through both foreign and domestic banks, no single country can control very much. And of course one major reason for going international in this way is just to avoid some petty control in some country, maybe even your own. It is frustrating for regulators, but such international markets do serve a useful purpose of allocating scarce capital on a world rather than local basis.

Government Capital Sources

Since many feel that they cannot get capital, and since some persons are in a position to apply political pressures, we often find government programs that provide capital for specific purposes. Thus in the United States, there are special agencies to channel capital to home-building (Federal Mortgage Association) and to build rural electric facilities (Rural Electrification Administration); in 1970 a new agency was established to provide capital to operate passenger trains. We also have a Small Business Administration, which provides capital for smaller companies that may be unable to get funds from conventional sources.

Often such government lending takes the form of guarantees rather than cash. Thus if you want to build ocean-going ships, you may qualify for special government guarantees. If the loan goes sour, the lender can get his money back from the federal government. Since the government's credit is good, a private lender may be willing to act.

As with everything else connected with capital, this is an extremely complicated area. Literally hundreds of government programs exist that either lend directly or guarantee loans, and it would take hundreds of pages just to describe them. The basic reasons for such activities is public disappointment in private markets. If something is not being done, or is being done badly, a new program is started to remedy the deficiency.

Private firms lend money to make money, and they normally will not make loans that appear to them to be unsound. If better opportunities exist, the loan will go there. The reason a shipbuilder or a homeowner cannot get his loan is because, given the risks, rates of return, and other factors, the lender prefers to make the loan elsewhere. In short, capital allocations are not necessarily made on the basis of what is socially desirable.

Special programs that reallocate scarce capital in this way tend to be inefficient. One good measure of how well any country allocates its resources is the rate of return on investment. If a government loan earns 2 percent, while good private loans yield 8 percent, some capital is being misemployed. We may get better houses or low-earning ships, but our wealth increases more slowly as a result. At the extreme, if all capital were put in no-return places, we would not grow at all, although we might be richer in some noneconomic sense, such as having more assets that earn no return, such as museums, parks, and public monuments. And of course, if we grow more slowly, we have less income to spread around to all.

This is not a serious problem in the United States, since government capital programs do not take many resources. But some countries (Great Britain is one) where the public sector is large, and where much capital is invested in loss-producing or low-return enterprises, find it difficult to figure out why their economy grows so slowly, even though billions of dollars are being invested every year.

Government loan programs tend to be forced savings for many firms and individuals. Because they must pay their taxes, they may be forced to finance government loan programs that use some of their tax money. The taxpayer might have preferred to pay less taxes and spend the money as he sees fit, but he cannot. Such programs stem from the political rather than the economic processes, and although they reflect what citizens generally want, they can be very unproductive.

Note again the moral issue here. If a society wants to invest in anything at all, it can do so. Citizens may well feel that such things as schools, monuments, or rapid transit systems are desirable. But the usual paradox arises: what makes a society rich and what is ethically desirable do not necessarily coincide. One may well have to pay the piper in the end.

Firm Financial Activities

To this point, we have considered only the capital markets, with all of their rich complexities. Firms have to get at such markets to obtain

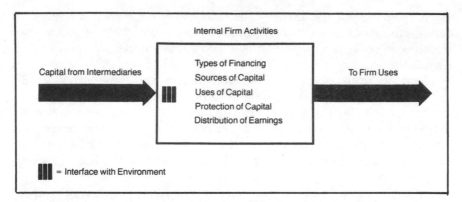

Figure 3. Firm Financial Activities.

needed funds. The way they do this is to demonstrate to suspicious intermediaries that they know how to use capital wisely and well and that they will earn large profits and pay back the loans.

To do this, any firm must perform its critical internal financial activities efficiently. Figure 3 shows what is needed. The firm must make the correct decisions about the critical elements of the financial process which are shown in Figure 3.

A handful of major corporations do this job so well that their ability to obtain capital is virtually unlimited. But this does not mean that they can expand indefinitely or take over the world. The major reasons they are so reputable financially is that they always do well, and the main reason they have always done well is that they rarely try anything that has a high probability of not paying off. This means that in addition to capital, they can obtain all other inputs too.

This is the rub. The usual limiting factor for such firms is the shortage of good management, which is a type of labor input. Somehow, even though billions of dollars are available, the managers who can make the billions pay off are not. Firms with such managers can and do expand at perhaps 5 to 10 percent per year, but those growing faster are extremely rare.

But most firms, including virtually all smaller ones, see capital as the absolute constraint. Somehow they can never find enough money to do what they really want to do. Hence their extreme interest in all relevant capital markets and intermediaries. If the money can be obtained, everything else falls in place.

Note also that the financial elements are very closely interrelated to all other managerial critical elements. One can plan the uses of capital extremely well, but if the production department, which is a major user of funds, falls down on its job, the plan may fail. Or if proper technicians and managers are not hired, the company cannot do its job, and it quickly gets into financial trouble. A few mistakes like this, and money becomes very hard to come by. Also, many firms do not have any successful experience to refer to when bargaining for funds, so they have difficulty convincing lenders that their promises can be kept.

Conclusion

Money is the lifeblood of any business, so firms pay close attention to capital sources. If they cannot get funds, they are dead.

What is always happening in financial markets is the allocation of scarce resources. More of us want money than there is available. How does society allocate it? This is a question that every country has to solve, one way or the other. It is commonly assumed that communist countries do not have to worry, but all that is happening in them is that the allocation mechanism is somewhat different from what it is in the United States. No society ever had so much money that it could avoid this problem.

The United States has the most intricate and complex capital markets of any country, which is logical, given its large economy and vast capital resources. Hence any serious study of money raising here must necessarily be more involved than anywhere else. Firm managers and intermediary managers have to study very carefully all options open to them before making the correct moves.

And finally, one can never escape the ethics of capital. Whatever is done will be disagreed with by many for moral, rather than economic, reasons. Some uses of capital will be seen as immoral or frivolous, and many suggestions for improvements will constantly be made. One result of such pressure in the United States has been the creation of special government markets in many areas where private capital has not gone, in the hope that in this way various socially useful aims will be achieved.

Al expected Mr. Goldberg's office to be pretty plush, and he wasn't disappointed. It was actually on Wall Street. Al figured that anyone who could find a billion dollars for you could probably afford the best. The firm of Ricks and Goldberg obviously could.

"I read your pamphlet on money, Mr. Goldberg. It gave me a lot of useful information. One thing I noticed was that it didn't sound like a bunch of conservative bankers talking. I mean, you actually seemed to recognize that there are other points of view about what you do."

Mr. Goldberg smiled. He was a man in his late fifties or early sixties, trim, extremely well dressed in a conservative way, wearing rimless glasses.

At last, Al thought, one of my images is correct. Mr. Goldberg looked exactly the way Al felt a conservative moneyman should.

"Well, Mr. Faber, that little booklet was written for average investors, not bankers. We are well aware that brokers and underwriters do not, ah, have a noble image in this modern world. We might as well face this fact and consider why this is so."

"As you say, anyone with money is both a minority and easy to get mad at," Al commented. "I have trouble understanding your point that capital is limited. Everywhere I look I see plenty of it."

"But it is limited just the same. Many revolutionaries have thought differently, until they came to power. Only then, when *they* had to ration scarce resources, did they realize that what we have been saying for centuries is really true. Consider Lenin, in Russia, in 1919."

Al remembered something. "Say, are you the Jason Goldberg who wrote *Crisis in Russia: The Capital Crunch in the Twenties?* I remember that *Newsworld* ran a quite favorable review of it a few months ago."

"Yes, I am. You seem surprised. You see, my father came from Russia in 1908, after a political crisis. I've always been interested in the Soviet Union, and of course I'm particularly interested in how they ration their capital and deal with their money problems."

It's a strange world, Al thought. Bankers write scholarly books, women audit accounts, and blacks run computers. "I see why your pamphlet tends to be broad," Al said. "You have a scholarly interest in what's going on."

"Oh, yes. But please, I don't want to bore you with my scholarly ramblings. How can I help you?"

"I'm looking at RVA."

"Yes, so Lamont Baxter said."

"I see that you're about to underwrite a $180 million bond issue for RVA. I can understand from your booklet the general problem, but exactly how do you go about finding $180 million?"

Mr. Goldberg smiled. "Actually the process starts long before we find the money. We have been working with RVA for over twenty years, and we have underwritten a number of their stock and bond issues. As a result, we have a great deal of knowledge about the company. We know the management people well, and we know their accounting and financial people very well too. By the way, how is Miss Masters these days?"

I'm glad I don't have to keep any secrets around these guys, Al thought. "Oh, she's fine. We're going to a show tonight, in fact."

"Give her my regards. She has a fine financial mind, unusual in a woman." Mr. Goldberg stopped and grinned sheepishly. "I suppose that is a sexist comment. I'm too old, Mr. Faber, too old. I was educated the wrong way. In any case, we are quite aware of what RVA is doing, and what it is planning to do. We are aware of their financial record, their cash position, and how well they forecast their activities. If they are promising you that they will pay back $180 million in five years, you can see that knowing how well they can forecast might be critical. We are aware of their asset positions, and we are quite aware of what their books really mean."

"What do you mean by that?" Al asked. "Aren't their books audited?"

"Of course, and we know their auditors well, too. But remember that accounting conventions and law require statements which may not be correct. For example, land and buildings are carried at historic costs. Thus, the RVA headquarters building, which is wholly owned by RVA, cost $16.7 million some eighteen years ago. We know that its present value is over $75 million. This asset is actually worth much more than the books show. On the other hand, certain land RVA purchased for $4.7 million in 1975 in New Mexico is now only worth about $2.1 million. You see, if we had to foreclose to get our money, such information would be very useful."

"I can see that. So you follow the company closely. Then what?"

"We are quite confident that RVA can easily carry the extra debt. The rating agencies, Poor's and Moody's, agree. RVA bonds have a rating of A, which is quite good, not the best, but good. Potential investors will look at these ratings before they buy."

"One thing puzzles me, Mr. Goldberg. Why does RVA want to issue

> Rating Agencies — organizations which rate the risk of new bond issues for potential buyers. Poor's and Moody's are the largest and best known.
>
> Ratings are letter grade. The higher the rating, the less risky the bond, and hence the lower the interest rate. A triple A (AAA) bond rating is best, while a B is pretty risky.
>
> Buyers watch ratings very closely. Raters must have impeccable reputations!

bonds now, instead of stock, or possibly preferred stock? According to Mr. Baxter's pamphlet, common stock would seem to be a better deal."

"Possibly. But the actual choice depends on RVA's financial structure right now. There is a point in tax law which is important here, and a second point for existing shareholders."

"Please explain."

"Interest paid on fixed interest securities is a cost, and hence tax deductible. Suppose that we have an interest rate of twelve percent on that $180 million. This would mean that $21.6 million in new interest expense would be incurred by RVA, and this money is deducted from net profits before income taxes are computed."

Al thought for a moment. "I see what you mean. If they issued $180 million in common stock and made the $21.6 million, they would have to pay corporate income taxes on that. If the tax rate is 40 percent, that could get expensive."

"Correct, Mr. Faber. But then consider the issue from the standpoint of present stockholders. If RVA issued more stock, then their equity would be diluted. By issuing bonds, the present owners maintain their existing share of power."

Al asked about equity dilution, and Mr. Goldberg explained. "You see, it does matter which type of capital you raise. But to raise capital by selling bonds, you have to have good credit."

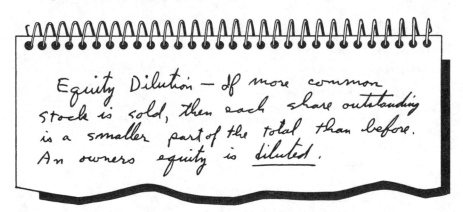

Equity Dilution — If more common stock is sold, then each share outstanding is a smaller part of the total than before. An owners equity is <u>diluted</u>.

"I suppose that you'll have one of those tombstone ads for this issue," Al said.

"Yes, you'll see one soon in such financial papers as the *Wall Street Journal*. Remember that we are very carefully regulated by the SEC as to what we can say about new issues. Those ads are not very exciting, but they do inform potential investors as to what is happening."

"If you were selling a stock issue instead of a bond issue, would the process be very different?" Al asked.

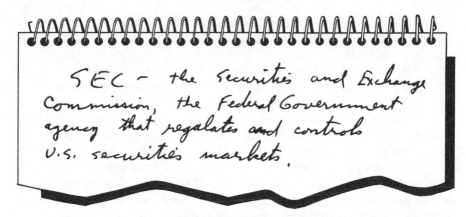

SEC - the Securities and Exchange Commission, the Federal Government agency that regulates and controls U.S. securities markets.

"No, not really. We would possibly work with different buyers, who might have different views of risk, but essentially we do the same things."

"OK, suppose that we now know that this RVA bond issue is a good deal. What next?"

"We begin to think about marketing and pricing. The price is the interest rate on the bonds. Obviously we have to be in line with other prices. No one will buy a $1,000 bond paying nine percent a year when he or she can buy a similarly risky bond paying twelve percent."

"I certainly wouldn't, assuming I had the money, which I don't," Al said. "I suppose that you follow interest rates very closely?"

"Certainly, and they have been changing rapidly in recent years. Going from ten percent to eleven percent doesn't seem like much, but that is a ten percent increase in the cost of money. One percent extra for $180 million is $1.8 million per year. Note our problem. We can't offer the issue at too high a price, or two things will happen. The issue will be oversubscribed, and RVA will be very upset. They pay more for their money than they have to, and we are not likely to remain their underwriter for long. But if we offer the issue at too low a price, we are stuck with the bonds, since no one will buy them."

"So you actually guarantee RVA that the bonds will be sold?"

"Yes we do, and one of our biggest risks is that we misjudge the market badly. It has happened, even to us."

"And that is one reason why you get a nice commission for selling RVA's bonds," Al commented.

"Yes. Another reason is that we know where to sell them. We also spend a lot of time worrying about who buyers might be. We cultivate buyers as assiduously as we cultivate RVA. You see, we are in the middle. To underwrite this issue successfully, we have to balance between seller and buyer. If we do our job, we earn our commission. RVA could not do this work, since they lack the knowledge and skills. The typical investor, even a large investor, could not do it either. We help both out."

"Where do you find the kinds of people who can spare $180 million?" Al asked. "I know you're not talking to any of my friends. Most of them couldn't spare eighty cents!"

"Do you contribute to your pension fund at *Newsworld*?"

"Sure, about thirty dollars a month. The company puts in the same amount."

"Your *Newsworld* pension fund receives over two million dollars a month. Its investment committee and its board of directors are anxious to invest this money at interest in safe and sound securities. In this way, your pension will be guaranteed. I can assure you that *Newsworld*'s pension fund will receive a copy of the RVA prospectus. They might well buy, let us say, a million dollars' worth of this issue, and you will have invested in spite of yourself. Similarly, if you have insurance policies . . ."

"I do," Al said.

". . . those companies also invest for the purpose of increasing the value of their reserves. We even sell an occasional bond to some wealthy individuals. Pension funds, trust funds, insurance companies, union pension funds, other large companies with surplus cash, a few foreigners, brokerage houses, and quite a few others will be buying these bonds."

"So you let them know about it, and they buy."

"We send them a copy of the prospectus, and you know that we are very carefully controlled by law as to what we can say. I'll send you a copy of the RVA prospectus if you wish. It will be ready in a few days."

"Thanks, I'd like to see one," Al said. "Now, if you have it all figured out right, RVA gets its bonds sold, some big institutional investors get some interest, and you get a commission. Capital has been rationed, as your booklet says."

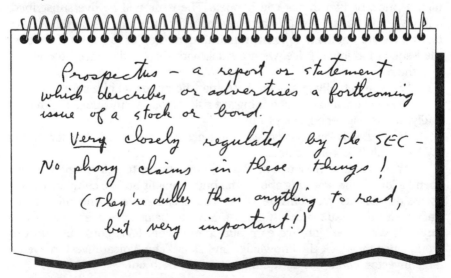

Prospectus — a report or statement which describes or advertises a forthcoming issue of a stock or bond.

Very closely regulated by the SEC — No phony claims in these things!

(They're duller than anything to read, but very important!)

"That is correct," Mr. Goldberg said. "And RVA will use this money to expand several plants, modernize another one, and build a small new facility in Oklahoma. A few more people will be employed, some contractors will hire still more people to expand those plants, and in the end, RVA should make more money. It's been following this pattern for many years now, with considerable success. You see, Mr. Faber, RVA is one of those companies that has learned to use money wisely and well. As a result, it tends to get more. I suppose that the rich keep getting richer, but it is one way to make sure that our capital gets used properly."

"You wouldn't do all of this for an untested company, would you?"

"Probably not, although we occasionally do try to underwrite an issue for a smaller company, often for the first time in its history. We did this with RVA only twenty-two years ago, and look what has happened. This is the way we keep growing ourselves. If we don't find newcomers, we may discover that we cannot grow ourselves."

"That sounds odd, Mr. Goldberg. After all, once you're rich and powerful, you stay that way forever."

"Just how many of the fifty largest American firms in 1917 do you think are still in the top fifty today?"

Al shrugged. "Probably all of them, except a few that merged."

"You should study more history. Only four or five are left. Most of the rest have gone bankrupt or been absorbed by rivals that did not even exist in 1917. No, being big and rich is not guaranteed. It is very easy to get set in your ways, sedate, suspicious of new ideas ... and then some other minor company comes along and wipes you out. RVA itself is an example."

"It only dates from the mid-1920's, and its first products didn't exist in 1917. OK, I see what you mean. But it still sounds like you pander to the successful."

" 'Pander' is such an ugly word, but I really suppose that we do. We, and our clients, have a bad habit of wanting our money back. Going with tested people and companies is a way of assuring that."

"Well, I want mine back too, so I'm sympathetic," Al said. But he really wasn't too sure he was.

DISCUSSION QUESTIONS

1. Obtain any copy of the *Wall Street Journal* for a recent day. Take a close look at it, and then consider these questions:

What kinds of financial markets are covered in the *Journal*? List all of them.

Note one advertisement stating that a new bond or stock issue is being offered. What information is presented here? What seems to be missing that you might want to know?

Find the section on foreign bonds and see what issues are being offered and for what prices and interest rates. Why would any American want to buy such risky things as foreign government bonds?

On most days several companies announce their dividends for the past quarter or year. Find one of these and state what happened. Why would a lender be interested in such a statement?

In the news part of the *Journal*, there are usually announcements of firms offering new production processes, or marketing agreements. Find one of these and see what is being reported. Why would any investor care about such things?

Pick any stock you wish and plot its performance for a month. What happened to the stock? Did it go up or down? Could you have made money by buying or selling it? Show how.

Pick any corporate bond you want and plot its price for a month. Could you have made any money here? How?

The *Journal* always carries some news items about various environmental factors. Much of the focus is on economic and legal news. Pick any such item and suggest why investors and borrowers might be interested in the information.

2. If you ever had a savings account at a bank, you have taken part in the capital formation process. Why did you put your money in a bank? What did you get for it? What safety factors exist in law and regulation to make you feel more secure about your money?

3. Where would a life insurance company get so much money to lend to firms? Check around your library to see if you can find out why such an institution has so much ready cash.

4. Your state uses much capital to build highways. Much of this money comes from taxpayers who buy fuel, and part of it is borrowed from the money market in some years.

Would you regard these expenditures as an investment? Why or why not? Why would a bank, insurance company, or corporation buy state bonds for this purpose? What do they get out of it? What risks do they take?

5. For many years the federal government has lent money at very low interest rates to nonprofit rural electric cooperatives to build electric power systems. Such systems make money only because they get loans at very low interest rates. It is common for the federal government to borrow at ten percent to relend at four percent to these cooperatives.

Do you like this idea? Why or why not? What virtue does this plan have from a business viewpoint? From a social viewpoint?

6. Select any one of the financial intermediaries listed in Figure 1 of the Ricks and Goldberg pamphlet and do a report in depth about it. Indicate exactly how this intermediary is organized, what laws regulate its behavior, what kinds of loans it can make, and if possible how much money it makes. Also suggest what are now seen as major problems in this area. What kinds of reforms, if any, are being proposed?

7. Visit your local commercial bank and find out what is needed to obtain a small business loan. What kinds of firm financial plans or other information does a banker want to see before he decides to make a loan? What security is he or she likely to insist on? Why? If he did make the loan, what interest rate would he charge?

8. Visit your local savings and loan association and find out what kinds of loans they make. What kinds of security do they want? What interest rate would they charge for a loan? Why is this rate so much higher than the rate they offer on their savings accounts?

9. Your college or university probably has a pension fund for its employees. Visit this office, if possible, and find out what the pension fund does with its money. Do you think that these investments are good and safe? Why or why not? What other options are available to the fund?

10. Consider carefully Mr. Goldberg's discussion of how his firm allocates capital. Is this fair?

Suppose RVA was going to use the money to build a factory to make slot machines to use in Atlantic City casinos. Is your answer the same? Why or why not?

Suppose that RVA was going to use the money to build a plant to manufacture a new type of kidney dialysis machine that will save hundreds of lives per year. RVA will of course make a big profit on the sale of each machine. Is your answer the same? Why or why not?

11. What is a financial intermediary?

12. What is an underwriter?

13. What does the SBA (Small Business Administration) do? Do you think that this agency serves a useful purpose?

17

SOCIAL RESPONSIBILITY

Well, so much for RVA's super-efficiency," Joe Chapman said, as the elevator shuddered, then stopped. The lights dimmed, then came on again.

"I think you're bad luck, Joe," Jack Tribble said. "I've been on these elevators a thousand times, and nothing ever happened."

"No, Al's the bad luck," Joe replied. "What are you doing this time, besides chasing Vicki?"

Al sighed. "I was going up to talk to James Marer."

"Wow!" Joe said. "The board chairman. All the way to the top!"

"Be quiet, guys," Vicki said. She was working the emergency phone. She told someone what had happened, listened for a minute, then hung up.

"They're checking it out, something about a burnt out bearing in the lift cable. He said that it will take a while, so we wait. The lights and air conditioning will stay on."

Al glanced around the elevator. Joe, Vicki, Jack, and the little old janitor, plus himself. No plan here, just some people who happened to get on the same elevator going up to the 40th floor. "As someone once said, you may wonder why I called this meeting," he said.

"Yeah, why did you call it?" Joe asked. "It's a bit too pat to just have happened. I think you planned the whole thing."

The emergency phone rang, and Vicki answered it. "They say it will take an hour or so, and to just relax and take it easy."

"OK, we take it easy," Jack said. "What do we talk about?"

"Al, what were you going to see Marer about?" Joe asked. "You have an expert panel here on just about everything, and we even have a real live member of the working class here." He looked at the janitor. "What's your name?"

"Wojciechowski, Stanislaus Wojciechowski."

"Ah, from the old country, eh?"

"Yes, I come from Poland, long ago."

Joe turned to Al. "OK, you have your panel. What's the subject?"

"I was going to talk to Mr. Marer about corporate social responsibility,"

Al replied. "I've been looking around RVA for quite a while now, and it's time to think a bit about whether or not you're responsible."

"Why ask Marer?" Joe asked. "He'll just give you the usual public relations stuff about how great and noble RVA is. Why not talk to the working stiffs?"

"OK, let's talk about social responsibility. How do you want to do it? Open ended discussion, or do you want to give speeches?"

"I like speeches," Vicki said. "Otherwise, Joe would monopolize the conversation."

"I yield to the lady," Joe said, bowing. "Vicki, you're first. Tell us all about how socially responsible RVA is."

Al took out his notebook. "And anything you say can be used against you, or RVA."

"Lots of people seem to think that profits are inherently evil," Vicki began, "and as a result, any private, profit seeking organization is inherently evil. Some people think that bigness is the key, that it's OK to make money if you run a little garage or fish shop, but wrong if you're big and powerful. And lots of people keep asking questions like, 'If you're so smart, why don't you fix up the ghettoes, or teach kids to read, instead of peddling soap or shoes or TV cassettes?' If people think that you're inherently evil, the discussion doesn't get very far."

"This is a fix," Joe muttered. "Vicki, it sounds like you memorized that spiel."

"Shut up and listen," Jack Tribble said. "You agreed to speeches, and you'll get your turn."

"But if you really want to talk about social responsibility, you have to start talking about goals. What are corporations for?" Vicki went on.

"To make money," Joe said.

"To make stuff, I guess," Al said.

"Yes, that's the historical reason," Vicki said, "and it's still important. People and organizations have roles to fill. Doctors cure the sick, surveyors prepare maps, and corporations produce goods and services. No one complains when Sam's Bicycle Shop, run and owned by Sam, does nothing more than fix up bicycles and does a good job. If Sam makes money, that's his business. But if you get big and powerful, people expect more. Besides, there may be a monopoly implication. Sam will never have the only game in the whole country for bicycles, but a big company may be huge and oligopolistic or monopolistic, too."

"OK," Al said. "So you start with goals. RVA's are pretty clear cut. The company tries to make money. Most of what I've seen involves searching for profitable markets. If you're smart and competent, and maybe lucky, you make money, sometimes big money."

"Long ago," Vicki went on. "That's all there was to it. But now, people want more. They want us to be responsible. Now, back to goals. Responsible to whom? For what?"

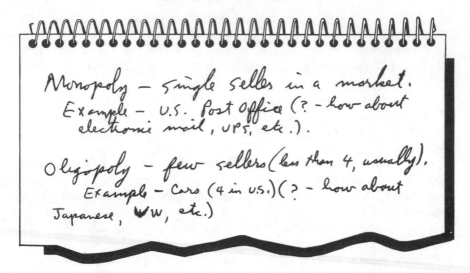

Monopoly — single seller in a market.
Example — U.S. Post Office (? — how about electronic mail, UPS, etc.).

Oligopoly — few sellers (less than 4, usually).
Example — Cars (4 in U.S.)(? — how about Japanese, VW, etc.)

"There are plenty of problems around," Al said. "Poverty, unemployment, discrimination, rotting cities, crime..."

"Sure, but do you really want RVA messing around with the police force? We don't know a thing about police forces."

"You do sell alarm systems and safes, though," Al said, thinking of Mr. Suzuki and what he might make of all this.

"But we don't really know how to do a better job of crime fighting than professional criminologists and police experts. So we pay taxes and let the proper people do it. If society wants to spend more money on crime, then raise taxes and do it, or shift taxes around. You don't ask a lawyer about your health, you ask your doctor."

Al nodded. "So you're saying that RVA should just go about its business making money, if it can, pay its taxes, observe the law, and let others do the dirty work, right?"

"That's about it." Vicki fished in her purse and found a lozenge. "This is all the food supply I have."

"It's funny you should take that conservative position, Vicki," Jack said. "If that had been the case, neither you nor I would be around this company. RVA, like most big companies, was pretty much male chauvinist and racist not too long ago. If they had just 'obeyed the law,' as you say, we'd probably still be looking for jobs."

"No, Jack, Vicki's right on that one," Al replied. "As I recall, RVA didn't do very much about job discrimination until the Civil Rights Act of 1964 was passed. They even dragged their feet for quite a while after that. But then the legal heat got turned on, and RVA decided to change. So your company observes the law, just as Vicki says. There's no big responsibility in that."

"Hey, Al, I thought we were making speeches," Joe said. "I want to hear Vicki finish. It's rare these days to hear a real reactionary talk, particularly a pretty one."

"Are you done, Vicki?" Al asked.

"Not quite. Remember Mr. Beeman's PARF loops?"

Everyone but Mr. Wojciechowski groaned. "Who doesn't?" Joe asked.

Vicki threw a paper clip at Joe. "Nevertheless, remember how they work. If you have a nice, quantifiable goal, and if you plan, operate, etc., right, you can get good results. You see, Al, profits are the major feedback loop. They tell you what to do. If a corporation has the central goal of long-term profit maximization, then all its activities are in line with that overall goal. You know when to quit and when to expand. That's really why profit maximizing organizations do so well. They *always* know what to do. Now, you tell me, 'End poverty,' and I don't know what poverty is!"

"It's lack of money," Jack said. "Believe me, I know."

"It's that, Jack, but it's much more. No one pays much attention to poor college students, and boy, they can be poor! But they usually won't be for long. No, poverty is poor health, lack of education, despair, and so on. We've been trying to get people out of poverty for a long time, and we still have plenty of poverty. I don't know what the problem is, so I don't know how to structure my goals, so I just mess around with the problem."

"Yeah," Al added. "Mr. Beeman said something like that. How many souls can your church save? How many should it save? How can you tell?"

"You're right," Vicki said. "If you stick a modern, profit seeking corporation with some nebulous social goals, you'll get in trouble fast. Either the company gets bogged down in the new problems and doesn't get anywhere, or it ignores them. Either way, nothing much gets done."

"Consider the U.S. Post Office," Joe said.

"That's exactly it," Vicki continued. "People get mad at it all the time and claim that it's inefficient. But the real problem is that the goals of the Post Office are so mixed up. They want to pay their workers well, so costs go up. They want to deliver mail to everybody, so people way out in the sticks get a twenty cent letter delivered for ten dollars. They want to be known for their technological advances, so they buy lots of expensive capital equipment that might not pay off. And, by the way, they want to break even, or make some money. You just can't have it all ways. Actually, the Post Office has some really first rate managers. Their problem is that they just don't know what's important."

Jack Tribble nodded. "Vicki's right there. A close friend of mine works for the Post Office, and he's absolutely first rate, brilliant. But he has trouble figuring out what he should be working on." Trib leaned back into the corner of the elevator. "Actually, that's about the only thing I do agree with Vicki about. You're wrong on all counts."

"Good," Joe said. "I was afraid that we'd all agree, and then what would we talk about? Mr. Chairman, can we give Jack the floor?"

"Go ahead, Jack," Vicki said. "I'm done, for the moment."

Jack waved his hands. "Sure, Vicki's right when she talks about how
hard it is to fix goals for social causes. She may even be right when she talks
about trying to get at infinite goals, like happiness, or saving souls, with finite
resources. But it's a cop out to think that you can just do your job and
nothing more. Most things in this world are non-business things. Religion,
art, music, the whole human condition ... that's what matters. Sure, we
produce soap and cassettes and locks and earth movers, because these jobs
have to be done. But a corporation, particularly a giant corporation, is a part
of this world, and it has to live with every part of it, not just the production
part."

"So what should we do, Jack?" Vicki asked. "Give some money to the
New York Symphony?"

"Sure, and we should give some more to the Harlem street musicians.
We might even commission a painting or two. But much more importantly,
we should try to figure out what the world is and where it's going, and then
get up at the head of the line, not wait until someone passes a law and tells
us what to do. RVA should have been hiring blacks and women for responsible positions forty years ago, not just since 1970."

"You did," Al commented. "Mr. Suzuki did it a long time ago."

"Sure," Jack said. "To save money, because he could get them cheaply.
Suzuki's no moral hero, Al. Didn't you talk to his production man, John
Jefferson? And anyway, the rest of RVA didn't. We should be thinking about
how to revitalize cities, not how to get out of them, as we're doing. We
should be thinking a lot about poverty, and how to prevent it, instead of just
paying taxes reluctantly."

"There's real money in poverty these days," Joe said. "That's what a
friend of mine at a consulting firm said a while back. You figure out a good
poverty study, and then you get a million-dollar federal grant to do the
research. No one gets out of poverty, except my friend, but then he wasn't
poor to start with."

Jack sighed. "Joe, that comment shows exactly what's wrong with RVA,
and for that matter, the whole society. We're cynical, or we try to figure out
what's in it for Number One, instead of trying to figure out how to change
people for the better. That probably explains why the Reagan administration
is cutting back on those poverty funds and other social benefits. It's a lot
easier to say to hell with it than it is to find good solutions to really important
problems."

"You go to church to do that," Vicki said. "You can't expect a company
to start figuring out how to make their employees more moral."

"No man is an island," Jack said. "You have to try. You always have
to try. If your society's rotten, then it's your job, as an individual or a corporation, to make it better."

"Look, Jack, I'm a busy man," Al said. "Suppose I agree with you, and philosophically, I think I do. Just what do I do to begin? Do I join a club that tries to end discrimination? Do I spend two hours a week meditating on the evils of man? Do I try to talk my boss into carrying more stories about the poor and downtrodden of this world?"

"Every person has to do it his or her own way," Jack replied. "But you have to try."

"Jack, you're back in a time and money sink," Vicki said. "You can't do it all, alone or as part of a group, and you can't figure out your priorities. So you muddle around, wasting time and money, and maybe you feel good. But nothing much happens."

Jack shook his head. "No, Vicki, you try. I'd like to see somebody important in this corporation get up, just once, and say that RVA will hire more minorities than the law requires, or put some money, even at a loss, into ghetto jobs, or start a training program for young minority kids, who couldn't get any kind of job right now. I'd like to see someone volunteer to clean up a river we polluted before the government made us."

"One man's meat is another man's poison," Joe said.

"What does that mean?" Al asked.

"I don't even agree with some of Jack's goals. We shouldn't be rebuilding crummy old cities, we should be scattering people out, in nice suburbs and small towns. Who needs Harlem? It should be torn down! You see, Al, a real problem here is that half the time, maybe ninety percent of the time, we can't even agree on what's worth doing. Besides, it's unfair to stick RVA with all the world's externalities."

"Now what are externalities?" Al asked.

Joe told him, and he wrote it down. "OK, so you're not responsible for the whole world. But what exactly are you responsible for?"

"Hey, I was talking," Jack said, "and I'm not finished."

"Go ahead, you've got the floor," Al said.

"Joe's got a point. We don't agree on all things. But we simply can't go hide under the rug and pretend the world isn't there, as Vicki suggests. We're a part of it. If no one's responsible, then things fall apart. Sure, it's tough to be responsible, and it's tough to figure out what to do first, second, and third. But you can't hide. There's a legitimacy question here, Al. Corporations have charters, and they have the right to do certain things. They have responsibilities, too. If they don't carry out their responsibilities, they can become illegitimate, that is, society can revoke their charters. I think that RVA, and lots of companies like it, are in real trouble, because society is demanding lots more from them than it used to, and the companies just don't want to respond."

"They just can't," Vicki said. "For all the reasons I gave. Society is going to be in real trouble if they force their productive units to carry the burden of the world. Look what happens in communist countries. Produc-

Externalities — Costs born by persons _outside_ the person or organization producing them.

Example — One driver creates a ~~B~~ small amount of pollution with his car, and this doesn't bother him — but 100 million vehicles collectively foul up the whole atmosphere. No one driver bears the pollution costs.

Clean up costs are _external_ to those creating them, hence _externalities_

tion stagnates, and worse, you end up with a police state, because there's only one official morality. Look at Iran, where religious fanatics are killing each other every day. If Joe and you disagree about a social goal, then what? Do we send one of you to a concentration camp? Remember, once RVA or any other corporation gets an official goal, then it becomes the party line. I'd rather vote for a politician who wants something and take my chances, than to discover that I have to believe something, or *else*, right inside RVA."

"Well, the issue is joined," Al commented. "But let's get back to this externalities thing. I see every so often that if you really try to get everything cleaned up totally, you end up with trade offs. For example, a big steel company had to clean up one of its old Ohio plants. Five thousand men got laid off. Now, what do you want? A bit of pollution, or no jobs?"

"You've bought the party line, Al," Jack said. "That company should have made the investments and kept the plant open, no matter if they lost a bit of money. That's a part of their responsibility, too."

"So the company loses a bit of money, and the Japanese or German, or even South Korean steelmakers, who don't have those external costs, take the market?" Vicki asked.

"Then we should tax imports and make them pay up," Jack said.

"And how about Third World markets?" Vicki asked. "We can't make the Mexicans or Brazilians pay more for our steel just because we want Ohio to be clean. If you force companies to make low profit, or zero profit investments, then you're saying that you want them to stagnate."

"I hope we're smarter than that," Jack replied. "We should be able to figure out how to produce at lower costs and keep things clean."

Joe nudged Jack. "You're sitting down there in New Jersey thinking up new things, Jack. How are you doing?"

Jack shrugged. "It's tough, Joe, but at least we're in there trying."

"Just look at the fast growing companies around the world, Jack," Vicki said. "They're the ones making big money. The stagnant, low profit, or even loss making companies don't go around giving money to charities, or giving jobs to young people who need them. The trouble with your ideas is that they're utopian. You want it both ways. You want lots of fast growth and productivity, so lots of people can go to work, make good money, and get out of poverty, and then by the way, don't change anything unless no one gets hurt, which is another way of saying don't change anything. Except maybe to spend lots of money on nonproductive things like cleanups."

"Hey, we were making speeches," Joe said. "Are you finished, Jack?"

"I'll never convince you people about anything, so I'm done," Jack said.

"Joe, it's your turn," Al said.

Joe drew a diagram on the back of an envelope and passed it around. "This is the way the corporation looks," he said. "You see, we have eight different clienteles to serve, and every group wants something different. The suppliers want stable, long term contracts at good prices. Remember, Jack, that has a minority tone now, too. We are trying to find good minority owned firms to supply us with all sorts of stuff. But the consumers want safe, high quality goods at low prices; the stockholders want big profits and fat dividend checks; and the employees want more money and fringes and better working conditions. Lord only knows what all the governments want—plenty, I guess. Tax money, cleanups, safety, you name it.

"But we can't satisfy everybody. If we pay big wages, profits go down.

JOE'S DIAGRAM ON THE BACK OF AN ENVELOPE

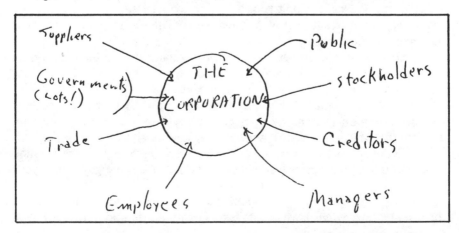

If we give juicy contracts to suppliers, we can't pay as much in wages, or profits go down again. If we hire unskilled and inexperienced labor, our productivity nosedives, and there go profits again. Maybe there goes quality products, since how can unskilled people make high quality goods?

"In the end, what you get is a lot of noise and not much action. People talk a good game, but what they're really out for is just what people have always been out for, namely money, prestige, and power. If you can get some suckers to listen to you, maybe you can win. Consider Vicki's arguments. She says just make money, no matter what. If you buy that, then the managers and the company can do what they please, subject to whatever laws are actually enforced, and lots of them aren't. It's a great game, if you can get away with it.

"Then consider Jack's points. He's arguing for other groups, such as customers, workers, society at large, who want more of the action. If he wins, we get more blacks or women, or some loafer gets some more cash to fool around with. But in the end, it's just shifting the gravy around a bit."

"You sound as if you think no one is really sincere," Al commented.

"Oh, someone out there may believe the stuff, but in the end, it all boils down to money and power. Have you ever watched what happens to people who win? Look at Jack here. He sounds like a church deacon, and not too long ago, he was a raving radical. Now that he's got a good job and a chance to get more status and get promoted, he's turned conservative, in spite of what he's saying. Vicki thinks she can move way up in the company, so she spouts the line that she figures will get her to the top. You people are all after the usual things. Al, you're here because if you do a great job on this story, you'll be a hero and win. In the end, we are all cynics and selfish."

"You sure act out your parts well," Al said. "I mean, you talk to managers and technicians at RVA, and you get a feeling that people, at least most of them, really believe in what they're doing. You're saying that they just sit back and figure out how to be sincere, and then play the part."

"Sure," Joe said. "Don't you?"

"Joe, you're really a cynic," Vicki said. "There's an interesting point here about honest managers."

"You mean like that guy we had in Uguland who bribed the prime minister to get the TV contract?" Joe asked.

"Yeah, a really honest bunch!" Jack said.

"We did fire him," Vicki said. "But the point is that you can't go very far with dishonest or immoral managers. If my boss was a crook, I'd quit, or blow the whistle. I couldn't work in that kind of situation."

"Come on, Vicki," Joe said. "With your drive, you'd stay. Come to think of it, you might blow the whistle, if it would get one more guy out of your way."

"I hate to agree with you, Vicki, but I do," Jack said. "I once worked for a real crook, when I was in college. He would lie and cheat and steal whenever he could. He paid out plenty of bribe money, too. But in the end, he couldn't build an organization. No honest person would work for him long, and the crooks he did manage to hire had to be watched so closely that the company finally folded."

"If you steal and cheat on others, you might do it to yourself," Al said. "I covered a story like that just before this one came up. A crooked contractor was paying off some city officials out west. His key man knew about it and helped out. But then the assistant started stealing from the company. Before long, the guy went broke." He took out his handkerchief and blew his nose. "Hey, who's raising the dust?"

"Big corporations demand a lot from subordinates, as we all know," Vicki said. "And if you plan to be in the game for a long time, you had better get some top people who are reasonably decent and honest. You're right, Al. You could end up stealing from yourself."

"But there's a bigger morality than just being honest," Jack said. "How about racial or sex discrimination? Sure, maybe the old time RVA managers were moral, in the sense that they didn't pay bribes, and they were nice to their employees. But they had cultural blinders on. Nice people just didn't hire blacks. That's what I meant when I talked about trying to be socially oriented. You can be a nice guy, but you can be culturally totally immoral at the same time."

"I had the floor, such as it is," Joe said. "But Jack's right, and that's what I mean. People can even believe that they're honest and moral and all of that, but in the end they somehow end up justifying what gets them money and power. And Jack, that goes as much for a black preacher as it does for an RVA vice president. No, in the end we're all out for Number One."

"In the end, though, we have to work for everyone, like it or not," Vicki said, "because that's the only way to maximize profits. If you cut everyone's throat, you can't get good workers, you can't find reliable suppliers, and you can't even hang on to your customers. That's exactly the point. You have to work for everyone in order to achieve what appears to be a selfish goal."

Joe nodded. "Straight out of Adam Smith, old girl. That line just won't wash, even though in the end I agree. We talk a great game, but in the end, we're inherently selfish."

Jack stretched. "Man, I'd like to get to the bathroom! Al, you've listened, and now it's your turn. What's your view of corporate social responsibility?"

"Yeah, Al," Joe said. "Give us something, instead of taking. It won't hurt."

"OK," Al said. "I've looked around lots of organizations, public and private, as a reporter. I've snooped out poverty, covered bribe stories, and tried to figure out what's going on. I've seen some real crime, and it's not too pleasant."

"We know you have the right credentials, Al," Joe said, "but what do you think about it?"

"I guess if I was pressed, I'd have to agree with Jack. There are all sorts of social and moral problems, big and little, that have to be attacked."

"Golly, I've been going with a socialist," Vicki said. "You can't really believe that, can you, Al?"

"As Jack said, you have to try. But Vicki, maybe you're right, in that if you don't know where you're going, then any amount of money, and any direction, won't get you there. I can see how tough it is to figure out what to do. Should RVA hire more women? The way you people hire, which is very slowly, that means you might hire fewer blacks."

"And that's a lousy idea," Jack said.

"It is not!" Vicki retorted.

Joe said. "I think we should hire more good Swedes."

"That's exactly my hang up," Al went on. "Which of you is right? Besides, there's a subtle assumption that when you need an accountant or a toolmaker, there are lots of highly trained and capable blacks, women, and maybe even Swedes out there to be hired. They're all equal, except for race or sex. But one thing I've learned around RVA is that this ain't necessarily so. Suppose the best accountant is a Swede? Do you hire someone almost as good who's a woman? If you do, some other company will cream you, sooner or later."

"Female accountants are all superior to males," Vicki said.

"I like Swedes, myself," Joe said, and Vicki made a face at him.

"I have the floor, remember?" Al said. "Now, Jack has a major point. You can be perfectly honest and moral, yet in some major way, totally immoral, like the old RVA managers who just never hired blacks, no matter how good they were. But the ethical problem is to figure out what that higher morality is. I know a guy who hates communists so much he would just love to drop atomic bombs on every communist country. If they retaliate, they wipe out the world, and he figures that it's better to die for the cause than to live in a wicked world. I disagree with him strongly, but who's right?"

"You are," Jack said.

"Sure, but suppose he was in power at RVA? Should he be giving company money to all sorts of fanatical right-wing organizations? Vicki's right on that point. You have to let everyone in on the act. Let's vote on such things, not just give power to decide morals to someone you don't even trust."

"Well, I'm glad that you agree with me on just one small point," Vicki said to Al, waspishly.

"I've been in a couple of those police states that Vicki talked about, and believe me, it's no fun when one group decides what's moral. But Jack, basically you're right. You have to try."

"Tell me how to try, and I will," Vicki said. "Can't you see, Al? You just have no way to resolve the moral issues."

"We seem to be going in circles now," Jack said. "No matter what we say, you can figure out some way around it. In the end, you can't logically debate morality. It's more a matter of believing in something."

"But governments do legislate morality," Al said. "They pass civil rights acts, they make you clean up your industrial mess, and they even define what a bribe is, and send you to jail if they catch you doing it."

"That's my point," Vicki said. "You just have to do what society says is right. If you start making your own moral decisions, you end up nowhere."

"Oh no you don't," Jack said. "But now that we've all said our piece, where are we?"

"On a stuck elevator," Joe said, looking at his watch. "But we still have one more speaker." He turned to the janitor. "Mr., ah . . . Stan, wasn't it?"

"Stanislaus."

"OK, Stan, what do you think? You're a part of this team, too."

Mr. Wojciechowski rubbed his bald head. "No one cares about the way an old man thinks, especially if he is just a janitor."

"No, Joe's right," Al said. "I care. It's your company, too, if all the propaganda RVA puts out about its happy family of employees is correct. What do you think?"

"I think that you have given me a very nice retirement party. Next Tuesday, I will be 65, and I retire. But it is so nice to hear you all. Such lovely words! They flow, and they tangle, and they sparkle. You are such very smart young people. You, Mr. Chapman . . ."

"Say, how do you know my name?" Joe asked.

"I clean up your office. It is almost five, and I start work at four, until midnight. Excuse me, I read your memos in the wastebasket. You are so clever, but so dumb, too."

"Hey, what's my being dumb have to do with social responsibility?" Joe asked.

"Oh, a lot. You see, Mr. Tribble mentioned that we are all a part of the whole. You fall in love, you marry that lovely girl in the legal department. But it is not quite right for you, or for her. And you are not so smart in many little ways, political ways, and you discover that you are not going very much farther in this company. So you get so cynical, so bitter, so convinced the world is against you. You want things both ways, to be rich, successful, powerful, and to be what you are. In RVA, this is not possible. But you have a wife now, and you think you need the money. So you stay. Before long, you will be too bitter, too cynical. It will destroy you, unless you go elsewhere. But you do not. You are so dumb."

"He's really got your number, Joe," Vicki said.

"We are all part of the whole, as Mr. Tribble says," Mr. Wojciechowski said. "So what you believe is not just what RVA is, but what you personally are. You, Miss Masters, you are so tense, so determined, so anxious to get ahead. I think you may not, because you try too hard. Mr. Chapman may be right. You try to be more like RVA than RVA. Maybe it pays off, but maybe not. I know that you have compassion ... I see it in some of your memos. But even when you write three drafts of the memo about firing that incompetent person, in the end it comes out cold and hard and efficient."

"Hey, I think we need a paper shredder around here," Joe said. "This guy's been reading too much mail!"

"I apologize, Mr. Chapman. But never before do I tell anyone. It is an old man's weakness."

"You said you came from Poland?" Al asked. "Were you always a janitor?"

"Once, long ago, I studied law. Then I was a soldier in the Polish army, against the Nazis. Then I was a prisoner of war, and much later, after the war, I get to the United States."

"You have a wife?" Al asked.

"Killed, in the war."

"Children?"

"One ... killed in the war. I am a lucky man. So many Poles killed, and I survive. It is so nice, just to be alive. And what use is Polish law in New York City? So I become a janitor, and I stay a janitor. But I still like to listen to good arguments, and you have a good one here. The words flow so nice, and you are all so smart and well educated!"

"So far, all you've said is that we believe what we do because we're complete people, not just RVA products," Al commented. "What else?"

"Ah, the cool reporter again! You are an interesting man, Mr. Faber, wandering around RVA, scaring people with your innocent questions! But you, too, are not so cool. You are quite insecure, Mr. Faber, and you really do not know what you want. Besides, can you make a great news story out of all this RVA material? Who wants to? Your deadline approaches, and it bothers you almost as much as you bother these RVA people."

"Go on, Stan," Joe said. "The party's getting interesting."

"You are not too sure what you think, Mr. Faber. But then most newspeople really aren't. You see the seamy side of life, and you wish it were not so. And your peers think that certain truths are real, so you believe too. But I wonder if you really do. I wonder. You are wishy-washy, and you are outside of everything. You want to be inside, but you cannot be. So you take cool and gentle moral truths and speak them as if they were real and mattered. I am not so sure that they do, to you. The world for you is a big puzzle, because you keep seeing just a bit here, and a piece there. So, your thoughts about morality and responsibility are like that, incomplete and tentative. But, as you say, at least you try, and I respect you for that."

"Thanks, I guess," Al said.

Mr. Wojciechowski turned to Jack. "Mr. Tribble, you are very interesting. A brilliant black man with a fine education, full of guilt for your success. You work so hard for your education and your position, and you know that you deserve it. But you are haunted by all those black people who were not so lucky, or so smart, or who did not work so hard. It is easy to say all sorts of noble things about what should be done, about all the injustices that have been committed. But I can tell you about real ghettoes, not the silly things you have here, where people by the hundreds of thousands marched to the gas chambers to achieve a madman's idea of moral perfection. I can tell you about those German businessmen in the 1930's who supported Hitler because he seemed likely to bring law and order to a disturbed country. I was there."

"Hey, are you really a guilt-ridden black liberal?" Joe asked Jack.

"Can it," Jack said tensely.

"I am sorry, Mr. Tribble," Mr. Wojciechowski said. "I hurt you. But you see, your thoughts are not those of just you, but of your culture, your race, and your family. You cannot escape what you are. Because you are all so smart and well educated, you say your thoughts so nicely, but in the end, what you think, or what you say you think, is more than you really believe."

"Interesting, Stanislaus, but what do you think?" Al asked. "You're being wishy-washy yourself, putting the burden on us. Sure, we're a part of something bigger, and sure, we all have our hangups, but what's yours?"

"A long time ago, I used to argue like you do now, but in Polish. I was very young, and the world seemed so imperfect! It really was, too. We would sit in the coffee house and have long, long talks about the way the world was, and how rotten it was. Then, later, I found out really how bad it was. But somehow I survived, and just to be alive was enough. I lost my interest in changing the world. Perhaps it had beaten me. Perhaps I realized that the world is neither good nor bad, but simply is. You take what you want, and you pay. The price is sometimes very high. But now, I walk down the street and watch people. I listen to you here, and I have a good meal sometimes. I learned long ago that someone else was going to change the world, maybe, but not me. So I accept it as it is. I vote for politicians that seem to agree with me, as Miss Masters says, and they almost always lose. When they win, they always disappoint me. You see, things change so very slowly, but they change. Perhaps I should go around making speeches, or join clubs to promote what I think is right, but I do not. The world just is, and I just am. It is enough. You people can worry about those great changes, and I will watch, and maybe I will agree, and maybe not, and then I will go about my job, wondering about the foibles of men and women."

"I suppose," Al said, "that most people would agree with you. Not too many want to change the world or even talk about it."

"You are right, Mr. Faber. It is hard enough to resolve one's personal affairs. You worry about getting a job, or a promotion, or passing an examination, or fixing your car. These little things are very real. You can touch them, play with them, and make them the way you want, or try to. But in the end, things just are. You cannot really change much. You, Mr. Faber, try to change Miss Masters, and she tries to change you, but it does not work too well. If you cannot talk a young lady into changing her mind, just how do you expect to change the world?"

"With great difficulty, I guess," Al said, noting Vicki's smile.

"But please, do not take my advice. As Mr. Tribble says, you have to try, even if you know you cannot do too much. Keep on arguing and debating and voting and joining. These things, too, are a part of being. Just because problems are so very difficult, this does not mean that you should not try to solve them. You are all very gifted people, and you have an obligation to do what you can, as you see best."

Joe patted Stan on the back. "Now that gets at a good point. Stan, you sound like an old Calvinist church sermon. Work hard, do your best, and try to succeed, even though you know that you may fail."

"The Calvinists are too grim for me," Mr. Wojciechowski said. "You need a sense of humor too. So many things are absurd. You have to be able to laugh at yourself once in a while, to see how silly you are. This is what is wrong with you, Mr. Chapman. You lost your sense of humor someplace. Mr. Tribble, Miss Masters, you too are on the way to becoming far too serious. I am not sure about you, Mr. Faber. Maybe you have lost it, or are losing it. People who cannot laugh at themselves are always very tense and unhappy. And the worst of all worlds is the one run by people with no sense of humor. So make a little joke once in a while, on yourself, and remember that if you were never even born, it would not matter so much. The world would still be about the same."

The elevator gave a slight jerk and began to move upward.

"I think we're back in the real world," Joe said.

It moved up a floor, and the door opened. A technician was waiting for them. "All out here," he said. "Sorry we couldn't get you out quicker. I hope you weren't too inconvenienced."

Joe, Al, Vicki, and Jack watched Mr. Wojciechowski walk off down the hall with his mop and bucket. "He might have said goodbye," Joe said.

"Why?" Al asked. "It really wasn't his party."

"Say, did old Stan bother you in there?" the technician asked. "He's a funny old guy, drinks too much. He claims that he lost his family during the war, but I think he just uses that as an excuse. He can be pretty weird sometimes."

"No," Vicki said thoughtfully. "He didn't bother us at all."

"Are you still going to see Mr. Marer?" Jack asked Al.

"If he has time. Our adventure wrecked my schedule. It's after five."

But Mr. Marer did see Al, and they had a long talk about RVA's posture toward corporate social responsibility. Al made lots of notes, and he heard a lot of good, subtle thinking about what problems a modern corporation faces in this area. But somehow the elevator ride was more fun, and a lot more interesting.

DISCUSSION QUESTIONS

1. A steel mill is pouring 500 tons of junk per day into what was once an attractive river. Five hundred other firms and towns have also been polluting the river, to the point where it is now totally polluted. How would you suggest getting at the job of cleaning it up? What kinds of government or private actions could be taken to get on with the job?

2. Your car is a major polluter along with 90 million others. Should you stop driving? Why or why not?

3. Your college burns a lot of garbage in open incinerators. If the new antipollution law is passed, it will have to spend $750,000 for new special burning equipment. This works out (including operating costs) to about $75 per student per semester. Are you willing to pay that much extra tuition to keep the air clean? Why or why not?

4. Go to your library or bookstore and find a book about some type of pollution or environmental problem. Read it and write a report from the business firm's point of view, indicating the following.

What is the problem seen here?

How will private firms be affected if the problem is solved the way the author suggests?

How soon will the pollution problem become so severe as to require immediate crisis action to correct it?

How will jobs be affected if the solution is carried out? Consider both lost jobs and new ones.

5. What are externalities? Who cares?

6. Big firms often are oligopolies. Does this make any difference to society, in terms of the social responsibility such firms have? Why or why not?

7. Sam ran a pretty good bicycle shop in a college town. He repaired bikes and sold new and used ones. His gross sales were around $60,000 per year, and he had no employees. For over thirty years, Sam stayed in business fixing bikes. He obviously did a good job, because people kept coming to him for his products and services.

But Sam was a cantankerous old guy. He refused to give any money to charitable causes, and he cheated as much as he could on his income tax. He cheated a lot on reporting his state sales tax, too. He did not belong to any church, nor did he give any money to any religious group. He felt strongly that what he earned was his, and he wasn't about to give it away. The only

political activity he engaged in was to object strongly to any new
or old tax laws.

Was Sam socially responsible? Why or why not?

8. A major, multibillion-dollar corporation with over 60,000
employees felt strongly that making money was its key purpose.
This company made and sold quality lines of industrial products,
and it kept on growing, and making more money, year after
year. But it gave no money to charity, nor did it support popular
social causes, such as hiring more women or minorities, or
cleaning up the environment. It tried, more or less, to obey
relevant law, and it paid its taxes due on time. Its profits and
dividends were high, and it paid the highest wages in its industry,
simply because the company felt that this was the way to get
superior employees.

When this company operated overseas, it took full advantage
of local law, and it did not help anyone except itself. Its products
stayed in high demand throughout the world because they were
so good. Last year, this company made a net profit, after taxes, of
over $300 million, which it partially reinvested in plant expansion
and partially paid out as dividends to stockholders.

Is this company socially responsible? Why or why not?

9. Do you agree with Jack, Vicki, Al, Joe, or Mr. Wojciechowski on the question of corporate social responsibility? Why?

10. Make a list of five socially important and relevant things
that in your opinion should be done. List them in their order of
importance. Now, compare your list with your classmates' lists.
How much agreement is there? How much disagreement? Which
are the "right" things to do?

18

CONCLUSION

Say, Vicki, will you marry me?" Al asked. They were driving down the freeway in Al's battered Olds. It was not exactly the best place to propose, but Al really couldn't figure out a better one.

"I thought you'd never ask," Vicki replied. "Why did you?"

"Well, I was afraid that you might ask me, for one thing. And then, I happen to love you, for another."

"What would you have said, if I had asked?"

"Damned if I know," Al replied.

"Honey, you sound pretty ambivalent about this."

"I am ambivalent. Remember how I was programmed. The wife stays home and keeps house, and the husband goes out and earns the money. Besides, I wasn't thinking much about getting married right now. You sort of snuck up on me. And I guess that you're all wrong, too. At least I never thought that I would fall in love with an accountant!"

"Are accountants all bad?"

Al sighed and glanced over at her. "You certainly aren't. But look, you make a lot more money than I do. You'll probably go right to the top of dear old RVA, or at least end up way up there someplace. I'll probably stay a reporter for a long, long time. I like it. I'm not sure that I really want my wife to be a lot more successful than I am. Gee ... to be known as Vicki Masters' husband!"

"The world's different, dear," Vicki said, smiling.

"Baby, you really trapped me. In spite of your overwhelming achievement drive, your cold-blooded political maneuvering, and all the cracks I keep hearing about how you worked your way into my assignment, I still fell in love with you."

"Maybe you did because I am what I am, not because I'm not what you wanted."

Al sighed. "That's what bothers me. You've forced me to reexamine all my premises, and that's never any fun. I've dated plenty of girls that had all the things I thought I wanted, and somehow they were pretty dull. You know, you're a lot like the rest of RVA ... some good, some bad, some greys, some nastiness, plenty of femininity, charm, and ..."

"Al, dear, that doesn't sound much like a passionate declaration of love!"

Al glanced over at her. "You're absolutely correct, as usual." He found an off ramp, drove into a quiet street, parked, and did it right.

Some months later, Al got a letter from Joe Chapman:

Dear Al,
    Well, I finally left RVA, and now I'm working for Radebaugh, Arpan, Schweikart, and Chung, which is a big accounting firm which has a large consulting operation as well. I work in Cleveland for the consulting group. I could see that my future at RVA was pretty dim, and I sensed that no one was really sorry to see me leave. But this job has everything I wanted. I can do my thing without getting trapped in a bunch of petty politics. My boss, Jim Chung, has given me a pretty free hand, and already we've managed to save a couple of companies millions of dollars through better organization.
    As you know, it's plenty tough to get a really good job these days, but I managed, thanks, oddly enough, to my wife, Judy. It seems that her skills as a legal secretary were very much in demand, and RAS & C hired her along with me. If it hadn't been for her, I'd still be fussing around at RVA, I guess.
    If that scandal sheet of yours ever needs some top-notch, super-sophisticated consulting work, let me know. For a big fee, we'd happily straighten you out. Just call me collect at (335) 968 2347, extension 43. I've been reading your articles on RVA, and believe me, that isn't the company I thought I was in. Boy, you must have talked to a bunch of strange people to come up with the ideas you did. But it's good stuff, and I can see why old Jason McKeever picked you for the assignment. You should sell a lot more magazines as a result.
    Be good, old buddy, and say hello to Vicki for me. Now that I'm out of it, I hope she gets to be CEO of RVA soon. At least I know her, and maybe I can sell her some consulting services. Boy, does RVA need them! Keep in touch.

                                        Yours,

                                        Joe

About the same time, Al saw this note in the *Financial Reporter:*

RVA Names Beeman CEO, Wilson Board Chairman

NEW YORK: Donald A. Beeman, 56, was elected president and chief executive officer of RVA, Inc., a diversified industrial company. William S. Wilson, 64, was appointed to the newly created post of chairman. Mr. Beeman previously was executive vice president for RVA's consumer goods division, and Mr. Wilson was CEO. Mr. Beeman joined RVA's predecessor company in 1949. He has been in charge of RVA's cassette television developments since their inception. Mr. Wilson has served with RVA since 1959.

Well, Al thought, sometimes people do get what they want. He thought about the conversation he had had with Mr. Beeman, and the plush offices, the chauffeured cars, and the pressure. But he wished him well anyhow, even though it probably meant that Vicki would be moving up and onward, too.

Al received all sorts of materials on his job, and a news item in the San Jose, California, *Post Dispatch* caught his attention:

Local Businessman Sets Up Foundation on Retirement; Gives $5 Million

Mr. Daniel Suzuki, president and founder of Snap-Kwik Lock Company, Inc., announced the formation of the Japanese-Italian Cultural Foundation, whose purpose is to promote better understanding between the two countries. Mr. Suzuki stated, "I spent considerable time in Italy during World War II, and then and now, the two peoples need much more interaction. I hope that our new foundation will be able to promote such understanding."

Mr. Suzuki has given the new foundation $5 million of RVA stock. Snap-Kwik was sold to RVA, a diversified conglomerate, nine years ago, but Mr. Suzuki remained as president. Mr. Suzuki is now retiring to devote his time to his various cultural interests.

There was a picture of Mr. Suzuki passing a check to Antonio Gionetti, the director of the new foundation.

Even for the man who had achieved beyond his wildest dreams there could be still more, Al mused. He tried to imagine Mr. Suzuki arguing with a bunch of excited Italians, but gave up. Besides, most of his images had turned out so wrong that perhaps it should be an excitable Mr. Suzuki arguing with a bunch of sober Italian academics. No, that didn't fit either. But in any case, it was fun to see what a man did when he had it made. Al would have happily settled for ten percent of that grant!

So the assignment was just about finished. Al had spent five months in and around RVA, trying to figure out what it was all about. He had met many people, talked to more experts than he ever thought existed, and socialized more than he ever figured he would with RVA people. Most of them were pretty decent, he thought, and while a few were probably crooks or corrupt, the majority seemed very interested in getting the job done right. Quite a few were new friends of his, and one or two were very special friends.

One thing he had learned was that his earlier ideas about corporations were pretty simplistic. It wasn't easy to sell a TV cassette system, or get it designed or into production. Booby traps were everywhere, and only the really competent could get it right most of the time.

AL'S SKETCH OF RVA

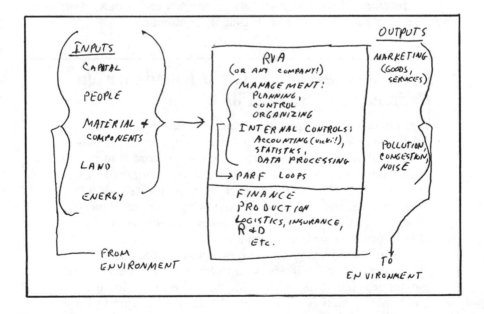

But this pondering didn't get his stories written. He had even figured out, on his own, pretty much what the system was about, and he idly sketched it on his scratch pad. But such diagrams might satisfy professors or managers, but not the readers of *Newsworld*, and certainly not his editor. No, he had to write stories about RVA that were newsworthy, that were sexy, that would excite people. He thought about the conversations he had had with various RVA executives and technicians. Those patient explanations of how things worked were not the stuff to make dramatic news stories, for sure. No, he would have to look elsewhere to find his news materials.

Al stared at his new, expensive typewriter/word processor. It was a nice perk, but darn it, you had to know what to say before you could use it. He stared for a long, long time, and then sighed and began. And this is the story he wrote...

QUESTIONS FOR DISCUSSION

1. Should Al marry Vicki? Why or why not?

2. Should Vicki marry Al? Why or why not?

3. Al has a problem, since the sorts of things he found out about RVA are not exactly the type of materials that make for great news stories. Take a look at some recent copies of such magazines as *Time, U.S. News and World Report,* and *Newsweek,* and help Al out.

Suggest three topics which he might use for stories. Why do you think that these stories would be attractive to the general public?

Now suggest three topics which might not be very interesting to the general public, but which are important to RVA and its managers. Why are these topics less appealing?

INCIDENT 1: WHO WANTS TO SEE IT, TOO?

Martin Baxter turned on the light, rubbing his eyes. "Robert, I have to admit that your ... television works. At least I could almost make out the figures most of the time. But golly, it's tough on the eyes!" They were both blinking.

"It still needs a lot of work, Mr. Baxter," Robert Brown admitted. "But remember, we've just been working on it since 1930 ... only four years ago, and we figure that we can get it ready for market by 1938. What do you think?"

Martin sighed. "Robert, I always admired you, even though you are sometimes a bit impractical in your inventions. Television! Who would possibly want to sit in their living room and watch a little ten inch picture, when they can go to the movies for 35 or 40 cents and see a huge screen? And I hear that those color experiments are working out well. By 1938, all movies will be in color. You'll be trying to compete with this $1,000 monster that no one can afford anyhow, which only shows black and white pictures. There is no way it will work. People listen to the radio at home, and they go to the movies to see things. That's the way it will always be. Why, those movie producing companies are just about the most profitable in the country right now, and they will stay that way forever!"

"We might be able to get the cost down a bit, just as radio did. Why, those first sets around 1922 cost over two hundred dollars, and now they cost under twenty, even for a pretty good set. By 1950, we should be down to maybe six hundred dollars for a good television receiver."

"And that's still five hundred too much," Martin said. "Be reasonable! You want me to finance this thing, and you claim that some day television will be big. But consider ... first you have to set up broadcasting stations, and you tell me that they are ten times as complicated as radio stations. Who will do that? The country's in a depression, and no one will put out hundreds of dollars for something they can't possibly pay for. The whole technology is so much more costly than radio that advertisers will never pay for ads. And then the theaters will kill you anyhow, because going downtown to the movies is something Americans will never stop doing. It's just too much fun."

"They sure will, once they realize that they can see and hear the programs in their own homes. And they can see things no movie house could ever show. Live sports, news, political debates, plays ... I tell you, we have a real winner here!" Robert turned as he smelled something burning. He rushed over to unplug his set. It was smoking.

Mr. Baxter smiled. "Well, you need about a million dollars and at least ten years of work before you have a product. I must admit that we did make a lot of money on some of your patents on radio tuning circuits. That's why I agreed to come by and see this thing. But this time, I'm sorry. You're a hundred years ahead of your time. Look, you made some good royalties on your circuits. Why don't you put that money into a really sound investment? RKO is building a new major movie house downtown. You could invest in that and make a good return for fifty years." Martin sighed, shook Robert's hand, and left.

Robert kicked the still smoking television set. Darn it, these bankers were so very conservative! Where on earth could he get $900,000? Maybe Mr. Baxter was right ... perhaps he was a hundred years ahead of his time. Still ... he sighed and began to strip the set. If he could only get more reliable components, then maybe he could make this thing work the way it should!

1. What happened to all of those huge downtown movie palaces? Did the rapid growth of television have anything to do with this development?

2. About 98 percent of American homes now have TV sets. Why? What does a TV set have that a movie doesn't have?

3. There are still many movies being made, and the industry is still more or less profitable. Why? What does a movie have that TV doesn't have?

4. Why do you think that an intelligent, perceptive banker of 1934 might believe that TV would never catch on? In retrospect, Mr. Baxter was mistaken, but then most bankers in 1934 would have agreed with him. Do you have to see something to figure out just how TV might affect people?

5. A promoter has been trying to sell you stock in a company that will manufacture two way telephone TV sets. The sets will cost about three hundred dollars, plus a service charge of about ten dollars per month. Once installed, they will allow people talking on the telephone to see each other on a picture screen. The picture can be turned off if desired. This promotor feels that this new product will take off fast, and that this company will grow and make huge profits.

Do you agree? What's good about this idea?

What's bad about it? Would you invest your hard earned money in this company?

INCIDENT 2: THE TEACHER AS MANAGER

A business professor who often received very good teaching ratings from her students once commented about how she did it. She really wasn't very verbal, and she certainly wasn't charismatic, but somehow students liked her courses.

"It's rather easy, actually, to be a good teacher, even if one's interpersonal skills aren't too good," she said. "What I do is simple. The day the class starts, I give my students a complete outline of the course, along with a sheet that schedules all events, such as examinations, the days papers are due, etc. I also have another handout that tells my students what they are expected to do, and what the course is supposed to accomplish. My outline has all the readings and assignments on it.

"Then we begin the course, and I follow the outline carefully. When an examination occurs, I make very sure that the students get theirs back quickly, usually the next time the class meets. People like to know what grade they received, even if it is bad news. Then I let anyone who feels abused complain, but only in writing. Talk is cheap, but a student who takes time to write out an argument as to why a question was poor deserves careful attention. If the student is right, he or she gets credit.

"I always re-announce things days in advance, so no one is ever surprised. At least, if the student shows up, he or she isn't! Everyone knows what is going on all the time, and all students know what they are getting. When the course is over, I try to give out final grades as quickly as possible.

"This pattern of teaching seems to work very well. I have heard others complain that they like surprises, but given the grade pressure most students face, and given their ignorance of the materials to begin with, most of them prefer not to be surprised. Knowing what you are doing makes it easier to do well."

This professor was once nominated for a teaching award. Another nominee was a charming, charismatic professor who really could talk. He held his students spellbound, and he loved his subject matter. This professor never handed out an outline; he often changed his mind about what to teach a few minutes before class; sometimes he forgot to give midterm examinations, and when he did, he rarely gave them back to students until after the final exam; and he occasionally would give surprise quizzes. He refused to discuss grades or examination questions with students, noting that what was done was done, and there was no point in worrying about it. Often he turned in final grades weeks late, and sometimes he never turned them in at all. Yet his course was always crowded, since he was such a brilliant speaker and teacher.

1. Analyze the teaching pattern of the first teacher in terms of PARF loops. What are the plans here; the activities; the feedback loops? Do you think that these are good or bad? Why?

2. Do the same for the second professor. What kinds of problems might a student get into with this gifted teacher?

3. Which professor would you rather take a course from, assuming that these professors were teaching parallel sections of the same course? Why?

INCIDENT 3: LONG TERM PLANNING FOR YOUR CHILDREN

Two neighboring familes both had children in 1976. In one family both parents are working, the wife as a nurse and the husband as a business manager. These parents started planning their daughter's future from the time she was born. They purchased an annuity for their child, payable at age 18, from a private insurance company. They felt that when their daughter reached college age, this money would pay for her education. They also felt it was extremely important that the girl get into a very good, very exclusive, and very expensive private university, and they are now planning to hire special tutors so that she can be properly prepared for high achievement in education. Without a really good university degree, these parents feel, their child will not do so well in life.

Their next door neighbor is a professor of history, and he is doing very little for his son, except to provide him with basic necessities and much affection. "Look," this professor said, when discussing how to raise children, "my son will be 18 in 1994. For all I know, there won't even be a world in 1994. Perhaps schooling won't be important. Perhaps my son will be stupid, or an underachiever. My neighbors bought an annuity that pays their daughter $20,000 in 1994. At the present six to ten percent inflation, that won't buy a cup of coffee in 1994! Besides, the government will either give or lend the necessary money to any person who can get into a decent university. It makes no sense to plan for 14 or 15 years into the future, because things will change so much that no one really knows what to do. The best thing to do for any child these days is to have fun with the kid, make sure that he or she socializes well, and hope for the best. Any kind of long term planning is stupid, given this crazy, mixed up world!"

1. Is it really true that parents cannot make long term plans for their children? Why or why not?

2. What critical planning premises about the future did the parents of the girl make? Are these valid?

3. What critical planning premises is the father of the son making? Are these valid?

4. What critical planning premises (if any) did your parents make about you? Were these valid?

INCIDENT 4: ENGINEERING AND DEPRECIATION

To begin with, Bill Smathers was an engineer by training. He was pretty good, good enough to wind up running a trucking company in a small Middle Eastern country newly arrived to the modern world. The company was owned by Mohammed Al Safra, a traditional but clever merchant. Bill was smart enough to insist on ten percent of the profits as his bonus as long as he managed the company.

Bill received a salary of $48,000 per year. The first year Bill's twenty heavy trucks, which cost $80,000 each, made a nice profit. The company had gross revenues of $1,875,000, with costs of $1,600,000. Hence net profits were $275,000, and Bill got a bonus of $27,500. This small country had no modern accounting tradition, and neither Bill nor Mr. Al Safra had ever heard of depreciation, so it was not included in costs.

The second year Mr. Al Safra hired a local accountant, trained at Indiana University, who told them a lot about depreciation. The accountant observed that heavy trucks operating in sand and dirt road conditions would not last more than five years. Bill agreed, noting that he would have to maintain them very well to have them last this long. But now Bill is really upset. Somehow, using a five-year life of equipment and taking straight line depreciation, he isn't going to get a bonus this year. Indeed, now the company is going to lose money, and Mr. Al Safra is upset, too. Bill might even get fired.

"Hey," Bill said to a sympathetic engineering friend one night, "somehow a lot of money has disappeared, and it's mine. We do just as well this year as we did last year, and yet now we're losing money! I don't get a bonus, and Mr. Al Safra is ready to fire me! I've done nothing different, except maybe perform better, and I'm in trouble. That crazy accountant is doing all this with mirrors, or something! How can we lose money by doing the same things we did before, when we made plenty? Besides, we have over $320,000 in the bank in cash now, whereas last year, we took that money in dividends and bonuses from profits. It doesn't make any sense at all, to pile up that cash that's mine."

1. Did Bill's trucking company *really* make a profit the first year? Why or why not? The second year, assuming that all the numbers were the same, except for depreciation? Why or why not?

2. Suppose that at the end of the fifth year, Bill was right, and the twenty trucks are junk. They cost $80,000 each when new, and they were written off (depreciated) totally over five years. If no depreciation were taken, and if Mr. Al Safra did not want to invest new capital in this venture, what would likely happen? Why?

3. Mr. Al Safra invested $1.6 million of his own money in those trucks at the beginning of year 1. Where would he be financially at the end of year 5, assuming that no depreciation expense were taken? Would he *really* have made a profit for those five years?

4. Did Bill deserve his profit bonus? Why or why not?

INCIDENT 5: EXPORT, WHERE ARE YOU NOW?

Westland Electronics is a small Ohio firm with annual sales in the $10 to $15 million range in recent years. This company manufactures some highly specialized instrumentation for steel mill uses. A single package of instruments sells for a minimum of $10,000, and single sales often go as high as $100,000. Customers are major steel companies all over the world, so the firm typically relies on a small number of highly skilled technical salesmen and relatively few orders.

In recent years, exports have been climbing very fast. Before 1971, Westland rarely sold in export markets, since it really didn't know much about foreign steelmakers. Besides, the dollar was overvalued. But as the dollar declined in value after 1971, and with some important technical innovations in the product line, Westland has been doing very well in exports. In 1982, total sales were $14.8 million, of which $6.2 million were foreign. In 1971, total sales had been $11.2 million, and exports were $55,300.

Until 1976, Westland merely turned its export orders over to an agent, who handled all details of packing and shipping. Fees ran as high as fifteen percent of orders, and Mr. Harris, Westland's president, decided that year to hire an export manager. He picked as his export manager a young woman who worked for the company as a secretary and happened to have studied Spanish in college at The University of Toledo.

Miss Wilcox proved to be a very capable saleswoman in her foreign territories, and much of the foreign sales increase could be credited to her. She made sure that foreign buyers were aware of the product line; she actively corresponded in four languages with potential clients; she had the company exhibit its products in a number of trade fairs abroad; and she followed up eagerly on all leads. She even dragged Mr. Morris to Caracas, Venezuela, to talk to a potential big customer, and he was surprised to get a big order, even though most of the conversations were in Spanish, which he didn't know.

The export tail is beginning to wag the domestic dog at Westland. Miss Wilcox reported directly to Mr. Morris until 1980, when he became very involved with other activities. He then had her report to his marketing vice president, Mr. Sampson.

This worked reasonably well, but now Mr. Puccini, the production manager, is upset. As export sales have risen, he finds that he has to make extensive product modifications with little notice. Foreign electric voltages and cycles are often different than in the U.S., and most buyers want metric, not English measurement calibrations. Mr. Puccini claims that he never finds out about foreign orders until it is too late, and then there are extra costs and delays. Recently, several important foreign orders were delayed in shipment, and important customers were very annoyed.

Mr. Jackson, the treasurer, is also upset. He finds that he is spending more time worrying about letters of credit, sight drafts, currency conversions, and other international matters than he does on domestic business. As an old timer who finds that anything but dollars is a sort of funny money, this bothers him. It bothers Westland's bank too. The bank is a small local operation, and it has to pay large correspondence fees to a big Cleveland bank to handle many foreign exchange transactions for Westland. Moreover, Mr. Jackson often doesn't find out what is happening before it is too late. Just last month, he received an irrevocable letter of credit from Venezuela in bolivares, and it took him four days to figure out that this represented a very nice $1.3 million order. It took him another three days to find a banker willing to make a short term loan on the basis of this odd letter of credit.

Mr. Morris recently called a meeting to discuss just who should report to whom in export. Mr. Sampson argued that export should be in marketing, since after all, this was sales, and marketing was totally responsible for these. Mr. Puccini argued that export should report to production, since so much that was different was involved in export sales, and Miss Wilcox really didn't have anything to do with the domestic marketing operation. She spent more time with him working out technical problems than she ever did with Mr. Sampson.

Mr. Jackson argued that export really belonged in finance, since the problem of payments was so critical. Moreover, if the company really wanted to get involved in foreign exchange and other odd foreign currency matters, he should know immediately what was going on, so that he could arrange to finance these transactions.

1. Where does the export department belong? Why?

2. Wherever you put the export department, what kinds of coordination are needed here? Set up an information flow system for Westland, starting with a first inquiry from a foreign customer, that would let everyone know what is going on at the right time.

INCIDENT 6: THE IMPORTANCE OF BEING UNIMPORTANT

In the 1970's, most major business textbook publishers realized that they could do best by focusing their efforts on mass markets. Their analysis showed that business school enrollments were rising at about 8 to 10 percent per year, and that sales of business texts would rise approximately by that amount. It was a pretty good business to be in, assuming that the company's product met the quality standards expected by professors. Remember that professors tell the students what to buy, and hence these professors largely determine total demand.

But the textbook publishers also noted that some fields grew faster than others. Certain required areas, such as basic marketing, finance, accounting, and management, which virtually all schools had their students take, were among the fast growing areas. Fields such as transportation, international business, and insurance grew very slowly.

The full line publishers gradually lost interest in these slow growth fields. Books that they had published went out of print, and their new books were mainly in the required fields. When they planned their marketing and products well, these bigger firms made good profits.

But one smaller publisher figured that if the big boys were going north, he might as well go south. He began to specialize in business texts for slow growth or no growth fields. His market was much smaller. Where a good basic marketing text might sell 25,000 copies per year, a good transportation text might sell 2,000 copies per year. In effect, this specialty publisher decided to stay small and specialize in minor materials. As he once noted to a marketing student, "We'll never get rich doing what we're doing, but at least we can survive and make good money. I can make fifteen percent on sales, whereas a major company is lucky to make five percent. My growth potential is just a fraction of what the bigger companies can expect. But my competition is nil, while theirs is very tough. The odds are that we can survive, while quite a few of those bigger companies could actually go broke. There is just too much competition for the mass market in business texts."

1. What do you prefer, 15 percent of $500,000, or 5 percent of $50 million? Why would a company deliberately choose to get into this unimportant field?

2. Did this market segment that the small company chose make sense? Why or why not?

3. This smaller company had a text in international business, which for years was a very small market. The big companies left this field alone. Now in the 1980's the international business field is growing very fast, and the small company is doing extremely well. But several bigger companies are planning new texts in this field, since it has become so large. Should the smaller company duck out of the area as a result, or should it dive in and compete with the giant firms? Why or why not?

INCIDENT 7: WHO NEEDS PEOPLE?

"For gosh sakes, they are working pretty well," Maxine Miller said, as she watched the altered chimpanzees carefully assembling the transceivers on Allied Electronics' assembly line. Maxine was Vice President for Production Systems at Allied.

"They do for a fact, don't they?" Dr. Warren Borris said happily. "You know, Maxine, when our Dr. Felderfine first began to mess around with genetic splices back in 1984, few people took him, or his research team, very seriously. But now, only seven years later, look ... we have successfully altered these chimps so that they can work on our production lines. We got their IQs up to about 65, and changed a few of their nastier personal habits, and now we don't need people anymore. Forget the union and $25 an hour pay rates. These chimps will work for a couple of bananas a day."

"Fine, if you can get us lots of them." Maxine watched the five chimps laboring away. One looked up and grinned at her, waving, yet not missing a production move. Maxine hesitated, then waved back. "We would need about 500 of them, Warren. How soon can you get them?"

"Give us ten million in cash and two years, and I think that we could give you your whole factory full. We hope."

Maxine thought about that. "I suppose that as usual, you're being optimistic, Warren. Figure four years and thirty million, right?"

Warren shrugged. "You know how it is in research. You can never really tell."

"You people don't have to live with the consequences, either," Maxine mused. "Already the union has got wind of this experiment, and they're upset. We can't just fire 500 people, Warren. There will be a lot of termination benefits to pay."

"That's your problem. I'm just a scientist."

"Already the Congress is talking about an altered animal restriction act. We might go ahead with the project and find out that it's illegal by the time we finish. But it could save over 60 percent of our production costs."

"If it's illegal here, we can shift production to France," Warren said. "Over there, they seem more eager to accept such things. Then the French branch would be able to export all over the world, including back to the States, for prices no one here could match. If the French don't go along, we can set up our animal production line in Brazil, or Hong Kong, or Sweden. That shouldn't stop us."

"Still, we could be in trouble if we go ahead," Maxine replied. "You figure that we may save ten million or so per year using these characters. But you have to figure total costs, and I don't think that you are."

"Maxine, we're scientists, not cost accountants. You do the figuring. But I tell you that this altered animal research could have payoffs bigger than you ever thought of."

1. Should Allied Electronics go ahead and develop a full range of altered animals to work on production lines? Why or why not?

2. What kinds of costs beyond direct development costs would Allied possibly face here?

3. Suppose that the U.S. bans such altered animals and their work. Could this country control this development effort on a world scale as well? Why or why not?

4. What are the social costs here? The social benefits?

Pete Williams was an excellent mechanic, really a superb one. His reputation grew in the small city he lived in, and before he was 25, he had set up his own repair shop. Within five years, he had acquired excellent modern equipment, a nice large shop building, and a growing clientele of highly satisfied customers. He had hired five other mechanics, and he was grossing over $220,000 per year and netting $30,000. Clearly here was a person who would be highly successful.

But the market potential for auto repairs in Pete's small city was limited, particularly for the premium priced, high quality services Pete supplied. In looking for ways to expand, Pete discovered that some affluent auto collectors were quite willing and able to pay high prices to get their antique autos restored. Pete attended a few auto shows, discussed this business with a few knowledgeable friends, and discovered that such autos could be restored even if they had to be shipped hundreds of miles to his shop. An avid collector was willing to pay for the best.

Pete landed one contract to restore a 1936 Cadillac convertible. As usual, he did a great job, and the pleased client spread the word to his friends that at last here was a mechanic who really cared! Within a few months, Pete had over twenty delightful antique cars sitting around his shop awaiting total restorations. Since the average billing for each car came to about $20,000, Pete obviously was in very good shape. He and his able crew began to restore these cars. A typical total restoration could take about six months, given that the entire vehicle had to be totally disassembled, and then reassembled with new parts.

At this point, Pete almost went broke. He explained it this way: "When I finish those twenty cars, I will receive about $400,000. My direct costs for labor and materials will be about $180,000, so this can be a very profitable business. But I've discovered a small problem, which is about to wipe me out.

"What is happening is that I have to put out that $180,000 to pay my mechanics and craftsmen and buy those parts before I collect from my customers. And often it is a long, long time before I can collect, since I have to finish the car before I get paid." He gestured at a gleaming 1933 Packard sitting in a corner. "That car is just about totally finished, and the bill is about $21,350, but I need a headlight lens to finally finish the car. Do you realize how hard it is to find a 1933 Packard headlight lens? We've been looking for it for two months. A guy in Montreal has one, maybe, and I hope to get it from him next month. But meanwhile, I've got over $14,000 tied up that I've paid out in cash, and I can't collect. My banker is very nervous, and I have a loan of $25,000 already overdue with him; my suppliers are demanding to be paid, and I'm late with them, too. I'm even having trouble meeting the payroll from time to time. Here I am, sitting on a gold mine, and I'm going broke! If I can somehow survive this cash crunch, I'll be in clover!"

1. Help Pete out by suggesting some type of financial planning he might do to get out of the trouble he is in. What sorts of credit and capital do you think he might need?

2. Pete recently visited a bank to discuss his financial problems. If you were the banker, what further information would you want from Pete before you seriously considered extending him some credit?

3. Pete also visited an underwriter to discuss the possibilities of making a stock offering to the general public for additional financing. Do you think that this type of company might be able to float a successful issue in the money market? Why or why not?

INCIDENT 9: GREEKS BEARING GIFTS

Nancy Bradshaw, a widow in her forties, was doing very well as an assistant purchasing agent for Leesone Electronics. After a few months of total confusion when she first took the job, she learned the ropes and began to save her company money. She had been out of the work force for many years raising her two children. One of her purchasing areas was for cleaning materials—solvents, soaps, mops, and various other items used in keeping both factories and offices extremely clean. Cleanliness was not only close to godliness; it was also close to quality control, since many components Leesone manufactured required very clean and dust free conditions to avoid contamination.

Nancy always talked to potential new suppliers, and about a year ago she met Mr. Stravros Stanovolopous, who owned a small company manufacturing special solvents to his own formulae. She purchased a small order of these solvents, and the production people quickly told her that they were the best they had ever used. So she continued to purchase these solvents from Mr. Stanovolopous, who not only quoted competitive prices, but also delivered on time. By the end of the year, Leesone had purchased over $85,000 worth of solvents from him.

Nancy also liked Stavros. A widower in his early sixties, he had immigrated from Greece in 1948, and he occasionally took Nancy to a business lunch. He was a charming man, with a fund of stories about Greece in the old days, along with plenty of gossip about people in the trade. Nancy was concerned about these lunches, but her boss, Mr. Chen, assured her that an occasional lunch with a prospective seller was perfectly all right. Leesone felt that no one would sell out for a lunch, even an expensive one, which was the only kind Mr. Stanovolopous ever took her to. And they did discuss business, some of the time. Indeed, it was during these lunches that Nancy could point out to Mr. Stanovolopous some of the problems that her production people were having keeping certain items clean, and one result was that Mr. Stanovolopous changed the formula of one of his solvents, making it even more superior for Leesone's purposes.

Nancy's purchasing plans included purchases of over $150,000 worth of these special cleaning solvents in the coming year. She had been buying them from two sources, but she had been receiving complaints about the other source. Stavros's solvents were much better and not any more expensive. Leesone did not like to rely entirely on a single source of supply for most items, but in this case, the Greek's product was outstanding. Nancy had discussed the possibility of placing all orders with Mr. Stanovolopous with Mr. Chen, and they had agreed that this was one situation where single sourcing might make sense.

A few days before Christmas, Nancy received an insured small package at her apartment. It was a solid gold, diamond encrusted wristwatch (Nancy figured that it must have cost at least $2,500 wholesale) from Mr. Stanovolopous. A small card enclosed thanked her so much for her kindness and consideration over the past year and wished that their relationship could continue. Stavros also noted that he fondly hoped that they could get together for an evening without business sometime in the near future.

1. What should Nancy do? Be very specific!

INCIDENT 10: JUST THE NUTS
AND BOLTS QUESTION

Nuts and bolts are not exciting, but the Smarton Engineering Company worries a lot about them, since it uses about 1.3 million bolts and 342,000 nuts per year in making its products. These products are component parts for specialized types of forklift trucks and other off-road heavy trucks.

Up to 1982, Smarton has purchased these nuts and bolts from two major suppliers, at an average cost of forty cents per dozen bolts and thirteen cents per dozen nuts. Usage rates for the next three years are expected to be about the same as for the past few years.

Michele Farber, the new young purchasing agent, has been discussing these nuts and bolts with Paul Hansen, the production manager. Paul is a bit old fashioned, and he really doesn't think that a lady knows much about nuts and bolts, but Michele did go to college, and she seems sharp. She has done a cost study which suggests that Smarton can manufacture all their own bolts by purchasing a special machine costing $26,000. Installation would cost $3,000, and Michele thinks that direct manufacturing costs would be between 9.3 and 11.2 cents per dozen.

Michele also has found out that for an additional $7,300, this machine can be adapted to make all the nuts the company needs. Direct manufacturing cost would be between 5.1 and 6.2 cents per dozen nuts.

1. Should Paul agree with Michele and ask top management to begin making these nuts and/or bolts, rather than buying them?

2. What other facts would you want to know before making this decision?

INCIDENT 11: MOTIVATIONAL PROBLEMS

A business professor at Indiana University was depressed every time he watched a basketball game. "Look at those young men!" he would say. "The basketball team has twelve perfectly motivated people playing for it. Our coach is sensational, at least in terms of getting young men to try. Even when we lose (which isn't too often), the guys play with total intensity."

The professor sighed. "Now, consider my management course. I have fifty students. Twenty of them could care less. Half the time, they don't even show up for class. Perhaps five or six are really trying, while the rest just try to get by. Yet management is much more important than basketball! What has the basketball team got that I haven't got? Why is it that I can't motivate students to try like those players do? If they did, they would all be important managers making big money within a very short period of time."

1. What does a college basketball team have, in terms of motivating players, that a management course doesn't have?

2. Is this type of motivation transferable? Could the business professor do anything that an athletic coach does that might make his students more motivated?

"We're damned if we do and damned if we don't," said A. L. Lerner, chief executive officer of the Allied Gear Company, shaking his head.

"We have to go," said Pete Merchant, his treasurer.

"We can't take the risk," said Sam Baxter, his executive vice president. "The board would never go along."

"Look," Mr. Lerner said, "we've taken this company and made it move, really move, in the past ten years. We've grown from $10 million a year in gross sales to $140 million. You fellows have gone all the way with me, and I trust and value your advice. But you, Sam, you admit that we've run out of market here in the States. And you, Pete, you argue that we have to make that overseas jump, and soon. But Nigeria? Couldn't we pick a safer place?"

"Safe? Nigeria has a stable government. It guarantees foreign investments. It wants high technology investment, just the sort of thing that we do. And the country's income has been growing from ten to twenty percent per year in real terms. What more do you want?"

Sam Baxter shook his head. "Pete, you're proposing that we should put $25 million of our own money into a place none of us have ever seen, and no one really wants to see. You admit yourself that with foreign currencies floating all over the place we could never be sure of our rates of return. And what do we know about Nigerian labor?"

Pete shoved the report across the table. "You've seen the figures. The Nigerian currency is strong—well, not too good in the past year, but for a decade it's been as good as the dollar. There's a good chance that it will rise relative to the dollar. And we can bring in all the technical staff we want."

"I can just see Pete Maxwell," Sand said, "with his wife and three kids, when we tell him that his next assignment is Lagos. He's never been out of Illinois, and we send him halfway around the world to mess around with a bunch of workers that probably don't speak English. Oh, boy!"

"He'll live," Pete said dryly. "Lots of Americans have gone overseas before, and lots will again."

"Pete, Sam, we've been through this before," Mr. Lerner said. "In the end, it boils down to this ... do we really want to start being a multinational corporation? We've done exporting, and we've licensed some of our processes in a few countries, but we've never made any direct investments abroad. Now we know that we can't expand much more in our traditional markets here. If our growth is to continue, we have to go abroad."

"Not true, A. L.," Sam said. "We can still expand, take over some companies in other fields..."

"You know how antitrust is going these days, Sam," Mr. Lerner replied. "We might get away with it for a little while, but we're getting big enough to be noticed now. We're just not a ten million dollar peanut stand anymore. Besides, our competition is going overseas fast, and I noticed that Fabrikwerke, our German competitor, is building a plant in Toledo. Big companies just have to go global."

"The big thing that scares me is people, A. L." Sam said. "We just don't have anyone around that has any foreign experience. We'll get into more new problems than we can handle. That's to say nothing of money. With our cash position the way it is, the board will really take a close look at any new investments in foreign currencies."

"Our cash flow won't improve much unless we get some high payout production," Pete said, "and that Nigerian venture is projected to yield 45 percent a year."

"Projections aren't facts, Sam, and you know it."

"Our next best investment is that deal in California. It pays out 14 percent," Pete added.

"Yeah, but it's a lot more certain than going to a funny money country." Mr. Lerner sighed. "Well, we have to make up our minds. The board meeting is next month, and we'll have to firm up these recommendations. Let's make our decision now."

1. Is it really true that a fast growing firm in this size range only has multinational options? What local options does it have, assuming that it now controls about as much of its various local markets as it can, given antitrust law and tough competition?

2. Suppose Allied does decide to go to Nigeria. What new kinds of problems will it face in Accounting, Finance, and Personnel? Make a complete list.

3. What new risks will Allied face if it goes to Nigeria? Can the company successfully plan to avoid these risks?

4. Look up some data on Nigeria. Does it make sense for a high technology, fast growing American company manufacturing various types of sophisticated machine tools used in metal fabrication to go to such a country? Why or why not?

INCIDENT 13: PROTECTING CAPITAL

These days even apparently low-income people can have quite substantial assets. A young woman was fond of her old widowed aunt, and she often visited her during college holidays. The aunt's husband had worked in an auto factory all his life, and the aunt only had a small social security pension, plus a little bond interest, to live on.

Last year the aunt died, and Sally Martin was surprised to discover that the aunt had left her her estate. By the time her aunt's house had been sold, along with her astoundingly valuable antiques (depression glass, 1928 furniture, etc.), Sally was informed that she now had a cash nest egg of $126,423.24. Last week the executor for her aunt's estate wrote Sally, saying that this amount had been deposited in her account. Sally is a fine arts major at your school, and her account typically had about $43.28 in it.

Sally doesn't know a thing about money, business, investments, or anything else connected with money management. Yet she is vaguely aware that leaving all this money in a checking account is a bad idea. "I really need some advice," she said to you over coffee. "What do I do? I want to go to graduate school and keep on studying for at least five more years. I'd like to earn some interest or something, but how do I know who's honest? A friend of mine keeps talking about the stock market, but I've heard that all you do there is lose money. Still, it would be nice to do the best I can with my money."

1. Help Sally out by suggesting a good investment portfolio for her. She wants to preserve her capital and gain the highest income consistent with safety. What would you suggest that she invest in?

2. Suppose Sally decided that she wanted to take a few risks and go for capital appreciation. What would you advise her to invest in?

To answer these questions, consult the *Wall Street Journal* for advice. Make a list of the securities, bank deposits, certificates of deposit, or whatever you suggest.

At the end of the semester or quarter, check back on your advice. Was it any good? Why or why not?

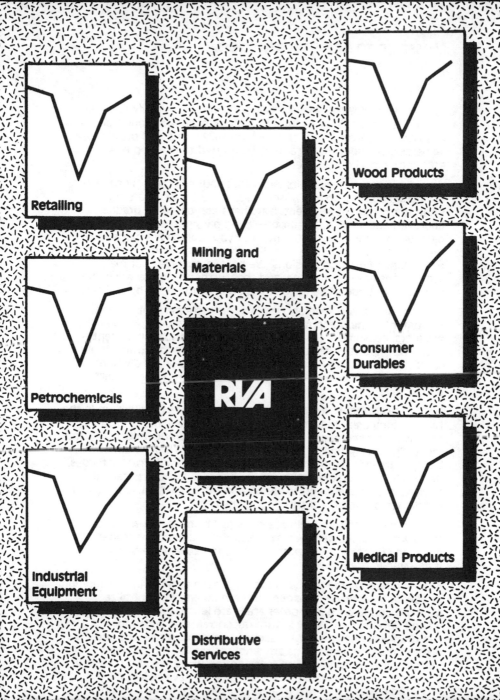

Annual Report

Retailing

Mining and Materials

Wood Products

Petrochemicals

RVA

Consumer Durables

Industrial Equipment

Distributive Services

Medical Products

1983

Message to the Stockholders

ACCOMPLISHMENTS: In 1983 RVA continued to move toward all-time high earnings, in spite of difficult economic conditions. Sales increased 12 percent from already high 1982 levels, and profits rose 14 percent, as your management continued to develop new efficiencies in all our divisions.

We believe that these results show that your company is properly diversified and in a strong position for the troubled years ahead. Profit improvement in recent years has been based on gradual improvements in all our eight operating divisions. In prior years, particularly during the 1960's, most of your company's gains were made through acquisitions and diversifications into new areas, plus expansions of existing divisions. We believe now that our major acquisitions have been made, and that further progress will come from efficient operation and expansion of our current businesses.

These basic markets, namely retailing, petrochemicals, industrial equipment, mining and materials, distributive services, wood products, consumer durables, and medical products, all present excellent opportunities for growth and profits in the future. While several of them were hard hit during the recession, all divisions are now profitable, and many have hit new highs in profitability during 1983.

FUTURE PLANNING FOR GROWTH: Your company is now well up in the top 500 companies in terms of total sales. We have moved from a small industrial company in 1950 to one of the world industrial giants today. This fact suggests why future acquisitions will be difficult. We now are large enough to present a target for antitrust activities. Hence more future expansion will be internal. But our potential markets are large enough to allow room for expansion, and we plan to take full advantage of this opportunity.

If the general economic climate remains favorable, we will continue to do well in all markets. We have long been among the leaders in our many fields, and we intend to take full advantage of our leadership in the future.

As a major conglomerate, we have long been a leader in development of new decentralized management techniques. We centralize planning and finance, but other areas are left to division managers for full development. They in turn decentralize activities to sub-divisional managers. We believe in payment for results and our division management teams are amply rewarded for excellent performance by bonuses and stock option plans. We also believe in developing new managers internally, and we have successfully recruited most of our new managers from within our divisions.

Foreign business now accounts for over 24 percent of total sales, and we believe that this growth will continue. We have fourteen overseas manufacturing facilities, largely located in Western Europe (one electronics plant is in Taiwan). No single country has more than three plants, so we are well placed in the event of local disturbance.

RVA GOALS: Our company objectives will continue to be A) to behave responsibly as a corporate citizen; B) to earn a superior return on stockholders' equity; and C) to achieve superior gains in earnings per share. While achieving these objectives has been difficult in recent years, we feel that they can be achieved in the future, particularly if the economic climate is favorable.

A real problem for us in the past decade has been rapid changes in government regulation, particularly in the field of employee safety and environmental concerns. We have invested over $72.7 million in pollution and safety equipment in the past three years, and these funds, while necessary, do not yield a net return to stockholders. However, it appears now that within two years we will meet existing and planned future requirements in both of these environmental areas. If proposed new rules and regulations, particularly in mining, should be applied, it will be quite difficult to meet our earnings objectives

OUTLOOK FOR 1984: We anticipate another good year for your company, as we are now well placed to take full advantage of market growth both at home and abroad. We have ample productive capacity to expand production in most of our major markets.

Cost inflation has been dropping since 1981, as have interest rates, and these developments are quite favorable for our future. High unemployment, particularly among younger people, now is a key constraint on many of our divisions in terms of potential markets, and resolution of this problem at the national level could lead your company to still greater sales.

We feel that your company will continue to expand and grow with the American economy in 1984 and beyond.

James M. Marer
Chairman of the Board

William S. Wilson
President and Chief Executive Officer

The Year in Review

SALES: Sales for your company reached an all-time high in 1983. Every division except Distributive Services had all-time high sales. Distributive Services sales declined only 1.7 percent, mainly because of a trucking strike and certain problems connected with computer rentals of the new X473B high speed computer. The largest gain in sales came in the Consumer Durables Division, which had an 18.6 percent increase. This gain came largely through high sales for Xeno tools and continued recovery in household furniture. Masefield Furniture also took full advantage of this trend and increased its market share.

PROFITS: Five of our eight divisions showed sharp gains in profits, contributing to our overall profit gain. Fierce competition in both food sales and discount operations affected our Retailing Division; inflation and a new labor contract depressed our Industrial Equipment Division profits slightly; and Distributive Services also had a small profit decline.

The 1983 profit results show the wisdom of diversification. Although some problems were encountered in a few divisions, others gained strength. As a result, overall profits rose significantly. We expect to overcome the difficulties in the three divisions whose profits declined slightly in 1983, resulting in improved results for 1984.

NET EARNINGS: Net earnings reached $284.5 million, or $1.66 per common share. This is the second best year on record for your company.

FINANCIAL POSITION: Net assets reached an all-time high of $2.4 billion. In 1983, your company invested $451.5 million in new facilities and equipment, also an all-time high.

Our strong financial position will be important in helping your management achieve success in years to come.

Total Markets
(millions of dollars)

Group	Sales		Profits	
	1983	1982	1983	1982
Retailing	$ 951.25	$ 779.13	$ 11.72	$ 8.73
Petrochemicals	371.55	296.29	38.34	36.98
Industrial Equipment	360.11	375.49	48.90	34.37
Mining and Materials	722.88	632.01	17.80	15.06
Distributive Services	119.27	90.12	7.38	5.13
Wood Products	642.21	495.72	57.87	46.59
Consumer Durables	898.08	818.21	31.39	42.11
Medical Products	672.26	597.29	147.13	121.42
TOTALS	$4,737.61	$4,084.26	$360.53	$310.39

Retailing

Your company's retailing operations had a difficult year because of fierce competition in major markets. Profits on sales of slightly over one percent were not considered adequate, and management is taking steps to improve marketing and cut costs to achieve higher margins.

Year	Sales (millions)	Net Profits (millions)
1983	$951.25	$11.72
1982	779.13	8.73
1981	255.30	3.15
1980	922.64	11.37
1979	980.82	12.08

The Minimax Discount Stores Division added six new stores in high volume shopping centers in the mountain states, and start-up costs also contributed to somewhat lower than desirable margins. However, these new stores, each in the 60,000 to 80,000 square foot superstore range, should contribute to profits in years to come.

Your company opened two experimental Minimax Discount Stores in England in 1981, which have been profitable. However, the lower value of the pound sterling adversely affected their earnings in 1982 and the first half of 1983. The recovery of the pound should put these stores in a highly profitable position.

Wide West Groceries has been following its long term policy of closing smaller, poorly located stores and opening fewer, but much larger supermarkets in desirable shopping center locations. In 1982, 29 stores were closed and 8 were opened. Start-up costs and closing costs adversely affected margins.

The Outlook: Your company plans to continue its present policies of opening new stores in high potential areas and closing marginal stores. By 1984, this long term policy should be almost complete, and margins should rise rapidly.

Cost inflation has plagued the division, and current trends toward lower inflation rates should be a major contributor to future profits.

Peter Kamp, President
Minimax Discount Stores

Peter Stevens, President
Wide West Groceries, Inc.

Petrochemicals Division

Profits and sales rose to an all-time high in 1983, as the petrochemical industry recovered rapidly from the 1981–82 recession. Synthetic fiber sales rose rapidly, particularly in Europe and Japan. The Anacine Film Division did particularly well with its new color film, which was placed on the market for the first time in

Year	Sales (millions)	Net Profits (millions)
1983	$371.55	$38.34
1982	296.29	36.98
1981	99.72	9.10
1980	360.37	37.19
1979	383.10	39.53

late 1982. This film, which allows for faster developing times and lower cost to the consumer, was widely used in industrial photography applications, and the sales outlook continues excellent.

Wilmount Chemical Division continued to have troubles in sulphuric acid sales, long a mainstay of this division. Increasing supplies of sulphur derived from various air pollution control systems have been dumped on the market, depressing sulphur prices and causing considerable problems in this industry.

The Outlook: If the forecast economic recovery continues, your company expects to continue to grow in sales and profits. Currency instabilities in Western Europe and Japan have temporarily helped the company, since it operates plants in West Germany, Sweden, and the Netherlands, where our management has been able to forecast currency fluctuations to our advantage. Turbulent international money markets are a serious concern to your management, and little relief is expected from this problem, which could cause serious future problems for your company.

A new synthetic fibers plant is being constructed in North Carolina, and it should be on stream in late 1984. Market and profit expectations for this new $115 million facility look excellent.

Serious competitive problems are expected in the sulphur industry for some years to come, and your management is actively exploring new business activities for Wilmont Chemical.

William C. Patton, President
Neutro Fibers, Inc.

John Hayashi, President
Anacine Fibers, Inc.

Jason Childers, President
Wilmont Chemical Company

Industrial Equipment

Although sales reached an all-time high for this division, cost inflation caused by a new labor contract, plus completion of several fixed cost long term contracts, depressed profits significantly. Ross & Vogel completed work on the Hungarian tool agreement, which was a major factor in lowered profits for

Year	Sales (millions)	Net Profits (millions)
1983	$375.49	$48.90
1982	360.11	34.37
1981	96.65	13.12
1980	349.28	47.43
1979	371.30	50.42

the year. This contract, signed in 1978, did not contain adequate inflation safeguards for rapid inflation of labor, materials, and energy costs.

Ace Engine Company continued to have record sales and profits, as it continued to shift out of auto and light truck systems to heavy duty automated systems. It expanded two brake systems plants in Western Europe, and it is building two new factories, one in Ireland and one in France, to better handle its growing European business.

Ace is also building a new plant near Phoenix, Arizona, to expand production of its electronic braking systems for heavy trucks and buses. These three plants should come on stream in 1984 or early 1985.

The Outlook: Federal safety standards for heavy trucks and buses means more new business for Ace Engine. The lagging investment pattern in Western Europe and the United States has hurt Ross & Vogel on its advanced machine tool line, but if investment turns up as expected, both sales and profits should increase.

Both Ace Engine and Ross & Vogel are at the forefront of technology in their major areas. Research and development expenditures continue to be high, and new product lines are close to full development for commercial markets. Your management is confident that future potentials for this group are excellent, and it will take full advantage of its leading position in relevant industries.

Helmut Schollhammer, President
Ross & Vogel, Inc.

Arland Garland, Jr., President
Ace Engine Company, Inc.

Mining and Materials Division

While sales and profits reached an all-time high for this division, profit margins were eroded badly in the second half because of sharply lower prices for copper and zinc. Energy cost increases also adversely affected results.

Year	Sales (millions)	Net Profits (millions)
1983	$722.88	$17.80
1982	632.01	15.06
1981	194.01	4.78
1980	701.14	17.26
1979	745.35	18.35

Peters Coal continued to expand steadily, reflecting new markets for coal. The new Wyoming Aterford Mine, opened in November, 1983, should contribute significantly to profits in future years, as demand for low sulphur Western coal increases. However, this mine opened too late in the year to affect significantly 1983 financial results.

The Outlook: The world copper industry continues to be plagued by excess capacity and low prices. There is no sign that this difficulty will end in the near future. Accordingly, it is likely that one or two of our three U.S. mines will be closed in the near future.

Zinc and lead demand continued reasonably strong. Profit potential looks excellent for our Zumont company for the next few years.

While American authorities in theory call for more coal use, in practice coal demand has risen quite slowly. Pollution problems in burning coal have been very difficult to resolve. However, Peters Coal has signed several long term supply contracts with major utility companies this year, and expansion of output and sales will continue for several years.

Peters Coal is also involved in a major coal gassification project, in cooperation with the U.S. Bureau of Mines and several other major industrial coal users. It is too early to determine the commercial applications of this research, but results to date appear promising, and further research and development will continue at high levels.

Cost uncertainties surrounding Peters Coal strip mining reclamation efforts continue. Until more experience is gained with existing and new Federal reclamation guidelines, it is not certain what effect these requirements will have on output or profits. Seven of the nine Peters Coal mines are strip operations.

Coal demand also remains very uncertain. On the one hand, government pressure to shift to coal is positive; on the other, environmental controls tend to limit extensive expansion of coal burning facilities.

Mark X. Rai, President
Peters Coal Company, Inc.

John S. Wright III, President
Zumont Lead & Zinc Company

Peter Goodenow, President
United Copper Company

Distributive Services

Your company had a troubled year caused by cost inflation, recession in key markets, and transition difficulties caused by changeovers to new types of computers and services in Hamlin Computer Rental Division. These difficulties have been largely overcome, and your management expects a return to the rapid growth in profitability and sales experienced in the past ten years.

Year	Sales (millions)	Net Profits (millions)
1983	$119.27	$7.38
1982	90.12	5.13
1981	32.01	1.98
1980	115.68	7.16
1979	122.98	7.61

Sesame Rentals disposed of a number of marginal retail outlets and continued to concentrate on industrial equipment rentals. Hamlin Computer Rental has now completely phased out its X39X line, which caused numerous problems, and has introduced the new X42X line, which has achieved excellent consumer acceptance in the past seven months. Pioneer Technical Training continues to grow in the field of proprietary computer training, and Maddock Trucking has made a complete transition from the regulated to the relatively deregulated environment in which it now works.

The Outlook: With most of its troubles behind, your division expects several years of fast growth in sales and profits. Outlooks for all the major fields in which it is involved are excellent. Marginal products and services have been discontinued, and resulting losses written off. As a result, poorly performing activities will not be a drag on the divisions as they have been in the past.

Richard McKibbon, President
Hamlin Computer Rental, Inc.

Daniel P. Simmonds, President
Pioneer Technical Training

Ulysses J. Baker, President
Maddock Trucking, Inc.

John R. Puri
Sesame Rentals, Inc.

Wood Products Division

Sales and profits reached an all-time high, due mainly to export orders for our complete line of mobile homes and special hospital equipped mobile units. Middle Eastern and Latin American markets were particularly active, but results were hampered by the increase in the value of the dollar relative to many foreign

Year	Sales (millions)	Net Profits (millions)
1983	$642.21	$57.87
1982	495.72	46.59
1981	172.36	15.53
1980	622.89	56.13
1979	662.17	59.67

currencies. Costs for lumber dropped sharply in the wake of the housing market collapse in the U.S., which helped us maintain profit margins.

Development of our new Easi-light fireplace logs, made from previously unused sawdust and other byproducts, coupled with very rapid increases in the use of wood stoves, also helped sales. Plywood demand in the U.S. has been deeply depressed by conditions in the housing industry. Credit and interest rate problems have also depressed mobile home sales.

The Outlook: Declines in interest rates which started in 1982 give our mobile home and timber product sales areas a bright future, if these dropped rates lead to continued increases in housing starts. Our export sales, which have been the main area for our growth, are now being seriously affected by the rapidly rising value of the U.S. dollar in terms of foreign currencies, but we are hopeful that our new export oriented mobile housing, office building, and hospital lines will continue to be popular in important world markets.

Mark E. Smith, President
Kline Lumber Company

Jack F. Dicer, President
Vicksburg Mobile Homes, Inc.

Mark U. Hays, President
Churchman Lumber Company

Consumer Durables Division

Sales and profits reached an all-time high for the division, reflecting strong consumer demand for our cassette TV system and our other electronics products, including games. Consumer spending on other durables rebounded strongly, as replacement needs increased, and your company's divisions were

Year	Sales (millions)	Net Profits (millions)
1983	$898.08	$42.11
1982	818.21	31.39
1981	241.03	8.42
1980	871.07	30.45
1979	925.99	32.37

able to take full advantage of the trend. Sales of Marchand Electronics' new line of video tape cassette systems and games for home TV use far exceed estimates.

Slight increases in housing starts aided Masefield Furniture sales, and their line of restoration products for older homes also did extremely well. The home handicraft demand growth continued, and Xeno Tool, with its superior line of power tools for the handyperson, benefitted accordingly.

The Outlook: The recent recession has led many consumers to postpone purchases of routine items, and as this market gathers strength in the years to come, Masefield Furniture and Whirlwind Electric could benefit strongly. Trends in home crafts and electronic home equipment are strongly up in our Marchand Electronics and Xeno Tool Company lines, and we expect to continue to obtain bigger market shares with our attractive products. Snap-Kwik Lock Company does the bulk of its business in security areas, which will continue to show strong growth, and its new security systems for autos show promise.

All groups in the Consumer Durables Division have shown themselves able to compete effectively and to gain market shares in their highly competitive markets. Your management expects that it can continue to perform effectively in the future.

Your company is expanding its Taiwan electronics assembly plant to meet higher demand, and this work should be complete by early 1984. A new factory has been purchased in Buffalo, New York, for expanded production of Whirlwind Electric Company energy saving space heaters. This plant, constructed in 1972, is being modified to meet Whirlwind's needs, and will be in full production by mid-1984.

Marcus M. Sharkey, President
Masefield Furniture Company

Victor M. Goh, President
Xeno Tool Company

Daniel M. Suzuki, President
Snap-Kwik Lock Company

Jean Flaherty
President, Whirlwind Electric Company

Medical Products Division

Your company's Medical Products Division had all-time sales and profits records for 1983. Extensive development of new models of hospital diagnostic centers (the one-stop diagnostic system) were well received by hospitals and clinics, and sales more than doubled from 1982. Export sales were even higher, increasing by over three hundred percent.

Year	Sales (millions)	Net Profits (millions)
1983	$672.26	$147.13
1982	597.29	121.42
1981	180.54	39.49
1980	652.04	142.70
1979	693.16	151.70

Our new drug Xanathin, for relief of certain types of arthritis, finally approved by the FDA in late 1982, was widely accepted, and sales were higher than initially forecast.

The Outlook: Your company has four new drugs under intensive development and testing, and your management hopes for FDA approval in the near future. Two of these drugs have already been approved for sale in European markets, and initial sales are very promising.

Hospital construction shows a declining trend, but Lewis Hospital Supply Company expects to maintain sales and profits through extensive development of new products, plus sales for modernization of older hospitals. Export markets should remain strong as well, and promising developments in electronic/computer diagnostic systems are now under intensive testing.

Mark V. Simon, President
Lewis Hospital Supply Company

Barbara A. Bates, President
Macer & Van Ormand, Inc.

Opinion of Independent Auditors

To the Stockholders and Directors of RVA,
Incorporated:

In our opinion, the accompanying consolidated
balance sheet, consolidated income statement,
and consolidated statement of sources and
applications of funds present fairly the
financial position of RVA Incorporated for the
year ended December 31, 1983. Our examination
of these statements was made in accordance
with generally accepted accounting standards,
and accordingly included such tests of the
accounting records as we considered
necessary in such circumstances.

Radebaugh, Arpan, Schweikart, and Chung
New York, N.Y.
February 14, 1984

Consolidated Balance Sheet
(millions of dollars)

	1983	1982
Current Assets:		
Stated on basis of realized values:		
Cash	$ 34.43	$ 39.61
Short term investments	135.19	31.75
Receivable from customers and others	524.96	489.73
Prepaid expenses and income taxes		
allocable to the following year	86.02	129.03
	780.60	690.12
Stated on basis of cost using principally		
"last in, first out" method:		
Inventories	1,043.76	1,008.37
	1,824.36	1,698.49
Deduct: **Current Liabilities:**		
Notes payable	70.71	25.02
Payable to material suppliers and others	548.94	504.39
Taxes based on income	144.34	112.27
Long-term debt due within one year	10.21	23.49
	774.20	665.17
Net Current Assets	1,050.17	1,033.32
Buildings, Machinery and Equipment—Net	1,574.24	1,338.04
Land—at original cost	45.02	37.83
Investments in affiliated companies	44.47	47.06
Investments in and advances to subsidiary		
credit companies	14.26	16.36
Other assets	17.58	16.28
Total assets less current liabilities	2,745.74	2,488.89
Deduct:		
Long term debt due after one year	818.91	837.62
Deferred taxes based on income	29.16	9.15
Net Assets	$1,897.67	$1,642.11
Outstanding shares	135.05	132.03
Profit employed in the business	1,760.62	1,510.08
	1,895.67	1,642.11

Consolidated Statement of Income and
Retained Earnings (millions of dollars)

	1983	1982
Sales	$4,737.61	$4,084.26
Costs:		
Inventories brought forward from previous year	1,008.37	958.55
Materials, supplies, services purchased, etc.	2,468.80	2,139.86
Wages, salaries and contributions for employee benefits	1,426.98	1,264.65
Depreciation	170.51	149.12
Interest on borrowed funds	77.27	60.19
Taxes based on income	270.62	210.68
	5,522.55	4,783.05
Deduct: Inventories carried forward to following year	1,043.77	1,008.37
Costs allocated to year (1)	4,378.79	3,774.68
Profit of consolidated companies	358.83	309.58
Equity in profit of affiliated companies	.24	—
Profit of subsidiary credit companies	1.46	.81
Profit for year-consolidated	360.53	310.39
Profit employed in the business at the beginning of the year	1,510.08	1,301.19
	1,870.61	1,611.58
Dividends paid	110.00	101.49
Profit employed in the business at beginning of the year	$1,760.61	$1,510.08
Profit per share of common stock		
Assuming no dilution	4.18	3.60
Assuming full dilution	4.04	3.49
Dividends per share of common stock	1.28	1.18

Consolidated Statement of Sources and
Uses of Funds (millions of dollars)

	1983	1982
Operations:		
Profit for year	$ 360.53	$310.39
Add or (Deduct) items not involved in net current assets:		
Depreciation	170.50	149.12
Deferred taxes based on income	20.01	18.96
Equity in profit of affiliated companies	(.24)	—
Profit of subsidiary credit companies	(1.46)	(.81)
Net current assets provided from operations	549.34	477.66
Long-term debt	9.88	183.54
Capital assets sold or scrapped	2.52	3.40
Common stock sold for cash under stock options	5.02	7.05
Dividends from affiliated companies	2.83	1.62
Dividends from subsidiary credit companies	.81	.81
Reduction in advances to subsidiary credit companies	4.05	—
	574.45	674.08
Cash dividends	110.00	101.49
Land, Buildings, Machinery & Equipment	418.28	400.95
Long-term debt	28.59	35.24
Other	.73	.24
	557.60	537.92
Net current assets at beginning of year	16.85	136.16
Net current assets at end of year	$1,033.32	$897.16
Cash and short-term investments	98.25	(26.89)
Receivable from customers and others	35.23	102.63
Prepaid expenses and income taxes allocable to the year	(43.01)	48.12
Inventories	35.40	49.82
Net change in current assets	125.87	173.66
Notes payable	45.68	(22.36)
Payable to material suppliers and others	44.55	58.16
Taxes based on income	32.07	(18.63)
Long-term debt within one year	(13.28)	20.32
Net change in current liabilities	109.02	37.50
Increase in current assets during year	$ 16.85	$136.15

Notice to the Stockholders

The annual meeting of stockholders will be
held at 1:00 p.m., June 1, 1984, at Wilmington,
Delaware. A notice of the meeting, proxy
statement, and proxy voting card will be sent
before the meeting to all stockholders of
record.

RVA Incorporated

Incorporated in Delaware in 1952

Board of Directors

Chairman: James M. Marer
L. M. Glowacka
P. Lamont Cort
A. B. Banerjee
Daniel B. Chu
Bertha Cool
Arnold R. Lombardi
Donald P. Lam
John J. Kim
David Parkly Truitt
Siko Suzuki
J. C. Howard
M. C. Hyer

Corporate Officers

President and Chief Executive Officer

William S. Wilson

Chief Executive Vice President

Jason C. Korth

Vice Presidents

Peter B. Byrnes
Richard Gardner
Michael McComb
S. R. Wysocki
Robert A. Beeman
Franklin A. Mee

Controller

Lamont Baxter

Treasurer

Wallace C. Harrington

Secretary

Wilma Bryant

General Offices

> 67927 Avenue of the Americas
> New York, N.Y. 92303

Independent Accountants

> Radebaugh, Arpan, Schweikart, and Chung
> 44 Nexus Place
> New York, N.Y. 33758
>
> *General Counsel*
>
> Metzger, Donnell, and Heineman
> 357 C Street
> New York, N.Y. 99878

Stock Transfer Agent

> Midtown Investment Bank
> 434 B Street
> New York, N.Y. 99878

Transfer Agent

> Union Bank
> 477 B Street
> New York, N.Y. 99878

GLOSSARY

ABC: Audit Bureau of Circulation, an agency that audits circulation figures for magazines.

Accounting: the art and science of keeping records of financial activities in generally accepted ways.

Accounts Payable: the amounts of money owed to creditors as the result of goods or services purchased on account.

Action System: how the necessary actions are to be taken to achieve the plan.

Actuarial Calculation: a mathematical forecast of an event based on carefully organized historical data.

Actuary: a professional trained to perform actuarial calculations.

Affirmative Action Programs: mandatory programs established by the federal government for the hiring of females and minority groups.

Affluent: rich.

After Sales Services: services performed by the seller for the buyer after the sale is made.

Allocate: to apportion for a specific purpose, ration.

AMTRAK: the U.S. Government-owned company that operates most passenger trains in the U.S.

Antitrust Laws: a group of laws which are designed to prevent the formation of a trust or grouping of businesses which maintains monopolies and restricts free competition.

Arbitrator: a neutral observer who has been designated to judge and rule on a dispute between opposing parties.

Asset Accounting: the part of accounting that deals with measuring assets. Shown in the Balance Sheet.

Assets: items owned by a company, including cash.

Audit: to check and verify accounts.

Auditor: a person appointed and authorized to examine accounts and records, to verify results.

Authority: the right to make decisions.

Balance of Payments: the statement of all international transactions in a given time period.

Balance Sheet: the accounting statement that shows a company's assets, liabilities, and owner's equity.

Batch Process: production system whereby products are produced in stages with buffers of inventories separating the stages.

Behavioral Research: study of human behavior.

Board of Directors: a group of persons, elected by the stockholders of a corporation, who conduct the business of the corporation.

Bond: a certificate of indebtedness, issued by the debtor. Commonly issued by corporations and various divisions of government.

Bottom Line: the final line on the income statement, which shows net profit.

Brain-Renters: firms that basically sell nothing but the services of their very talented staffs (e.g., advertising agencies, management consultants, etc.).

Budget: a financial plan on how to spend money.

Capital Gain: profit made from selling a capital asset, such as stocks. Capital gains are taxed at a lower rate than income.

Capital Intensive: using significantly more capital equipment than labor to produce goods.

Capital Market: the money market, i.e., where rates for lending and borrowing are set.

Capital Structure: the financing of a firm by debt, preferred stock, and net worth (including capital, capital surplus and retained earnings).

Cash Flow: flows of actual money in and out of the organization.

Casualty Insurance: insurance covering non-life events, such as fires, floods, collisions, etc.

CEO: abbreviated form for Chief Executive Officer; usually the president.

Certificate of Deposit: a negotiable certificate of a time deposit in a commercial bank, earning a specified rate of interest over a given time.

Channel Theory: this theory helps the firm decide which distribution system to use in moving the product from the manufacturer to the final consumer.

Charter: a grant from government to perform certain functions.

Civil Rights Act of 1964: the federal law which bans job and hiring criteria based on race, sex, or religion.

Closed Loop Feedback: information about activities returned to a unit (i.e., computer) that automatically adjusts for deviations.

Closed Systems: systems closed or isolated from external events and influences.

COBOL: an acronym for Cobol Business Oriented Language. A procedure oriented business computer language.

Collusion: secret agreement or cooperation for an illegal or deceitful purpose (e.g., between two companies trying to eliminate competition from others).

Commercial Paper: short term promissory notes of highly reputable business firms.

Common Carrier: a transportation company that serves the general public.

Common Stock: an ownership share in a corporation.

Computer: an electronic device which performs various mathematical manipulations.

Computer Programs: plans to solve problems by using the computer.

Computer Terminal: a system (machine) that enables the computer operator to enter data directly into the computer.

Conglomerate: a grouping of many separate businesses into a single, unified company with a central strategy and central control.

Consumer Behavior: in marketing, the study of why consumers act as they do in buying or not buying.

Consumerism: a movement designed to protect consumers from exploitation.

Contingency Management: management which considers the possible effects of external events, and attempts to react to and evaluate such impacts.

Contract: an agreement between two or more parties to do or not do some specific thing.

Contract Carrier: a transportation company that serves a few clients on a specific contract basis.

Control: an attempt to impose order, according to some set of rules, on a disorderly world.

Convertible Currency: a local money freely convertible to any other country's money at the prevailing exchange rate.

Convertible Debenture: a bond convertible to stock under given circumstances.

Corporate Income Tax: a fixed rate of tax set by the government on the profits of corporations.

Corporation: a business owned by its stockholders and characterized by limited liability, state legal charters, a continuous existence, ability of shareholders to buy and sell stock, an elected board of directors who run the company, and corporate tax rates.

Cosmopolitan: marked by interest in many parts of the world.

Cost Benefit Analysis: process of weighing costs and gains in making a decision.

Cost Producers: firms that are primarily interested in getting production costs down.

Craft Union: a union whose members are mainly skilled craft workers (e.g., electricians, plumbers).

Creative Accounting: taking every advantage of the accounting rules to create the best possible opinion.

Culture Bound: tied to a given set of beliefs, attitudes, and mores, regardless of facts or logic.

Customer Profiles: a list of the key characteristics of a group of customers.

Cybernetics: the science of communication and control theory concerned with the comparative study of automatic control systems.

Data: collection of statistics, or raw information to be processed when needed.

Deficit: the precise excess of liabilities over assets, or of expenditures over receipts.

Deflation: decrease in money supply over a period of time, causing prices of goods and services to decline.

Demand: the quantity wanted by buyers at a given price.

Demand Forecasting: a method whereby a firm predicts how many customers will buy how much of a particular product in the near future.

Demographic Variables: population characteristics (e.g., age, sex, income).

Depreciation: a decrease in value due to decay or obsolescence.

Development: the evolution of something already known.

Deviation: variance from a norm.

Direct Foreign Investment: investment by a foreign company which also involves control and management of the investment.

Distribution Costs: costs associated with selling a product, as contrasted with production costs.

Distributor: a firm that distributes and sells a product.

Dividend: a payment to the owners of a corporation normally in cash, but sometimes in shares.

Double Taxation: system whereby the government taxes corporate profits and then taxes this same money a second time as individual income after it has been distributed to stockholders in the form of dividends.

Duty: see import duties.

Early Adopters: persons who buy a new product as soon as it is available.

Economies of Scale: lowering of production costs as output expands.

EEC: European Economic Community, a group of European countries which have agreed to have free trade among themselves.

Effluent: something that flows out; waste material (e.g., smoke, sewage) discharged into the environment.

EFTA: European Free Trade Association, a group of European countries which have agreed to have free trade among themselves.

Entrepreneur: someone who organizes, manages, and assumes the risks of a business or enterprise.

Equal Opportunity: the requirement to treat all employees equally, without regard to race, sex, religion, or ethnic origin.

Equitable: fair, equal, and just.

European Economic Community: See EEC.

Exchange Control: government regulations about how the country's money can be changed into other countries' money.

Exchange Rate: the actual rate at which one country's money can be converted into another country's money.

Expedite: to speed up the progress of something.

Express Warranty: warranty spelled out in the contract of sale.

Expropriation: the action of the state in taking the property of an individual.

Externalities: costs borne by persons outside the person or organization creating the costs.

Factor Endowment: relative supply of capital and land (agricultural and raw materials) per capita; size and general health of the work force.

Federal Trade Commission: the federal government agency responsible for regulating advertising.

Feedback: return of information to the planner (manager), for potential corrective action.

Finance: to provide money or funds.

Financial Intermediary: an institution (e.g., commercial bank, credit union, finance company, etc.) that reallocates savings into other uses.

Fiscal Policy: pattern of government spending and taxing, which may be varied to control the economy.

Flexible Budget: a budget which adjusts to changes in plans.

Flow Process: capital-intensive production process having its own internal feedback loops that operate fairly independently of people; used in oil refineries and chemical plants.

Footloose Firms: companies that can locate anywhere because either the good or service produced is composed of easily found materials or the costs of moving both inputs and outputs are a small part of total costs.

Forecasting: prediction of the costs and/or revenues that allow the manager to make a pro forma income statement for the coming period.

Foreign Exchange Rates: the ratio of the value between two national currencies, as the British pound and the U.S. dollar.

FORTRAN: an acronym for *FORmula TRANslation*. This is a procedure oriented computer language usually used to perform mathematical operations.

Fortune 500: a list of the 500 largest American corporations, published annually by *Fortune* magazine.

Four P's: in Marketing, key factors - Product Policy, Place Decisions, Price Mechanisms, and Promotional Activities.

Franchise: permission granted by a manufacturer to a distributor or retailer to sell his products.

Functional Subsystem: the subsystem which concerns the structure of the functional divisions of the firm like marketing, production, etc.

Gantt Chart: a time plan to accomplish a task.

GATT: General Agreement on Trade and Tariffs. Agreement among a group of countries that meet from time to time to negotiate reductions in tariffs and other trade barriers.

Gold Plate a System: to make a system using only the best parts and components, regardless of cost.

Gross National Product (GNP): the sum total value of a country's goods and services produced.

Hardware: computer machinery.

Historic Cost: the original money cost of an asset.

Implied Warranty: in a sale, a legal although unwritten assumption; for example, that the candy bar you get from a machine will be fit to eat.

Import Duties: taxes on products coming into a country from other countries.

Income Statement: the accounting statement that shows revenues and costs.

Independent Auditors: see public accounting firms.

Industrial Union: a union whose members work in a specific industry (e.g., auto workers, steel workers).

Inflation: an economic condition where the purchasing power of the dollar declines as the general level of prices for goods and services increases.

Information: data that has been processed into reports, sorted, and directed to those who use it, usually in summary form.

Information System: the structured organization of data and data retrieval.

Informational Subsystem: the subsystem which concerns the proper flows and accumulations of information in the firm.

Initial External Perception (IEP): creative act performed by a manager in deciding what to plan about (leads into the PARF loop).

Input: mathematical data put into the computer.

Input Control: control of what enters the system.

Insolvent: unable to pay debts as they fall due in the usual course of business.

Instruction Deck: a set of punch cards which tells the computer what to do.

Interest: payment for the use of money, for a given time period. Expressed as a percentage.

International Constraints: in international business, environmental factors that influence a company's internal affairs and prevent them from doing certain things.

International Monetary Fund (IMF): an international organization designed to facilitate international payments among nations.

Inventory Control: the process of trying to keep adequate materials in stock while minimizing inventory carrying costs.

IRS: *Internal Revenue Service.* The government agency which is responsible for collecting the income tax.

Ivy League Schools: a group of exclusive old private universities in the east, which includes Yale, Harvard, Princeton, Columbia, among others.

Job Lot: production process which constructs a few products at once, usually controlled by human feedback.

Lease: a term contract to rent a property, subject to the conditions stated in writing.

Liabilities: sums owed to others by a company.

Licensing: buying the right to use another company's patents, trademarks, or know-how.

Limited Liability: a situation in which a law or laws will permit the owners of a business to pay less than the whole indebtedness of the business.

Line Manager: a manager directly in authority. One who is responsible for results.

Liquidity: in finance, the ability to sell any asset for cash at any time.

Listed Stock: a stock bought and sold on a formal, organized stock exchange.

Logistics: *see* physical distribution.

Long-Term Debt: money owed and payable more than a year from the present date.

Madison Avenue: a street in New York City where many ad agencies are located, hence used as a short-hand term for the advertising business.

Make or Buy Decision: a decision to buy an item or make it yourself.

Man-Machine Symbiosis: the interrelated human and non-human elements in a productive system.

Management by Objective: to manage something with a view to achieving specific, measured goals, or objectives.

Management Featherbed: a few comfortable jobs where incompetents are sent out to pasture with impressive titles, full pay, and no important duties.

Managerial Accounting: accounting that shows costs and revenues. Shown in the *Income Statement.*

Market-Oriented Firms: companies whose primary concern is being close to their markets (e.g., retail stores, service-oriented firms).

Market Saturation: a situation when all buyers already have the product.

Market Segmentation: the strategy of directing the marketing efforts of the firm toward a certain portion of the entire market. It identifies the part of the market which has the best customers for the firm's product.

Market Share: percentage of the total sales in one sector that a company has.

Materials-Oriented Firms: companies to whom the cost of raw materials is so important that they tend to locate their plants near them (e.g., steel mill).

Media: agencies, means, or instruments. In advertising, types of communication to be used.

Merger: the union of two or more formerly independent business firms.

Metric Standard: using the metric system (millimeters, meters, etc.) for all measurements and precise dimensions, such as hole sizes.

Micro-circuitry: reduction of electrical computer circuits to extremely small size.

Minicomputer: a small computer with *relatively* limited capacity.

Mixed Capitalistic System: economic system that has publicly as well as privately owned firms, but relies primarily on customers' free choice.

Model: a structured representation of reality.

Monetary Policy: one means by which a government controls the economy; increasing or decreasing the supply of money.

Monopoly: a market with a single seller.

Moonlighting: working part-time on a second job.

Motivation: the reasons people have or the driving forces which lead to activity and choice of activity.

Multinational Firm: a corporation with major investments and sales in many countries. Also called MNF's; MNC's (companies); MNE's (enterprises).

Nationalization: government takeover of a sector of the economy.

NATO: North Atlantic Treaty Organization, a military alliance of European countries and the U.S.

Net Cash Flow: the difference between total cash receipts and total cash expenditures.

Non-Cash Cost: a cost which is not actual money paid out in the given period.

Oligopoly: a market with only a few competitors.

One-Offs: items produced one at a time.

Open Loop Feedback: information about activities returned to a human operator, who then decides what to do.

Open Systems: systems which are exposed to external events and influences.

Opinion of Independent Auditors: a statement as to the correctness of a company's accounting reports for a given time period by an independent, separate accounting firm.

Opportunity Cost: implicit cost to a firm of forgoing the benefits of one alternative in order to choose another alternative.

Order of Priorities: order of things to be done, beginning with the most significant.

OSHA: Office of Safety and Health Administration. The federal government agency responsible for administering federal laws pertaining to the health and safety of employees.

Out of Stock: not in the store when the customer wants to buy it; said of an item commonly carried by a store.

Output: processed data put out by the computer.

Owner's Equity: the net amount of the company owned by its owners.

PARF Loop: Planning, Activities, Results, and Feedback. A complete management system. See Management by Objective.

Partnership: a business owned by two or more persons characterized by unlimited liability, personal taxes or profit shares, dissolution upon death of a partner, and limitations upon a partner's ability to sell his interest in the partnership.

Patent: a grant of exclusive use of an invention to the inventor for 17 years.

Peer: an equal, a member of the same group.

Pension: a payment to a retired person.

Per Capita: per person.

Perquisites: any non-money benefit given an employee, such as use of a car. Also perks, for short.

PERT: Program Evaluation and Review Technique. A plan to accomplish a task, taking into account all interrelationships of production components.

Physical Distribution: the movement and storage of goods within the firm, plus related functions such as plant movement, terminals, loading and unloading facilities, and packing. Sometimes called logistics.

Plan: a scheme of action or procedure.

Political Subsystem: the informal subsystem of politics and maneuvering for improved position in the firm.

Poor's and Moody's: financial books giving investors basic financial information about publicly held companies.

Post-Purchase Analysis: study of buyers after they buy.

Predictive Standards: the norms used for future planning.

Preferred Stock: a stock that has a fixed interest payment per year.

Premise: something assumed or taken for granted.

Premium: the price of an insurance policy.

Preventive Maintenance: routine work done on a car in advance of breakdowns, designed to prevent mechanical problems.

Private Carrier: a firm that carries only its own goods.

Probability: the relative likelihood that an event will occur.

Product Liability: a firm's responsibility for its product after it has been sold.

Product Mix: the array of items being produced in a given plant.

Production Management: taking inputs such as labor, materials, and energy, and transforming them into usable outputs.

Profit Center: a unit of a company that calculates its own net profit.

Programmer: a person who designs, writes, maintains, and tests computer programs.

Proprietary Part: an item which cannot be reproduced by a competitor because of patent or copyright restrictions.

Proprietorship: a single ownership business characterized by unlimited liability, personal taxes, individual property ownership, and liquidation upon death of the owner.

Prospectus: a written explanation of what a company intends to do; used by individuals in deciding whether to invest in the company.

Provincial: a person of local or restricted interests or outlook.

Public Accounting Firms: accounting firms that audit the books of publicly owned corporations.

Qualified Statement: an independent auditor's opinion which is qualified, meaning that the auditor feels the company's accounting statements do not truly reflect the facts.

Quota: a maximum or minimum limit.

R & D: Research (activities involved in the discovery of some new process of scientific development) and Development (evolution of something already known).

Random Sample: an item chosen from a set which has an equal chance of being chosen among all items.

Rate of Return: the profit earned, stated as a percentage, on a given project per year. Also ROI (Return on Investment).

Ration: see allocate.

Reactionary: a very conservative person.

Real Growth Rates: growth in physical terms, not in inflated money.

Receivables: sums of money owed to a company.

Repugnance: deep aversion, strong dislike.

Research: the activities aimed at the discovery of a new process or product.

Retailing: the business function of selling the product to the final buyer.

Retained Earnings: the part of corporate profits which is not paid to stockholders but is retained by the firm.

Risk: likelihood that some future event will occur; can be accurately predicted, and hence is insurable.

ROI: Return On Investment. See rate of return.

Sampling: selection of a small group to study from a larger group.

Self-Insurance: accepting risk oneself, without buying insurance; said of a company or person.

Selling Dead Horses: trying to sell a product or service that very few people want now or might want in the future.

Seniority: stronger position held by an employee due to longer time spent in the organization.

Site Analysis: predicting the sales potential of establishing a retail store at a certain geographic location. Firms use site analysis to determine where to locate a retail outlet.

Social Overhead Capital: availability and quantity of power supplies, water, communications systems, transportation, public warehousing, physical transfer facilities, housing, etc.

Social Security System: a U.S. government program which provides income for various groups, most notably retired persons and those incapacitated in accidents.

Social Subsystem: the informal subsystem of friends and groups of people in the firm.

Sociotechnical Systems: systems involving interrelated human and technical elements.

Software: computer instructions or programs.

Sources and Uses of Funds Statement: the accounting statement showing actual cash inflows and outflows for a given period.

Sovereign: possessed of controlling power; ruling, predominant.

Specs, Specifications: description of requirements.

Speculator: one who deals to make a profit from fluctuations in price.

Staff Personnel: the experts, technicians, and advisors who advise line managers.

Statistics: a science dealing with the collection, classification, analysis, and interpretation of numerical facts or data.

Stockholder: a person who owns at least one share of a corporation, by purchase from the corporation or from another stockholder, and who generally has a vote in electing the Board of Directors.

Strategy: the pattern of decisions in a company that defines goals, produces policies and plans, and decides on courses of action.

Subcontracting: contracting with a third party to carry out all or part of work specified in an original contract.

Suboptimization: maximizing one component of a system at the expense of another.

Subsidy: money granted by the government to make up the difference between the "free market" price and the government-fixed price.

System Noise: extraneous signals, information, static, and similar obstructions to information.

Tariff: a tax on imports.

Tax Concessions: special benefits given by a government to encourage business.

Taxonomy: the systematic ordering and naming of goups within a field.

Tolerance Limits: stated measurements within which the item measured must remain.

Total Marketing Concept: philosophy that the customer's wants and needs should be the focal point of a firm's activities. First, the firm finds out what the customers want and need, and then each department of the firm, such as finance, marketing, engineering, etc., devotes its efforts to satisfying the need.

Turnkey Project: project in which a firm builds a complete facility to sell to a foreign country or firm.

Uncertainty: a future event which cannot be predicted with accuracy based on current data, and hence is uninsurable.

Unemployment Rate: the percentage of those persons in an economy who are able to work but are not employed.

Unions: a group of non-managerial workers formed to gain stronger bargaining power in dealing with management.

Unlimited Liability: the condition of being bound in law to pay an indebtness without limitations.

Value Analysis: analysis of a component or part to determine whether an acceptable substitute can be had at a lower cost.

Vendor: a seller of something.

Vocational Guidance: counseling about a person's work skills and employment prospects.

Volume Minima: lowest weight accepted for a given rate.

Voting Rights: the ability of the owners of a corporation to elect its directors.

Wagner Act (1935): legislation that outlawed "yellow-dog" contracts, made labor organization legal, and established the National Labor Relations Board.

Warranty: a seller's guarantee to the buyer.

WASP: White Anglo Saxon Protestant.

Wholesaler: a firm that sells to retailers for final sale to ultimate buyers.

Wholesaling: the business function of buying goods from the manufacturer and in turn selling to the retailer or final buyer. The wholesaler often specializes in distribution of the product.

Working Capital: money kept on hand for the purpose of paying current obligations before payment is received for sales.

Yellow-Dog Contract: a document prospective employees were required to sign before being hired forcing them to agree not to join a union on threat of immediate dismissal. Yellow-dog contracts were outlawed in 1935 by the Wagner Act.

Zoning Code: a set of rules for a locality, specifying land use.

BIBLIOGRAPHY

Chapter 2
The Formation and Growth of a New Business

Anderson, R. A., and Kumph, W. A. *Business Law,* 9th ed. Cincinnati: Southwestern Publishing Company, 1972 (Parts VIII and IX).

Barber, Richard J. *The American Corporation.* New York: Dutton, 1970.

Barker, Theodore C. *Business History.* London: Historical Association, 1971.

Establishing and Operating Your Own Business. Superintendent of Documents, Small Business Division, U.S. Department of Commerce, Washington, D.C. 1975.

Hicks, Herbert G., Pride, William M., and Powell, James D. *Dimensions of American Business.* New York: McGraw-Hill, 1975.

Hoag, Edwin. *How Business Works.* New York: Bobbs, 1978.

Klug, John R. *The Basic Book of Business.* Boston: Cahners Books International, 1977.

Krainin, H. L. *What You Should Know About Operating Your Business As a Corporation.* New York: Oceana, 1967.

Lusk, H. F. *Business Law: Principles and Cases,* 3d U.C.C. ed. Homewood, Illinois: Irwin, 1974 (Parts V and VI).

Preston, Paul. *Business: An Introduction to American Enterprise.* New Jersey: Prentice-Hall, 1976.

Robinson, W. R. *Fundamentals of Business Organization.* New York: Hive, 1974.

Seligman, Ben B. *The Potentates.* New York: Dial Press, 1974.

Sobel, Robert. *The Entrepreneurs: Explorations Within the American Business Tradition.* New York: Weybright, 1974.

Tate et al. *How to Start and Manage Your Own Business.* New York: Dow Jones-Irwin, 1977.

Van Home, J. C. *Fundamentals of Financial Management,* 2nd ed. New Jersey: Prentice-Hall, 1974.

Chapter 3
What Do Managers Do?

Albers, Henry. *Principles of Organization and Management,* 4th ed. New York: John Wiley and Sons, 1974.

Brightman, Richard. *Information Systems for Modern Management.* New York: Macmillan, 1971.

Flippo, Edwin B., and Munsinger, Gary. *Management,* 4th ed. Boston: Allyn and Bacon, Inc., 1978.

Koontz, Harold, and O'Donnell, Cyril. *Principles of Management,* 5th ed. New York: McGraw-Hill, 1972.

Newman, William, Summer, Charles, and Warren, Kirby. *The Process of Management,* 3rd ed. Englewood Cliffs, New Jersey: Prentice-Hall, 1972.

Richman, Barry M., and Farmer, Richard N. *Management and Organizations.* New York: Random House, 1975.

Schmidt, Warren. *Organizational Frontiers and Human Values.* Belmont, California: Wadsworth, 1970.

Starr, Martin. *Management: A Modern Approach.* New York: Harcourt Brace Jovanovich, 1971.

Chapter 4
Control: Accounting

Arens, Alvin A., and Loebbecke, James K. *Auditing: An Integrated Approach.* New Jersey: Prentice Hall, 1976.

Benjamin, James Joseph, Francia, Arthur J., and Strawser, Robert H. *Financial Accounting.* Dallas: Business Publications, 1975.

Cushing, Barry E. *Accounting Information Systems and Business Organization.* Massachusetts: Addison-Wesley, 1974.

Hopwood, Anthony G. *Accounting and Human Behavior.* New Jersey: Prentice-Hall, 1974.

Horngren, Charles T. *Cost Accounting: A Managerial Emphasis.* New Jersey: Prentice-Hall, 1977.

Internal Revenue Code. Chicago: Commerce Clearing House, 1978.

Kaluza, Henry J. *Accounting: A Systems Approach.* New York: McGraw-Hill, 1976.

Kieso, Donald E., and Weygandt, Jerry J. *Intermediate Accounting.* New York: John Wiley, 1977.

Plevyak, Paul P. *Exploring Accounting Careers.* Cincinnati: South-Western, 1976.

A Survey in 46 Countries: Accounting Principles and Reporting Practices. New York: Price, Waterhouse, 1975.

Chapter 5
Control Statistics and Data Processing

Anderson, Ronald Gordon. *Data Processing and Management Information Systems.* London: MacDonald and Evans, 1974.

Brown, Rex V., Kahr, Andrew S., and Peterson, Cameron. *Decision Analysis for the Manager.* New York: Holt, Rinehart, and Winston, 1974.

360

Cabot, A. Victor, and Harnett, Donald. *An Introduction to Management Science.* Massachusetts: Addison-Wesley, 1977.

Elliot, Clarence Orville, and Wasley, Robert S. *Business Information Processing Systems: An Introduction to Data Processing.* Illinois: Irwin, 1975.

Hamburg, Morris. *Statistical Analysis for Decision Making.* New York: Harcourt, Brace, Jovanovich, 1977.

Harnett, Donald Lee. *Introduction to Statistical Methods.* Massachusetts: Addison-Wesley, 1975.

Maniotes, John, and Quasney, James S. *Computer Careers: Planning, Prerequisites, Potentials.* New Jersey: Hayden, 1974.

McAllister, Harry E. *Elements of Business and Economics: Learning by Objectives.* New York: Wiley, 1975.

Sanders, Donald H. *Computers in Society.* New York: McGraw-Hill, 1977.

Winkler, Robert L., and Hays, William L. *Statistics: Probability, Inference and Decision.* New York: Holt, Rinehart and Winston, 1975.

Chapter 6
Organization

Becker, Selwyn W. *The Efficient Organization.* New York: Elsevier, 1975.

Berkman, Harold W. *The Human Relations of Management.* Encino, California: Dickenson, 1974.

Bowers, David G. *Systems of Organization: Management of the Human Resource.* Ann Arbor: University of Michigan Press, 1976.

Caplow, Theodore. *How to Run an Organization.* New York: Holt, Rinehart and Winston, 1976.

Chandler, Alfred D. *The Managerial Revolution in American Business.* Cambridge, Massachusetts: Belknap, 1977.

Drucker, Peter F. *Management: Tasks, Responsibilities and Practices.* New York: Harper & Row, 1974.

Famularo, Joseph J. *Organization Planning Manual.* New York: American Management Association, 1971.

Gannon, Martin J. *Management: An Organizational Perspective.* Boston: Little, Brown, 1977.

Gelb, Gabriel M. *Research at the Top: Better Data for Organizational Policy Making.* Chicago: American Marketing Association, 1975.

Gibson, James L. *Organizations: Behavior, Structure, Processes.* Dallas: Business Publications, 1976.

Graham, Gerald H. *Management: The Individual, the Organization, the Process.* Belmont, California: Wadsworth, 1975.

Jackson, J., and Morgan, C. *Organization Theory: A Macro-Perspective for Management.* P - H, 1978.

Kast, F. E., and Rosenzweig, J. E. *Organization and Management: A Systems Approach.* New York: McGraw Hill, 1974.

Khandwalla, Pradip N. *The Design of Organizations.* New York: Harcourt Brace, 1977.

Silber, Mark B. *Managerial Performance and Promotability.* New York: AMACOM, 1974.

Smith, Peter B. *Groups Within Organizations.* New York: Harper & Row, 1973.

Tosi, Henry L. *Management: Contingencies, Structure and Process.* Chicago: St. Clair Press, 1976.

Uris, Auren. *The Executive Deskbook.* New York: Van Nostrand, Reinhold, 1976.

Chapter 7
Marketing

Broome, C. L., and B. M. Enis. *Marketing Decisons: A Bayesian Approach.* Scranton, Pa.: International Textbook Company, 1971.

Brown, Milton P. *Problems in Marketing.* New York: McGraw-Hill, 1968.

Buzzell, Robert D. *Marketing Research and Information Systems.* New York: McGraw-Hill, 1969.

Darden, W. R., and R. P. Lamone. *Marketing Management and the Decision Sciences: Theories and Applications.* Rockleigh, N.J.: Allyn and Bacon, 1971.

Davis, Kenneth R. *Readings in Sales Force Management.* New York: Ronald Press, 1968.

Hess, John M. *International Marketing.* Homewood, Ill.: Richard D. Irwin, 1966.

Kotler, Philip. *Marketing Management,* 4th ed. Englewood Cliffs, N.J.: Prentice-Hall, 1980.

Kotler, Philip. *Principles of Marketing.* Englewood Cliffs, N.J.: Prentice-Hall, 1980.

Mandell, Maurice I. *Advertising,* 3rd ed. Englewood Cliffs, N.J.: Prentice-Hall, 1980.

Chapter 8
Retailing

Davidson, William R., Doody, Alton F., and Sweeney, Daniel. *Retailing Management,* 4th ed. New York: Ronald Press Company, 1975.

James, Don L., Walker, Bruce J., and Etzel, Michael J. *Retailing Today: An Introduction.* New York: Harcourt Brace Jovanovich, 1975.

Pintel, Gerald, and Diamond, Jay. *Retailing.* Englewood Cliffs, New Jersey: Prentice Hall, 1977.

Richert, G. Henry, et al. *Retailing: Principles and Practices,* 6th ed. New York: Gregg and Community College Division, McGraw-Hill, 1974.

Will, R. Ted, and Hasty, Ronald W. *Retailing.* San Francisco: Canfield Press, 1973.

Chapter 9
Insurance and Research and Development

Allison, David, ed. *The R & D Game: Technical Men, Technical Managers, and Research Productivity.* Cambridge, Massachusetts: MIT Press, 1969.

Bickelhaupt, David Lynn. *General Insurance, 9th ed.* Homewood, Illinois: R. D. Irwin, 1974.

Dean, Burton Victor. *Evaluating, Selecting, and Controlling R & D Projects.* New York: American Management Association, 1968.

Gerstenfeld, Arthur. *Effective Management of Research and Development.* Reading, Massachusetts: Addison-Wesley Publishing Company, 1970.

Greene, Mark Richard. *Risk and Insurance, 3rd ed.* Cincinnati: South-Western Publishing Company, 1973.

Henke, Russell W. *Effective Research and Development for the Smaller Company.* Houston, Texas: Gulf Publishing Company, 1963.

Heyel, Carl. *Handbook of Industrial Research Management, 2nd ed.* New York: Reinhold, 1968.

Legg, Howard W. *A Brief Outline of Insurance, 3rd ed.* Indianapolis: Rough Notes, 1971.

Vaughan, Emmett J., and Elliott, Curtis M. *Fundamentals of Risk and Insurance, 2nd ed.* Santa Barbara: Wiley, 1978.

Williams, Chester Arthur, and Heins, Richard M. *Risk Management and Insurance, 3rd ed.* New York: McGraw-Hill, 1976.

Chapter 10
Financial Management

Bank of America. *Money Market Instruments and Investment Vocabulary.* San Francisco, 1974.

Friedman, Seymour. *Principles of Financial Management.* Cambridge, Massachusetts: Winthrop Publishers, 1978.

Haley, Charles W., and Schall, Lawrence D. *The Theory of Financial Decisions.* New York: McGraw-Hill Book Company, 1973.

Mao, J. C. T. *Corporate Financial Decisions.* Palo Alto, California: Pavan Publishers, 1976.

Chapter 11
Physical Distribution

Attwood, Peter R. *Planning a Distribution System.* London: Gower Press, 1971.

Aylott, John D., and Brindle-Wood-Williams, Digby. *Physical Distribution in Industrial and Consumer Marketing*. London: Hutchinson, 1970.

Ballou, Ronald H. *Business Logistics Management*. Englewood Cliffs, New Jersey: Prentice-Hall, Inc., 1973.

Bowersox, Donald J., LaLonde, Bernard J., and Smykay, Edward W. *Physical Distribution Management: Logistic Problems of the Firm*, rev. ed. New York: The Macmillan Company, 1968.

Davis, Grant M., and Brown, Stephen W. *Logistics Management*. Lexington, Massachusetts: Lexington Books, 1974.

Heskett, James L., Glaskowsky, Nicholas A., Jr., and Ivie, Robert M. *Business Logistics: Physical Distribution and Materials Management*, 2nd ed. New York: Ronald Press Co., 1973.

Johnson, James C., and Wood, Donald F. *Contemporary Physical Distribution*. Tulsa, Oklahoma: PPC Books, 1977.

Sawdy, L. C. W. *The Economics of Distribution*. New York: Halsted Press, 1972.

Smykay, Edward W. *Physical Distribution Management*, 3rd ed. New York: The Macmillan Company, 1973.

Taff, Charles A. *Management of Physical Distribution and Transportation*. 5th ed. Homewood, Illinois: Richard D. Irwin, Inc., 1972.

Chapter 12
Purchasing

Alijan, George W. (ed.). *Purchasing Handbook: Standard Reference Book on Purchasing Policies, Practices, Procedures, Contracts and Forms*. 2nd ed. New York: McGraw-Hill, 1966.

Barlow, C. Wayne. *Purchasing for the Newly Appointed Buyer*. New York: American Management Association, 1970.

Bohlinger, Maryanne Smith. *Merchandise Buying: Principles and Applications*. Dubuque, Iowa: W. C. Brown Co., 1977.

Cantor, Jeremiah, and Loda, Frank. *Mechanized Purchasing Systems*. AMA Management Bulletin #104. New York: American Management Association, 1967.

Combs, P. H. *Purchasing Handbook of International Buying*. Boston: Cahners Publishing, 1970.

Diamond, Jay. *Retail Buying*. Englewood Cliffs, N.J.: Prentice-Hall, 1976.

Farrell, P. V., and Heinritz, S. F. *Purchasing: Principles and Applications*. Englewood Cliffs, N.J.: Prentice-Hall, 1971.

Hersker, Berry J. *The Purchasing Agent's Guide to the Naked Salesman*. Boston: Cahners Books, 1975.

Lee, Lamar. *Purchasing and Materials Management: Text and Cases*. New York: McGraw-Hill, 3rd ed., 1977.

Wingate, John Williams. *The Management of Retail Buying*. Englewood Cliffs, N.J.: Prentice-Hall, 2nd ed., 1978.

Chapter 13
Production

Adam, E. E., and Ebert, R. J. *Production and Operations Management.* Englewood Cliffs, N.J.: Prentice-Hall, 1978.

Biegel, J. E. *Production and Control: A Quantitative Approach.* Englewood Cliffs, N.J.: Prentice-Hall, 1971.

Buffa, E. S. *Modern Production Management: Managing the Operations Function.* New York: Wiley, 1977.

Chase, R. B., and Aquilano, N. *Production and Operations Management.* Homewood, Ill.: Richard D. Irwin, 1977.

Greene, James H. *Production and Inventory Control Handbook.* New York: McGraw-Hill, 1970.

Hoffmann, T. R. *Production: Management and Manufacturing Systems.* Belmont, Calif.: Wadsworth Publishing, 1971.

Marshall, Paul W., et al. *Operations Management.* Homewood, Ill.: Richard D. Irwin, 1975.

Niland, Powell. *Production Planning, Scheduling and Inventory Control.* New York: Macmillan, 1970.

Vollman, T. E. *Operations Management.* Reading, Mass.: Addison-Wesley, 1973.

Chapter 14
Personnel

Barnard, Chester I. *The Functions of the Executive.* Cambridge, Mass.: Harvard University Press, 1938. Chapter 12.

Dalton, Gene W., and Lawrence, Paul R. *Motivation and Control in Organizations.* Homewood, Ill.: Richard D. Irwin, 1971.

Gray, D. E., and Guilford, J. S. *Motivation and Modern Management.* Reading, Mass.: Addison-Wesley Publishing, 1970.

Koontz, Harold, and O'Donnell, Cyril. *Principles of Management.* 3rd ed. New York: McGraw-Hill, 1964. Chapters 24-27.

Lawler, E. E. "Compensating the New Life-style Worker," *Personnel* (1971), 19-25.

Likert, Rensis. *New Patterns of Management.* New York: McGraw-Hill, 1961.

Maslow, A. H. "A Theory of Human Motivation," *Psychological Review*, 50 (1943), 370-396.

Reitz, H. Joseph. *Behavior in Organizations.* Homewood, Ill.: Richard D. Irwin, 1977.

Stroh, T. F. *Managing the New Generation in Business.* New York: McGraw-Hill, 1971.

Chapter 15
International Business

Apilado, Vincent P., and Gies, Thomas G. *Banking Markets and Financial Institutions.* Homewood, Ill.: Richard D. Irwin, 1971.

Blough, Roy. *International Management: Environment and Adaptation.* New York: McGraw-Hill, 1966.

Clough, Shepard B. *The Economic Development of Western Civilization.* New York: McGraw-Hill, 1962.

Ewigg, David W. "MNCs on Trial," *Harvard Business Review,* 50 (May-June 1972), 130-143.

Farmer, Richard N. *Incidents in International Business.* Homewood, Ill.: Richard D. Irwin, 1980.

Farmer, R. N., and Richman, B. M. *International Business,* 3rd edition, 1980.

Fayerweather, John. *International Business Management.* New York: McGraw-Hill, 1969.

Fisher, R. *International Conflict for Beginners.* New York: Harper and Row, 1970.

Grosset, Serge. *Management: European and American Styles.* Belmont, Calif.: Wadsworth Publishing, 1970.

Kolde, Endel J. *International Business Enterprise.* Englewood Cliffs, N.J.: Prentice-Hall, 1968.

Kramer, Roland L. *International Marketing.* 3rd ed. Cincinnati: South-Western Publishing, 1970.

"The Multinationals Ride a Rougher Road," *Business Week,* December 19, 1970, pp. 57-146.

Prather, Charles L., and Wert, James E. *Financing Business Firms.* Homewood, Ill.: Richard D. Irwin, 1971.

Stahl, Sheldon W. "The Multinational Corporation: A Controversial Force," *Monthly Review,* Federal Reserve Bank of Kansas City, January 1976, 3-10.

Webber, Ross A. *Culture and Management: Text and Readings in Comparative Management.* Homewood, Ill.: Richard D. Irwin, 1969.

Chapter 16
Capital Markets

Barger, Harold. *Money Banking and Public Policy.* Chicago: Rand McNally, 1962.

Dougall, Herbert E., and Gaumnitz, Jack E. *Capital Markets and Institutions.* Englewood Cliffs, N.J.: Prentice-Hall, 3rd ed., 1975.

Goldsmith, Raymond W. *Financial Institutions.* New York: Random House, 1968.

Hutchison, G. S. *Financing Corporate Growth.* New York: Presidents Publishing

Kaplan, Gilbert Edmund, and Welles, Chris. *The Money Managers*. New York: Random House, 1969.

Kaufman, George C. *Money, The Financial System, and The Economy*. Chicago: Rand McNally, 1973.

Pesek, Boris P., and Saving, Thomas R. *Money, Wealth, and Economic Theory*. New York: Macmillan, 1967.

Robbins, Sidney M., and Terleckyj, N. E. *Money Metropolis*. Cambridge, Mass.: Harvard University Press, 1960.

Robinson, Roland I. *Money and Capital Markets*. New York: McGraw-Hill, 1964.

Chapter 17
Social Responsibility

Backman, Jules, ed. *Social Responsibility and Accountability: An In-Depth Look at the Policy Issues*. New York University Press, 1975.

Beesley, Michael, and Evans, Tom. *Corporate Social Responsibility*. Croom Helm Publishers, 1978.

Berle, Adolf A., and Means, Gardner. *The Modern Corporation and Private Property*. Harcourt Brace Jovanovich, 1968.

Farmer, Richard N., and Hogue, W. D. *Corporate Social Responsibility*. Palo Alto, California: SRA, 1973.

Harper, John D. *The Corporate Role in Society*. Columbia University Press, 1977.

Jacoby, Neil H. *The Corporate Power and Social Responsibility*. Macmillan, 1973.

Nader, Ralph, and Green, Mark. *Taming the Giant Corporation*. Norton, 1976.

————. *Corporate Power in America*. Viking Press, 1973.

Sethi, S. Prakash. *The Unstable Ground: Corporate Social Policy in a Dynamic Society*. John Wiley and Sons, Inc., 1974.

Annual Reports

Bernstein, Leopold A. *Financial Statement Analysis: Theory, Application and Interpretation*. Homewood, Ill.: Irwin, 1974.

Foster, Louis Omar. *Understanding Financial Statements and Corporate Annual Reports*. Philadelphia: Chilton, 1968.

Greenleaf, Robert W. *An Introduction to Corporate Financial Statements*. Indianapolis: Orchard House Press, 1974.

How to Read a Financial Report. New York: Merrill, Lynch, Pierce, Fenner and Smith, Inc., 1973.

Manning, Bayless. *A Concise Textbook on Legal Capital*. New York: The Foundation Press, 1977.

Rogers, David C. D. *The Manager's Guide to Finance and Accounting: A Concise Introduction to the Language of Business*. Michigan: Landis Press, 1972.

Sources of Composite Financial Data: A Bibliography. Philadelphia: Robert Morris Associates, 1971.

INDEX

May we introduce other Ten Speed Press books you may find useful . . .
over three million people have already.

What Color Is Your Parachute? by Richard N. Bolles
The Truth Option by Will Schutz
The Damn Good Resume Guide by Yana Parker
The Three Boxes of Life by Richard N. Bolles
Where Do I Go From Here With My Life?
by John C. Crystal and Richard N. Bolles
Who's Hiring Who by Richard Lathrop
Don't Use a Resume by Richard Lathrop
Mail Order Know-How by Cecil C. Hoge, Sr.
Mail Order Moonlighting by Cecil C. Hoge, Sr.
The Student Entrepreneur's Guide by Brett M. Kingstone
Computer Wimp by John Bear
Better Letters by Jan Venolia
Write Right! by Jan Venolia
Finding Facts Fast by Alden Todd

You will find them in your bookstore or library,
or you can send for our *free* catalog:

TEN SPEED PRESS
P O Box 7123   Berkeley, California 94707